THE MISSIONARY MOVEMENT
IN CHRISTIAN HISTORY

THE MISSIONARY MOVEMENT
IN CHRISTIAN HISTORY

Studies in the Transmission of Faith

Andrew F. Walls

Orbis Books
Maryknoll, New York

T&T Clark
Edinburgh

Seventh printing, September 2003

Published by Orbis Books, Maryknoll, New York 10545, U.S.A. and T&T Clark Ltd, 59 George Street, Edinburgh EH2 2LQ, Scotland.

Permission to publish chapters and journal articles from the publishers listed at the foot of the first page of many chapters in this book is gratefully acknowledged. Special thanks are owed to Ecclesiastical History Society for permission to reprint chapters 8, 13, 15, and 16. They first appeared in *Studies in Church History* volumes 14, 17, 19, and 28. Mention of the Society was inadvertently omitted in the first printing of this book.

Manufactured in the United States of America.

Library of Congress Cataloging-in-Publication Data is available from the Library of Congress, Washington, D.C.

British Library Cataloguing-in-Publication Data is available from the British Library.

Orbis/ISBN 1-57075-059-9

T&T Clark/ISBN 0 567 08515 5

TO DOREEN
"For thy sweet love remember'd such wealth brings,
That then I scorn to change my state with kings."

Contents

Abbreviations

BMS	Baptist Missionary Society
BNTC	Black's *New Testament Commentaries*
CIM	China Inland Mission
CMS	Church Missionary Society
EJCSK	Eglise de Jésus-Christ sur la terre par le Prophete Simon Kimbangu
FRCS	Fellow of the Royal College of Surgeons
HIEC	Honourable East India Company
HJ	*Hibbert Journal*
JICH	*Journal of Imperial and Commonwealth History*
LMS	London Missionary Society
MMS	Methodist Missionary Society
NS	New Series
PG	*Patrologia Graeca*
PL	*Patrologia Latina*
SCH	*Studies in Church History*
SCM	Student Christian Movement
SPCK	Society for Promoting Christian Knowledge
SPG	Society for the Propagation of the Gospel
SVMU	Student Volunteer Missionary Union
TNTC	Tyndale *New Testament Commentaries*
USPG	United Society for Propagation of the Gospel
WMC	World Missionary Conference (Edinburgh, 1910)

Preface

This volume brings together a selection of pieces written over a twenty-year period. Most were originally prepared for oral delivery; nearly all have appeared in print before, and one or two have even been granted the dignity of translation. For some time, friends have asked for a collection of such papers, which had appeared in various settings and in several countries. The book arises from deference to their judgment, and in response to their insistence, rather than from any confidence of my own.

Raking over the embers of the past in this way inevitably raises editorial decisions. I have taken the opportunity of correcting some transmissional misfortunes, smoothing over some stylistic infelicities, and removing a particularly blatant error or two. That has been the easy part. I have also striven, with only partial success and without wholesale re-writing, to adopt more inclusive gender language, as far as this is attainable by one who learned his writing in a less enlightened age. More fundamental questions arise concerning the geological time marks of earlier decades, and the intellectual fossils embedded in their strata, and concerning the repetitions of views, arguments, statements and even wording that occur when one talks on similar topics on different occasions. In the end, friends whose instincts I have learned to trust, notably Lamin Sanneh and Bill Burrows, have persuaded me to let such things take their course. Save for the minor alterations already mentioned, therefore, the papers are reproduced in substantially their original form. I have not attempted to update the bibliographical references.

That the book has actually come into being is due to the insight, patience and perseverance of Bill Burrows, Managing Editor of Orbis Books. Its acceptability has been enhanced by the skill and perception of the Orbis copy editors. At the Centre for the Study of Christianity in the Non-Western World, Anne Fernon has, as always, efficiently coped with my most unreasonable requests with unfailing good humour. For the material itself, I have a legion of creditors in a host of friends, colleagues and students in different parts of the world. Of those long departed I especially cherish the memory of G. T. Manley, C. P. Groves and Max Warren (there were giants in the land in those days), who set me forward in early stages of my journey. Of later travelling companions, I am conscious of how much I owe to Kwame Bediako, Jonathan Bonk, Richard Gray, John Hitchen, Åke Hultkrantz, Olav Guttorm Myklebust, Andrew Ross, to the late Harry Sawyerr and Bengt

Sundkler, and to many associated in one way or another with the Universities of Aberdeen and Edinburgh and with Yale Divinity School. Stephen Peterson first introduced me to the last-named institution, and has been a more important source of encouragement and stimulus than he is probably aware. The Day Missions Library at Yale has much enhanced the quality of my life, and Yale friends such as Charles Forman, Martha Smalley, Paul Stuehrenberg, and Joan Duffy have further enriched it. The Overseas Ministries Study Center, New Haven, Connecticut, the launchpad for many important projects in mission studies, has been a frequent place of refuge, its large-hearted staff ever-welcoming. Much of what I have written, including some of the pieces in this book, would not have been completed without the vision and generosity of its Director, Gerald Anderson, and his mastery of the gentle arts of persuasion and blackmail.

To three close associates in particular I owe an immeasurable debt. The incisive mind and rigorous standards of Harold Turner, a colleague in Sierra Leone, Nigeria, and Scotland, and still vigorously leading the Gospel and Cultures Trust in New Zealand, have been an influence for nearly forty years. Wilbert Shenk, now of Fuller Seminary, has been a regular source of ideas, and initiatives. Prophets do not necessarily make architects, but he manages to combine those vocations. And Lamin Sanneh, once of Aberdeen and now of Yale, has been an ever-flowing spring, an abiding source of refreshment and sustenance, who brings fertility to parched ground. These three friends all urged the making of this collection; I hope against hope that the outcome will not betray them.

Underlying everything has been the activity of my wife Doreen, who has succeeded where, in the lamentable case of Humpty Dumpty, the best efforts of all the king's horses and all the king's men were of no avail.

Introduction

This book is a collection of fragments, itself a selection from a larger collection of fragments. It therefore offers no systematic account of anything; and even as regards the topics it includes, it omits much that is crucial. Insofar as it has a single theme, it is to be heard in a symphonic combination of the three movements into which it is divided. The first of these is a reflection on the nature of the Christian faith, seen from the perspective of its historical transmission. The second looks at that transmission process in relation to the special case of Africa, and considers the special place of Africa in Christian history. The third focuses on the missionary movement from the West as a model of what happens—to both partners in the process—as the transmission of faith takes place.

Study agendas are usually a matter of personal or institutional biography, and this one is no exception. I arrived in West Africa in my thirtieth year, with an assignment to teach those in training for the ministry in Sierra Leone, and in particular to be responsible for teaching them church history. I had received, as I thought, a pretty good theological education; and my graduate work had been in patristics at Oxford, under the venerable F. L. Cross. I was, as Paul put it, circumcised on the eighth day, of the tribe of Benjamin and all the rest of it, and had sat at the feet of Gamaliel. And I shared the conventional wisdom of the 1950s about church history teaching; that church history was full of lessons to be imparted to the "younger churches" from the accumulated wisdom of the older ones.

I still remember the force with which one day the realization struck me that I, while happily pontificating on that patchwork quilt of diverse fragments that constitutes second-century Christian literature, was actually living in a second-century church. The life, worship and understanding of a community in its second century of Christian allegiance was going on all around me. Why did I not stop pontificating and observe what was going on? In this I had an advantage not open to all my expatriate colleagues; though a preacher of my church, I was a layman, and thus could fit unobtrusively into the local church structures, and frequently be unnoticed or forgotten. The experience changed this academic for life; instead of trying to extrapolate from that ancient corpus of literature and apply it, I began to understand the second-century material in the light of all the religious events going on around me.

A further revolution of outlook was at hand. It was obviously necessary to learn, and indeed to teach (so far as a curriculum basically made in Europe allowed), something of the history of Christianity in the area in which I now worked. It therefore seemed only right to devote some research time to the same topic. When I began, I intended this as no more than a polite nod to the local Christian community; as far as I was concerned, such research would be a sideline, indeed a hobby. Such things were hardly real church history; real church history needed Greek and Latin. It was soon clear, however, that work on the African materials was not only "real" church history, but was going to be as demanding and laborious, and require as firm a grasp of techniques and sources as patristic studies. And there were fewer guidelines, fewer precedents, hardly any instruments of study, and no F. L. Cross to be my Gamaliel. It also involved addressing the forms of African religion and society, a study which I had hitherto found rather uninteresting, at least in terms of its literature. Why was I surprised? I had always recognized that study of the literatures, history, and religion of the later Roman Empire was essential for patristic studies; I should not have expected that African church history would provide an easier ride.

Some years later, I found myself with new responsibilities in a different part of Africa. In a national university in newly independent Nigeria I was to arrange for a Department of Religion. As a national university, it was to provide for the study of all the religious traditions of Nigeria, and it would have Christians and Muslims on its staff. It developed programs in Christian and Muslim studies in parallel, each aiming at the heart of the respective traditions. All students were required to take courses in the primal religions of Africa. And all were required to undertake work in the phenomenology of religion in order to consider what constitutes religion and to examine basic forms and concepts such as prayer or sacrifice. As for research, the crying need seemed to be to be able to understand the local situation. Why were there 331 churches in a five-mile radius in one small town? How had these congregations come into being? What was the significance of the fact that in recounting the origins of any congregation in the area hardly anyone in that congregation ever mentioned a missionary?

By the time the Nigerian Civil War began, I was in my own country, once again teaching church history to students who were to be ministers. The traditional Scottish method of church history involved three years of teaching. The first year was for the early Church; the second, the Reformation; the third, Scotland—after all, what else is there? To have gone to such a post ten or twelve years earlier would have been delight; now it was mortification.

Of course, I was welcome to teach an optional course on African church history (not that anyone would be likely to opt for it). But the worrying thing was the deforming nature of such a syllabus of church history. It obstructed students from ever learning what the church was, or where the church was. The abundant evidence was on every hand of the decline of Christianity in Britain; but how would these future ministers ever realize that the Christian faith was actually expanding in most of the rest of the world, that most Christians would soon be living in the southern continents? Above all, the syllabus kept them from understanding Scotland's place in the world church. Gradually I found myself drawn into a new discipline, to which Africa had induced the first faltering steps. From church history, Christian duty led to the history of religions.

Quite unexpectedly came an invitation to open a new department of religious studies in a university which already had a faculty of divinity. It was 1970, and a post-Christian generation of students was finding a new interest in religion. Some indeed were highly committed believers; others highly uncommitted, but intensely interested. This generation was not rebelling against the church, because it had never been a part of it. The uncommitted were interested in prayer, meditation, devotion; and they expected to learn about such things if they learned about Indian religion. For such people, prayer and devotion were things that Hindus did; they had never associated them with the grey old churches that some of their parents still attended. The graduate program offered another dimension; for the people in it, often Africans, or, if Westerners, people with long service in Africa or the Pacific, were concerned with the religions of Africa, or the interactions of those religions with the Christian faith, or the history and life of churches or movements shaped by those conditions.

My duty was now to be, not a church historian, but a historian of religions whose principal concern was Christianity. It was a salutary experience to try to teach about Christian faith and history under the same conditions as I or my colleagues would teach about Islamic or Buddhist faith and history. It occurred to me that no one—certainly no Muslim or Buddhist—would offer an introductory course in Islamic or Buddhist history in the way the average New Testament 101 course was offered. Surely traditional theological teaching was selling Christianity short? More and more I was forced to consider what held the incredible cultural diversity of historic Christianity together. What united observant Pharisaic Jews of the post-Pentecost period, Greek theologians at Nicea, wild Irish ascetic monks, zealous Victorian supporters of missions, and white-robed Nigerian congregations chanting in the streets about the power of the Spirit? For all these culturally diverse groups were historically and organically linked in the chain of the transmission of the Gospel.

And in parallel with this went the study of the primal religions—first of Africa, then of the Pacific and the Americas. All other considerations apart, the historical study of Christianity demanded it. Throughout Christian history so far, the overwhelming majority of new Christians have come from the primal religions—far more than from Hinduism or Buddhism, incomparably more than from Islam.

Combining these areas of study brought another realization, matching the earlier realization that came in Sierra Leone about the patristic period. It was that texts still existed—many in Latin, others in Old North European languages—that reflected, directly or indirectly, the process of interaction between the Christian faith and the primal religions of Europe. What was the process by which my own ancestors, and those of most Western Christians, came to appropriate the Gospel? What were the structures of the old primal religions of Europe, and how parallel were they to the primal religions of today? More importantly, was it possible to understand those old texts (including those of well-known, widely translated writers such as Bede or Gregory of Tours) better in the light of the encounters of religions presently visible in Africa? And might the same texts which revealed those old human responses to the Christian faith help to understand what was going on in Africa now? One way of finding out was to spend a little labour in the study of Old Norse. Another was to bring together a mixed group of Western and African students to read these texts together. It was a revelation to see how African Christians responded to these documents which reflected the origins of Western European Christianity, and the insights they brought to them.

I now work in a centre of graduate studies where everyone is concerned with some aspect of Christian history, life or thought in Africa, Asia, Latin or Caribbean America, or the Pacific. There are 40 or 50 people, belonging to 15 or 20 nationalities, most of them experienced in teaching or ministry. The palefaces are always in a minority, and often there is hardly a native Scot to be seen. In such a group, everyone is a teacher and everyone a student. Such a group can help to uncover not only their own, but one another's Christian history; a history in which the missionary period is now only an episode. To be involved in such work is to be permitted to watch the Christian Gospel penetrating and interacting with the cultures of Africa, Asia and the Pacific in a way analogous to that by which in the patristic period where my studies began, it penetrated and interacted with the Greek.

The bewildering paradox at the heart of the Christian confession is not just the obvious one of the divine humanity; it is the twofold affirmation of the utter Jewishness of Jesus and of the boundless universality of the Divine Son. The paradox is necessary to the business of making sense of the history of the Christian faith. On the one hand it is a seemingly infinite series of cultural specificities—each in principle as locally specific as that utterly Jewish Jesus. On the other hand, in a historical view, the different specificities belong together. They have a certain coherence and interdependence in the coherence and interdependence of total humanity in the One who made humanity his own.

It is in the moments of transition, the process of diffusion across cultural boundaries, the points at which cultural specificities change, that the distinctive nature of the Christian faith becomes manifest in its developing dialogue with culture. The process is clearly visible within the New Testament itself. The Synoptic Gospels, rooted as they are in the soil of Palestine, set forth the Good News of Jesus in terms of the themes he himself preached, the Kingdom of God and the work of the Son of Man. But how rarely the letters of Paul, addressed to the Hellenistic world of West Asia and Southern Europe, employ the term Kingdom of God; and they never once speak of the Son of Man. Such Palestinian titles had little immediacy in the world of the new Christians; they required footnotes. In order to explain in the Greek world who Christ is and what he did and does, a new conceptual vocabulary had to be constructed. Elements of vocabulary already existing in that world had to be commandeered and turned towards Christ. And once that happened, and Hellenistic people began to see Christ in their own terms, a host of questions arose that Palestinian Jews, even those who had had a Hellenistic education and were at home in the language, felt no need to raise. Christian preaching and Christian understanding moved beyond the category of Messiah—which for many of the earliest believers must have seemed the heart of the Gospel—to embrace such categories as Logos and Pleroma to explain the significance of Jesus.

And the process was hugely enriching; it proved to be a discovery of the Christ. As Paul and his fellow missionaries explain and translate the significance of the Christ in a world that is Gentile and Hellenistic, that significance is seen to be greater than anyone had realized before. It is as though Christ himself actually grows through the work of mission—and indeed, there is more than a hint of this in one New Testament image (Eph. 4:13). As he enters new areas of thought and life, he fills the picture (the Pleroma dwells in him). It is surely right to see the process as being repeated in subsequent transmission of the faith across cultural lines.

The cultural diversity of Christianity is widely acknowledged today and perhaps now needs little new defence. Perhaps we need, however, to remember that this diversity exists not only in a *horizontal* form across the contemporary scene, but also in a *vertical* form across history. Christianity is a generational process, an ongoing dialogue with culture. Just as diversity of Christian expression and its ultimate coherence combine in the contemporary scene, so they are across the generations. We belong to the ancestors —and to our grandchildren, and this is as true of the Church as a whole as of any local segment of it. The full-grown humanity of Christ requires all the Christian generations, just as it embodies all the cultural variety that six continents can bring. As the writer to the Hebrews puts it, Abraham and the patriarchs have even now not yet reached their goal. They are waiting for "us" (Heb. 11:39-40).

In the pages that follow it is urged that the divine saving activity can be understood in terms of translation. Divinity is translated into humanity, but into *specific* humanity, at home in specific segments of social reality. If the Incarnation of the Son represents a divine act of translation, it is a prelude to repeated acts of re-translation as Christ fills the Pleroma again—other aspects of social reality. And the proper response to such activity is conversion. Conversion is turning; and Christian conversion is turning towards Christ. This means that the process of conversion involves turning what is already there.

The second and third parts of the book are simply explorations of the same theme in specific territories. The exponential growth of the Christian faith in the African continent in the past century or so seems to me to raise the question whether this massive encounter with a new body of thought and network of relationships may not be as determinative of the future shape of Christianity as was the encounter with the Greek world.

The missionary movement from the West offers another way of approach. It seems a particularly valuable one since we seem to be reaching the end of this particular chapter, and it may be possible to look at it in better perspective than before. No informed historian today is going to confuse missionary history with the church history of Africa or Asia.

Missionaries had a double identity. They were representative Christians trying (and in the process demonstrating all the elements of human fallenness and all the limitations of human vision and foresight) to do Christian things, things that were specifically, characteristically Christian. They were seeking to share the knowledge of Christ; and more than any other group of Westerners in the period of Western expansion, they were trying to make Christian choices and live in a Christian way. But they were also representative Westerners, shaped by Western history and conditions and values, and Western social networks and intellectual discourse. Today, Christians are no longer necessarily representative Westerners, and Westerners are not necessarily representative Christians; and that makes the period of double identity the more interesting. In fact the missionary movement was crucial to the way the Western world learned of the non-Western, because the missionary movement had perforce to engage with the cultures of the rest of the world in a more fundamental way than any other part of Western society.

Studies arising directly out of the work of mission in the nineteenth and early twentieth centuries had an immense impact on Western learning, opening new fields of study, pioneering new methods and disciplines, and adding new dimensions to those that already existed. It was the leading edge of the West's intellectual meeting with the non-Western world. It started within the Western world; the missionary movement was itself part of the intellectual discourse of the West. There was no other way open; none of us can begin to take in new ideas except in terms of ideas we already have. It was the conviction that Christ belonged to all humanity, and that the good news of Christ could be intelligibly received by all humanity, that motivated engagement with non-Western cultures at perhaps the most fundamental level Westerners attained during the colonial period.

But what began as a specific act of translation became part of a discovery of Christ. Once again the attempt to transmit faith in Christ across linguistic and cultural frontiers revealed that Christ had meanings and significance never guessed before, and revealed another glimpse of the glory of the completed, redeemed humanity. But there was no escape from the labour of translation, with its complexities, its ambiguities, and in the last analysis, its impossibility. The cost in application and agony was incalculable. The fundamental missionary experience, by which the endeavour stands or falls, is to live on terms set by someone else. This is as true in the intellectual realm as elsewhere.

Our own situation is quite different from that of an earlier time. The process of transmission no longer takes place necessarily from the Western intellectual discourse. It is multicultural in its personnel; it will be increasingly multicultural in expression and application. I do not claim to know where that may lead. But it is worth noticing from the story of the missionary movement how often early mission studies—while originating within and never independent of the Western intellectual tradition—frequently expanded, revised, contradicted and subverted that tradition. This took place because the practitioners were seeking—as they believed, trusted and prayed—to follow Christ where no one had been before. It is time to do it again. At a time when Christianity is itself increasingly marginal to Western intellectual discourse, that discourse needs to come to terms with Christianity as a non-Western religion.

Part One

THE TRANSMISSION OF CHRISTIAN FAITH

1

The Gospel as Prisoner and Liberator of Culture[1]

Is There a "Historic Christian Faith"?

Let us imagine a long-living, scholarly space visitor—a Professor of Comparative Inter-Planetary Religions perhaps—who is able to get periodic space-grants which enable him to visit Earth for field study every few centuries. Let us further assume that he wishes to pursue the study of the earth-religion Christianity on principles of Baconian induction, observing the practices, habits, and concerns of a representative sample of Christians, and that he exploits the advantage he has over any earthbound scholar by taking his sample across the centuries.

Let us assume his first visit to be to a group of the original Jerusalem Christians, about 37 CE. He notes that they are all Jews; indeed, they are meeting in the Temple, where only Jews can enter. They offer animal sacrifices. They keep the seventh day punctiliously free from work. They circumcise their male children. They carefully follow a succession of rituals, and delight in the reading of old law books. They appear, in fact, to be one of several "denominations" of Judaism. What distinguishes them from the others is simply that they identify the figures of Messiah, Son of Man, and Suffering Servant (figures all described in those law books) with the recent prophet-teacher Jesus of Nazareth, whom they believe to have inaugurated the last days. They live normal family lives, with a penchant for large, close families; and they have a tightly knit social organization, with many common meals taken in each other's houses. Law and joyful observance strike our spaceman observer as key notes of the religion of these early Christians.

His next visit to Earth is made about 325 CE. He attends a great meeting of Church leaders—perhaps even the Council of Nicea. The company come

[1]This article was first published in *Faith and Thought* 108 (Nos. 1 and 2, 1982): 39-52. A slightly revised form appeared in *Missionalia* 10 (No. 3, 1982).

from all over the Mediterranean world and beyond it, but hardly one of them is Jewish; indeed on the whole they are rather hostile to Jews. They are horrified at the thought of animal sacrifices; when they talk about offering sacrifices they mean bread and wine used rather as it was in the house meals our observer noticed in Jerusalem. They do not have children themselves, since Church leaders are not expected to marry, and indeed most of them regard marriage as an inferior, morally compromised state; but they would regard a parent who circumcised his children as having betrayed his faith. They treat the seventh day as an ordinary working day: they have special religious observances on the first day, but do not necessarily abstain from work or other activities. They use the law books that the Jerusalem Christians used, in translation, and thus know the titles Messiah, Son of Man, and Suffering Servant; but "Messiah" has now become almost the surname of Jesus, and the other titles are hardly used at all. They give equal value to another set of writings, not even composed when the Jerusalem Christians met, and tend to use other titles, "Son of God," "Lord," to designate Jesus.

Their present preoccupation, however, is with the application of another set of words to Jesus—words not to be found in either set of writings. The debate (and they believe it of absolutely fundamental importance) is over whether the Son is *homo-ousios* with the Father, or only *homoi-ousios* with Him.

The dominant factors which the outsider notices as characteristic of these Christians are the concern with metaphysics and theology, an intense intellectual scrutiny, an attempt to find precise significance for precise terms. He thinks of the Jewish Christians in the Temple nearly three centuries back, and wonders.

The best cure for his wonderment is the still greater wonder of a journey to Ireland some three centuries later still.

A number of monks are gathered on a rocky coastline. Several are standing in ice-cold water up to their necks, reciting the psalms. Some are standing immobile, praying—with their arms outstretched in the form of a cross. One is receiving six strokes of the lash because he did not answer "Amen" when the grace was said at the last meal of brown bread and dulse. Others are going off in a small boat in doubtful weather with a box of beautiful manuscripts and not much else to distribute themselves on islands in the Firth of Clyde, calling the astonished inhabitants to give up their worship of nature divinities and seek for joy in a future heavenly kingdom. Others are sitting quite alone in dark caves by the seashore, seeking no intercourse with men.

He ascertains from these curious beings that their beautiful manuscripts include versions of the same holy writings that the Greek fathers used. He notices that the Irish use the same formula that he heard being hammered out in Nicea in 325 CE; somewhat to his surprise, because they do not in general seem very interested in theology or very good at metaphysics. They attach great importance to the date on which they celebrate their main festival, Easter; an outsider is most likely to notice their desire for holiness and their heroic austerity in quest of it.

Our spaceman delays his next visit until the 1840s, when he comes to London and finds in Exeter Hall a large and visibly excited assembly hearing speeches about the desirability of promoting Christianity, commerce, and civilization in Africa. They are proposing that missionaries armed with Bibles and cotton seeds be sent a distance of four thousand miles to effect the process. They are also proposing a deputation to the British Government about the necessity of putting down the slave trade, raising a subscription to promote the education of Black mechanics, agreeing that letters be written, pamphlets and articles published. The meeting has begun with a reading from the same book (in English translation) that the other Christians used, and there have been many other quotations from the book; indeed, a large number of people in the meeting seem to be carrying it. On enquiry, the observer finds that most also accept without question the creed of Nicea. Like the Irish, they also use the world "holy" quite a lot; but they are aghast at the suggestion that holiness could be connected with standing in cold water, and utterly opposed to the idea of spending life praying in an isolated cave. Whereas the Irish monks were seeking to live on as little as possible, most of this group look remarkably well fed. What impresses the outsider is their activism and the involvement of their religion in all processes of life and society.

In 1980 he comes to Earth again, this time to Lagos, Nigeria. A white-robed group is dancing and chanting through the streets on their way to their church. They are informing the world at large that they are Cherubim and Seraphim; they are inviting people to come and experience the power of God in their services. They claim that God has messages for particular individuals and that his power can be demonstrated in healing. They carry and quote from the same book as the Exeter Hall gentlemen. They say (on being shown the document in a prayer book) that they accept the creed of Nicea, but they display little interest in it: they appear somewhat vague about the relationship of the Divine Son and the Holy Spirit. They are not politically active and the way of life pursued by the Exeter Hall gentlemen is quite foreign to them; they fast like the Irish, but only on fixed occasions and for fixed purposes. The characteristic which springs most readily to the spaceman's mind is their concern with power, as revealed in preaching, healing, and personal vision.

Back in his planetary home, how does our scholar correlate the phenomena he has observed? It is not simply that these five groups of humans, all claiming to be Christians, appear to be concerned about different things; the concerns of one group appear suspect or even repellent to another.

Now in no case has he chosen freakish examples of Christians. He has gone to groups which may, as far as such statements can be permissible at all, be said to reflect representative concerns of Christians of those times and places, and in each case the place is in the Christian heartlands of that period. In 37 CE most Christians were Jews. Not only was Jerusalem the Christian center; Jerusalem Christians laid down the norms and standards for other people. By 325 CE few Christians were Jews, the main Christian centers lay in the Eastern Mediterranean and the key language for Christians was Greek. By 600 CE, the balance had shifted westward, and the growing edge of Christianity was among the northern and western tribal and semi-tribal peoples—and Ireland was a power center. In the 1840s Great Britain would certainly be among the outstanding Christian nations, and certainly the one most notably associated with the expansion of the Christian faith. By 1980, the balance had shifted again, southwards; Africa is now the continent most notable for those that profess and call themselves Christians.[2]

So will our visitor conclude that there *is* no coherence? That the use of the name Christian by such diverse groups is fortuitous, or at least misleading? Or does he catch among the spheres some trace of Gilbert Murray's remark that representative Christians of the third, thirteenth, and twentieth centuries would have less in common than would a Catholic, Methodist, and Free-thinker, or even (glancing round the College Common Room and noting the presence of Sir Sarvepalli Radhakrishnan) "a well-educated Buddhist or Brahmin at the present day?"[3] Is shared religion in the end simply a function of shared culture?

Our spaceman may, however, note that between the five groups he has visited there is a historical connection. It was Christians scattered from Jerusalem who first preached to Greeks and founded that vast Greek edifice he observed in 325; it is in Eastern Christianity that we must seek some of the important features and some of the power of Celtic Christian religion. That Celtic religion played a vital part in the gradual emergence of the religion of Exeter Hall. And the Cherubim and Seraphim now in Lagos are ultimately a result of the very sort of operations which were under discussion at the Exeter Hall meeting.

But besides this historical connection, closer examination reveals that there are other definite signs of continuity. There is, in all the wild profusion of the varying statements of these differing groups, one theme which is as unvarying as the language which expresses it is various; that the person of Jesus called the Christ has ultimate significance. In the institutional sphere, too, all use the same sacred writings; and all use bread and wine and water in a special way. Still more remarkable is the continuity of consciousness. Each group thinks of itself as having some community with the others, so

---

[2]See David B. Barrett, "A.D. 2000: 350 Million Christians in Africa," *International Review of Mission* 59 (1970): 39-54; A.F. Walls, "Towards Understanding Africa's Place in Christian History," in J.S. Pobee, ed., *Religion in a Pluralistic Society: Essays Presented to Professor C.G. Baëta* (Leiden, 1976), pp. 180-189.

[3]Gilbert Murray, *Five Stages of Greek Religion* (1935), p. 174.

different in time and place, and despite being so obviously out of sympathy with many of their principal concerns. Still more remarkable, each thinks of itself as in some respect continuous with ancient Israel, even though only the first have any conceivable ethnic reason to do so, and though some of the groups must have found it extremely hard to form any concept of ancient Israel, or any clear idea of what a Jew might be or look like.

Our observer is therefore led to recognize an essential continuity in Christianity: continuity of thought about the final significance of Jesus, continuity of a certain consciousness about history, continuity in the use of the Scriptures, of bread and wine, of water. But he recognizes that these continuities are cloaked with such heavy veils belonging to their environment that Christians of different times and places must often be unrecognizable to others, or indeed even to themselves, as manifestations of a single phenomenon.

The "Indigenizing" Principle

Church history has always been a battleground for two opposing tendencies; and the reason is that each of the tendencies has its origin in the Gospel itself. On the one hand it is of the essence of the Gospel that God accepts us as we are, on the ground of Christ's work alone, not on the ground of what we have become or are trying to become. But, if He accepts us "as we are" that implies He does not take us as isolated, self-governing units, because we are not. We are conditioned by a particular time and place, by our family and group and society, by "culture" in fact. In Christ God accepts us together with our group relations; with that cultural conditioning that makes us feel at home in one part of human society and less at home in another. But if He takes us with our group relations, then surely it follows that He takes us with our "dis-relations" also; those predispositions, prejudices, suspicions, and hostilities, whether justified or not, which mark the group to which we belong. He does not wait to tidy up our ideas any more than He waits to tidy up our behavior before He accepts us sinners into His family.

The impossibility of separating an individual from his social relationships and thus from his society leads to one unvarying feature in Christian history: the desire to "indigenize," to live as a Christian and yet as a member of one's own society, to make the Church (to use the memorable title of a book written in 1967 by F.B. Welbourn and B.A. Ogot about Independent churches in Africa) *A Place to Feel at Home.*

This fact has led to more than one crisis in Christian history, including the first and most important of all. When the elders at Jerusalem in the council of Acts 15 came to their decision that Gentiles could enter Israel without becoming Jews, had they any idea how close the time would be when *most* Christians would be Gentiles? And would they have been so happy with their decision had they realized it? Throughout the early years the Jerusalem Church was in a position to set the standards and to make the decisions, because of its direct connection with the Savior, and its incomparably greater knowledge of the Scriptures. And when its historic decision opened the door wide for Gentile believers in the Jewish Messiah, there must have been many who assumed that nevertheless Gentile Christians, as they matured, would come to look as much like Jerusalem Christians as was possible for such benighted heathen. At least Acts 21:20 suggests that, while being decently glad of the "mission field" conversions recounted by Paul, they continued to think of Jerusalem as the regulative center of God's saving word. What were the thoughts of those who fled from Jerusalem as the Roman armies moved in to cast down the Temple? Did they realize that the future of Messiah's proclamation now lay with people who were uncircumcised, defective in their knowledge of Law and Prophets, still confused by hangovers from paganism, and able to eat pork without turning a hair? Yet this—and the fact that there were still many left to speak of Jesus as Messiah—was the direct result of the decision of the Jerusalem Council to allow Gentle converts "a place to feel at home." So also was the acceptance of Paul's emphatic teaching that since God accepts the heathen as they are, circumcision, food avoidances, and ritual washings are not for them. Christ has so made Himself at home in Corinthian society that a pagan is consecrated through his or her Christian marriage partner (1 Cor. 7:14). No group of Christians has therefore any right to impose in the name of Christ upon another group of Christians a set of assumptions about life determined by another time and place.

The fact, then, that "if any man is in Christ he is a new creation" does not mean that he starts or continues his life in a vacuum, or that his mind is a blank table. It has been formed by his own culture and history, and since God has accepted him as he is, his Christian mind will continue to be influenced by what was in it before. And this is as true for groups as for persons. All churches are culture churches—including our own.

The "Pilgrim" Principle

But throughout Church history there has been another force in tension with this indigenizing principle, and this also is equally of the Gospel. Not only does God in Christ take people as they are: He takes them in order to transform them into what He wants them to be. Along with the indigenizing principle which makes his faith a place to feel at home, the Christian inherits the pilgrim principle, which whispers to him that he has no abiding city and warns him that to be faithful to Christ will put him out of step with his society; for that society never existed, in East or West, ancient time or modern, which could absorb the word of Christ painlessly into its system. Jesus within Jewish culture, Paul within Hellenistic culture, take it for granted that there will be rubs and frictions—not from the adoption of a new culture, but from the transformation of the mind towards that of Christ.

Just as the indigenizing principle, itself rooted in the Gospel, associates Christians with the *particulars* of their culture and group, the pilgrim principle, in tension with the indigenizing and equally of the Gospel, by associating them with things and people outside the culture and group, is in some respects a *universalizing* factor. The Christian has all the relationships in which he was brought up, and has them sanctified by Christ who is living in them. But he has also an entirely new set of relationships, with other members of the family of faith into which he has come, and whom he must accept, with all their group relations (and "disrelations") on them, just as God has accepted him with his. Every Christian has dual nationality, and has a loyalty to the faith family which links him to those in interest groups opposed to that to which he belongs by nature.

In addition—as we observed to be the case in all the spaceman's varied groups of representative Christians—the Christian is given an adoptive past. He is linked to the people of God in all generations (like him, members of the faith family), and most strangely of all, to the whole history of Israel, the curious continuity of the race of the faithful from Abraham. By this means, the history of Israel is part of Church history,[4] and all Christians of whatever nationality, are landed by adoption with several millennia of someone else's history, with a whole set of ideas, concepts, and assumptions which do not necessarily square with the rest of their cultural inheritance; and the Church in every land, of whatever race and type of society, has this same adoptive past by which it needs to interpret the fundamentals of the faith. The adoption into Israel becomes a "universalizing" factor, bringing Christians of all cultures and ages together through a common inheritance, lest any of us make the Christian faith such a place to feel at home that no one else can live there; and bringing into everyone's society some sort of outside reference.

The Future of Christian Theology
and Its Cultural Conditioning

In the remainder of this paper I would like to suggest something of the relevance of the tension between the indigenizing and the pilgrim principles for the future of Christian theology.

First, let us recall that within the last century there has been a massive southward shift of the center of gravity of the Christian world, so that the representative Christian lands now appear to be in Latin America, Sub-Saharan Africa, and other parts of the southern continents. This means that Third

---

[4] " . . . the first fact of the Church [is] that we are Gentiles who worship the God of the Jews" — with *their* psalms, in Gentile languages but their concepts (Paul van Buren, "The Mystery and Salvation and Prayer," *Ecumenical Institute for Advanced Theological Studies Yearbook* [Jerusalem, 1977-78], pp. 37-52).

World theology is now likely to be the representative Christian theology. On present trends (and I recognize that these may not be permanent) the theology of European Christians, while important for them and their continued existence, may become a matter of specialist interest to historians (rather as the theology of the Syriac Edessene Church is specialist matter for early Church historians of today, not a topic for the ordinary student and general reader, whose eyes are turned to the Greco-Roman world when he studies the history of doctrine). The future general reader of Church history is more likely to be concerned with Latin American and African, and perhaps some Asian, theology. It is perhaps significant that in the last few years we have seen for the first time works of theology composed in the Third World (the works of Latin American theologians of liberation, such as Gutiérrez, Segundo, and Miguez Bonino) becoming regular reading in the West—not just for missiologists, but for the general theological reader. The fact that particular Third World works of theology appear on the Western market is not, however, a necessary measure of their intrinsic importance. It simply means that publishers think them sufficiently relevant to the West to sell there. Theology is addressed to the setting in which it is produced.

This is perhaps the first important point to remember about theology: that since it springs out of practical situations, it is therefore *occasional* and *local* in character. Since we have mentioned Gutiérrez, some words of his may be quoted here. Theology, he says, arises spontaneously and inevitably in the believer, in all who have accepted the gift of the word of God. There is therefore in every believer, and every community of believers, at least a rough outline of a theology. This conviction leads to another: whatever else theology is, it is what Gutiérrez calls "critical reflection on Christian praxis in the light of the word."[5] That is, theology is about testing your actions by Scripture.

In this, of course, we are hearing the typical modern Latin American theologian, who is stung by the fact that it has taken Marxists to point out things that Amos and Isaiah said long ago, while Christians have found good theological reasons to justify the position of Jeroboam, Manasseh, and Dives, and is nagged by the remark of Bernanos that "God does not choose the same men to keep his word as to fulfil it." But it is likely to be the way of things also in Africa. The domestic tasks of Third World theology are going to be so basic, so vital, that there will be little time for the barren, sterile, time-wasting by-paths into which so much Western theology and theological research has gone in recent years. Theology in the Third World will be, as theology at all creative times has always been, about *doing* things, about things that deeply affect the lives of numbers of people. We see something of this already in South African Black Theology, which is literally

---

[5]Gustavo Gutiérrez, *A Theology of Liberation* (Maryknoll, N.Y.: Orbis Books; London: SCM, 1973; rev. ed., with new introduction, 1988), pp. 6-15.

about life and death matters (as one South African Black theologian put it to me, "Black Theology is about how to stay Christian when you're a Black in South Africa, and you're hanging on by the skin of your teeth"). There is no need to go back to wars of religion when men shed blood for their theologies: but at least there is something to be said for having a theology about things which are worth shedding blood for. And that, Third World Theology is likely to be.

Because of this relation of theology to action, theology arises out of situations that actually happen, not from broad general principles. Even the Greek Church, with centuries of intellectual and rhetorical tradition, took almost 200 years to produce a book of theology written for its own sake, Origen's *De Principiis*. In those two centuries innumerable theological books were written, but not for the sake of producing theologies. The theology was for a purpose: to *explain* the faith to outsiders, or to point out where the writer thought someone else had misrepresented what Christians meant.

It is therefore important, when thinking of African theology, to remember that it will act on an African agenda. It is useless for us to determine what we think an African theology ought to be doing: it will concern itself with questions that worry Africans, and will leave blandly alone all sorts of questions which we think absolutely vital. We all do the same. How many Christians belonging to churches which accept the Chalcedonian Definition of the Faith could explain with any conviction to an intelligent non-Christian why it is important not to be a Nestorian or a Monophysite? Yet once men not only excommunicated each other, they shed their own and others' blood to get the right answer on that question. The things which we think are vital points of principle will seem as far away and negligible to African theologians as those theological prize fights among the Egyptian monks now seem to us. Conversely the things that concern African theologians may seem to us at best peripheral. Remembering the emergence of theology at a popular level, it is noteworthy how African Independent churches sometimes seem to pick on a point which strikes us by its oddity or irrelevance, like rules about worship during the menstrual period. But this is usually because the topic, or the sort of topic, is a major one for certain African Christians, just as it apparently was for the old Hebrews, and it needs an answer, and an answer related to Christ. There often turns out to be a sort of coherence in the way in which these churches deal with it, linking Scripture, old traditions, and the Church as the new Levitical community—and giving an answer to something that had been worrying people. In short, it is safe for a European to make only one prediction about the valid, authentic African Biblical theology we all talk about: that it is likely either to puzzle us or to disturb us.

But is not the sourcebook of all valid theology the canonical Scriptures? Yes, and in that, as the spaceman found, lies the continuity of the Christian faith. But, as he also found, the Scriptures are read with different eyes by people in different times and places; and in practice, each age and community makes its own selection of the Scriptures, giving prominence to those which seem to speak most clearly to the community's time and place and leaving aside others which do not appear to yield up their gold so readily. How many of us, while firm as a rock as to its canonicity, seriously look to the book of Leviticus for sustenance? Yet many an African Independent church has found it abundantly relevant. (Interestingly, Samuel Ajayi Crowther, the great nineteenth-century Yoruba missionary bishop, thought it should be among the first books of the Bible to be translated).

The indigenizing principle ensures that each community recognizes in Scripture that God is speaking to its own situation. But it also means that we all approach Scripture wearing cultural blinkers, with assumptions determined by our time and place. It astonishes us when we read second-century Christian writers who all venerated Paul, and to whom we owe the preservation of his writings, that they never seem to understand what we are sure he means by justification by faith. It is perhaps only in our own day, when we do not read Plato so much, that Western Christians have begun to believe that the resurrection of the body is not the immortality of the soul, or to recognize the solidly material content of biblical salvation. Africans will have their cultural blinkers, too, which will prevent, or at least render it difficult for them to see some things. But they will doubtless be different things from those hidden in our own blind spots, so they should be able to see some things much better than we do.

That wise old owl, Henry Venn of the Church Missionary Society, reflecting on the Great Commission in 1868, argued that the fullness of the Church would only come with the fullness of the national manifestations of different national churches:

> Inasmuch as all native churches grow up into the fullness of the stature of Christ, distinctions and defects will vanish. . . . But it may be doubted whether, to the last, the Church of Christ will not exhibit marked national characteristics which, in the overruling grace of God, will tend to its perfection and glory.[6]

Perhaps it is not only that different ages and nations see different things in Scripture—it is that they *need* to see different things.

The major theological debate in independent Africa[7] just now—Item 1 on the African theological agenda—would appear to be the nature of the African past. Almost every major work by an African scholar in the field of

---

[6]Instructions of the Committee of the Church Missionary Society to Departing Missionaries, June 30, 1868, reproduced in W. Knight, *The Missionary Secretariat of Henry Venn* (1880, p. 284).

[7]"Independent Africa" is here distinguished from South Africa, where different conditions have produced different priorities and a different debate.

religions—Harry Sawyerr,[8] Bolaji Idowu,[9] J. S. Mbiti,[10] Vincent Mulago[11]—
is in some way dealing with it. Now each of the authors named was trained
in theology on a Western model; but each has moved into an area for which
no Western syllabus prepared him, for each has been forced to study and
lecture on African traditional religion—and each has found himself writing
on it. It seems to me, however, that they all approach this topic, not as
historians of religions do, nor as anthropologists do. They are still, in fact,
Christian theologians. All are wrestling with a theological question, the
prime one on the African Christian's intellectual agenda: who am I? What
is my relation as an African Christian to Africa's past?

Thus, when Idowu concludes with such passion that the *orìṣas* are only
manifestations of Olódùmare, and that it is a Western misrepresentation to
call Yoruba religion polytheistic, the urgency in his voice arises from the
fact that he is not making a clinical observation of the sort one might make
about Babylonian religion: he is handling dynamite, his own past, his
people's present. One can see why a non-Christian African writer like Okot
p'Bitek, who glories in pre-Christian Africa, accuses John Mbiti and others
so bitterly of continuing the Western missionary misrepresentation of the
past.[12] It is as though he were saying "They are taking from us our own
decent paganism, and plastering it over with interpretations from alien
sources." Here speaks the authentic voice of Celsus.

The mention of Celsus reminds us perhaps that African Christians are
not the first people to have a religious identity crisis. Gentile Christians had
precisely the same issue to face—an issue that never faced the Jewish
missionaries, Paul, Peter, Barnabas. They knew who they were ("circumcised the eighth day, of the tribe of Benjamin . . . "), just as Western
missionaries for more than 150 confident years knew who *they* were. It is
our past which tells us who we are; without our past we are lost. The man
with amnesia is lost, unsure of relationships, incapable of crucial decisions,
precisely because all the time he has amnesia he is without his past. Only
when his memory returns, when he is sure of his past, is he able to relate
confidently to his wife, his parents, or know his place in a society.

Early Gentile Christianity went through a period of amnesia. It was not
so critical for first-generation converts: they responded to a clear choice,
turned from idols to serve the living God, accepted the assurance that they

---

[8]See Harry Sawyerr, *God—Ancestor or Creator?* (1970).

[9]See Bolaji Idowu, *Olódùmare: God in Yoruba Belief* (1962) and *African Traditional Religion: A Definition* (1973).

[10]See John S. Mbiti, *New Testament Eschatology in an African Background* (Oxford, 1971); *African Religions and Philosophy* (1969); and *Concepts of God in Africa* (1970).

[11]See Vincent Mulago, "Christianisme et culture africaine," in C.G. Baëta, ed., *Christianity in Tropical Africa* (1968), pp. 308-28.

[12]See Okot p'Bitek, *African Religions in Western Scholarship* (Kampala, 1971).

had been grafted into Israel. It was the second and third generations of Christians who felt the strain more. What was their relation to the Greek past? Some of them (some indeed in the first generation, as the New Testament indicates) solved the problem by pretending their Greek past did not exist, by pretending they were Jews, adopting Jewish customs, even to circumcision. Paul saw this coming and roundly condemned it. You are *not* Jews, he argues in Romans 9-11; you *are* Israel, but grafted into it. And, defying all the realities of horticulture, he talks about a wild plant being grafted into a cultivated one. But one thing he is saying is that Gentile Christianity is part of the *wild* olive. It is different in character from the plant into which it is grafted. Such is the necessity of the indigenizing principle.

Later Gentile Christians, by then the majority in the Church, and in no danger of confusing themselves with Jews, had a major problem. Yes, they were grafted into Israel. The sacred history of Israel was part of their history. Yes, the idolatry and immorality of their own society, past and present, must have nothing to do with them. But what was God doing in the Greek world all those centuries while he was revealing himself in judgment and mercy to Israel? Not all the Greek past was graven images and temple prostitution. What of those who testified for righteousness—and even died for it? Had God nothing to do with their righteousness? What of those who taught things that are true—that are according to reason, *logos*, opposed to the Great Lies taught and practiced by others? Had their *logos* nothing to do with The Logos, the light that lighteth every man coming into the world? Is there any truth which is not God's truth? Was God not active in the Greek past, not just the Jewish? So Justin Martyr and Clement of Alexandria came up with their own solutions, that there were Christians before Christ, that philosophy was—and is—the schoolmaster to bring the Greeks to Christ, just as was the Law for Jews.

This is no place to renew the old debate about continuity or discontinuity of Christianity with pre-Christian religion, nor to discuss the theology of Justin and Clement, nor to consider the correctness of Idowu and Mbiti. My point is simply that the two latter are wrestling with essentially the same problem as the two former, and that it seems to be the most urgent problem facing African Christians today, on their agenda. Until it is thought through, amnesia could make African Christianity tentative and unsure of its relationships, and unable to recognize important tasks. More than one answer may emerge; the early centuries, after all, saw the answer of Tertullian as well as of Clement. And there may be little that outsiders can do to assist. Once again Paul saw what was coming. "Is He not," he asks his Jewish interlocutor, and on the most thoroughly Jewish grounds, "the God of the Gentiles also?" (Rom. 3:29f.).

The debate will certainly reflect the continuing tension between the indigenizing and the pilgrim principles of the Gospel. Paul, Justin, and Clement all knew people who followed one without the other. Just as there were "pilgrims" who sought to follow, or to impose upon others the modes of thought and life, concerns and preconceptions which belonged to someone else, so there were Greek-educated "indigenizers" who sought to eliminate what they considered "barbarian" elements from Christianity such as the Resurrection and the Last Judgment. But these things were part of a framework which ultimately derived from the Christian faith, and thus they played down, or ignored, or explicitly rejected, the Old Testament, the Christian adoptive past. Perhaps the most important thing to remember about the opponents of these Gnostics is that they were just as Greek as the Gnostics themselves, with many of the same instincts and difficulties; but they knew instinctively that they must hold to their adoptive past, and in doing so saved the Scriptures for the Church. Perhaps the real test of theological authenticity is the capacity to incorporate the history of Israel and God's people and to treat it as one's own.

When the Scriptures are read in some enclosed Zulu Zion, the hearers may catch the voice of God speaking out of a different Zion, and speaking to the whole world. When a comfortable bourgeois congregation meets in some Western suburbia, they, almost alone of all the comfortable bourgeois of the suburbs, are regularly exposed to the reading of a non-bourgeois book questioning fundamental assumptions of their society. But since none of us can read the Scriptures without cultural blinkers of some sort, the great advantage, the crowning excitement which our own era of Church history has over all others, is the possibility that we may be able to read them together. Never before has the Church looked so much like the great multitude whom no man can number out of every nation and tribe and people and tongue. Never before, therefore, has there been so much potentiality for mutual enrichment and self-criticism, as God causes yet more light and truth to break forth from his word.[13]

---

[13]I have quoted here sentences from my paper "African and Christian Identity," which first appeared in the Mennonite journal *Mission Focus* and was later reprinted in W.R. Shenk, ed., *Mission Focus—Current Issues* (Scottdale, Penna.: Herald Press, 1980).

2

Culture and Coherence in Christian History[1]

From Pentecost to the twentieth century, Christian history may be divided into six phases. Each phase represents its embodiment in a major culture area which has meant that in that phase it has taken an impress from that culture. In each phase the expression of the Christian faith has developed features which could only have originated in that culture whose impress it has taken within that phase.

Jewish—the First Age

For one brief, but vital, period, Christianity was entirely Jewish. The Christians of the first generation were all Jews—diverse, perhaps, in background and outlook, Hebraist and Hellenist, conservative and liberal—but without the slightest idea that they had "changed their religion" by recognizing Jesus as Messiah. It remains one of the marvels of the ages that Christianity entered its second phase at all. But those unnamed "men of Cyprus and Cyrene" introduced some Greek-speaking pagans in Antioch to the Jewish national saviour, and those law-righteous apostles and elders at Jerusalem agreed that they might enter Israel without becoming Jews. The result was that Christianity became Hellenistic-Roman; the Messiah, Saviour of Israel, was recognized to be also the Lord, Saviour of souls. It happened just in time, for soon afterwards the Jewish state disappeared in the early holocausts of AD 70 and AD 135. Only the timeous diffusion of faith in Jesus across cultural lines gave that faith any continuing place in the world. Without its diffusion at that time its principal representatives would have been the Ebionites and similar groups who by the third and fourth centuries lay on the very fringe of the Christian movement, even if they themselves could claim to be the enduring legacy of James the Just and the Jerusalem elders.

---

[1]This chapter was delivered in 1982 as the Finlayson Lecture in Edinburgh.

In the process of transmission the expression of that faith changed beyond what many an outsider might recognize. To see the extent of the change one has only to look at the utterances of early Jewish Christians as reflected in the New Testament, the utterances which indicate their priorities, the matters most on their hearts. "We had hoped that he would be the one to set Israel free," says the disillusioned disciple on the way to Emmaus (Luke 24:21, TEV). On the mount of ascension, the preoccupation is the same. Realizing that they stand at the threshold of a new era, the disciples ask, "Lord will you at this time give the Kingdom back to Israel?" (Acts 1:6). Statements and questions like these could be uttered only by Jews, out of centuries of present suffering and hope deferred. They can have no meaning for those who belong to the nations, whether in the first or the twentieth century. These come to Jesus with quite different priorities, and those priorities shape the questions they ask, even about salvation. A first-century Levantine Gentile would never have brought to Jesus as a matter of urgency the question of the political destiny of Israel; though he might have raised that of the destiny of the soul. The fact remains that Jesus Christ fulfilled the different statements, and answered the different questions; or rather, he convinced his Jewish and his Gentile followers, as he convinces his followers today, that the answer to their deepest questions lay with him, even when the question and the answer did not seem to fit. No doubt the words of Cleophas on the Emmaus road, or of the disciples on the mountain, betray an inadequate understanding of his person and work. Nevertheless, he does not reject that understanding as altogether misplaced. He does not say, "I am not in the business of giving the Kingdom back to Israel, you should keep out of politics and concentrate on inner spiritual realities." He accepts the statement and the question in the terms in which they are posed—terms which centuries of peculiar experience had conditioned Jews to frame. But—"it is not for you to know when" (Acts 1:7). There is no reason to think that Gentile statements about the ultimate will be any more final, or Gentile questions about it any more penetrating, than Jewish ones. There is no reason to suppose that Christ's answer to our own fundamental statements and questions, conditioned by quite different experiences, will be any less oblique than those he gave to Cleophas or the disciples. We know only that the full answer must ultimately be no less satisfying.

Those Christian Jews in Antioch who realized that Jesus had something to say to their pagan friends took an immense risk. They were prepared to drop the time-honoured word Messiah, knowing that it would mean little to their neighbors, and perhaps mislead them—what concern was the redeemer of Israel, should they grasp the concept, to them? They were prepared to see the title of their national saviour, the fulfillment of the dearest hopes of their people, become attached to the name of Jesus as though it was a sort of surname. They took up the ambiguous and easily misunderstood word "Lord" (Acts 11:20; contrast, e.g., Acts 9:22, which relates to a Jewish audience). They could not possibly have foreseen where their action would lead; and it would be surprising if someone did not warn them about the disturbing possibilities of confusion and syncretism. But their cross-cultural communication saved Christian faith for the world.

Hellenistic-Roman—the Second Age

The second of the six phases of Christianity was Hellenistic-Roman. This is not, of course, to say that within that age Christianity was geographically confined to the area where Hellenistic-Roman culture was dominant. Important Christian communities lay, for instance, in Central Asia, and East Africa, and South India. But the dominant expression of the Christian faith for several centuries resulted from its steady penetration of Hellenistic thought and culture during a period when that culture was also associated with a single political entity, the Roman Empire.

The second phase, has, like the first, left its mark on all later Christianity. Of the new religious ideas which entered with the Christian penetration of Hellenistic culture, one of the most permeative for the future was that of orthodoxy, of a canon of right belief, capable of being stated in a series of propositions arrived at by a process of logical argument. Such a feature was not likely to mark Christianity in its Jewish period; Jewish identity has always been concerned either with what a person *is* or what he *does* rather than with what he believes. But when Christian faith began to penetrate the Hellenistic Roman world, it encountered a total system of thought, a system to which it was in some respects antipathetic, but which, once encountered, had to be permeated. The system had a certain inbuilt arrogance, a feature it has never quite lost despite the mutations through which the Hellenistic-Roman legacy has gone in its transmission over the centuries to other peoples, and despite the penetration effected by Christian faith. Basically it maintained that there is one desirable pattern of life, a single "civilization" in effect, one model of society, one body of law, one universe of ideas. Accordingly, there are in essence two types of humanity: people who share that pattern and those ideas, and people who do not. There are Greeks—a cultural, not an ethnic term—and there are barbarians. There are civilized people who share a common heritage, and there are savages who do not.

In many ways the Jews and their religion already represented a challenge to this assumption. Whatever degree of assimilation to it many Jews might reflect, the stubborn fact of Jewish identity put them in a different category from almost all of the rest of the Hellenistic-Roman universe. Alone in that universe they had an alternative literature, a written tradition, of comparable antiquity. And they had their own dual classification of mankind: Israel, *the* nation, and the nations. Hellenistic-Roman Christians had no option but to maintain, and to seek to reconcile, aspects of both their inheritances.

The total system of thought had to be penetrated by the Gospel, Christianized. This meant the endeavour to bring the intellectual tradition into captivity to Christ and using it for new purposes, and it also meant putting the traditions of codification and of organization to the service of the Gospel. The result was orthodoxy: logically expounded belief set in codified form, established through a process of consultation, and maintained through effective organization. Hellenistic-Roman civilization offered a total system of thought, and expected general conformity to its norms. The Christian penetration of the system inevitably left it a total system.

Barbarian—the Third Age

Hellenistic-Roman civilization lived for centuries in the shadow of fear; fear of the day when the centre could not hold, when things fell apart, when the over-extended frontiers collapsed and the barbarian hordes poured in. Christians fully shared these fears. Tertullian, who lived in the age of persecution, though he would not countenance Christians in the army— Christ has unbelted every soldier, he says—prayed for the preservation of the Empire; for when the frontiers collapsed, the Great Tribulation would begin. For the people living under the Christian Empire the triumph of the barbarians would be equated with the end of Christian civilization.

Two great events brought about the end of Hellenistic-Roman Christianity. One had been widely predicted—the collapse of the Western Roman Empire before the barbarians. The other no one could have predicted—the emergence of the Arabs as a world power and their occupation of the Eastern provinces where the oldest and strongest Christian churches lay. The combination of these forces led to the end of the Hellenistic-Roman phase of Christianity. That it did not lead to the slow strangulation of the total Christian presence in the world was due to the slow, painful, and far from satisfactory spread of Christian allegiance among the tribal peoples beyond the old frontiers, the people known as barbarians, the destroyers of Christian civilization. What in fact happened was the development of a third phase of Christianity, what we may call a barbarian phase. Once again, it was only just in time: centuries of erosion and attrition faced the peoples of Christianity's Hellenistic heartlands. Once again, Christianity had been saved by its cross-cultural diffusion.

The cultural gap to be bridged was quite as great as that between Jew and Greek, yet the former faith of classical civilization became the religion of peasant cultivators. The process was marked by the more or less ready acceptance by the new Christians of a great deal of the cultural inheritance of the classical civilization from which they derived their Christianity. Further, when they substituted the God of the Bible for their traditional pantheons, the language and ideas had passed through a Greek-Roman filter before reaching them. The significance of this we must consider later.

Nevertheless, the barbarian phase was emphatically not a simple extension of the Christianity of the patristic age, but a new creation, conditioned less by city-based literary, intellectual, and technological tradition than by the circumstances of peasant cultivators and their harsh, uncertain lives. If they took their ideas from the Hellenistic Christian world, they took their attitudes from the primal world; and both ideas and attitudes are components in the complex which makes up a people's religion. As with their predecessors, they appropriated the Christian faith for themselves, and reformulated it with effects which continued amid their successes after their own phase had passed away. If the second phase of Christianity invented the idea of *orthodoxy*, the third invented the idea of the *Christian nation*. Christian Roman Emperors might establish the Church, might punish heretics, might make laws claiming allegiance to Christ, might claim to represent Christ, but tribal peoples knew a far stronger law than any Emperor could enforce, that of custom. Custom is binding upon every child born into a primal community; and non-conformity to that custom is simply unthinkable. A communal decision to adopt the Christian faith might take some time in coming; there might be uncertainty, division, debate for a while, but once thoroughly made, the decision would bind everyone in that society. A community must have a single custom. It was not necessarily a case of strong rulers enforcing their own choice. In Iceland, which was a democracy with no central ruler, the Assembly was divided down the middle between Christians and non-Christians. When the decision for Christianity was eventually made, the non-Christians felt bitter and betrayed, but no one suggested a division into communities with different religions. Religion in fact is but one aspect of the custom which binds a society together. There can be only one Church in a community. And so barbarian Christianity brings to fruition the idea of the Christian nation.

Once the idea of the Christian nation was established, a new hermeneutic habit easily developed: the parallel between the Christian nation and Israel. Once nation and Church are coterminous in scope, the experiences of the nation can be interpreted in terms of the history of Israel. In Western Christianity this habit has long outlived the historical circumstances which gave it birth and has continued into the age of pluralism and secularization.

Western Europe—the Fourth Age

The fourth cultural phase of Christianity was a natural development of the third. Inter-action between Christian faith and practice in its Hellenistic-Roman form and the culture of the northern peoples produced a remarkably coherent system across Western and Central Europe. When the Eastern Roman Empire, which effectively prolonged the Hellenistic phase of Christianity for several centuries in one area of the world, finally collapsed before the Muslims, the new hybrid Western form of Christianity became the dominant representation of Christianity. In the sixteenth century this Western formulation was to undergo radical revision through the movements of Reformation. The Protestant version of this was particularly radical (not least through its emphasis on vernacular Scriptures), in stressing the local encounter of man with the Word of God. Reforming Catholicism, on the other hand, stressed the universal nature of the Church, but unconsciously established its universality on the basis of features which belonged essentially to Western intellectual and social history and, indeed, largely to a particular period of it. Both forms, however, belonged unmistakably to Western Europe; their very differences marked a growing cultural divergence between the north and the south of the area.

One major development that took place within the West over those centuries set a challenge to Christian faith as hitherto received in Europe and required its reformulation. As we have seen, a necessary feature of barbarian Christianity was communal decision and mass response. But Western thought developed a particular consciousness of the *individual* as a monad, independent of kin-related identity. Christianity in its Western form adapted to this developing consciousness, until the concept of Christian faith as a matter of individual decision and individual application became one of the hallmarks of Western Christianity.

Expanding Europe and Christian Recession—the Fifth Age

This Western phase of Christianity developed into another phase, with which it should probably be taken: the age of expanding Europe. The population of Europe was exported to other continents and the dominance of Europe extended, until by the twentieth century people of European origin occupied, possessed, or dominated the greater part of the globe. During this vital period, Christianity was the professed and, to a considerable extent, the active religion of almost all the European peoples.

Seen in the context of Christian history as a whole, this period saw two remarkable developments. One was a substantial *recession* from the Christian faith among the European peoples. Its significance was not at first manifest, because it was not regular and steady. Beginning in the sixteenth century, it had reached notable proportions by the eighteenth century. During that century, however, and for much of the nineteenth, there was a Christian counter-attack, which halted the movement of recession in Europe and brought spectacular accessions in the new towns of North America. The sudden quickening of the recession, therefore, in the twentieth century took observers by surprise—though predictions of its extent had been current a couple of centuries earlier. Only in the twentieth century did it become clear that the great towns which were the source and the sign of Europe's dominance had never really been evangelized at all.

The other major development of the period was the *cross-cultural transplantation* of Christianity, with varying degrees of success, to multitudes of people outside Europe. It did not look overwhelming by 1920: the high hopes once entertained of the evangelization of the world in one generation had by that time drained away into the trenches of the First World War. But we can see now that it was enough. The seeds of Christian faith had been planted in the Southern continents; before long they could be seen to be fruiting abundantly. All the world Empires, except the Russian, have now passed away; the European hegemony of the world is broken; the recession of Christianity among the European peoples appears to be continuing. And yet we seem to stand at the threshold of a new age of Christianity, one in which its main base will be in the Southern continents, and where its dominant expression will be filtered through the culture of those continents. Once again, Christianity has been saved for the world by its diffusion across cultural lines.

Cross-Cultural Transmission—the Sixth Age

Let us pause here to consider the peculiar history of Christianity, as compared with other faiths. Hindus say with some justice that they represent the world's earliest faith, for many things in Indian religion are the same now as they were before Israel came out of Egypt. Yet over all those centuries, the geographical and cultural centre has been the same. Invaders like the Aryans have come and made their mark, great innovative movements like that of the Buddha have come, and flourished awhile, and then passed on elsewhere. The Christians and the Muslims with their claims to universal allegiance have come and made their converts. But still the same faith remains in the same place, absorbing all sorts of influences from without, not being itself absorbed by any.

By contrast, Iranian religion has been vital enough to have a moulding effect at certain crucial times on Hinduism, Judaism, Christianity, and Islam in succession; and yet as a separate, identifiable phenomenon in the world, its presence today is tiny. Christianity, on the other hand, has throughout its history spread outwards, across cultural frontiers, so that each new point on the Christian circumference is a new potential Christian centre. And the very survival of Christianity as a separate faith has evidently been linked to the process of cross-cultural transmission. Indeed, with hindsight, we can see that on several occasions this transmission took place only just in time; that without it, the Christian faith must surely have withered away. Nor has its progress been steadily outwards, as Muslims may claim of their faith. Its progress has been serial, with a principal presence in different parts of the world at different times.

Each phase of Christian history has seen a transformation of Christianity as it has entered and penetrated another culture. There is no such thing as "Christian culture" or "Christian civilization" in the sense that there is an Islamic culture, and an Islamic civilization. There have been several different Christian civilizations already; there may yet be many more. The reason for this lies in the infinite translatability of the Christian faith. Islam, the only other faith hitherto to make a comparable impact in such global terms, can produce a single recognizable culture (recognizable despite local assimilations and variations) across its huge geographical spread. This has surely something to do with the ultimate untranslatability of its charter document, the Qur'an. The Christian Scriptures, by contrast, are open to translation; nay, the great Act on which Christian faith rests, the Word becoming flesh and pitching tent among us, is itself an act of translation. And this principle brings Christ to the heart of each culture where he finds acceptance; to the burning questions within that culture, to the points of reference within it by which people know themselves. That is why each phase of Christian history has produced new themes: themes which the points of reference of that culture have made inescapable for those who share that framework. The same themes may be beyond the conception of Christians of an earlier or another framework of thought. They will have their own commanding heights to be conquered by Christ.

Diversity and Coherence in Historic Christianity

If we were to take samples of *representative* Christians from every century from the first to the twentieth, moving from place to place as will be necessary if our choice is to be representative, would they have anything in common? Certainly such a collection of people would often have quite different priorities in the expression of the faith. And it is not only that the priorities are different; what appears of utmost importance to one group may appear intolerable, even blasphemous, to another. Even were we to take only those acknowledged as forming the tradition of Christianity represented by Western Evangelicals—how does the expression of the faith compare among Temple-worshipping Jew, Greek Council Father, Celtic monk, German Reformer, English Puritan, Victorian Churchman? How defective would each think the other on matters vital to religion?

And yet I believe we can discern a firm coherence underlying all these, and indeed, the whole of historic Christianity. It is not easy to state this coherence in propositional, still less in credal form—for extended credal formulation is itself a necessary product of a particular Christian culture. But there is a small body of convictions and responses which express themselves when Christians of any culture express their faith. These may perhaps be stated thus:

(1) The worship of the God of Israel. This not only defines the nature of God; the One, the Creator and the Judge, the One who does right and before whom humanity falls down; it marks the historical particularity of Christian faith. And it links Christians—usually Gentiles—with the history of a people quite different from their own. It gives them a point of reference outside themselves and their society.

(2) The ultimate significance of Jesus of Nazareth. This is perhaps the test which above all marks out historic Christianity from the various movements along its fringes, as well as from other world faiths which accord recognition to the Christ. Once again, it would be pointless to try to encapsulate this ultimacy forever in any one credal formula. Any such

formula will be superseded: or, even if adopted for traditional reasons, it may make no impression on believers who do not have the conceptual vocabulary the formula will imply. Each culture has its ultimate, and Christ is the ultimate in everyone's vocabulary.

(3) That God is active where believers are.

(4) That believers constitute a people of God transcending time and space.

These convictions appear to underlie the whole Christian tradition across the Christian centuries, in all its diversity. Some of the very diversity of expression, indeed, has arisen from the pressure of the need to set forth these responses in terms of the believers' framework of thought and perception of the world. To them we should perhaps add a small body of institutions which have continued from century to century. The most obvious of these have been the reading of a common body of scriptures and the special use of bread and wine and water.

Southern Cultures and the Christian Future

Once more the Christian faith is penetrating new cultures—those of Africa and the Pacific and parts of Asia. (The Latin American situation is too complex for us to pause to consider its peculiar significance here.) The present indicators are that these southern expressions of Christianity are becoming the dominant forms of the faith.

This is likely to mean the appearance of new themes and priorities undreamt of by ourselves or by earlier Christian ages; for it is the mark of Christian faith that it must bring Christ to the big issues which are closest to men's hearts; and it does so through the structures by which people perceive and recognize their world; and these are not the same for all. It must not be assumed that themes which have been primary in the Christian penetration of former cultures will remain primary for all the new ones. They may not possess those points of reference which made orthodoxy, for instance, or the Christian nation, or the primacy of individual conscience, absolutely crucial to the capture by Christ of other world views. Various early Jewish Christians would have found their Greek successors strangely cold about Israel's most precious possession, the Law of God and its guide to living. Many of them would have been equally disturbed by the intellectual complexities into which christological discussion was leading Greek Christians. In each case what was happening was the working out of Christian faith within accepted views of the world, so that those world views—as with the conversion of believers—are transformed, yet recognizable.

As the process continues in the Southern continents, Christians whose tradition has been shaped by other factors will still be able to look out for the signposts of historic Christianity so far: the worship of the God of Israel, the recognition of the ultimate significance of Christ, the knowledge that God is active among the believers, the acknowledgment of a people of God transcending time and space; and join in the common reading of the Scriptures, and in the special use of bread and wine and water.

In this survey I have left on one side a vital theme. I have talked of the transmission of Christianity across cultural frontiers and the way that this has produced a series of Christian transformations across the centuries. These transformations may be seen as the result of the great principle of translatability which lies at the heart of Christian faith and is demonstrated both in the Incarnation and in the Scriptures. It might be valuable to link this process with Paul's vision in Ephesians 4 of the full-grown humanity unto which we are to grow together—as though the very diversity of Christian humanity makes it complete. The image is hard for us to appropriate because of the very individualism which is so crucial a part of our own world view. But it looks as though Paul was less impressed by the passing of faith to the Gentiles—mightily as he rejoiced in it, still less by the new shape which Christian faith took in Gentile hands—much as he himself may have been responsible for this, than by the fact that through Christ one nation had been made out of two. Jew and Gentile, who had not in centuries been able to eat in each others' houses without calling the whole covenant of God into question, now sat down together at the table of the Lord. It was a phase of Christian history that did not last long. Not long after Paul's time, Gentiles so dominated the Christian Church that in most areas Jews were hardly noticeable in it. Christianity became a Gentile matter, just as in its earliest days it had been a Jewish matter. But, for a few brief years, the one-made-out-of-two was visibly demonstrated, the middle wall of partition was down, the irreconcilables were reconciled. This was, surely, not simply a historic episode, but a paradigmatic one, to be repeated, even if briefly, again and again. It is repeated as people separated by language, history and culture recognize each other in Christ. And the recognition is not based on one adopting the ways of thought and behaviour and expression, however sanctified, of the other; that is Judaizing, and another Gospel. Christ must rule in the minds of his people; which means extending his dominion over those corporate structures of thought that constitute a culture. The very act of doing so must sharpen the identity of those who share a culture. The faith of Christ is infinitely translatable, it creates "a place to feel at home." But it must not make a place where we are so much at home that no one else can live there. Here we have no abiding city. In Christ all poor sinners meet, and in finding themselves reconciled with him, are reconciled to each other.

3

The Translation Principle in Christian History[1]

Translation and Incarnation

Politics is the art of the possible; translation is the art of the impossible. Exact transmission of meaning from one linguistic medium to another is continually hampered not only by structural and cultural difference; the words of the receptor language are pre-loaded, and the old cargo drags the new into areas uncharted in the source language. In the end the translator has simply to do his best and take risks in a high risk business.

In the light of the frustrations inherent in the translation process, it is the more astonishing that God chose translation as his mode of action for the salvation of humanity. Christian faith rests on a divine act of translation: "the Word became flesh, and dwelt among us" (John 1:14). Any confidence we have in the translatability of the Bible rests on that prior act of translation. There is a history of translation of the Bible because there was a translation of the Word into flesh.

In the other great faiths of the world, salvation does not depend on translation in this way. India has long known faith in the divine presence in the universe, and faith in the divine saving intervention in the universe. But if, as is characteristic of old India, salvation lies in attaining or realizing identity with the divine, no act of divine translation takes place. Meaning is not actually transferred from the divine to the human sphere, for the human sphere has no permanent significance, or, indeed, reality; the phenomenal world is just what Hindu sages have long said it is, illusion, *maya*.

Even Judaism and Islam, which come from the same Semitic matrix as Christianity, and share the Christian characterization of God's manward activity as speech, do not represent it as *translated* speech. In Islamic faith

[1]First published in Philip C. Stine, ed., *Bible Translation and the Spread of the Church* (Leiden: E.J. Brill, 1990), pp. 24-39.

God speaks to mankind, calling to obedience. The sign of that speech is the Qur'an, the direct speech of God, delivered in Arabic at the chosen time through God's chosen Apostle, unaltered and unalterably fixed in heaven for ever. In prophetic faiths God speaks to humanity: in Christian faith, God becomes human. This conviction conditions the Christian attitude even to prophetic speech. Though the earliest Church was Jewish and retained the Jewish Scriptures, the Christian approach to the Bible is not identical with the historic understanding of the Torah. The Christian Scriptures are not the Torah with an updating supplement. The translation of the speech of God, not just into human speech but into humanity, implies a different type of encounter with the divine. Much misunderstanding in Christian-Muslim relations has occurred from the assumption that the Bible and Qur'an have analogous status in the respective faiths. But the true Christian analogy with the Qur'an is not the Bible, but Christ. Christ for Christians, the Qur'an for Muslims, is the Eternal Word of God; but Christ is Word Translated. That fact is the sign that the contingent Scriptures (also describable as Word of God), unlike the Qur'an, may and should constantly be translated.

Incarnation is translation. When God in Christ became man, Divinity was translated into humanity, as though humanity were a receptor language. Here was a clear statement of what would otherwise be veiled in obscurity or uncertainty, the statement "This is what God is like."

But language is specific to a people or an area. No one speaks generalized "language"; it is necessary to speak a particular language. Similarly, when Divinity was translated into humanity he did not become generalized humanity. He became *a person* in a particular locality and in a particular ethnic group, at a particular place and time. The translation of God into humanity, whereby the sense and meaning of God was transferred, was effected under very culture-specific conditions.

The implications of this broaden if we take the Johannine symbol of the Word made flesh along with the Pauline symbol of the Second Adam, the Ephesian theme of the multi-ethnic New Humanity which reaches its full stature in Christ, and with Paul's concern for Christ to be formed in the newly founded Gentile churches.[2] It appears that Christ, God's translated speech, is re-translated from the Palestinian Jewish original. The words of the Great Commission require that the various nations are to be made disciples of Christ.[3] In other words, national distinctives, the things that mark out each nation, the shared consciousness and shared traditions, and shared mental processes and patterns of relationship, are within the scope of discipleship. Christ can become visible within the very things which constitute nationality. The first divine act of translation into humanity thus gives rise to a constant succession of new translations. Christian diversity

---

[2]See, for example, Rom. 5:12-6:14; 1 Cor. 15:20-28; Eph. 2:11-22, 21:7-16; Gal. 4:19.

[3]Mt. 28:19. Note that it is the *nations*, not some people within the nations, who are to be discipled.

is the necessary product of the Incarnation.

Further, as Christian faith is about translation, it is about conversion. There is a real parallel between these processes. Translation involves the attempt to express the meaning of the source from the resources of, and within the working system of, the receptor language. Something new is brought into the language, but that new element can only be comprehended by means of and in terms of the pre-existing language and its conventions. In the process that language and its system is effectively expanded, put to new use; but the translated element from the source language has also, in a sense, been expanded by translation; the receptor language has a dynamic of its own and takes the new material to realms it never touched in the source language. Similarly, conversion implies the use of existing structures, the "turning" of those structures to new directions, the application of new material and standards to a system of thought and conduct already in place and functioning. It is not about substitution, the replacement of something old by something new, but about transformation, the turning of the already existing to new account.

Thus in the Incarnation, the Word becomes flesh, but not *simply* flesh; Christian faith is not about a theophany or an avatar, the appearance of divinity on the human scene. The Word was made *human*. To continue the linguistic analogy, Christ was not simply a loanword adopted into the vocabulary of humanity; he was fully translated, taken into the functional system of the language, into the fullest reaches of personality, experience, and social relationship. The proper human response to the divine act of translation is conversion: the opening up of the functioning system of personality, intellect, emotions, relationship to the new meaning, to the expression of Christ. Following on the original act of translation in Jesus of Nazareth are countless re-translations into the thought forms and cultures of the different societies into which Christ is brought as conversion takes place. Conversion is not the substitution of something new for something old (in the great act of translation into humanity, Christ took nothing away from humanity made in God's image); nor the addition of something new to something old (in the great act of translation, Christ added nothing *to* humanity as made in God's image). Conversion is the turning, the re-orientation, of every aspect of humanity—culture-specific humanity—to God. For Christ was the full expression of God in human medium. Of its nature, then, conversion is not a single aoristic act, but a process. It has a beginning; we cannot presume to posit an end.

Bible translation as a process is thus both a reflection of the central act on which the Christian faith depends and a concretization of the commission which Christ gave his disciples. Perhaps no other specific activity more clearly represents the mission of the Church.

The parallel of Scripture and Incarnation is suggested in the opening words of the Epistle to the Hebrews on the relation between the partial, episodic, occasional words of God spoken through the prophets and the complete and integrated Word spoken all at once in the Son (Heb. 1:1-4). The issues and problems of Bible translation are the issues and problems of Incarnation. The struggle to present writings embedded in languages and cultures alien to the present situation of every people is validated by the act which translated God into a medium of humanity. As the Incarnation took place in the terms of a particular social context, so translation uses the terms and relations of a specific context. Bible translation aims at releasing the word about Christ so that it can reach all aspects of a specific linguistic and cultural context, so that Christ can live within that context, in the persons of his followers, as thoroughly at home as he once did in the culture of first-century Jewish Palestine. We may take it that the endemic hazards and problems of translation are a necessary part of the process of Christian mission. Key words or concepts without an obvious equivalent in the receptor language, central biblical images rooted in the soil or history of the Middle East or the usages of the Roman Empire, the shift of meaning in apparently corresponding words, the luggage that receptor language terms carry with them—these are the means by which the word about Christ is applied to the *distinctives* of a culture, and thus to its commanding heights. New translations, by taking the word about Christ into a new area, applying it to new situations, have the potential actually to reshape and expand the Christian faith. Instead of defining a universal "safe area" where certain lines of thought are prescribed and others proscribed or ignored (the natural outcome of a once-for-all, untranslatable authority), translatability of the Scriptures potentially starts *inter*actions of the word about Christ with new areas of thought and custom. Again the contrast with the Qur'anic Word is manifest.

In this respect translation resembles conversion; indeed, it is a working model of conversion, a turning of the processes of language (with the thought of which that language is the vehicle and the traditions of which it is the deposit) towards Christ. And like conversion, it has a beginning but no end. However effective the impact, it is never good enough; and as social life and language change, so must translation. The principle of translation is the principle of revision.

There is one exception to the revision principle. The translations of Christ that take place as believers within different cultures respond to him are *re*translations. These incarnations of Christ are contingent on that first Incarnation with its firm anchorage in time and space, its "crucified under Pontius Pilate." Similarly, biblical translation is re-translation, with the original always at hand. The various translations can always be compared, not only with the original, but with other translations made from the same original. Though each act of translation, like each process of conversion, takes the original into new territory and potentially expands it, the absence of a family resemblance among the products would properly give rise to suspicion. Diversity arising from the penetration of new culture complexes is not incompatible with coherence arising from the fact that the various translations have been made from a common original. And in this, too, biblical translation mirrors Christian mission. It is not possible to have too much of the localizing and indigenizing principle which makes the faith thoroughly at home, nor too much of that universalizing principle which is in constant tension with it, and which links that local community with its "domestic" expression of faith in the same Christ of Christians of other times and places. It is possible only to have too little of either.

Perhaps a comparative history of translation would be an illuminating way of approaching the history of Christian mission and expansion—not only in the geographical and statistical sense of the spread of the Church, but the dynamic expansion of the influence of Christ within the Church that comes from the attempts at the radical application of his mind within particular cultures. What follows must of necessity be restricted to some early examples which illustrate the theme.

The translation principle was at work even in Christianity's ante-natal period. At least by the second century before the Christian era, the Jewish Scriptures were being turned into Greek. It is significant both that the traditional Jewish story about the origin of the Septuagint translation ascribed to that translation a missionary purpose, and that the reality of its origin probably has little to do with any Jewish mission to the Gentiles. The likely origin of the Septuagint lies in the fact that Greek was fast becoming the first language of so many Jews in Alexandria and other extra-Palestinian Jewish communities; it was, in fact, a Jewish vernacular translation. Nevertheless, the generally accepted account came to be that Ptolemy Philadelphus, King of Egypt, a Gentile who had conceived an abundant veneration for the Scriptures, had sought the translation, and that God had rewarded him and demonstrated the divine approval of the undertaking by means of a signal miracle. The translation of the Scriptures into Greek is seen in these stories as being as manifestly the work of God as the tables given to Moses on Sinai.

That earliest translation committee must remain the envy of all its successors. Although it consisted of seventy (-two) translators, the work was complete in seventy-two days. Still more remarkably, the learned Alexandrine Jew Philo, living early in the first Christian century, tells us that the versions, prepared individually, were word for word identical, "as though dictated to each by an invisible prompter." And he goes on:

> Who does not know that every language, and Greek especially, abounds in terms, and that the same thought can be put in many shapes by changing single words and whole phrases . . . ? This was not the case, we are told, with this law of ours, but the Greek words used corresponded literally with the Chaldean [i.e., Hebrew], exactly suited to the things they indicated. . . . The clearest proof of this is that, if [Hebrews] have learned Greek, or Greeks [Hebrew] and read both versions, the [Hebrew] and the translation, they regard these

with awe and reverence as sisters, or rather as one and the same, both in matter and words, and speak of the authors not as translators, but as prophets and priests of the mysteries, whose sincerity and singleness of thought has enabled them to go hand in hand with the purest of spirits, the spirit of Moses.[4]

There is no doubting Philo's sincerity in these convictions (though there is more than a little whether he knew any Hebrew). But one cannot read him long before realizing how steeped is this Jewish Alexandrine in Plato, and how well acquainted with Stoic writers. If for him Moses is the purest of spirits, Athens as much as Sinai has set and shaped his mind. In other words, even among Jews the field of reference of the Scriptures has been extended, and Moses and the prophets given new intellectual company. Philo can use them as authoritative when he explores the thought world of the host community of Alexandria whose speech and much of whose education he shares. The most precious possession of his people, the Torah, becomes *nomos*, or rather *The Nomos* in Greek, and Greek-speaking Jews (who have themselves to deal with Alexandrian law, and with Roman law) find themselves with a contribution to the Platonic and Stoic debates on the nature of law, which could never have arisen without the translation of the Scriptures. And Philo's Hellenistic surroundings taught him that Greeks stumbled at questions about the nature of reality because they were unaware of what every Jewish child knew from infancy, the activity of the sovereign God in creation. He knew also that they often could not hear the plain words of the prophets about God stretching out the heavens like a curtain, because of questions which could occupy no one brought up solely in Hebrew learning. The phenomenal universe is material, and hence alien to Spirit: how can Pure Spirit be responsible for matter? Philo—following a line developed by other Greek-speaking Jews before him[5]—finds a key to such Greek questions within the Scriptures themselves. The key lay not indeed in the affirmations of Deutero-Isaiah about the creator, nor primarily within the creation narratives of Genesis (though he noted how God "spoke" there), but in the Book of Proverbs, in the passages personifying wisdom or showing God's use of "wisdom" in His creation. Gradually the widely canvassed Greek idea of Word/Reason (*logos*) coalesces with the biblical theme of wisdom, until Philo can present *Logos* as a sort of shock absorber between the transcendent God and His creation. "To his Word, chief messenger, highest in age and honour," says Philo, "the Father of all has given the special prerogative, to stand on the border and separate the creature from the Creator."[6] The *Logos* thus becomes the point at which

---

[4]See Philo, *Life of Moses*, trans. F.H. Colson and G. H. Whittaker (Loeb), 2:26-42.

[5]Most obviously in the *Book of Wisdom* (for example, ch. 7) belonging to the previous century.

[6]Philo, *Who Is the Heir of Divine Things?* trans. F.H. Colson and G.H. Whittaker, (Loeb), 205.5.

human contact is possible with the Sovereign Lord. By the use of the Jewish Scriptures in an essentially Greek philosophic discourse, the transcendent God, the God of Israel, is introduced into the heart of thoroughly Greek questions. Greek thinkers using only Greek resources would have left the God-factor on the periphery of those questions; devout Jews using only untranslated Scriptures would have dismissed the questions themselves as so much Gentile profanity. No wonder Philo rejoiced in the story of Ptolemy Philadelphus and the Septuagint. In due time countless Christians were to follow his path.

Early Christianity was thus already touched by the translation principle. Not even Jewish Palestine could be culturally and linguistically sealed off from the Hellenistic world; and the very words of Jesus come to us in Greek dress. The radical Stephen slashes at the heart of traditional Judaic religiosity about the Temple with the sabre of the Septuagint;[7] and the process which called the Septuagint into being is given Gospel authentication as the Pentecost crowd of Dispersion Jews hears the wonderful works of God, not in the sacred language of the Temple liturgy (the object of their pilgrimage), but in the languages of the various nations that were their real mother tongues (Acts 2:11).

The time came when traditional Judaism rejected the Septuagint; most probably because the Christians had got hold of it. More literal translations, such as those of Symmachus and Theodotion, were used when Greek was absolutely necessary. In due time there was a retreat from translation altogether. The delighted legends of the miraculous origin of the Septuagint gave place to grudging recognition of the event as an exception to the general rule, a sign for the particular benefit of Ptolemy Philadelphus rather than a pointer to the salvation of the world.[8] Eventually we reach the bald statement that the Torah cannot be turned into Greek, an absolutism that Islam was later to echo.[9] But by this time the Septuagint was afloat in the world under new colours, in the care of a Christianity that was now as overwhelmingly Hellenistic and Greek speaking as it had once been overwhelmingly Jewish. And it was to aid in a variety of ways in the application to Hellenistic culture of the Christ event. That application was to take Christian faith into a vast complex of ideas, principles, and relationships, to seek their subjection to Christ.

The cultural translation of Christianity gave the Scriptures a new status

---

[7]Acts 7:2-53. Cf. Acts. 15: 16ff., where the argument of James the Just turns on the Septuagint text.

[8]*Megillah* 9a quotes Rabbi Judah as indicating that only the Pentateuch can be translated into Greek, because of the precedent of King Ptolemy.

[9]According to Sepher Torah 1:8, "Seventy elders wrote the Law in Greek for King Ptolemy, and that day was as bad for Israel as the day in which they made the calf, for the Law could not be translated corresponding to all requirements" (C.K. Barrett, trans., *The New Testament Background* [London, 1956], p. 213).

and purpose. They were no longer ethnically Jewish; their field of application was universal. Justin tells how, when he had tried all the philosophical schools and found himself as far as ever from the true end of philosophy, the vision of God, he met an old man who urged him to read the Jewish prophets— "more ancient than all those who are esteemed philosophers . . . who . . . foretold what would come to pass, even what is now coming to pass."[10] Justin took the advice, and it led him to Christ. His contemporary Tatian similarly testifies:

> Some barbaric writings came into my hands which were too old for Greek ideas and too divine for Greek errors. These I was led to trust, owing to their very simplicity of expression and the unstudied character of their authors, owing to their intelligible descriptions of creation, their foreknowledge of the future, the excellence of their precepts and the fact of their embracing the universe under the sole rule of God. . . . They furnish us . . . with something which had been received but which, thanks to error, had been lost.[11]

Both Justin and Tatian, well versed in conventional philosophy, are impressed by the antiquity of the Jewish Scriptures, which they knew only because of the Septuagint, by their predictive content (related directly to the person of Christ) and their relevance to the most urgent questions of intellectual discourse. The fact was that the Septuagint was the only alternative literature in the Greek world which could claim comparable antiquity with the Greek corpus. The antiquity of the literature used by the Christians was important: the world view of Hellenistic civilization rested on the conviction that every important question had been canvassed; in itself Christianity thus stood condemned by its very novelty. The demonstration therefore that the Christians had writings older than Socrates, that Moses wrote before Plato, nay (as the boldest apologists could assert) Plato got some of his best passages from Isaiah, was a major apologetic consideration.

By their translation into Greek and use by converted Hellenistic Gentiles, the Hebrew Scriptures took on a new purpose and were applied within a new universe of thought. They became an authoritative sourcebook for Greek Christians seeking to build a coherent world view. The Greek translation of the Scriptures may have been necessary in various ways to the Dispersion Jewish scholar Philo, the Hellenistic Jewish Christian Stephen, the ambicultural missionary rabbi Paul, but each of them could claim another history and another spiritual homeland. Justin and Origen had no such other home; the Scriptures in Greek were necessary to them for the building of a cultural and intellectual house that they could recognize as

---

[10]Justin, *Dialogue with Trypho*, 7.
[11]Tatian, *Oration* 29.

home. They could neither wholly abandon the Hellenistic world of their inheritance, nor leave it in the form it had for their unreconstructed contemporaries. Justin, the eclectic philosopher, continues as a teacher of philosophy from his conversion to his martyrdom; for Christianity is simply divine philosophy, a philosophy which leads (as in Plato's teaching true philosophy does) to the vision of God. The Scriptures—including (and in some ways, because of their antiquity, especially) the Jewish Scriptures— provide him with an authoritative text for the radical criticism of his heritage. That his heritage was corrupted and full of demonic things he had no doubt. But there was truth there too. There had been Greeks before Christ like Socrates, who had rejected the false gods and suffered for it. Surely such as Socrates had spoken according to *Logos*, reason? And if they did, must not this reason of theirs come from the source of all reason, the *Logos*, the Divine Son of the Father?[12] And so the daring *Logos* symbol taken by the Fourth Evangelist, as already foreshadowed by Philo, appears in a new context and with a differently freighted significance. The *Logos* of the Fourth Gospel may not be the *Logos* of Philo's liminal shock-absorber; its most important component may well be the active Hebrew *Dabhar Yahweh*, the Word of the Lord. But it is the *Dabhar Yahweh* translated, and translated into a medium where the term is already loaded, and in a setting in which much of the original significance can probably not be heard. The load in the translation propels it towards Justin, who, with other early Hellenistic Christian writers takes it further into realms which neither Philo nor the Fourth Evangelist reached. It becomes an indispensable tool by which to bring Christ into contact with the Greek heritage; and Christ becomes the criterion of truth within that heritage. The prior loading of the word *Logos* may have meant that Greeks who spoke no Hebrew (that is, nearly all of them) missed many important things about the *Logos* as the active Word of God, but it did not mislead them about their salvation. Indeed, it enabled them to see that salvation.

But the loading of words is not a one-directional process. We have only to think of a still more daring piece of translation risked quite informally by Jewish Christians in the first recorded sustained encounter between the word about Christ and Greek-speaking pagans. According to the Book of Acts unnamed believers originating from Cyprus and Cyrene spoke to Greeks in Antioch about "the Lord Jesus" (Acts 11:20). In all previous proclamations, Jesus had been presented as the Messiah, the Saviour of Israel. In this new, Hellenistic-pagan context, he is given the title *Kyrios*, the title Hellenistic pagans gave to their cult divinities. One might have expected (did any of their more cautious contemporaries predict?) that the result would be the recognition of the Lord Jesus as one more cult divinity alongside the Lord Serapis or the Lord Osiris. The major reason this did not

---

[12]Justin, *1 Apology*, 46.

happen was undoubtedly that those pagans who responded were brought into a community where the Septuagint was constantly read, and the biblical associations of *Kyrios* penetrated their minds and attached themselves to the cult divinity title. But in the first encounter, the loading of *Kyrios* with the cult divinity idea was vital. It is doubtful whether unacculturated pagans in the Antiochene world could have understood the significance of Jesus in any other way. None of us can take in a new idea except in terms of the ideas we already have. Once implanted, however, this understanding of the word received a set of controls from its new biblical frame of reference. In time much of the original loading of the word disappeared altogether.

Another feature of the Septuagint took on a new significance as that translation progressed under Christian auspices towards the heart of Hellenistic culture. In the Hebrew text of the Old Testament, of course, the divine name is represented by the Tetragrammaton, for in the Old Testament God has a personal name. But centuries of Jewish reverence did not allow that name to be pronounced, and in the Septuagint that reverence is given concrete form. The Tetragrammaton is replaced by *Kyrios*. God in the Septuagint has no name.[13]

This sharpened the confrontation of early Christianity with the popular religion of the Greco-Roman world. God was *not* Zeus/Jupiter, or Saturn/Kronos, or any amalgam of the gods. He was *ho Theos, the* God, over and against them all. If this gave force to the rejection of the gods of popular religion it also lubricated the connection of Christianity with that indigenous philosophical tradition which also had rejected popular religion, which had spoken of the ultimate principally in abstract terms or in negatives. That connection was to have momentous consequences for the whole of Western theology.

Altogether the effect of that first pre-Christian translation was crucial for the development of an indigenous Hellenistic Christianity. But it was also exemplary for the whole history of Gentile Christianity, a direction indicator for the encounter of many peoples in their subsequent interaction with the Christian faith. Many of the issues that have occurred since within or as a result of the work of Bible translation, are foreshadowed in that first great movement of cross-cultural Christian diffusion. Hellenistic people could not be converted without the conversion of the whole universe of Greek thought. That universe was the construction of centuries. There was no question of its being abandoned or substituted—no such option really existed. There was no alternative for Hellenistic Christians but the conversion of Hellenistic culture itself, the steady application of Christ and the word about Christ to its processes and priorities—another work of centu-

---

[13]*Kyrios*, of course, appears in the Septuagint as the title of the Sovereign God, but this would not be an aspect which a pagan was likely to seize on; nor is it likely that these early Greek Christians who are depicted in Acts would do so.

ries. In that process the existence of the Septuagint was critical. The New Testament, itself partly a work of translation into Greek from a Jewish medium and conveyed through Jewish minds, could hardly have had the radical effect it did except for its association with the Greek translation of the ancient Jewish literature, the alternative classical corpus.

Oral Recital in a Literary Culture

The Greco-Roman world had an established literary culture, a large literate community, and a widespread and efficient mechanism for book production. Christian literature came to a market and to reading habits already shaped by the uses of non-Christian literature. It developed, however, some uses of its own.

The old man who told Justin to read the Hebrew prophets clearly assumed that he would be able to get access to them and to the Gospels. And Justin himself, explaining to a Greek audience (in a book, of course, which he clearly hopes non-Christians will read) what it is that Christians actually do in their meetings, explains that the memoirs of the apostles and the writings of the prophets are read for as long as time permits.[14] (There are indications in early Christian literature that this was often quite a long time.) The Church's Scriptures are those read in church, and it was this public reading of Scripture, a natural continuation of synagogue practice, which must have been normative for most members of the early Christian communities. The practice was maintained by the earliest Christian communities outside the Greek world. The oldest surviving document of North African Christianity records the trial of a group of Christians on July 17, 180. The accused have a box which they say contains The Books, and the letters of Paul, a righteous man.[15] Since the record is in Latin, the books presumably represent an early vernacular translation. In the Great Persecution a hundred and twenty years later, in the same part of Latin-speaking Africa, the magistrates were carrying out a Government order that all Christian books should be confiscated. The Mayor tells the bishop to hand over the writings of the law and "anything else you have," but search reveals only one large volume; the clergy say the readers have the rest. Examination of the readers' houses produces four books from one, two from another, none from a third.[16] In other words, a few years before Constantine's accession the fundamental importance of the books for the vitality of Christianity is recognized even by the Government. But the books

---

[14]Justin, *Dialogue with Trypho*, 11-14.
[15]*Acts of the Sicilian Martyrs.*
[16]*Gesta apud Zenophilum* (text in *Corpus Scriptorum Ecclesiasticorum Latinorum* 26, 186-88).

are primarily for *public* reading; even the clergy do not possess their own copies. Books belong to congregations, and there is an order of ministry specially responsible for their care and for public reading. Even in this literary culture, the process of communication for most Christians was essentially oral, and its auditorium was the regular worship of the Church. And as literary compositions, the pre-Vulgate Latin translations do not even read well; they bear all the marks of later "missionary" translations. The young Augustine, a Latin-speaking African who found Greek heavy going, turned from them in disgust as unworthy of comparison with Cicero. The Latin Scriptures may, of course, have sounded better in public recital; as it was, the mature Augustine found a theological rationale in their "lowliness."[17]

Christianity and Northern Oral Culture

In its next great cross-cultural diffusion of Christianity, a faith which had made its home in a long-established literary culture with a Mediterranean history and priorities had to make terms with the world-views of the disintegrating tribes, settled or semi-settled marauders and peasant cultivators who bordered the Roman Empire and brought about its gradual dissolution. Among the new Christians there was no indigenous literary culture, no large literate community, and no market-oriented book production.

Nor was there any over-arching missionary strategy for the evangelization of the West. The conversion of the West took place as a result of a variety of disparate initiatives from Church authorities (most famously Pope Gregory the Great), political expansionists (most notoriously Charlemagne), and a stream of inspired ascetics (of whom Celtic Christianity produced a prodigious number). Amid centuries of muddled response, and a linguistic situation in constant flux, it is not surprising that there were different attitudes to translation. For our present purposes two contrasting examples must suffice. They are not exactly contemporary, but the conditions in which they worked were broadly parallel and the central figures themselves had much in common.

Ulfilas, or Wulfila as he was among his own people, was Gothic by birth though descended from Christian captives taken from Asia Minor. He was the leading figure in the Gothic Christian community which emerged from these captives from the Hellenistic-Roman world, and spoke both Greek and Gothic. Not surprisingly, he was Arian, for this would be the natural expression of the Christianity of his origins. At the age of 30 he was consecrated Bishop of the Goths, at that time living beyond the fringe of the

---

[17]Augustine, *Confessions* 3.5: "My swelling pride shrank from their lowliness, nor could my sharp wit pierce the interior thereof" (Pusey's translation).

Roman Empire. His vigorous evangelism was only too successful, and he and many of his people eventually moved to form a Gothic enclave within the Empire. With the complex history of the Visigoths we are not here concerned, nor with the precise part which Wulfila played in their conversion. There seems no reason to doubt the stories which credit him with bringing to birth a complete translation of the Bible into Gothic; complete, that is, apart from the Books of Kings, which he is said to have left aside because his people needed no more instruction as to warfare. Before he could produce his translation he had to design an alphabet for Gothic.[18]

In other words, Wulfila is an early example of what was to be a regular feature of the later missionary movement. He was the creator of literature within a culture otherwise entirely oral. Once created, it had to be sustained, which meant the creation of a literate class (there was no hope for many years to come of a literate *community*). The natural model was the Hellenistic one, of an educated clergy, with a rank of readers who might graduate to higher things.

The Goths became a Christian people, spread out over a vast area. They impinged more and more on the Empire, and the time came when the Goths provided the Emperor. And throughout Gothdom, in and beyond the Empire, Wulfila's version of the Scriptures was read. It is the sole monument of Gothic literature. Though Wulfila was an Arian, and though the Goths were long Arian, there is nothing particularly Arian about it. But then, no characteristically Gothic theology has come down to us. When Gothic Arians discussed theology with Greek Nicenes, they presumably did so on Greek ground, with Greek intellectual weapons and bilingual texts; and the distinguished historian of the Visigoths has raised the question whether Wulfila did his people the best service by placing their access to Scripture in a vernacular which no non-mother tongue speaker had reason to learn. Alas that we do not know more of the life and thought of those early Gothic Christians who filled up the ranks of the laity and spoke no Greek or Latin.

A century after Wulfila, at the other end of Europe, Patrick began his strange career. There are parallels between them; Patrick, though not Irish by birth, was British and Celtic-speaking. He came from the Romanized Christian population left demoralized in Britain after the Roman Empire decided to reduce its overseas commitments. He also spoke and wrote Latin, though probably not as well as Wulfila, and he had no Greek, in which Wulfila was fluent. He first went to Ireland as a captive, just as Wulfila's forebears had gone to Gothdom. He was a slave there and came to a deep experience of God. He escaped and later returned as a missionary.

---

[18]For Wulfilia (floruit 340-370) there is a brief life by his pupil Auxentius and references in Philostorgius (*Ecclesiastical History* 2.5) and other fifth-century writers. See G.W.S. Fridrichsen, *The Gothic Version of the Gospels* (Oxford, 1926) and *The Gothic Version of the Epistles* (Oxford, 1936).

Ireland, unlike his homeland, had never been part of the Roman Empire, and lacked such characteristic Roman features as towns and administrative centers. Patrick, a Celt himself, shared the Celtic view of a universe packed with potentially hostile powers, which he confronted with the name of Christ. He did not behave like a Roman bishop; rather, he travelled as the Irish kings did, and Irish ecclesiastical organization was, in Roman terms, distinctly odd. He lamented his crude Latin and his ignorance of Greek; more polished Gallo-Latin Christians over the water raised their eyebrows at his rusticity and at an early sin which impeded his ordination, and may have found it hard to cope with a man who had quite such vivid experiences of the devil jumping onto his chest.[19]

Patrick, like Wulfila, needed to produce a class of readers and Scripture experts. Like Wulfila, he had to start by producing a small literate community, and we are told that he regularly taught alphabets. But these were *Latin* alphabets. Patrick, with all his closeness to Celtic life and thought, attempted no vernacularization of Scripture. Indeed—though he was clearly a Celtic preacher of immense power and presence—when he uses a Scripture passage almost as a curse on a chief who had kidnapped Christian women, he writes as though it will have special force in Latin.[20] He raised a group of followers who wrote better Latin than himself, who composed beautiful Latin hymns (not to mention beautiful Celtic ones), who produced books of unrivalled artistry, who set Ireland in the mainstream of Western culture, and made it a nation of scholars.

Patrick, rather than Wulfila, represents the dominant practice of this, the third phase of Christian expansion, at least as far as Western Europe is concerned.[21] The acculturative process which the evangelization hastened had the effect of taking the consciousness of the peoples of the north and west beyond locality and the kinship group which had traditionally bounded their societies. Eventually it was to lead to the concept of Christendom, the territorial Empire of Christ. The existence of a common language for Scripture, liturgy and learning was a powerful factor in this. "At the present time," says Bede in A.D. 731, "there are in Britain, in harmony with the five books of the divine law, five languages and four nations— English, British, Scots, and Picts. Each of these have their own language; but all are united in their study of God's truth by the fifth—Latin—which

---

[19]Patrick (c. 390-460?) is his own biographer. The references here are to his remarkable *Confession*.

[20]Patrick, *Letter to Coroticus* 20: "These are not my words, that I have presented in Latin, but those of God, of the apostles and prophets who never lied."

[21]Eastern Christianity followed a different path, though even here we see the growth of "special languages" such as Church Slavonic, as well as genuine vernacularization. For the most remarkable incident cf. A.P. Vlasto, "The Mission of SS. Cyril and Methodios and its Aftermath in Central Europe," in G.L. Cuming, *The Mission of the Church and the Propagation of the Faith* (Cambridge, 1970), pp. 1-16.

has become a common medium through the study of the scriptures."[22] The Church saved Latin, as it was to save or strengthen many languages in centuries to come through making them the vehicle of the Christian Scriptures and of Christian worship. But it was not Latin as a vernacular language that was saved; Latin emerged as a "special" language for Christians, the universal language of that literate class of Christians who conducted the liturgy and publicly read the Scriptures. It had other important effects also, besides uniting the disparate peoples of the Empire of Christ in a common Christian culture. It gave them a shared past by connecting their local and national story with that of the Christian Roman Empire and of the early Church; it gave them a shared intellectual heritage by connecting them with the history and literature of old Rome.[23] In the first Christian encounter with the Hellenistic world we are immediately conscious of the process of evangelization by translation. In the encounter with the northern peoples the process of evangelization by supplementation is often more obvious. The language of Scripture is less the motor for the penetration of an established culture than the vehicle for the appropriation and expression of a new identity.

But this is only part of the story. Vernacular exposition of the Scriptures remained an important duty as it had been for Patrick. The Anglo-Saxon missionary Boniface, serving under Frankish auspices in territory coming under Frankish control, insisted that the renunciation of the devil required by the baptismal vow should be explained in the vernacular, but the baptismal formula itself delivered in Latin.[24] Here is an early distinction between what demands the believer's comprehension and active participation and the representative acts of the Church which are the safest and strongest in the special language of the Church. And as vernacular languages themselves became written languages, vernacular translations naturally appeared as an adjunct to the official Church versions. Bede, most Roman in obedience yet most English in outlook, was at the time of his death preparing a translation of John's Gospel into the speech of Northumbria.[25]

The vernacular principle received its most rigorous assertion in the sixteenth century. Protestantism is essentially Northern vernacular Christianity. Its very diversity is related to the diversity of the local settings; it is Christianity translated, not only into local languages but into the local cultural settings of Northern Europe. It is probably no accident, as Fernand

---

[22]Bede, *Ecclesiastical History* 1.1, trans. L. Sherley Price.

[23]The Gallo-Roman bishop, Gregory of Tours, seamlessly joins history from the Fall to Clermont Ferrand via Jerusalem and Rome in his *History of the Franks* (I.1.).

[24]Cf. J.M. Wallace-Hadrill, *The Frankish Church* (Oxford, 1963): 377-89.

[25]Cuthbert, *Life of Bede*.

Braudel points out, that the line between Catholic and Protestant Europe so closely follows the line between the true provinces of the Roman Empire and the areas in which Roman rule was temporary, peripheral, or absent.[26] The principal exception is Ireland—Patrick's Ireland.

The period which produced this spectacular demonstration of the vernacular principle also saw two other developments with far-reaching consequences. One was technological: the development of printing made possible the widespread ownership of copies of the Scriptures. This opened the way for private, individual study to supplement public reading in the congregation. For many more Christians than formerly, private rather than public reading became the principal and most potent form of encounter with Scripture. The changes involved in moving from an oral to a literary relationship with Scripture, and from a communal to an individual one, require more consideration than can be given here. Perhaps the change of relationship assisted Christian penetration of Western culture in which individualization was becoming increasingly important.

The other critical development was the beginning of the next phase of Christian cross-cultural diffusion. It was eventually to lead to the situation in which we now stand, the passing of the Christian center of gravity from the West to the South, as Christian recession in Europe accompanied massive Christian adhesion in Latin America, Sub-Saharan Africa, the South Pacific, and a few areas of Asia.

The new era was to demonstrate all the translation questions of the earlier encounters of Christian faith with other cultures. The way of Wulfila and the way of Patrick are both evident in that era, and the distinction is not simply that between "Protestant" and "Catholic" approaches. Early Protestant history in West Africa raised the question for a time (a very short time!) whether a vigorous English-speaking African Church would not render African languages unnecessary,[27] and today one may well wonder whether English has not simply taken over from Latin as the special international language of theology. William Smalley has drawn attention to the phenomenon of language hierarchies, in which people use different languages for different purposes; including sacred purposes.[28] The relevance of this to the history of Christian expansion deserves further exploration.

In the latest phase of Christian expansion Wulfila has overtaken Patrick as in the previous one Patrick overtook Wulfila. Both now assume mass

---

[26]F. Braudel, *Civilization and Capitalism*, vol. 3, *The Perspective of the World* (English trans., London, 1984), p. 66.

[27]See "Black Europeans—White Africans," chapter 8 in this volume, for more on this issue.

[28]E.g., W.A. Smalley, "Thailand's Hierarchy of Multilingualism," *Language Sciences* 10 (No. 2, 1988).

readerships rather than seminal literate classes, since both now have the capacity to provide copies of the Scriptures in numbers. (Both must also take account of the extent to which oral cultures remain oral, and respond to Scripture orally, even when they possess a literature.) The measure of their effectiveness is how far the Word once more recognizably takes flesh in the cultures in which they work, and people behold *His* glory under human conditions.

4

Culture and Conversion
in Christian History[1]

The Human Auditorium

Let us begin with a visit to the theatre. It is a crowded theatre, with a huge stage, and a stream of actors passing across it. Everyone in the packed auditorium can see the stage, but no one sees the whole of it. People seated in one place cannot see the entrances left, though they can hear the actor's voice as he enters from the wings. Seated somewhere else, the view is obstructed by a pillar, or an overhanging balcony. Go up into the balcony, and the proscenium arch cuts off the top of the set. As a result, though everyone in the audience sees the same play and hears the same words, they have different views of the conjunction of word and action, according to their seat in the theatre. Those on one side get a sharply focused view of certain scenes which those placed elsewhere do not have to the same degree, and people in the balcony are puzzled to hear laughter in the stalls when they themselves have seen nothing to cause it. But the position is reversed when the scene changes, and the main action is on another part of the stage.

Of course, it is possible to get up and change one's seat; but while this may provide a different view of the stage, it will still not enable a view of the whole stage at once; and the way a person who changes seats understands the performance as a whole will still be affected by where they were sitting for the first act.

Certainly, some people will see more than others. Those who lean forward eagerly, those who crane round the obstructive pillar, will see more than those who loll back in their seats. Those who get up at the interval and compare notes with friends sitting elsewhere in the auditorium will per-

---

[1]This chapter was first given as a lecture at Mennonite Biblical Seminary, Elkhart, Indiana.

haps understand the action best of all. But it is a condition of being in the audience that what we see most clearly is governed by where we are sitting in the theatre.

The play we are watching is the drama of life. The whole human race can see the stage on which the drama is enacted; but the focus varies according to the place in the auditorium. Now this drama has a development which is vital to the plot, which we may call the Jesus Act. For this act the conditions are the same as for all the others; everyone sees the stage, but no one sees the whole stage. People in the auditorium view the Jesus Act on the part of the stage most open to them where they are sitting.

We may think this a strange theatre, and that God, the great actor-manager, might at least have provided better conditions for viewing that vital act. Since it is so crucial, could it not have been put on in a different theatre, without these inbuilt visual obstacles? Or could he not have made some other arrangement whereby everyone would see it in much the same way? A moment's thought, however, shows that this would not do. The Jesus Act is crucial to the drama of life. It is not a separate play. It is necessary to see the Jesus Act from the same seat in the theatre as we see the rest of life because it *belongs* to the rest of life.

Our seat in the theatre is determined by a complex of conditions: where we were born, where our parents came from, what language we speak at home, what our childhood was like, and so on. People who share broadly similar conditions form culture blocks—rather like blocks of seats in the theatre, from which the view of the stage is very similar. Culture is simply a name for a location in the auditorium where the drama of life is in progress.

Viewing the Jesus Act in that drama will involve some reading or hearing of the Christian Scriptures. Once again what we see or hear in the process will be affected by where we are sitting in the auditorium. People seated in another part of the house will see some things we cannot, and be unable to see some things that seem to us important. They cannot see them, not through blindness or wilfulness, but because they have been sitting in a different place. From that place they may well be seeing that the Jesus Act is fitting exactly into an earlier development that escaped our notice because of that overhanging balcony that interrupts our view so constantly that we have forgotten its existence.

This limitation is a necessary feature of our hearing the Gospel at all. For the Gospel is not a voice from heaven separate from the rest of reality; it is not an alternative or supplementary programme to the drama of life which we are watching. The Jesus Act, the Gospel, is *in the play*. That is the implication of the Incarnation. It has to be received, therefore, under the same conditions as we receive other communication, through the medium of the same faculties and capacities. We hear and respond to the Gospel, we read and listen to Scriptures, in terms of our accumulated experience and perceptions of the world.

The Constitution of Culture

C. S. Lewis relates in his autobiography, *Surprised by Joy*, a characteristic sample of the cross-purposes conversation that he frequently experienced with his father.

A certain church in Belfast has both a Greek inscription over the door and a curious tower. "That church is a great landmark," said I, "I can pick it out from all sorts of places—even from the top of Cave Hill." "Such nonsense," said my father, "how could you make out Greek letters three or four miles away?"

The story illustrates a common phenomenon: different perceptions of the same reality, different images recalled by the same name. If the mind is programmed to thinking of a certain church in terms of a Greek inscription, the vision of that inscription will recur when someone mentions that church, even if *they* are talking about the shape or height of the tower.

This programming of our minds, which determines our perceptions, gives us our seat in the theatre. It is the result of a complex process which includes our whole past, Our past is the clue to our identity. It has made us what we are, and without it we would not know ourselves. To lose one's memory is to lose one's past, to lose one's past means to be rootless, insecure, unable to form assured relationships. A person suffering from amnesia has lost the sense of identity which enables him to make such relationships. Is the man standing next to him an old friend or a new acquaintance? Is the woman now approaching him his wife—or a complete stranger? Without the memory of his past, he cannot tell.

But the programming of our minds, the establishment of our perceptions, is constituted not only by events and experiences but by relationships. The best clue to our identity is *to whom* we think we belong and *who* we think belongs to us. The influences which have made us what we are and determine our perceptions have themselves been mediated through relationships, some close and primary (family, teachers, intimate friends); others secondary but equally important—clan, tribe, race, nation, class, group. These relationships in one sense actually *constitute* the self. We can only identify the self by establishing its relationships to others.

This is easier to realize in some societies than in others. For centuries now, people in the West have tended to think of the self in terms of its individuality, the autonomous self existing in and of its self, making independent decisions; so that even the Gospel is necessarily proclaimed in terms of the salvation of the individual and preaching is directed to eliciting individual response. It is a natural consequence of the style of thinking which starts "I think; therefore I exist." In many societies elsewhere the starting point might be rendered, "I *belong*, therefore I exist." This solidarity of the self-in-relationship is a recurrent biblical theme—for instance in Paul's assertion of total human solidarity in Adam and in Christ as the vehicle both of death and of salvation.

Our consciousness and vision of the world is thus constituted by experiences and by relationships. The combination determines whether we see a tower or a Greek inscription when a particular church is mentioned. It is important to remember that each response is quite valid—the church really has both a tower *and* an inscription. To resume our initial metaphor, we are watching the same play, and in the Jesus Act we are hearing the same Gospel words, but the dominant images that result may differ because of the different parts of the stage most fully open to view.

It may be possible, for a time at least, to switch off all attention from the play, or to watch only some part of the action which appeals to us. Certainly it is possible to treat the Jesus Act as an interruption and try to make sense of the play without it, or abandon it as having no meaning. What is not possible is to see the Jesus Act, the Gospel, apart from the drama of life of which it is part, and outside the conditions imposed by the vision available on our side of it. If we are to find in the Jesus Act the key to the drama of life, then Christ must fill the stage *as we see the stage*. If everyone in the auditorium is to be able to find the key in the Jesus Act, then Christ must fill the stage as it is seen in every one of the different positions in the auditorium. We can only see, and it is essential that we do see, the Jesus Act in the theatre in relation to the play of life as a whole and in terms of the area of the stage we can see. That is, it is necessary that we hear the Gospel under, and in relation to, the conditions of our experiences and relationships, our environment and society—our culture in fact. Others seated elsewhere in the world theatre will see the same action, hear the same words; but their seating will enable them to see parts of the stage that we do not and will obscure some things which may seem to us crystal clear.

The Necessity of Christian Diversity

For if we cannot take the Jesus Act out of the theatre because it cannot be separated from life, it follows that it cannot be separated from life in a particular place, at a particular time, within a particular culture—because that is the only sort of life there is. The proper audience response to the Jesus Act is to devote complete attention to its progress through the whole action of the drama of life in the whole area of the stage visible to us; making sure, of course, that we are seeing as much as we can. It is essential that we see the Jesus Act under the same conditions as we see the rest of our life, because it is that life, with the experiences and relationships which constitute it, which is to be transformed by what Christ did in the Jesus Act. We therefore have a paradox: the very universality of the Gospel, the fact that it is for *everyone*, leads to a variety of perceptions and applications of it. Responsive hearers of the Gospel respond in terms of their own lives. They must make sense of the Jesus Act within the play as they have seen it, and on the part of the stage within their field of vision. By the same token, the very universality of the Scriptures ensures a variety of specific interpretations and applications.

Incarnation and Cultural Specificity

And this brings us to the very heart of Christian faith. When the Word was made flesh and dwelt among us, he became *an actual person*. He did not become generalized humanity, or a personification like the Buddha Amitabha, a towering embodiment of highest virtue. The Gospels show us a person, with a vivid personality, with the whole range of human emotions, and a localized human body. The Christ does not come recurrently into the world, like Vishnu setting successive ages to right. He came once, into a particular family at a particular period and place, spoke a particular language, shared in a particular culture—a culture which, if not the most parochial in the world at that time, was certainly not the most cosmopolitan either. Perhaps one of the hard sayings of Jesus, in the interview with the Syro-Phoenician woman, shows just how fully the Divine Son shared in the culture into which he consented to be born (Mark 7:37). If I may take the liberty of the language of my own analogy, the Lord accepted the limitation that taking a seat in the theatre of life means taking a *particular* seat.

At the heart of Jewish faith, as at the heart of Islamic faith, is the Prophetic Word—God speaks to humanity. At the heart of Christian faith is the Incarnate Word—God became human. The divine Word was expressed under the conditions of a particular human society; the divine Word was, as it were, *translated*. And since the divine Word is for all humanity, he is translated again in terms of every culture where he finds acceptance among its people. The unchanging nature of the Prophetic Word of the Qur'an, fixed in heaven for ever in Arabic, produces a single Islamic civilization recognizable, despite all the local variations, from Indonesia to Morocco. There can be no single Christian civilization; the Christian Scriptures are not, like the Qur'an, the Word of God only when delivered in the original languages. In Christian understanding The Word of God can be spoken in any language under heaven. The divine Son did not become humanity in general, but a specific man in a specific place and culture; he is, as it were, made flesh again in other places and cultures as he is received there by faith. Similarly with the Christian Scriptures; there is (for purposes of communication, at least) no such thing as language in general; to be understood, we must speak some *particular* language. For the process of translation of the Word into human life which constitutes Christian living, there is no generalized human condition and therefore no single Christian expression. The Word has to be translated in terms of specific segments of social reality.

Christian faith, then, rests on a massive divine act of translation, and proceeds by successive lesser acts of translation into the complexes of experiences and relationships that form our social identities in different parts of the world auditorium.

The Cultural Significance of the Great Commission

It is worth relating this realization to the words of the Great Commission recorded in Matthew 28:19, "Go then, and make disciples of all nations, baptizing them in the name of the Father, the Son and the Holy Spirit, and teaching them to observe all that I have commanded you."

The special history of the Church in the West in comparatively recent times has given rise to a habit of relating this text to overseas missions. In fact, Jesus gave no special commission for overseas missions. He gave only *one* commission. The words are not only or specially about overseas missionaries (still less about the duty of supporting them). They simply say what Jesus expects his followers to do.

The highly individualistic nature of contemporary Western culture has led to the interpretation of this passage as though it said "Make some disciples in each nation." No doubt this meaning can be validly deduced, but it does not represent the meaning of the words. According to the words of the Great Commission which we have, the task of the disciples of Christ is to *disciple the nations*, to make the nations disciples.

The associations of such words will be different in different parts of the human auditorium. A Jewish Christian believer of the first century—one of those for whom Matthew's Gospel was first written perhaps?—would recognize in the words "the nations" his usual collective term for Gentiles— "the nations" over against "the Nation"; that is Israel. And as a disciple of Christ, such a believer would learn from the words that the Messiah, the national deliverer of Israel, was to be the deliverer of Gentile outsiders also—those same outsiders who often caused Israel's suffering. In later centuries, the words would sound with a different resonance within a "christendom" which applied the Christian name to the whole of Western society. Nations loudly professed the Christian name, when the national life was full of oppression and cynical immorality. In these circumstances, to "disciple" the nations was to call one's own nation to righteousness. Later still, the founders of the modern missionary movement could take from these words the confidence that, despite all contrary appearances, places where no Christian community had been in 1800 years of Christian history should one day recognize the faith of Christ as their faith. As one of the great missionary figures of the nineteenth century puts it,

> The object set before us is . . . that all nations should gradually adopt the Christian religion as their national profession of faith, and thus fill the universal church by the accession of national churches.[2]

---

[2]Henry Venn, Secretary of the Church Missionary Society, in instructions dated June 30, 1868. See William Knight, *The Missionary Secretariat of Henry Venn . . .* (London, 1880), p. 282.

Each of these visions awakened by the Great Commission led to noble life and high endeavour, and each had a measure of fulfilment. What of our own century, which has known so much agony and ecstasy over nationhood? What, after all, is a nation?

Our minds pass first to the nation-state; to political units which have, or might have, a seat at the United Nations. But the nation-state is a comparatively recent concept; only within the present century has the world been fully organized into nation-states. And even nation-states frequently have several layers of national identity. Some nation-states have to hold a national identity forged in quite recent times, while at the same time maintaining a variety of national identities, perhaps with distinct languages, within their borders. Others impose a national identity of the majority upon minority peoples with quite different national identities. We must, then, go deeper than the nation-state.

Nationhood, whatever the size of the nation, implies commonality, the possession of features or attributes in common. A nation shares a location, a history, traditions, customs, a sense of belonging. This sense of belonging together marks them off from others who do not share that history and those features. Earlier, we thought about identity being constituted by experiences and relationships—to whom we belong, who we feel belongs to us. Nationality implies shared experiences and relationships, specific ways of doing things.

Discipleship and Nationhood

Is there any sense in which "nations" in this sense of the word can be made disciples? An answer requires some consideration of what is involved in discipleship.

Jesus was a rabbi; it is the title by which he is most frequently addressed in the Gospels. And, like other rabbis, he had disciples. Another famous rabbi, Johanan ben Zakkai, praised his own five celebrated disciples in terms which tell us something of the ideal characteristics of discipleship:

Eliezer ben Hyrcanus is a plastered cistern which loses not a drop; Joshua ben Hananiah—happy is she that bare him; Jose the priest is a saintly man; Simeon ben Nathaniel is fearful of sin; Eleazer ben Arak is an ever-flowing spring.[3]

The first and last of these characteristics are worth special attention. One excellent disciple was like a plastered cistern that does not lose a drop. Such an ideal disciple fills his mind with the holy word, and passes it on exactly

---

[3]Herbert Danby, trans., *The Mishnah*, tractate *Aboth* ("The Fathers"), 2.8 (Oxford, 1933), p. 448.

as received. But there is an alternative embodiment of the ideal disciple, one who is like an ever-flowing spring. The holy word has its own dynamic. Discipleship is not just traditionary, but creative. As new situations arise, the holy word is carried forward into new reaches of meaning—extends, as it were, to meet the new situation. Complete discipleship thus implies *both* the plastered cistern *and* the ever-flowing spring.

Though Jesus takes the ideal of discipleship beyond the rabbinic (the special marks of his disciples are love and servanthood, readiness to take the towel and basin and do the dirty jobs), Rabbi Johanan's praises of his own disciples may help us understand what discipleship is about. The holy word—the word of the Master, the word of Scripture—passes into the memory. The plastered cistern does not lose a drop. But that word is not a static once-for-all possession, secured by memory and repeated enunciation. It is a dynamic, developing, growing, creative factor in the mind; ever fresh, ever bringing out new things, never getting stuck in the past, never getting stale or out of date. The disciple is an ever-flowing spring. There are echoes of this in the Gospels. We are told more than once that the disciples of Jesus understood some word of his, or of Scripture, only at a later time. We are told also that a function of the Spirit is to lead the disciples into all truth, and bring his words back to their memory. So the holy word does not stay simply in the disciple's memory, to be passed on (though this is very necessary); it invades the disciple's whole personality, to bring its influence to bear on the developing situations in which that disciple becomes involved. Discipleship, that is, involves the word of the master passing through the disciple's memory and into all the mental and moral processes; the ways of thinking, choosing, deciding.

Let us now apply this understanding of discipleship to the task of making disciples of all nations. It is clear that more is implied than simply making the Master's word known to all peoples. That Word is to pass into all those distinctive ways of thought, those networks of kinship, those special ways of doing things, that give the nation its commonality, its coherence, its identity. It has to travel through the shared mental and moral processes of a community, the way decisions are made in that community. Christ is to become actualized—to become flesh, as it were—as distinctively, and may I say it, as *appropriately*—as when he lived as a Palestinian Jew in the early first century.

Every nation, in the sense adopted here, has a pattern of thought and life essentially its own. Long ago, Edwin Smith spoke of "the shrine of a people's soul."[4] He was thinking especially of language, and language is undoubtedly a major factor in what belongs to a people. But the *shrine* of a people's soul has more in it than language, considered simply as verbal

---

[4]Edwin W. Smith, *The Shrine of a People's Soul* (London, 1929).

communication. Within the shrine lie that people's history, its traditions, its corpus of recognized literature (oral or written). If a nation is to be discipled, the commanding heights of a nation's life have to be opened to the influence of Christ; for Christ has redeemed human life in its entirety. Conversion to Christ does not isolate the convert from his or her community; it begins the conversion of that community. Conversion to Christ does not produce a bland universal citizenship: it produces distinctive discipleships, as diverse and variegated as human life itself. Christ in redeeming humanity brings, by the process of discipleship, all the richness of humanity's infinitude of cultures and subcultures into the variegated splendour of the Full Grown Humanity to which the apostolic literature points (cf. Eph. 4:8-13). This means that the influence of Christ is brought to bear on the points of reference in each group. The points of reference are the things by which people know their identity and know where, and to whom, they belong. Discipling a nation involves Christ's entry into the nation's thought, the patterns of relationship within that nation, the way the society hangs together, the way decisions are made.

This has several implications. For one thing it means that discipling is a long process—it takes generations. Christian proclamation is for the children and grandchildren of the people who hear it. Just as personal discipleship involves the lifelong working of "holy word" through the personality, so national discipleship involves a generational penetration of the ways of thought, the springs of action, the points of reference, of people forming a nation.

Second, the application of the mind of Christ to these points of reference will mean that the master's word is constantly penetrating new realms of human reality. In consequence, the Christian expression in that "nation" will take a distinctive shape, have a distinctive set of priorities and concerns; because the word about Christ has to be applied to its *distinctives*. The word of Christ is accordingly for ever meeting new situations, going into conditions that Christians have never experienced before.

Proselyte and Convert

All too often those who have been the means whereby the Christian faith has spread across cultural frontiers have wanted new Christians to regard as important all the things that have been important to themselves. What could be more important to a Jewish believer than the Law, the brightest treasure of Israel? Or circumcision, the sign of the covenant of God with his own people? And so a significant number of early Christians concluded that non-Jewish converts should be circumcised and keep the Law. The Epistle to the Galatians tells us what Paul thought about that (Gal. 1:6-7, 2:11ff., 3:1-5:2); and the Acts of the Apostles tell us that, after due discussion, the early Church decided circumcision and Torah were for the old Christians, but not for the new ones (Acts 15:23-29). Often since, other good people, with the highest motives, have wanted other Christians to be scrupulous about all the things that mattered to themselves, that came out of the encounter of the word of Christ with their own history. And sometimes converts, desperately anxious to do the right thing, have been very ready to oblige; just as in New Testament times there were Gentile Christians quite ready to submit to circumcision in order to achieve full status as God's people.

To do this was to follow the way of the Jewish proselyte; the pagan who, in order to cleave to the God of Israel, had turned his back on his nation and entered the nation of Israel. Paul knew that the path of the proselyte was a blind alley for Gentile disciples of Jesus. They had to bring Christ to bear on areas of life of which people who had been observant Jews all their life knew nothing; and if they became proselytes, became in effect imitations of Jewish Christians, they would be disabled from bringing Christ to bear on those areas. The faith of Christ had immediately to be applied to situations quite outside the experience of the devout people who formed the backbone of the early Church. What were you to do if a pagan friend invited you to dinner, and the meat might—or might not—have previously been offered at a temple sacrifice? (Cf. 1 Cor. 10:27ff.) A devout Jewish believer was not going to be invited to dinner anyway; nor was a proselyte. Greek disciples had to be able to decide what to do. If they simply copied Jewish believers—the senior Christians, the experienced Christians, the best Christians of the time—there was no way left in which the word about Christ could enter Greek family and social life.

As the Christian faith took hold in Greek-speaking Asiatic families, other questions arose that no Jew had to face. Indeed, this is hinted at in the New Testament account of the first real encounter of Christian faith with the pagan world. This occurs in the eleventh chapter of Acts, where Luke quietly describes one of the most critical events in Christian history.[5] So far as we can see, it was no part of any grand missionary strategy on the part of the Church; it grew out of circumstances wholly unforeseen. Nor were the people who initiated it, so far as we know, any of the apostles and elders of Jerusalem who were the Church's pillars. It was a few Jerusalem Christians—we do not even know their names—who, driven away from home to Antioch, began to talk to their Greek pagan friends about Jesus, whom they and all other Christians of that time thought of as the Jewish national saviour. It would have been useless to labour at explaining the term Messiah—supposing an Antiochene pagan to have the interest to hear all about the messianic hope of Israel, it would still be far from clear what it all had to do with him. The Jewish believers in Jesus described in Acts 11 risked a dangerous translation. They presented Jesus by the title their pagan friends used for their cult divinities—that is *Kyrios*, Lord. That event

---

[5] Acts 11:19-23. Note in particular verse 20—Kyrios, not Christos.

marked the beginning of the conversion of the Greek world. It was not simply that the numbers of Christian believers multiplied; from now on the word about Christ, and the faith of Christ, began to work through the vast complex of Greek and Roman thought. That complex was a total system, undergirding the law, reflection, education, literature, intellectual life of a substantial section of contemporary humanity. So complete, so universally accepted was that system that only two classes of humanity were recognized: "Greeks" who were shaped by it, and "barbarians" who were outside it.[6] The whole system of thought, apparently so assured and final, had to go to school again with Christ. The process altered the expression of the Christian faith completely; for the word of Christ had now to be introduced into areas of thinking, and brought to bear upon ideas that Peter and John and James the Just never dreamed of and that Paul himself barely glimpsed.

It was impossible either to ignore the previous system of ideas, or to abandon it, or to leave it as it was. It had to be penetrated, invaded, brought into relation with the word about Christ and the Scriptures which contained it. The process meant a new agenda for Christianity. Matters which had never troubled the heads of the apostles and elders of Jerusalem became matters of life and death as the word about Christ encountered the established metaphysic of the Hellenistic world, while many things which were vital to the first generation of Christians in Jerusalem just dropped out of sight. Those Jewish Christians from Cyprus and Cyrene who had recognized that Jesus was also good news for their pagan friends began the discipling of a "nation." It involved the penetration of thought patterns, the entry of the Gospel into mental and moral processes. The penetration took centuries. It was never completed.

In our own day there are signs that African theologians are at a similar point in the application of the word about Christ to another vast complex of thought, action, and relationships to that which Greek Christian thinkers reached when they faced the problems posed by their cultural identity.[7] Christian Africa is now having to grapple with the meaning of the African past, and with what God was doing in it. African systems of thought and codes of symbols and nets of kinship are as formidable in this way as the Greco-Roman. The great travail of Christian Africa is over the conversion of the African past. Perhaps no conversion is complete without the conversion of the past.

The Twin Forces of Christian History

Throughout Christian history two forces are distinguishable in constant tension. One is an indigenizing principle, a homing instinct, which creates in diverse communities a sense that the Church belongs there, that it is

---

[6]Paul himself adopts the twofold designation on occasion, knowing the Romans will understand (Rom. 1:14).

[7]See Kwame Bediako, *Theology and Identity: The Impact of Culture upon Christian Thought in the Second Century and in Modern Africa* (Oxford, 1992).

"ours." The other is a "pilgrim" principle that creates within the Christian community the sense that it is not fully at home in this world, so that it comes into tension with its society from its loyalty to Christ. The one tends to localize the vision of the Church, the other to universalize it. The two principles are recurrent because each springs directly out of the Gospel itself. On the one hand God accepts us in Christ just as we are, with all our distinctives—even the things which mark us off from others—still on us. On the other he accepts us in order that we may become something different; that we may be transformed out of the ways of this world into the image of Christ. Either of these forces can be manipulated; we may make the Church so much a place to feel at home that no one else can live there, or we can use the sense of Christian identity to legitimate some group's economic and social interests. That is civil religion—and it is an ever-present peril when Christianity is well established in any community. When we give way to this we draw the teeth of the Scriptures so that they will not bite *us*, while still hoping that they will bite other people. The opposite error is to impose, in the name of some universal and historic orthodoxy, a set of requirements and inhibitions that arise from the Christian history of another community.

The homing and the pilgrim principles are in tension. They are not in opposition, nor are they to be held in some kind of balance. We need not fear getting too much of one or the other, only too little. To understand their relationship we have only to recall that both are the direct result of that incarnational and translational process whereby God redeems us through the life, death, and resurrection of Christ. It is his life which enters the life of each new community where he is received by faith, and which is to be realized through all the courses of that community's thoughts and traditions. One result is the rich diversity of Christian life and experience. Another is a new transcendent commonality, shared across diverse communities. The Scriptures, the medium by which the life of the Christian community is regulated, are inseparable from a specific historic experience, that of old Israel—a nation to which most Christians do not belong by birth. Thus Christians of all communities, with all their distinctive discipleships, are brought together "in Christ." If his likeness is to be formed in each community of Christians, some sort of family resemblance should be developing across them. All these cultures which they represent, all the nationalities belong alike to the fullness of Humanity described so graphically in the Epistle to the Ephesians. It is a delightful paradox that the more Christ is translated into the various thought forms and life systems which form our various national identities, the richer all of us will be in our common Christian identity. The Word became flesh, and dwelt among us—and we beheld *his* glory, full of grace and truth.

5

Romans One and the Modern Missionary Movement[1]

There is no telling what may happen when people begin to read the Epistle to the Romans. What happened to Augustine, Luther, Wesley and Barth launched great spiritual movements which have left their mark in world history. But similar things have happened, much more frequently, to very ordinary people as the words of this Epistle came home to them with power.

F. F. Bruce[2]

I

The explosive effect of the Epistle to the Romans has been as marked in the missionary movement as anywhere else. The number of nineteenth-century missionary sermons and appeals based on Romans 10:14f. alone is beyond calculation. A district secretary of the Church Missionary Society at the middle of the century[3] sees this section as the climax of the epistle. The opening has proved that Jews and Gentiles are equally guilty in God's sight, and thus in equal need of salvation; Paul goes on to state the method of salvation, justification by faith; and then to prove the importance and propriety of its publication to the Gentiles; and by the section 10:11-15, "binds all who have the gospel to send it to them."[4] Half a century later, A. T. Pierson, one of the formative influences on the movement of the 80s and 90s which transformed the size and nature of the European and American missionary forces, was characteristically speaking of Romans 10 as "The

---

[1] First published as "The First Chapter of Romans and the Modern Missionary Movement" in W.W. Gasque and R.P. Martin, eds., *Apostolic History and the Gospel* (Grand Rapids: Eerdmans; and Exeter: Paternoster, 1971).

[2] F. F. Bruce, *The Epistle of Paul to the Romans*, TNTC (London, 1963), p. 60.

[3] John Johnson, *Sermons* I (London, 1850), pp. 113ff.

[4] *Ibid.*, p. 115.

unparalleled missionary chapter of the Bible" and, equally characteristically, dividing its content alliteratively as The Market for Missions,
the Message of Missions, the Methods of Missions, and the Motive for
Missions.[5]

Another theme beloved of nineteenth-century preachers was that of
Romans 3:29, "Is he not the God of the Gentiles also?"—or, as W. Y.
Fullerton insisted, "God is the God of the heathen also."[6] But this affirmation proceeds directly from the argument of 1:18f. about the universality of
God's wrath,[7] and this section, especially that which refers specifically to
the pagan world (1:18-32) has not unnaturally had a history of its own in
missionary thought.

The Christian view of non-Christian religions reflects traditions of
thought which have come to be denominated respectively those of "continuity" and "discontinuity,"[8] the one stressing God's activity in the world
outside the sphere of Scripture or church, recognizing or seeking points of
contact between the biblical revelation and that activity, as certainly God's
own; the other stressing the radical difference between God's redeeming
actions in saving history and any system whatever of human thought or
life, seeing religion in itself under the judgment of God, sometimes denying
any affinity between that revelation and "religion" at all.[9] Both traditions
are very ancient, going back to the earliest Christian centuries, arguably
both to the New Testament.[10] The representatives of each, with their
favourite Scripture passages, have ever claimed to represent the mind of
the New Testament; and, further, have supported their views with a wealth
of empirical evidence about non-Christian religious thought and life.

---

[5]A. T. Pierson, "The Market for Missions," *Missionary Sermons: A Selection from
the Discourses Delivered on Behalf of the Baptist Missionary Society on Various Occasions*
(London, 1925), pp. 185 ff. The sermon was originally delivered in 1903.

[6]W. Y. Fullerton, "The God of the Heathen Also," *ibid.*, pp. 299-310. The sermon
was delivered in 1909.

[7]It is inappropriate to argue here the old question (for Calvin discussed a form
of it) whether 1:18-3:20 is in fact a digression. See C. K. Barrett, *The Epistle to the
Romans, BNTC* (London, 1957), p. 33.

[8]These terms were popularized through the discussions at the International
Missionary Council Meeting at Tambaram, Madras, in 1938; see especially *The
Authority of the Faith*, Tambaram Series I (London, 1939). Behind the discussions lay
Hendrik Kraemer's preparatory volume, *The Christian Message in a Non-Christian
World* (London, 1938). See also C. F. Hallencreutz, *Kraemer towards Tambaram: A
Study in Hendrik Kraemer's Missionary Approach* (Uppsala, 1966).

[9]Cf. on this whole question K. Barth, *Kirchliche Dogmatik* 1/2, especially c. 17
(*Church Dogmatics I: The Doctrine of the Word of God*, part 2 [Edinburgh, 1956], pp.
280-361); A. Th. van Leeuwen, *Christianity in World History* (London, 1964).

[10]P. Beyerhaus, "Religionen und Evangelium, Kontinuität oder Diskontinuität?"
Evang. Missions Magazin 3 (1967), pp. 118-135.

II

Romans 1:18 ff., save for the modern debate about the nature and extent of the knowledge of God implied in 1:20, has not been an exegetical battlefield between the traditions in the way provided, for instance, by the missionary content of the Iconium and Areopagus addresses in Acts.[11] Its special place in the missionary movement is due to the fact that at various times people saw there, or thought they saw there, the non-Christian world that they themselves knew; and at other times, assuming these verses to give the origin of non-Christian religion, they were puzzled to account for other features of non-Christian religion which did not apparently accord with such a picture. That Paul's intention in the section as a whole is to show the whole world under judgment has hardly been in doubt; that the specific details of 1:22-27 reflect a view of contemporary Graeco-Roman society in decadence has usually also been recognized. But what is the relation of these particulars to the general principle? Is Paul simply describing how the seamier side of contemporary pagan society came into being? Or is he describing the origin of all non-Christian religions—perhaps even of religion itself? Does he assume the wilful rejection of a universal primitive monotheism? And—given an answer to any of these—how are the phenomena of non-Christian religion actually in view at the time to be accommodated to it? It is such questions as these, or rather, the assumed answers to them, which underlie much of the debate arising from Christian evangelization.

For the early Christian missionary thinkers, it was not Romans I which expressed the most important Christian contact with the non-Christian world. For them pagan society and pagan popular religion was at least broadly similar to that which Paul knew; and the most liberal of them had no desire to declare affinity with it. Justin, who is quite prepared to believe that Socrates and anyone else who spoke according to *logos*, and inasfar as they did so, were Christians before Christ,[12] is also certain that the gods of the street corner are demonic parodies, the direct result of wicked impositions by evil spirits.[13] Such thinkers were much more concerned to maintain their affinity with the philosophical tradition, which for them represented the glory of their inheritance, and which rejected popular religion as strenuously as they did; in fact, it was a mark of the Logos at work in Socrates that he defied popular religion and, like the Christians, was branded an atheist for doing so.[14] Justin, in fact, has reached a place where many another missionary was to come over the next eighteen centuries: he has concluded

---

[11]Cf. B. Gärtner, *The Areopagus Speech and Natural Revelation* (Uppsala, 1955).
[12]*Apology* I.46.
[13]*Ibid.*, I.5.
[14]*Ibid.*, I.6.

that there is more than one type of non-Christian tradition. There is that which is palpably devilish; there is that which is compatible with the Gospel and strenuously opposed to what it opposes.

The long period during which Western Europe was almost insulated from the non-Christian world meant that, apart from Jews, the only non-Christian peoples of whom most Christians, at least in the countries which became Protestant, knew much were those same Greeks and Romans, brought to life again by the new learning. Paul's catalogue of loathsomeness could be amply documented from other sources ("Of these abominations thou hast with Lactantius, Eusebius and Augustine," says Calvin).[15] Other sources also revealed that some pagans stood aloof from these abominations: Calvin's first major work, after all, was a commentary on Seneca. But with no regular living contact with a self-consciously non-Christian society, it was easy for Reformed Christians to separate, as the early apologists did, the philosophic from the religious tradition of classical paganism. Romans 1:18 ff. could thus be taken to indicate how "idolatry"—i.e., all religion outside Israel and the Church—took its origin.

III

When, in North America, contact with a non-Christian people was resumed, there was little reason to question this judgment. As the colonists looked upon the Indians—often with a desire for their salvation[16]—they saw the darkened heart changing the glory of the uncorruptible God into an image, the bodies given up to lust and dishonour plainly enough.[17] There was not even a Seneca. The connection between ancient and modern heathenism was also apparent:

> Let us inquire into the records of *antiquity*, let us consult the experience of all ages, and we shall find, that those who had no guide but the light of nature, no instructor but unassisted reason, have wandered in perpetual uncertainty, darkness and error. Or let us take a view of the *present* state of those countries that have not been illuminated by the gospel; and we shall see, that notwithstanding the improvements of near six thousand years, they remain to this day

[15]In Rom. 1:23.

[16]R. Pierce Beaver, *Church, State and the American Indians* (St. Louis, 1966); "American Missionary Motivation Before the Revolution," *Church History* 31 (1962), pp. 216-26.

[17]Joseph Sewall, *Christ Victorious Over the Powers of Darkness . . . Preached . . . at the Ordination of the Reverend Mr. Stephen Parker* (Boston, 1733). Reprinted in R. Pierce Beaver, *Pioneers in Mission: The Early Missionary Ordination Sermons, Charges, and Instructions* (Grand Rapids, 1966), pp. 41-64 (see p. 47).

covered with the grossest darkness, and abandoned to the most immoral and vicious practices.[18]

Despite the clear manifestation of the "invisible things of God" some ancient heathen denied his existence, while the rest worshipped his creatures, and "even the most despicable beings in the order of nature."

> This was the state of the Gentile nations when the light of the gospel appeared to scatter the darkness that overspread the face of the earth. And this has been the case, so far as has yet appeared, of all the nations ever since, upon whom the Sun of righteousness has not arisen with healing in his wings. Every new discovered country opens a new scene of astonishing ignorance and barbarity; and gives fresh evidence of the universal corruption of human nature.[19]

For the preacher of missionary ordination sermons, viewing the Amerindians from without, this was no doubt enough. But those who penetrated more closely into Native American society, while unequivocal in their affirmation of human depravity, saw other factors also. So early a missionary as John Eliot (1604-1690), a man living close to the Indians and learning their language, is struck by the fact that this people, although idolatrous and immoral, did believe, despite first appearances, in the Deity; that they believed also in the immortality of the soul, and an eternity of happiness or misery—they even had a tradition of one man who had actually seen God. Eliot, like several of his Puritan colleagues, came to the conclusion that the Native Americans were a remnant of the ten lost tribes of Israel. This would also explain their food taboos and purification rites, and their story of a general deluge. Over the years an idea with breathtaking implications grew in him: might not the Amerindians be only a fragment of the Semitic peoples who had broken away from the rest? Might not the peoples of India, of China, of Japan also be descended from the ten tribes? Alas then, why do they not all talk Hebrew? Eliot can speak only of the local language, but at least its grammatical frame is nearer to Hebrew than to Latin or Greek. Perhaps Chinese, Japanese, the Indian languages, are all degenerate forms of Hebrew. Perhaps, far more important, the conversion of the Indians, of which his own labours were a pledge, is but the sign that God is going to break eastward for the conversion of Israel, the ten tribes as well as the two?[20]

---

[18]Ebenezer Pemberton, *A Sermon Preached in Newark, June 12, 1744, at the Ordination of Mr. David Brainerd*. An edition published in New Haven in 1822 has been reprinted in R. Pierce Beaver, *Pioneers in Mission*, pp. 111-24 (see p. 113).

[19]*Ibid.*, p. 114.

[20]This aspect of Eliot's thought is well documented by S. H. Rooy, *The Theology of Missions in the Puritan Tradition* (Delft, 1965), pp. 230 ff.

It is easy to laugh at the enthusiasms of this lonely missionary; but he is grasping at a rationalization of a fact of experience. On a simple reading of Romans 1:18ff., Native American religion ought to be unrelievedly idolatrous. But it is not. The presence of other elements, however, can be explained as survivals in debased form of part of the Jewish revelation. Not only so, but in other parts of the world—India, China, Japan—traces of the same redemptive revelation may be found. By elimination, only in Africa, and among other Hamitic peoples, will Romans 1 apply in all its rigour as a picture of religion.[21]

At a later period, Jonathan Edwards, a warm supporter of missions and no stranger to the Indians himself, again finds the truth of Romans 1:18ff. confirmed by his own observations:

> The doctrine of St. Paul, concerning the blindness into which the Gentiles fell, is so confirmed by the state of religion in Africa, America, and even China, where, to this day no advances towards the true religion have been made, that we can no longer be at a loss to judge the insufficiency of unassisted reason to dissipate the prejudices of the Heathen world, and open their eyes to religious truths.[22]

Whence, then, come such approximations to "religious truths" as any of these may have? Edwards answers, from outside. Heathenism since the fall has been so dark that such a custom as sacrifice for sin could not have originated there. It *must* have been derived from the Jews. In the paganism of the old world, Plato, though a lesser philosopher than Socrates, yet knew more than he about true religion. The reason is that Socrates, unlike Plato, never left Greece, and was thus less open to outside influences.[23]

On such an explanation of those elements in non-Christian religion which cannot be ascribed to wilful blindness, it would be, of course, in the devil's interest to isolate peoples as far as possible from infectious contact with revealed religion. And Edwards argues that this actually happened: America was first peopled by the direct action of the devil. Satan, alarmed at the success of the gospel in the first three Christian centuries, surprised by the fall of the heathen Empire in the time of Constantine, and fearing that his kingdom might be completely overthrown, led the Indians away into America so that he could keep them for himself.[24]

---

[21]Eliot, however, did not base his missionary work upon this theory, or advocate or practice any restriction of evangelization to his supposed "Semites." The call to preach Christ took precedence over all speculations as to how He would bring in His kingdom. Cf. Rooy, p. 235.

[22]Jonathan Edwards, *Works* (1817 ed.) VIII, p. 193.

[23]*Ibid.*, pp. 188ff. Cf. Rooy, p. 299.

[24]Rooy, pp. 300f.

IV

Meanwhile, in contemporary Europe, far away from the real heathen, the genteel debate about "natural theology" was going forward. The argument of the *consensus gentium* acquired fresh importance. "No nation without belief in God," said the theologian; and the sceptic made answer, "How do you know?"

The evidence of the Jesuit missionaries from China became an absorbing interest. On the face of it, it represented a triumph for orthodoxy, and for the presence of "natural" religion; for here was a people which had allegedly preserved the knowledge of God and obeyed a pure morality for more than two thousand years. Leibnitz, whom we do not usually think of as a herald of the missionary movement, wanted Protestant missionaries to teach revealed religion to the Chinese who had preserved natural religion so effectively. In the end, of course, the other orders defeated the Jesuits on the interpretation of the Chinese texts, and this particular source of evidence for natural theology (which was in any case inconveniently proving too much) passed out of view—though attention was always available for accounts by travellers of the beliefs of non-Christian societies.[25]

Only a small part of the debate about China was concerned with the exegesis of Romans or any other apostolic book; nor, despite the undoubtedly sincere plea of Leibnitz for a Protestant mission, was it really conducted with any idea of doing anything. The Chinese, like the Tahitians later, were being called in to help solve a European problem. By contrast, the members and agents of the missionary societies which began to form by the end of the century, were desperately concerned with action: action for the salvation of the souls of those to whom they went. The terms in which people spoke of non-Christian religions were transformed as a result. For one thing, the Evangelical Revival, which underlay the new movement, had brought a more radical view and more vivid sense of the nature of sin; for another, earnest men were transmitting accounts of what they actually saw.

And what they saw was not usually a grave, distant, polite people preserving over thousands of years the knowledge of God and pure morality—the terms of the earlier eighteenth-century debate—but human sacrifice, the immolation of widows, the pictorial representations of *lingam* and *yonni*, cult prostitution, the victims crushed beneath the car of Jagannath. The picture of Romans 1:18ff., in fact, emerged again, less from a theory of religion than from the effect of observation; and the words and phrases of Romans 1:18ff.

---

[25]On views of paganism, cf. F. E. Manuel, *The Eighteenth Century Confronts the Gods* (Cambridge, Mass., 1959); on the European debate on the Jesuit evidence, cf. E. L. Allen, "Missions and Theology in the Eighteenth Century," *HJ* 56 (1958), pp. 113-22.

ring out time and again as missionaries view the religion of non-Christian peoples.[26] Further, just as the early apologists shared with the philosophical tradition much of the polemic against popular religion, so the missionaries in India had allies—liberal intellectuals with burning desire for religious reformation, like Rajah Ram Mohan Roy, and angry young men like some of Duff's early converts, rebelling against the traditional practices.[27]

Africa likewise recalled Romans 1 for many observers. David Jonathan East, one of a small host of writers on West Africa in the 1840s, produces an imposing account (based on travellers' tales) of African slavery, drunkenness, immorality, and lack of commercial probity. He then quotes Romans 1:28-31. "What an awful comment upon this affecting portion of Holy Writ are the humiliating facts which these and the preceding chapters record."[28] In another place, however, East recognizes that African paganism, though reprehensible, is in one respect different from that of Romans 1. Though African peoples have images, they do not make images of the Supreme God: they simply ignore him for the subordinate divinities and spirits.

> Thus it appears, that if they have not "changed the glory of the incorruptible God into an image, made like to corruptible man, and to birds, and four-footed beasts and creeping things"—they have, in their view, excluded him from the government of his world, and substituted in his room the wild creatures of their own imaginations, identifying these professedly spiritual existences with what is material, and oft times grossly absurd.[29]

African paganism thus demonstrates the principles of Romans in 1:18 ff., but identity in detail is not demanded.[30]

---

[26]Some representative works describing Indian religion may be cited: William Ward, *An Account of the Writings, Religion and Manners of the Hindoos*, 4 vols. (Serampore, 1811), 2 vols. (London, 1817): "It is probable, indeed, that no heathen nation has made a single idol in honour of 'the living and true God', and that direct worship to Him was never offered by any heathen" (I, p. xiv); Claudius Buchanan, *Christian Researches in Asia* (London, 1811), and *An Apology for promoting Christianity in India* (London, 1813); A. Duff, *India and Indian Missions, Including Sketches of the Gigantic System of Hinduism* (Edinburgh, 1839). On the attack on idolatry, cf. K. Ingham, *Reformers in India, 1793-1833* (Cambridge, 1956), pp. 33-54.

[27]George Smith, *The Life of Alexander Duff* (London, 1881), chaps. 5-6. For the view of Hinduism of an Indian convert, cf., e.g., K. M. Banerjee, *Dialogues on the Hindu Philosophy* (1861); Nehemiah Goreh, *Rational Refutation of the Hindu Philosophical Systems* (Calcutta, 1862; Madras, 1897).

[28]D. J. East, *Western Africa: Its Condition and Christianity the Means of Its Recovery* (London, 1844), p. 71. The work is based on a collation of earlier writings.

[29]*Ibid.*, p. 148.

[30]The existence of a conception of a Supreme God in African traditional religion, spoken of but not regularly worshipped, was frequently recognized by early nineteenth-century observers. Cf. J. Beecham, *Ashantee and the Gold Coast* (London, 1841), chapt. 7.

V

As the nineteenth century proceeded, such missionary views came into contact, and sometimes, collision, with new patterns of thought. There was the new interest, itself partly a result of the missionary movement,[31] in the literature of Eastern religions. There was the regnant hypothesis, held with all the intensity of a newfound faith, of the evolution of religion. There was the whole new science, with evolution as its basis, of anthropology, and *The Golden Bough* to link them all together.

There were many points of conflict. The missionary affirmation of the idea of a supreme God was immediately suspect; for animistic peoples who had not reached the appropriate stage, such a conception could only be a missionary invention. The charge was quite unjustified, for, on the reading of Romans 1 which most early missionaries had, there was no need to invent a High God in any non-Christian religion. They found the High God in African religion because he was there, not because their theology demanded his presence.

As the evolutionist doctrine gained repute, the rival doctrine of a primitive monotheism, from which all nonbiblical religions were descended, was more clearly enunciated, and Romans 1:20 ff. was its prime source. Sir Monier Monier Williams, an influential Sanskrit scholar and himself a devout Evangelical, argued that, just because of the original monotheism behind all religions, one could expect to find fragments of truth.[32] No longer was it necessary to presuppose borrowing from Jewish sources to explain every acceptable element in non-Christian religion. At one point he went further, and declared that some of the essential doctrines of Christianity were present in germ in all religions, awaiting the development and fulfilment which only Christianity could bring.[33]

It was possible, however, to affirm a primitive monotheism without drawing all these conclusions. Principal (later Bishop) Moule, a deep influence on scores of the new type of missionary who went out in such numbers

---

[31]The greatest name is, of course, that of Friedrich Max Müller, certainly no pillar of evangelical orthodoxy or pattern of missionary zeal; but Sir Monier Monier Williams, Professor of Sanskrit at Oxford from 1860, was closely associated with the missionary movement, and James Legge, Professor of Chinese there from 1875, had been a missionary with the London Missionary Society in China. Missionary reports, studies, and researches were undoubtedly a major contributory factor to the discovery by the West of Eastern religious literature.

[32]M. Monier Williams, *Indian Wisdom, or Examples of the Religious, Philosophical and Ethical Doctrines of the Hindus* (London, 1875), pp. 143f. (4th ed., p. 132 n.).

[33]M. Monier Williams, *Modern India and the Indians* (London, 1887), p. 234. For this position, which Williams eventually rejected, cf. E. J. Sharpe, *Not to Destroy but to Fulfil* (Uppsala, 1965), pp. 50 ff.

in the 1880s, gave exegetical backing to such a view.[34] The great Johannes Warneck was among those who observed in paganism a memory tenuous and not understood, of the primeval revelation:

> Dispassionate study of heathen religions confirms Paul's view that heathenism is a fall from a better knowledge of God.

In early days humanity had a greater treasure of spiritual goods, but neglected its knowledge and renounced its dependence until nothing remained but a dim presentiment.[35] Not that all saw anything as formalized as a primitive monotheism in Romans 1. A.E. Garvie, a formative influence on several important missionary writers of the twentieth century, argued that the essence of Paul's argument had nothing to do with the origin of religions at all but simply with the "close connexion between false views of God and wrong standard of duty," and that the Roman society of which Paul was primarily speaking had, to common knowledge, suffered a decline.[36]

In fact, one arm at least of the missionary movement began to develop the line of argument indicated, though later repudiated, by Monier Williams. Long years of study of the classics of Eastern religions indicated that Christianity was in fact their fulfilment—the "crown," to use the expression of the outstanding protagonist of this school, John Nicol Farquhar.[37] To pass from Duff's description of Hinduism to Farquhar's is to move to a different world. Yet each is describing exactly what he saw. Of course, time had brought changes—some of what Duff had seen had gone forever. But the main difference lies in the fact that Farquhar had, as it were, met Seneca.

Farquhar's series "The Religious Quest" (the singular is significant) reveals the sources of change. Sydney Cave is thoroughly representative of the contributors when he declares that the first missionaries were disquali-

---

[34]"The believer in the holy Scriptures . . . will receive this view of the primeval history of Theism as a true report of God's account of it. Remembering that it concerns an otherwise unknown moment of human spiritual history, he will not be disturbed by alleged evidence against it from lower down the stream" (H. C. G. Moule, *The Epistle of Paul to the Romans*, Expositor's Bible [London, 1893], p. 45). Cf. also his Cambridge Bible commentary (1879) on Rom. 1:21.

[35]Quoted by S. M. Zwemer, *The Influence of Animism on Islam* (London, 1920). Cf. J. Warneck, *The Living Forces of the Gospel* (E.T. Edinburgh, n.d.), p. 98: "The heart of the heathen is like a palimpsest, the original writing of which is written over and become unseen. No one knows anything of the words of wisdom covered over there." Andrew Lang's theory of the High Gods, developed in opposition to the nature-myth school, took its origin from missionary and other reports. See W. Schmidt, *The Origin and Growth of Religion* (E.T. London, 1935), pp. 172ff.

[36]A. E. Garvie, *Romans*, Century Bible, *ad loc.*

[37]J. N. Farquhar, *The Crown of Hinduism* (Oxford, 1913). See E. J. Sharpe, *Not to Destroy, passim.*

fied from seeing the best in the non-Christian world because the sacred books were closed to them. When one looks at, for instance, the Saivite Temple in Tanjore one can understand the violent reactions of the pioneers; but the Hinduism we now face (1919) is very different from that of a century ago. "We are concerned with the 'Higher Hinduism.' Idolatry is doomed."[38]

Such judgments and such a viewpoint on Hinduism was the fruit of the study of its literature. It is thus hardly surprising that when the World Missionary Conference of 1910 came to discuss "points of contact" and "preparation for Christianity" in the religions, it was on "Animism," which has no literature, that there was most hesitation.[39]

As we have seen, Monier Williams came to retract his idea of a development of religions with Christianity as the crown; his last position stressed that a gulf—"not a mere rift across which the Christian and non-Christian may shake hands and interchange similar ideas in regard to essential truths"—lay between the Bible and the "so-called Sacred Books of the East."

> Be fair, be charitable, be Christ-like, but let there be no mistake. Let it be made absolutely clear that Christianity cannot, must not be watered down to suit the palate of either Hindu, Parsee, Confucianist, Buddhist, or Mohammedan, and that whosoever wishes to pass from the false religion to the true can never hope to do so by the rickety planks of compromise. . . .[40]

He spoke to the depths. For many missionaries the practical way of expressing an attitude to the religions came to be that, while elements of good remained, the *systems* stood condemned.

VI

It would be inappropriate here to take the story through Tambaram and beyond, though the Epistle to the Romans has always been in the background, and occasionally, as in the controversy over 1:20, right in its forefront. The traditions of continuity and discontinuity will, no doubt,

---

[38]S. Cave, *Redemption, Hindu and Christian* (Oxford, 1919).

[39]*World Missionary Conference, Edinburgh 1910: Report of Commission IV. The Missionary Message in Relation to Non-Christian Religions.* See especially chapt. 2: "Some deny the existence of any point of contact, or preparation for Christianity in any of the beliefs and rites of Animism—it may be noted that these witnesses find practically no religious content in Animism. . . ." Cf. Warneck, *Living Forces*, pp. 85ff. On the other hand, in 1900 an African Christian, the Rev. (later Bishop) James Johnson was telling missionary-minded students that Africa "is conscious of the existence of God, believes in divine providence, believes that every good and perfect gift comes from above, from Him who is the Father of us all. . . . Africa desires and intends to worship Him, but she knows not how to do it" (*SMP* [London, 1900], pp. 74f.).

[40]E. Stock, *History of the Church Missionary Society* III (London, 1899), p. 304.

continue to lock horns in the missionary debate, and the Epistle to the Romans will continue to challenge, quicken, and rebuke those who desire to declare the righteousness of God. As one reviews the place which the first chapter has hitherto had in the thought of the missionary movement, some features stand out which indicate its continuing relevance.

Christian evangelists have found themselves addressing people in societies with coherent patterns of thought—within systems of belief and activity. It has been convenient to provide names like "Buddhism" and "Hinduism" to cover numbers of these systems. The validity of this process is not a theme to discuss here; but at least we should not talk as if Paul used them himself. Perhaps too much of the debate about continuity or discontinuity has been concerned with systems. As a result, we have men, each genuinely describing what he saw, producing such different interpretations of "Hinduism" as those of Duff and Farquhar. When this is introduced into the context of Romans 1, we have one party inviting all to recognize that these non-Christian religions lie manifestly under the wrath of God for their manifest deeds, and another pointing to particular persons, books, or doctrines, and saying in effect (as Bishop Ryle said of the necessity of baptism by immersion for Eskimos), Let those believe it who can.

Argument about which is the correct, or the more correct, picture of "Hinduism" is beside the point in the light of Romans 1:18ff., for Paul's concern here is not with systems at all, but with men. It is *people* who hold down the truth of unrighteousness, who do not honour God, who are given up to dishonourable passions. It is upon men, who commit ungodly and wicked deeds, that the wrath of God is revealed.

As systems, and ultimately the collective labels for systems which we call the world religions, have slipped into the place of ungodly people in the interpretation of Romans 1, so Christianity, also conceived as a system, has sometimes slipped into the place of the righteousness of God. The true system has been opposed to false systems condemned there. It has sometimes, but not always, been realized that "Christianity" is a term formally identical with the other labels; that it certainly covers as wide a range of phenomena as most of them; that, if the principalities and powers work within human systems, they can and do work within this one. Man-in-Christianity lies under the wrath of God just as much, and for the same reasons, as Man-in-Hinduism. It was the realization of this which saved the earliest generations of the modern missionary movement from the worst sort of paternalism. Humanity was vile everywhere, not only in Ceylon. The Christian preacher had the same message of *repentance* and faith for the non-Christian world as he had been preaching in the Christian world;[41] for it was not Christianity that saves, but Christ.

---

[41]Cf., e.g., Sewall's sermon in Beaver, *Pioneers in Mission*, pp. 41-64. The missionary preacher's task is identical with that of the congregational minister.

This in turn relates to another point: the close connection of Romans 2 with Romans 1. The "diatribe" form of Romans 1-2 has often been re-marked, as has the indebtedness of the language to Wisdom 13-14 and its closeness to the normal, accepted Jewish polemic against idolatry.[42] The thrust of Romans 1 lies in Romans 2; not in the origin of paganism but in the hopelessness of the virtuous. And, before going on to show the free acceptance of men of all kinds through faith in Christ, Paul offers (Rom. 2:17ff.) a satirical commentary on Diaspora Judaism's understanding of its mission. Here was a busy, missionizing people: a guide to the blind, a light to those that sit in darkness, a corrector of the foolish, a teacher of children— the Wisdom of the opening chapters of Proverbs and the Servant of Isaiah 42 rolled into one—who yet for all their exaltation of the Decalogue, stole, committed adultery and sacrilege, and, as the Scripture said about the Jews of an earlier time, caused the heathen to blaspheme the name of God because of what they saw in his people. Some sharp things have been said from time to time to missionaries. Some of them are in the New Testament.

---

[42]Cf. Bruce, *Romans*, on 21:16: "We can almost envisage him as he dictates his letter to Tertius, suddenly picking out the complacent individual who has been enjoying the exposure of these sins he 'has no mind to', and telling him that he is no better than anyone else" (p. 86).

6

Origins of Old Northern and New Southern Christianity[1]

Christian history has seen many changes in the center of gravity of the Christian World. Three of these have been crucial, for each of them led to a transformation in Christian expression. The first was initiated when some unnamed Jewish Christians in Antioch presented the Messiah of Israel as the Lord of the Greeks (Acts 11:20); it reflected a massive movement of people nurtured in Hellenistic civilization to worship the God of Israel. The second came when the peoples of the north and west, whom Hellenistic Christians thought of as the barbarian destroyers of Christian civilization, came to the faith in Christ and substituted the God of the Christians for their traditional pantheons. The third has come to a climax in our own century, reflecting a process going on for considerably longer; it has been the massive movement towards Christian faith in all the southern continents—sub-Saharan Africa, Latin America, certain parts of Asia, the Pacific Islands—which means that Christian profession in the southern continents now outnumbers that in the northern.[2]

The obvious feature which these three great intakes of Christians have in common is that each has consisted overwhelmingly of adherents of the primal religions; by comparison, converts from the other religious traditions have been few. But there have been other similarities, too. The second and third have to be seen in the context of a major cultural impact of one civilization on another. The adoption of Christianity often accompanied

---

[1]Originally published in Hans Kasdorf and W. Müller, eds., *Bilanz und Plan: Mission an der Schwalle zum dritten Jahrtausend* (Bad Liebezell: Verlag der Liebezeller Mission, 1988).

[2]See David B. Barrett, ed., *World Christian Encyclopedia* (Nairobi: Oxford University Press, 1982), pp. 3ff., and Table 2 on the significance. Cf. A. F. Walls, "The Christian Tradition in Today's World," in Frank B. Whaling, ed., *Religion in Today's World* (Edinburgh: T. & T. Clark, 1987).

substantial social change and was often part of the mechanism of adjustment to social change.

Primal societies under the impact of social change through the presence
of an invader culture are particularly vulnerable at three points: values,
hierarchy of leadership, and the local point of reference. The adoption of
Christianity by the peoples of the north and west in earlier centuries, and
by primal peoples of the southern continents in later times, provided means
of coping with this fundamental social and psychic disturbance with all its
traumas. It provided, for instance, a new set of values to replace the old
(though the replacement was rarely exact, and in both north and south most
people were left with dual or overlapping value systems). It often provided,
or legitimated, an alternative hierarchy to one outmoded or discredited. It
provided a universal point of reference, linking the society with its traditionally local and kin-related focus to a universal order.

In Northern Europe, for a people to become Christian was for them to
enter Christendom, to be part of a fellowship of peoples owing allegiance
to Christ. In the West this allegiance was concretized through the acknowledgment of the West's only apostolic see. Entry to Christendom was also
entry to a literary culture preserved by and through the Church. It was a
literary culture based on Latin, the language of the sacred books and the
liturgy, the language of the literary tradition of the Western Roman Empire
which the peoples of the north and west had collectively destroyed.

In modern times, in the southern continents, the acceptance of Christianity by primal peoples has again gone hand in hand with entrance to a
literary culture, and often with an international language to match the
broadened horizons. But there has been a significant difference.

In ancient times, Southern and Eastern Christianity developed vernacular Christian literatures such as the Coptic and Slavonic; for the most part,
Northern Christianity did not. Liturgy and Scriptures remained in Latin.
The concept of a universal interconnected Christian body was thus
strengthened, but at the risk of sacred language becoming exotic. The fact
that Celt and Saxon alike used Latin may have helped to heal the breach
between the Saxons missionized from Rome and the Celtic Christians
whom the fathers of the missionized Saxons had suppressed. To Christianize was to Latinize, to bring people within the sphere of classical culture.

In modern times, the Christianizing process in preliterate societies in the
southern continents has similarly brought its recipients within the sphere
of literary culture and international communication. But, in principle anyway, it has favoured the growth of *vernacular* literature. Original expectations that Latin, or some Western language, would serve for most important
sacred purposes gave way to a recognition that Scripture and liturgy
belonged to the vernacular, that the language of prayer is most properly
the language of the home. The cultural effects of this are obvious; there are
many instances of cultural renaissance caused by the growth of vernacular

writing.[3] The specifically Christian "sacred" use of the vernacular has given some primal cultures a resilience against the solvent of rapid change leading to loss of identity, and enabled a preservation of part of the local focus in the very act of producing a broader identity. There are also theological side effects. The explanation and elucidation of the Christian faith in one's own vernacular, in dialogue with other vernacular speakers, is a wholly different matter from its recapitulation in an alien language of learned discourse, however correctly acquired.

The other great differences between the birth processes of old Northern and new Southern Christianity were even more fundamental. In the early preaching of Christianity, missionaries proclaimed God over against the gods, the one over against the many, the new Christ over against the old Thor. This was a continuation of the methods of preaching in the first great intake of Christians from the primal religions of the Hellenistic-Roman world. No one could think of Zeus/Jupiter as the God and Father of our Lord Jesus Christ; and as far as they accepted a *praeparatio evangelica* in pre-Christian religion, the missionaries found it in the philosophers' God and the code of the abstract good, rather than anything in mythology or cult. When the faith came north, it again found no shadow of itself in the faiths it displaced. Odin was not God, nor was Thor, nor Frey. Indeed the old religions of the north seem rarely to have had any place for a High God. Christian proclamation, therefore, forced a choice between old and new, God and the gods,[4] Christ and Thor. The Nordic graves tell their own story. In some, pieces of metal have been found carved as Christ's cross, in others as Thor's hammer. Some people evidently thought it prudent to look both ways; there are graves which contain both cross and hammer, and one or two which have a hammer-shaped cross.[5] In Iceland we hear of Helgi the half-Christian who worshipped Christ on land, but felt safer with Thor at sea; and in Norway the pious gesture regularly made by King Olaf the Good before taking food was variously interpreted by observers. This halfway state could not last for ever; as the White Christ established his kingdom in the north, refusing any rival, sharing his throne with no one, the Black Thor and the other old gods were condemned to death or forced into the spirit shadow world.

Generally speaking, the story of Southern Christianity has been differ-

---

[3]See Lamin Sanneh, "Mission and the Modern Imperative, Retrospect and Prospect," in Joel Carpenter and Wilbert R. Shenk, eds., *Earthen Vessels: Evangelicals, Culture and the American Missions Enterprise in the Last Century* (Grand Rapids: Eerdmans, 1988), pp. 301-16.

[4]Cf., in relation to eleventh-century runic inscriptions, E. Segelberg, "God Help His Soul," in *Ex orbe religionum. Studia Geo Widengren II* (Leiden: Brill, 1972), pp. 161-76.

[5]See the photographic plates in E. G. Turville-Petre, *Myth and Religion of the North: The Religion of Ancient Scandinavia* (London: Weidenfeld and Nicolson, 1964).

ent. In primal societies in quite diverse parts of the world, the Christian preachers found God already there, known by a vernacular name. Often associated with the sky, creator of earth and moral governor of humanity, having no altars or priesthood, and perhaps no regular worship, some named Being could be identified behind the whole constitution of the phenomenal and transcendental worlds. More often than not, that name has been used in Scripture translation, liturgy, and preaching as the name of the God of Israel and of the Church. Where this has happened, the coming of Christianity has not been—as in northern Christian experience—bringing God to the people, so much as bringing him near. The fact that, however severe the Christian judgment may have been about the religion and life of primal societies, the name of God was in so many instances retained, may yet have momentous consequences for the future shape of Christian theology.[6] God is "the God of the Gentiles also"[7] in a way which lies outside the experience of Western Christians.

It is worth reverting to the early experience of Northern Christianity and reflecting how long the conversion process went on. The primal religions predominated in most of Sweden until the twelfth century, in Finland still longer. Many areas acknowledged Christianity only to revert and start again. The author of the Orkneyinga Saga tells us of the first conversion of the Orkney Islands in a way which makes clear why a second conversion was needed:

> Olaf Tryggvason spent four years looting in the British Isles. Then he was baptized in the Scillies, and from there sailed to England where he married Gyda, the sister of [the Christian] King Kvaran of Ireland. . . .
>
> Olaf sailed east with five ships . . . until he reached Orkney. At Osmundswald he ran into Earl Sigurd [ruler of Orkney] who had three ships and was setting out on a viking expedition. Olaf sent a messenger to him, asking Sigurd to come over to his ship as he wanted a word with him.
>
> "I want you and all your subjects to be baptised," he said when they met. "If you refuse I'll have you killed on the spot, and I swear that I'll ravage every island with fire and steel."
>
> The Earl could see what kind of situation he was in and surrendered himself into Olaf's hands. He was baptised and Olaf took his son, called Hvelp or Hundi, as a hostage and had him baptised too under the name of Hlodvir. After that, all Orkney embraced the faith. Olaf sailed east to Norway taking Hlodvir with him, but Hlodvir

---

[6]For an important discussion of this see Kwame Bediako, *Theology and Identity: The Impact of Culture upon Christian Thought in the Second Century and Modern Africa* (Oxford: Regnum Books).

[7] Cf. Romans 3:29.

didn't live long and after his death Sigurd refused to pay homage to King Olaf.[8]

Olaf Tryggvason was King of Norway, and the saga writer gives a pretty fair indication of his methods of Christianization. In themselves they probably caused little particular offence; the Norsemen lived by the power of a strong right arm, and he who had the strongest could have what he wanted as long as it remained the strongest. Olaf may have been quite sincere in what he understood—through that shrewd, perverse, and bloodsoaked mind of his—concerning his new faith; the blessings it opened and the dangers from which it gave hope of rescue. He may well have believed that he was bringing the highest possible benefit to his subjects by forcing them to the new cult. But he was also building up the power of the monarch more than any King of Norway before him; and undoubtedly widespread adherence to the universal faith which he promoted so enthusiastically would assist the process of centralization. When he delivers to the Earl of Orkney his ultimatum about baptism he is implicitly laying claim as king to be the earl's overlord. The earl sees this, and bows to *force majeure*. But when the earl's son, the king's hostage, dies, there is nothing more to lose. The king is a long way off, and as the saga writer puts it, he "refused to pay homage to King Olaf." The writer does not think to mention what was equally true, that it was no longer necessary to follow King Olaf's religion. The Orcadians gave it up for a generation.

But the story as a whole simply shows that conversion at the point of the sword was not decisive for Christianity. That force was often used in the conversion of the northern peoples is undeniable, and it was used with a ferocity and violence beyond anything the *conquistadores* did in the Americas and far beyond anything that happened in modern Africa or Asia as a result of imperial association with Christianity. But, as in Orkney, the strong right arm might be counterproductive. It was precisely because Christianity was the pledge of loyalty to Olaf of Norway that the Orcadians rejected it as soon as they safely could, and waited until they were ready to receive it for their own reasons, not someone else's.

That time came during the long reign of Earl Thorfinn, who died in A.D. 1064. Here is the Orkneyinga Saga again:

> Earl Thorfinn was now the sole ruler of Orkney and the Other territories he had won. . . . From time to time the Earl would go on viking expeditions to the west of Scotland and to Ireland and also spent some time in England as leader of the King's bodyguard.
>   When Thorfinn heard that King Magnus had died, he sent envoys

---

[8]Orkneyinga Saga 12, trans. H. Pålsson and P. Edwards, *The History of the Earls of Orkney* (London: Hogarth Press, 1978).

east to King Harald in Norway with a message of goodwill, saying that he wanted the King's friendship. The King gave a favourable reply to the message and promised Thorfinn his friendship.

From there Thorfinn sailed south along the coast all the way to Denmark where, after a land journey, he met King Svein at Aalborg. The King invited Thorfinn to stay with him and feasted him in grand style. Then Thorfinn announced his intention to visit Rome. In Saxony he met the Emperor Henry who gave him a warm welcome and many fine gifts, including a number of horses.

The Earl began his pilgrimage and travelled to Rome, had an audience with the Pope and received absolution from him for all his sins. After that Thorfinn started back home and arrived safe and well in his own earldom.

By now he was finished with piracy and devoted all his time to the government of his people and country and to the making of new laws. He had his permanent residence in Birsay, where he built and dedicated to Christ a fine minster, the seat of the first bishop of Orkney.[9]

Here we are given a portrait of Earl Thorfinn as a young chief, securing his income by regularly looting Christian Ireland (a proper occupation for a venturesome Norse warrior who shared the booty). A few sentences later we meet Earl Thorfinn as elder statesman. He has made the long pilgrimage to Rome and received absolution from the Pope himself, building a cathedral on his bleak North Atlantic island next to his tidal fortress, and was celebrated as a legislator, a man who codified laws for the common good.

The transformation of Thorfinn is the transformation of his people. Over the critical half-century of Orcadian history that he dominated, not only he but his people "gave up piracy"; indeed, they recognized that the viking way of life, with its forays into richer, settled, largely Christian lands was piracy. Certainly this was associated with the process of the Orcadians becoming Christians; but the association is not simple and direct. It was not, for instance, a matter of simple moral reformation as a result of conversion, though in frequent individual cases this may well have been true. The fact was that the Viking age had to come to an end. Raiding is of its nature subject to a law of diminishing returns, and the raiding life is incompatible with other important activities. Christianity, among all its other aspects, provided a means of adjustment from raiding to farming. The worship of Odin had little relevance outside the warrior state. In Odin's Valhalla people spent all-day fighting and all-night drinking. The farmer who did that would never get through to a year's harvest. Thor's dynamic energy, or the old fertility couple Frey/Freya, might assist him (and indeed, the

---

[9]Orkneyinga Saga 31.

Black Thor was the last rival of the White Christ in the north). But better still, those who steadily work for their living get help from the worship of one God, who made both earth and skies.

The Nordic peoples were but the latest of many groups to follow a similar path. Over the centuries, other Germanic tribes had moved west led by warrior bands excited at vast new lands to plunder. But a time always came when the need was less to conquer and defend these lands than to farm and maintain them; and the change of life style was assisted by a change of faith and worship. It was not a steady or a regular movement. Bede tells us of a Christian king of the East Saxons who was put to death for forgiving his enemies.[10] In this case it looks as if the young warriors were disgruntled at the thoroughness of their master's conversion, since it reduced his willingness to go to war. It was precisely on war, with its access to booty, that their livelihood depended. Peace defrauded them of their just expectations. They killed their Christian king.

If conversion facilitated change of life style it also facilitated stable relationships with other peoples—a discourse of Christian nations. Not for nothing does the saga writer set the story of Olaf's conversion and Thorfinn's transformation in the context of their voyages, marriage alliances, and friendships. But the adoption of Christianity by the warlords and peasant cultivators of the north forced upon it situations, priorities, anxieties, and enquiries that it had never known in its centuries of steady penetration of the Hellenistic-Roman framework of civilization. Some puzzled letters from missionaries survive: Augustine of Canterbury among the English, Boniface (an Englishman) among the Friesians a century later refer to their respective Popes questions that have arisen from their missionary work.[11] Many of them are about marriage, a topic on which the missionaries were doubtless well-informed as regards standard theology and practice.

The new Christians, however, had formerly lived by a totally different set of rules, and it was by no means clear how far *all* the traditional rules had to change. (Could two brothers marry two sisters?) And there were questions dealt with in traditional northern codes which had never formed part of Christian theology at all. How soon should a woman enter church after childbirth? Can a leper receive communion? Should a man stay away from worship following nocturnal emission? Such questions were not in the Roman lawbooks and it was no use to say they were unimportant, that they had nothing to do with the substance of faith. They were questions of serious moment for the new Christians, and would not go away. For a whole world had toppled; a world of sacred places and sacred times and ritual acts, and with it had gone a form of security. For people to feel secure in their new faith

---

[10]Bede, *Historia Ecclesiastica* 3:22.

[11]*Ibid.*, 1:27; Gregory to Boniface in Migne, *PL* 89; trans. in C. H. Talbot, *The Anglo-Saxon Missionaries in Germany* (London, 1954), letter 14.

they must have satisfactory answers to the questions left by the old. The result, in the nature of the case, was going to be different from the expression of the faith embodied in the missionaries who taught it.

Those missionaries and their mentors in the cultured, well-organized older Christian centres in Italy and Gaul must also have had much heart searching regarding their "barbarian" colleagues. The chequered career of Patrick and the various strands of apology that come through his surviving writings are a case in point. It was not simply that he wrote bad Latin; that could be forgiven in a colonial setting. The fact that he had committed a major sin as a young man no doubt reinforced the idea that great care was necessary before entrusting church leadership to "natives." But what did his more sophisticated colleagues and referees make of Patrick's recognition of dreams as channel of God's guidance, of his vivid description of his being transfixed by the devil descending like a great rock upon his chest?[12]

Already in Patrick, who lived as early as the fifth century A.D., we can see that the Christianity of the new northern ex-primalists was going to take a quite different form from that of the literary civilization of North Africa. It was also to last longer, and a millennium and a half later missionaries from Patrick's own land were to express reservations about the products of African and Pacific Christianity not unlike those of the best conducted monasteries about Patrick and his like.

The conversion process which led to the formation of Northern Christianity is worth renewed study for the sake of understanding the current formation of new Southern Christianity. Indeed, at some points the observation of the Christian presence in primal societies in twentieth-century Africa, Asia, or the Pacific may cast light on the pages of Gregory of Tours and Bede and Snorri. The resemblances should never blind us to the differences, nor should they dull us to effects which lie outside the experience of old Northern Christianity, or of uninhibited vernacular Christian expression seen as God entering a people's past through his vernacular name. Or again, they should not blind us to the results of the breaking up of Christendom, of territorially identified Christianity, or of the discourse of Christian nations.

But we should also remain alert to the fact that a simple substitution of the culturally new for the culturally old is neither sufficient nor possible when the mental and moral fabric of a society is torn; or when people must live in different worlds of discourse at the same time; or when they are faced with moral and social obligations which belong to different orders, and when those obligations conflict with each other; or when they believe (or half believe) in different universes of power. If there is to be no wound, if people are to make clear moral choices and do so in the faith of Christ, they must be able to integrate their worlds, to knit together the new and the old.

---

[12]All mentioned in Patrick's brief *Confession*.

Part Two

AFRICA'S PLACE
IN CHRISTIAN HISTORY

7

The Evangelical Revival, the Missionary Movement, and Africa[1]

Evangelicalism and the Missionary Movement

The modern missionary movement is an autumnal child of the Evangelical Revival. Fifty years separate the great events of Northampton and Cambuslang from the formation of the earliest of the voluntary societies to promote Christian activity in the non-Christian world; yet, without the revival, the societies would have been inconceivable. The revival clarified the rationale for such activity by transmitting the understanding that there was no difference between the spiritual state of a pleasure-seeking duchess (though baptized and adhering to the prevailing religious system of the higher and middle classes) and that of a South Sea Islander. That spiritual parity of the unregenerate of Christendom and the heathen abroad had important missionary consequences. Like the admonition to Lady Huntingdon's titled friend, who did not want to enter the kingdom of heaven in the same manner as her coachman, it took a hatchet to some axiomatic superiorities. A consistent view of human solidarity in depravity shielded the first missionary generation from some of the worst excesses of racism.

The revival also supplied the logistic networks—interregional, international, interdenominational—that undergirded the movement. The chain that lead to William Carey's pioneering missionary initiative of 1792 was forged by a gift from a Scottish Presbyterian to an English Baptist of a book by a New England Congregationalist.[2] Another New Englander, David

---

[1] First published in M. A. Noll, D. W. Bebbington, and G. A. Rawlyk, eds., *Evangelicalism: Comparative Studies of Popular Protestantism in North America, the British Isles, and Beyond, 1700-1990* (New York: Oxford University Press, 1994), pp. 310-30.

[2] A. Fawcett, *The Cambuslang Revival: The Scottish Evangelical Revival of the Eighteenth Century* (London: Banner of Truth, 1971), pp. 223-36.

Brainerd, became the principal model of early British Missionary spirituality; his own work had been supported by the Society in Scotland for Promoting Christian Knowledge.[3] An unending stream of correspondence, crisscrossing the Atlantic, reveals just how important as a missionary factor were the African-Americans and Afro-West Indians.[4] The Church Missionary Society was hauled back from absurdity through the pastor of a German congregation in London who put them in contact with a seminary in Berlin.[5] Magazines on two continents gathered and disseminated "missionary intelligence" without regard to denomination or country of origin.[6]

Above all, the revival supplied missionaries. There had been various earlier schemes for missions, although none went further than paper because no one was likely to undertake them.[7] The first generation of the Protestant missionary enterprise was for practical purposes an evangelical undertaking. Jane Austen represents the bright society girl as saying to the earnest young clergyman: "When I hear of you next, it may be as a celebrated preacher in some great society of Methodists, or as a missionary into foreign parts."[8] Methodist preacher or foreign missionary—enthusiasm could go no further. By 1813 missions had some degree of official recognition implied by the charter (as renewed in revised form) of the East India Company, and by the 1830s serious Christians of every sort were ready to agree that missions were a good thing; well past the middle of the century, however, it was overwhelmingly evangelicals that staffed them. It may therefore be worth recalling some of the influences that shaped the early missionaries' own religion.

---

[3] J. van den Berg, *Constrained by Jesus' Love: An Enquiry into the Motives of the Missionary Awakening in Great Britain in the Period between 1698 and 1815* (Kampen: Kok, 1956), pp. 57-58, 91-92; S. H. Rooy, *The Theology of Missions in the Puritan Tradition: A Study of Representative Puritans* (Grand Rapids: Eerdmans, 1965), pp. 289-93. In 1816 the *Missionary Register*, of Anglican Evangelical provenance, serialized Jonathan Edwards's account of Brainerd.

[4] Cf. A. J. Raboteau and D. W. Wills, "Rethinking American Religious History," *Council of Societies for the Study of Religion Bulletin* 20 (1991): 57-61.

[5] E. Stock, *History of the Church Missionary Society*, Vol. 1 (London: CMS, 1899), pp. 82-83; Charles Hole, *The Early History of the Church Missionary Society to the End of 1814* (London: CMS, 1896), pp. 81-85.

[6] The best-known early example was the *Missionary Register*, published in London; a *Scottish Missionary Register* on similar lines appeared in 1820.

[7] Some examples appear in van den Berg, *Constrained by Jesus' Love*, pp. 15-28. For the sad story of Justinian Welz, see J. A. Scherer, *Justinian Welz: Essays by an Early Prophet of Mission* (Grand Rapids: Eerdmans, 1969). It is significant that the eighteenth-century Tranquebar mission, though supported in the highest circles of state (its formal originator was the king of Denmark) and church (its finances were administered by the Society for Promoting Christian Knowledge), relied on A. H. Francke's pietist establishment at Halle for its staff.

[8] Jane Austen, *Mansfield Park* (1814), Vol. 3, Chapt. 16 (Chapt. 47 in most modern editions).

Evangelical Religion and Christendom

Historic evangelicalism is a religion of protest against a Christian society that is not Christian enough. It is eloquently expressed in Wesley's hymn about blind churchmen:

> O wouldst thou, Lord, reveal the sins,
> And turn their joy to grief:
> The world, the CHRISTIAN world convince
> of damning unbelief.[9]

Evangelical preaching is primarily addressed to a world that is both Christian and unbelieving. Churchgoing, not always enthusiastic, is accepted within this world; to return to Jane Austen's *Mansfield Park,* even the smart set represented in the Crawfords are evidently regularly at church, and the reprobate Henry, who has "never thought on serious subjects," has nevertheless considered how certain passages of the liturgy should be read.[10] Regular, even intense religious observation can also be found in this world, as is clear from the accounts of evangelical conversions, which regularly feature parental piety or describe a career that includes devout periods. Furthermore, despite bouts of rhetorical alarm, open rejection of Christian doctrine is generally muted. Wilberforce saw "sceptics and unitarians" as a fringe—though he feared a broadening fringe—of society.[11] The evangelical bugbears were less professed infidelity than professed Christianity without the "distinguishing doctrines of the gospel."

Evangelical Christianity, in a word, assumes Christendom, the territorial conception of the Christian faith that brought about the integration of throne and altar that began with the conversion of the barbarians of the North and West. Perhaps we have not fully faced the extent to which all subsequent Western Christianity was shaped by the circumstances under which the people of northern Europe came into the Christian faith—coming not as individuals, families, or groups but as whole societies complete with their functioning political and social systems integrated around their ruler. *Individual* choice could hardly exist, even in concept. The ideal outcome could be pictured as the assembly of Christian princes and their peoples, all subjects to the King of Kings; it lead inevitably to the idea of the Christian nation, where each member of the nation is within the sphere of the church. The tension between the principle of Christendom and its realization in practice is the history of Western Christianity. It may be noted that the

---

[9] *Collection of Hymns for the Use of People Called Methodists* (London, 1780), No. 94.

[10] Austen, Vol. 3, Chapt. 3 (Chapt. 34 of modern editions).

[11] William Wilberforce, *Practical View of the Prevailing Religious System of Professed Christians In the Higher and Middle Classes of This Country Contrasted with Real Christianity* (London, 1797; many editions).

vernacular movement in the northern parts of Christendom that we designate the Protestant Reformation left the territorial principle intact and the tension unresolved.

Mainstream evangelicalism in the period in which the missionary movement was born accepted the idea of a Christian nation. The idea is fundamental, for instance, to William Wilberforce's *Practical View* (1797). The book is not a spare-time avocation of a public man who happens to be an evangelical Christian; Wilberforce writes *because* he is a public man. Only a revival of religion, he argues, can rescue both the Christian nation and its most prominent symbol, the established church. "Unless there be reinfused into the mass of our society something of that principle which animated our ecclesiastical system in its earlier days, it is vain to hope that this establishment will very long continue. But in proportion as vital Christianity can be revived, in that same proportion, the church establishment is strengthened."[12]

The evangelical legislator is concerned to bring the nation in reality to what it is already in principle, and, as he believed, by history also. Hence Wilberforce's equal application of his energies to issues of national righteousness (the slave trade), social righteousness (dueling, and the Society for the Suppression of Vice), and personal holiness. "Real Christianity" can be expressed in and through a national church, whose baptism is the birthright of everyone born in the nation.

The full title of Wilberforce's book is *Practical View of the Prevailing Religious System of Professed Christians in the Higher and Middle Classes of this Country Contrasted with Real Christianity.* The hallmark of evangelical religion is real Christianity over against its substitutes. Thus John Wesley arranges his 1780 hymnbook "according to the experience of *real* Christians" and includes in the section headed "Exhorting sinners to return to God" a subsection "Describing formal religion," lest the returning sinner get stranded in formal religion and proceed no further. A section "Describing inward religion" follows immediately. Evangelical faith is about inward religion as distinct from formal, real Christianity as distinct from nominal. In other words, the evangelicalism of the period takes its identity from protest, and in effect from nominal Christianity. Evangelical religion presupposes Christendom, Christian civil society.

That society is generally defective as regards "the distinguishing doctrines of the gospel," or as Wilberforce calls them, "the peculiar doctrines of Christianity." He identifies three: original sin and consequent human depravity; the atonement of Christ; and the sanctifying power of the spirit in the believer's life. The doctrines that distinguish evangelicals are anthropological and soteriological. They occur in a variety of wordings in the

---

[12]*Ibid.*

evangelical literature of the time.[13] They are reflected, for example, in Charles Simeon's summary of the aims of preaching: to humble the sinners, to exalt the Savior, and to promote holiness.[14]

The "prevailing religious system of professed Christians" does not understand the radical nature of sin. Consequently, it cannot understand the nature of the atonement that the church (and Prayer Book) confess; and it has no place for the life of holiness. By contrast, the evangelical paradigm of conversion begins with the personal knowledge of sin, moves to personal trust in Christ's finished work, and issues in godly personal life.

Evangelical religion stands in a long tradition of protest movements against superficial Christian profession, going back at least as far as the fourth century, when the desert fathers turned their backs on the attractive commodity then for the first time widely available—Christianity combined with self-indulgence. (If, as Khomiakov argued, the pope was the first Protestant, perhaps Saint Antony the Copt was the first evangelical.) But the Evangelical Revival is more than a protest movement; it represents a cultural development addressing the Christian message to its time and place as convincingly and appropriately as Antony ever did to his.

The Christendom concept as it had emerged over centuries was no longer adequate, and its practice was increasingly ambiguous. No longer was there a single Christian territory from Ireland to the Carpathians with a single sacred language accepting the rule of Christ as enunciated by a single church from a single apostolic see. Contrary to the first instincts of potentates and churchmen alike, states adopted compromises on religion and reluctantly recognized minorities. (Religious toleration is the offspring not of charity but of political realism.)

Religious pluralism was, however, only one factor pointing to the privatization of religion, its steady movement into the sphere of private judgment and personal decision. Intellectual and social developments pointed in the same direction. An increasing individualization of consciousness (where "I think, therefore I exist" can be an axiom), and an understanding of societies in terms of contracted mutual consent undermined the principle of territorial Christianity that had underlain Western

---

[13] *Hymns for the People called Methodists*, preface. The arrangement of the first part of the hymnbook suggests a logical, if not invariably chronological, progression of "real" Christian experience: Part I: Exhorting sinners to return to God—Describing (1) The pleasantness of religion; (2) The goodness of God; (3) Death; (4) Judgment; (5) Heaven; (6) Hell; (7) Praying for a blessing. Part II: Describing formal religion; Describing inward religion. Part III: Praying for repentance; For mourners convinced of sin; For persons convinced of backsliding; For backsliders recovered. Part IV deals with the life and activity of "Believers," and Part V with the activities of the Methodist society.

[14] W. Carus, *Memoirs of the Life of the Rev. Charles Simeon. . . With a Selection of His Writings and Correspondence* (London: Hatchard, 1847), p. 188.

Christianity (even in its Protestant form) since the time of the barbarian conversions.

Western Christianity therefore faced a cultural crisis—attrition of its basis in Western culture, with the weakening of the sanctions of the institutional church, the increasing efficiency of the centralized state, and the relegation of religion to the private sphere. The Evangelical Revival was perhaps the most successful of all the reformulations of Christianity in the context of changing Western culture. Not, of course, that it arose de novo. Besides renewing the call to radical discipleship so often sounded in earlier Christian history, it retained the medieval concern (deep rooted in the European psyche) for propitiation. It also extended and clarified the Reformation idea (particularly as developed by the English Puritans) of a life of holy obedience in the secular world and in the family. Above all, it combined the traditional framework of the Christian nation and the established church (whether with or without a formal *principle* of establishment was really a matter of locality) with serious recognition of individual selfhood and personal decision. That reconciliation bridged a cultural chasm in Christian self-identity. It helped to make evangelical religion a critical force in Western culture, a version of Christianity thoroughly authentic and indigenous there. To use the appalling current missiological jargon, the Evangelical Revival contextualized the gospel for the northern Protestant world.

Beyond Christendom: The Crux of the Missionary Movement

There is, of course, a lurking peril in all successful indigenizations. The more the gospel is made a place to feel at home, the greater the danger that no one else will be able to live there. And the missionary movement required people whose personal religion had become effectively (though critically) aligned with Western culture to transmit the Christian message in non-Western settings where the assumptions that had shaped their religion did not apply. In early days, missionary regions contained no Christendom, no Christianized society. There was no nominal Christianity to act as the reference group—indeed as the target group—of preaching. And in many, perhaps most, newly reached societies, the audience had no capacity to make individual choices without regard to the networks of kinship. Indeed, the encouragements or successes of early missions may have been more baffling to the understanding of evangelical missionaries and their supporters than the more frequent episodes of failure, heartbreak, and disaster. There were events that missionaries could ascribe only to the hand of God. How else could one interpret a whole island people rejecting their traditional worship and acknowledging Christ? And yet this could take place without any sign of the long-established patterns of evangelical conversion. When the missionaries on Tahiti—Congregationalists at that—ceased to record the names of converts on the ground of "the profession becoming national,"[15] it was a sign of the extension of the meaning of the word "conversion." It might now denote a wholehearted recognition of a change of religious allegiance; conviction of sin and longing for holiness might follow later. Time after time missionaries noted apparently sincere professions of faith that lacked these features. "I have came to the conclusion," said an American missionary by way of explanation, "that deep and pungent convictions are not to be looked for in the heathen when they first become converts to Christianity. 'By the law is knowledge of sin'; but this is imperfectly understood. It has not had time to work down into the heart."[16]

Nevertheless, taking it as a whole, in its Catholic as well as its Protestant aspect, the missionary movement has changed the face of Christianity. It has transformed the demographic and cultural composition of the church, with consequences not yet measurable for its future life and leadership and theology and worship. The most remarkable feature of this transformation has been in the African continent, minimal in Christian profession when the missionary movement began, but now, when so much of the West is in the post-Christian period, moving to the position where it may have more professing Christians than any other continent.[17] The instances that follow illustrate the encounter of evangelical Christianity with Africa; every incident bears a historical relationship to evangelical missionary endeavor. What makes them different comes from the interaction of the evangelical themes with factors at work in Africa.

Christianity and African Initiatives

The sheer size of its professing Christian community must be one reason for taking seriously the significance of Africa. But Christian mission is not simply about the multiplication of the church; it is about the discipling of the nations. It is about the penetration of cultures and ways of thought by the word about Christ. It is about translation—one might almost say the translation of the word into the flesh, since its starting point is the incarnation, which brought the Divine Son to live in the very culture-specific

---

[15]Cf. R. Lovett, *The History of the London Missionary Society, 1795-1895* (London: Henry Frowde, 1899), pp. 184-237. J. Garrett, *To Live among the Stars: Christian Origins in Oceania* (Geneva: World Council of Churches; Suva: University of the South Pacific, 1982), pp. 13-31.

[16]Congregationalist missionaries anointed and crowned the king in Tahiti and drafted national law codes in various islands.

[17]See the statistical analyses in D. B. Barrett, *World Christian Encyclopedia* (Nairobi: Oxford University Press, 1982); see also earlier pointers in D. B. Barrett, "A.D. 2000: 350 Million Christians in Africa," *International Review of Mission* 59 (1970): 39-54; and Roland Oliver, *How Christian Is Africa?* (London: Highway Press, 1956). Cf. A. F. Walls, "Towards Understanding Africa's Place in Christian History," in *Religion in a Pluralistic Society: Essays Presented to Professor C. G. Baeta*, ed. J. S. Pobee (Leiden: Brill, 1976), pp. 180-89.

situation of Jewish Palestine.[18] It is about the translation of Scripture into thought and action, as the word about Christ is brought to bear on the points of reference within each culture, the things by which people know themselves and recognize where they belong. Our attempted assessment of significance must thus take some account of the processes of translation as well as of multiplication; if the argument so far is correct, the Evangelical Revival is itself an example of such translation.

Modern African Christianity is not only the result of movements among Africans, but it has been principally sustained by Africans and is to a surprising extent the result of African initiatives. Even the missionary factor must be put into perspective.

There is something symbolic in the fact that the first church in tropical Africa in modern times was not a missionary creation at all. It arrived ready made, a body of people of African birth or descent who had come to faith in Christ as plantation slaves or as soldiers in the British army during the American War of Independence, or as farmers or squatters in Nova Scotia after it.[19] They were eleven hundred in number, arriving in 1792 in Sierra Leone, in the strip of land purchased by the Clapham philanthropists as a Province of Freedom. They marched ashore (it is said) singing a hymn of Isaac Watts—"Awake, and sing the song of Moses and the Lamb." Their choice of hymnody was significant. They had left the house of bondage, they had crossed the Red Sea, they were now entering the promised land. They brought their own preachers with them, and their churches had been functioning for nearly twenty years in Sierra Leone when the first missionary arrived. (Indeed, they ejected their second missionary as "too proud for a Methodist preacher," or, as he thought, because of their "American Republic spirit.")[20] Sierra Leone—a tiny country in the nineteenth century, not to be identified with the borders of the present republic—supplied African missionaries in quantities for the rest of West Africa and could even spare one or two to work elsewhere. (Sierra Leone missionaries were appointed to Kenya in the 1880s.)[21] Over a sixty-year period, Sierra Leone produced a hundred ordained men for the Church Missionary Society

---

[18]Cf. A. F. Walls, "The Translation Principle in Christian History," in *Bible Translation and the Spread of the Church in the Last Two Hundred Years*, ed. P.C. Stine (Leiden: Brill, 1990), pp. 24-39. Reprinted in this volume as chapt. 3.

[19]On the so-called Nova Scotian settlers in Sierra Leone, see Christopher Fyfe, *A History of Sierra Leone* (Oxford: Oxford University Press, 1962); and idem, *"Our Children Free and Happy": Letters from Black Settlers in Africa in the 1790s* (Edinburgh: Edinburgh University Press, 1991).

[20]A. F. Walls, "A Christian Experiment: The Early Sierra Leone Colony," in *The Mission of the Church and the Propagation of the Faith*, Studies in Church History 6, ed. G. J. Cuming (Cambridge: Cambridge University Press, 1970), pp. 107-30.

[21]T. A. Beetham, "A Sierra Leone Missionary to Kenya," *Sierra Leone Bulletin of Religion* 1, no. 2 (1959): 56-57.

alone, in addition to countless catechists, teachers, and other mission work-ers—all from a population of perhaps fifty thousand.[22]

On the other side of the continent, Louise Pirouet has drawn attention to the process of Christian expansion in the area that now forms the state of Uganda. It was Ganda evangelists who carried out the work, often operating far from home in areas quite different from their own in language, tradition, and food, as much "foreign missionaries" as any European.[23] It is a reminder of the vital importance of the evangelist and the catechist in African Christian history—a person usually without much formal educa-tion in the Western sense; not fluent, perhaps not literate, in English; but the terminal connection through which the Christian faith passes into African village society. But even the evangelist-catechist is only part of the story. I recall a survey of how the numerous congregations within one densely populated area of Nigeria had come into being. Time after time the seminal figure was a new court clerk who was a Christian, or a worker on the new railway, or a tailor, carrying his sewing machine on his head, or some other trader. Some such stranger, or a group of strangers, had arrived and had started family prayers, stopped work on Sunday, and sang hymns instead, and some local people got interested. Or perhaps the initial impetus came from people from that village who had gone elsewhere—to school, to work, to trade, in more than one case to jail—and on return home sought the things they had found in their travels. The survey yielded no instance of a congregation founded by a missionary, and hardly one founded by any official agent of the church at all. In most cases the role of the mission had been to respond—sometimes, through straitened resources, belatedly and minimally—to an initiative within the community.

Another factor in Christian expansion in Africa has been the emergence of dynamic figures who owed little in any direct way to church mission, and nothing to any commission from one. Such figures are especially important in West Africa between the First World War and the end of the Great Depression. The most celebrated of these figures, and by far the most important figure in Ivory Coast Christian history, is the Liberian prophet William Wadé Harris. In an important study, D. A. Shank calls Harris a prophet of modern times.[24] Certainly Harris was convinced of his prophetic call, and he meditated deeply on Scripture, which, as Shank shows, he read in a way quite different from that of the missionaries but one quite intelli-

---

[22]P. E. H. Hair, "The CMS 'Native Clergy' in West Africa to 1900," *Sierra Leone Bulletin of Religion* 4 (1962): 71-72; cf. idem, "Freetown Christianity and Africa," *Sierra Leone Bulletin of Religion* 6 (1964): 13-21.

[23]M. L. Pirouet, *Black Evangelists: The Spread of Christianity in Uganda, 1891-1914* (London: Collings, 1978).

[24]D. A. Shank, "William Wadé Harris: A Prophet of Modern Times." Ph.D. dissertation (University of Aberdeen, 1980). See also idem, "The Legacy of William Wadé Harris," *International Bulletin of Missionary Research* 10 (1986): 170-76.

gible within his own frame of reference. He called people to repentance; he persuaded thousands to abandon traditional African religious practices; he pointed them to the God of the Scriptures, which as yet they could not read, sometimes leaving King James Bibles as a sign of the source of the teaching to follow; he baptized with water and, by prayer and exorcism, triumphed over the spirits. Mission representatives, however much they might regret omissions in his teaching or deplore some features of it, still strove to get Harris's approval to be his successors in the work; yet he had set out on that work in response to what he believed the call of God, with no seal from any mission body.

The Methodist Church in Ashanti, Ghana, owes much to the preaching of a charismatic jailbird called Sampson Oppong.[25] Oppong always claimed that he had little knowledge of Christianity at all before his call as a preacher. The dramatic events that lead up to his entry on his vocation included a prophetic dream and its fulfillment the next day, an attempt to poison a Christian that failed because the intended victim vomited the substance after saying grace, and an alcoholic stupor during which Oppong was punitively kicked by a sheep he had stolen. The Methodist mission estimated that as a result of this man's preaching, twenty thousand people came under their pastoral care within five or six years. In Nigeria two major religious bodies, the Apostolic Church and the Christ Apostolic Church, derive eventually from the work of Joseph Babalola, a steamroller driver who found the divine imperative in the breakdown of his engine and became the key figure in a mass movement that stirred Yorubaland in the depression years.[26] Nor were such phenomena confined to West Africa. In Lesotho, for instance, at much the same time, the Paris Mission was recognizing that multitudes came into the church following the preaching of a young layman called Walter Mattita, who not long before had been at most a wayward and negligent church attender.[27]

None of these figures easily fitted into the structures of ministry and leadership of any of the mission churches, yet those same churches recognized their effectiveness. Each claimed a direct commission from God imparted by dream or vision and confirmed by signs following. The work of each led to a massive expansion of churches (and in all but Babalola's case, mission-led churches) that were already in existence. We might take another set of figures on the lowly rungs of the mission's ladder who

---

[25]G. M. Haliburton, "The Calling of a Prophet: Sampson Oppong," *Bulletin of the Society for African Church History* 2, No. 1 (1965): 84-96.

[26]Cf. H. W. Turner, *History of an African Independent Church: The Church of the Lord (Aladura)* (Oxford: Clarendon Press, 1967), pp. 16-32.

[27]S. N. Mohlomi, *Kereke ea Moshoeshoe: Lesotho's First New Religious Movement*. M. Litt. dissertation (Edinburgh: Centre for the Study of Chistianity in the Non-Western World, 1977).

instituted comparable Christian movements outside the missionary sphere altogether. There is Garrick Braide, otherwise known as Elijah II, Anglican catechist in the Niger delta, founder of the healing church, the Christ Army.[28] Most spectacular of all is the legacy of the Baptist catechist Simon Kimbangu, arrested for subversion by the Belgian authorities in Congo in 1917, after a few short months of preaching and healing. He spent the rest of his life in prison. The movement he began was proscribed, went underground, gave a Christian expression to the independence movement, and, as colonial rule collapsed, emerged under the leadership of a son of Kimbangu as L'Eglise de Jésus-Christ sur la terre par le Prophète Simon Kimbangu, claiming a membership over five million.[29]

Conversion in Context

The African reasons why Africans became Christians are manifold. In current historiography it is common to assert that the reasons were secular and ulterior—a means of access to the power possessed by Europeans or of acquiring desirable things dispensed from that source. A recent work by C. C. Okorocha argues that in the context of Igboland, where there was a particularly rapid response to Christianity, it is wrong to call such reasons secular.[30] Religion was always in Igboland directed to the acquisition of power; the gods were followed in as far as they provided it. So the combination of military defeat by the British, the desirable goods and capabilities in the power of the whites, and the association of all this with the power of the book now on offer to them declared the inferiority of the traditional religious channels. There was every *religious* reason to abandon them. To abandon them, however, did not require a complete redrawing of the map of the spiritual world. The Igbo had always recognized a Supreme Being— Chukwu or Chineke. Christian preaching seemed to offer direct access to Chukwu/Chineke; what it enjoined was a redirection of religion away from the now-discredited lesser divinities. This was, Okorocha argues, a genuinely religious response, a reordering of the relationship with the transcendent. It involved an act of decision, a break with part of the past, a new pattern of worship that was enthusiastically followed, and a code of dos

---

[28]G. O. M. Tasie, "The Prophetic Calling: Garrick Sokari Braide of Bakana," in *Varieties of Christian Experience in Nigeria,* ed. E. Isichei (London: Macmillan, 1982), pp. 99-115.

[29]Among the more important of a legion of works on Kimbangu and the movement and church that emerged from his work, see M. L. Martin, *Kimbangu: An African Prophet and His Church* (Oxford: Blackwell, 1975); and Werner Ustorf, *Africanische Initiative: Das aktive Leiden des Propheten Simon Kimbangu* (Bern: Lang, 1975).

[30]C. C. Okorocha, *The Meaning of Religious Conversion in Africa: The Case of The Igbo of Nigeria* (Aldershot: Avebury Gower, 1987).

and don'ts close enough to the traditional one to be recognizable (except perhaps for men important enough to have more than one wife). It provided immediate access to the book and the power it conveyed.

Okorocha's account of the Igbo story is, in fact, curiously reminiscent of the account given by Bede of the conversion of the English Kingdom of Northumbria. Edwin, the king, well disposed to Christianity himself, called a council to test the consensus. The first speaker was a priest of the old gods who put in his vote for Christianity. His argument ran thus: No one has served the gods more faithfully than I, yet I see many who enjoy much more of the royal favor than I do. I conclude, therefore, that there is nothing to be gained from their service. After the vote was taken, the priest was the first to defile the shrine of the gods who so let down their faithful worshiper.[31] In work not fully incorporated into his book, Okorocha detects a dual movement in Igbo Christianity. The first abandonment of the old divinities was marked by vigorous adhesion to Christian worship and what one might call a Deuteronomic theology: honor God, and he will honor you. A later generation knows the lurking feeling that there may be something in the old ways, but its Christianity includes a new emphasis on the cross and on taking up the cross. And Okorocha raises the question of the part played in this itinerary by the area's dreadful sufferings during the Nigerian Civil War.[32]

In Igboland and Northumbria alike, Christianitiy was first accepted in terms of a traditional worldview and in relation to traditional goals. It is impossible for any of us to take in a new idea except in terms of an idea we already have. But in Igboland and Northumbria alike, the new element adopted into the belief system had a dynamic of its own that entered deep into the traditional system and interacted with it.

The impact on Africa of alien influences from the Western world produced an array of reasons within the traditional framework of thinking to seek for radical religious adjustment and change. The religious effects of a river dam, of a concrete building constructed over the abode of the water spirit, of an exodus of young men to work for cash, of a virus caught from incomers for which the local society has no immunity—these things are potentially more shattering religiously than years of preaching to a stable and satisfied society. In stable primal societies the tradition of the elders—a body of knowledge, wisdom, and interpretation built up over centuries—provides the means of coping with every conceivable situation. But when situations arise for which the tradition has no answers, the society may be in danger of disintegration unless it can find either a means of containing

---

[31]Bede, *Ecclesiatical History* 2.13.

[32]C. C. Okorocha, "Salvation in Igbo Religious Experience: Its Influence on Igbo Christianity." Ph.D. dissertation (University of Aberdeen, 1982).

the invading elements or a new rule of life to act as an alternative or supplementary tradition. Without such a key to conduct, the relationships, the hierarchies, and the values of the society are alike disturbed. People are left in confusion—they face conflicting obligations, and ambiguities strew the path of proper conduct. Frequently in Africa the adoption of Christianity has been a means of adapting to burdensome and potentially dangerous situations. The search for a new key to life, a yearning to be able to make assured choices with a good conscience, is surely a thoroughly religious motive, even if it is not the one to which missionary preaching has been primarily addressed.

The search for a key to conduct perhaps lies behind the apparent legalism that has often followed in the wake of evangelical preaching. People who had turned from the old ways at the preaching of Harris or other African evangelists sometimes asked the newly arrived representative of the mission church whether there was special food that a Christian should eat, or whether it was necessary for Christians to sleep, as Europeans did, above the level of the ground. These were not trivial issues. Having abandoned the rules of one tradition, one must know all the demands of the one that is to replace it.[33]

Apparently Augustine, the Roman missionary in the English kingdom of Kent, faced a parallel situation. The questions that, Bede informs us, burst from the first English Christian converts and inquirers were on topics such as the possibility of two brothers marrying two sisters, or attendance at worship during pregnancy or menstruation or after intercourse.[34] No doubt their pre-Christian rituals were hedged by regulations concerning such things. If the gods who underwrote the sanctions on such prohibitions were being abandoned, it was necessary to know what the new God demanded in such matters. To be without an answer was to leave people confused and in fear of breaking a dangerous taboo. It is worth noting that many African Independent churches have explicit regulations on these very matters. Like Pope Gregory, to whom Augustine referred his questions, they have noticed that some of them are dealt with in the Holiness Code in Leviticus. Because of this they are able from the sacred book to build up the way of life of a neo-Levitical community. Are they not a kingdom of priests?

---

[33]For an example of the concerns, cf. G. M. Haliburton, *The Prophet Harris: A Study of an African Prophet and His Mass Movement in the Ivory Coast and the Gold Coast, 1913-1915* (New York: Oxford University Press, 1973), p. 222. On the place of the law in the Christian itinerary, see D. A. Shank, "African Christian Religious Itinerary: Toward an Understanding of the Religious Itinerary from the Faith of African Traditional Religion(s) to That of the New Testament," in *Exploring New Religious Movements: Essays in Honor of H. W. Turner*, ed. A. F. Walls and W. R. Shenk (Elkhart, IN: Mission Focus, 1990), pp. 143-62.

[34]Bede, *Eccesiastical History* 1.27.

Some African Christian Initiatives

A well-known feature of West African life is the prophet-healing churches (in West Africa often called *aladura*, a Yoruba word standing for "praying people").[35] These are constructed on a model of the church quite different from any Western one, a model that arises from an indigenous reading of the Scriptures and a lively apprehension of the priorities of many anxious people. Prophecy, healing, divination, and revelation feature regularly in their life. Church order is frequently intricate and precise, the members having differentiated uniforms with symbolic designs and assigned ranks and functions. There may be a charismatic leader; there will certainly be plenty of congregational participation. There may also be a detailed code of regulations, exhortations, and prohibitions, as well as vigorous spiritual exercises involving fasting and prayer. Most will combat witchcraft and sorcery; some will identify witches; still more striking, some will cure witches of their baleful powers.

It is worth remembering that the movement from which many of these spring began among mature lay Christians of evangelical Anglican vintage. It was as a revival prayer group that they first met; as Christians, they were searching for the demonstration of God's power amid human devastation (the influenza epidemic after World War I) and spiritual depression.[36]

Until recently these prophet-healing churches could be held the most significant and the fastest-growing sector of the indigenous churches. This is no longer so certain. Nigeria and Ghana, to name but two countries, are witnessing the rise of another type of independent church.[37] Like many prophet-healing churches, they have often originated as prayer or revival groups inside older churches. Like the prophet-healing churches, they proclaim the divine power of deliverance from disease and demonic affliction, but the style of proclamation is more like that of American adventist and pentecostal preaching. Gone are the African drums and the white

---

[35]On the origins of the Aladura movement, see Turner, *History;* and J. D. Y. Peel, *Aladura: A Religious Movement among the Yoruba* (London: Oxford University Press for International African Institute, 1968). Turner's companion volume, *African Independent Church: The Life and Faith of the Church of the Lord (Aladura)* (Oxford: Clarendon Press, 1967), gives the fullest account yet available of the life of a prophet-healing church.

[36]Turner, *History,* pp. 9-13.

[37]The movement is now beginning to attract due attention in the literature. Its importance is signaled by Rosalind Hackett, "Enigma Variations: The New Religious Movements in Nigeria Today," in *Exploring New Religious Movements,* ed. Walls and Shenk, pp. 131-42. For a study of a representative movement, cf. Matthews Ojo, "Deeper Christian Life Ministry: A Case Study of the Charismatic Movements in Western Nigeria," *Journal of Religion in Africa* 18 (1988): 141-62.

uniforms of the aladuras; the visitor is more likely to hear electronic keyboards and amplified guitars, see a preacher in elegant *agbada* or smart business suit and a choir in bow ties. Yet these radical charismatic movements are African in origin, in leadership, and in finance. They are highly entrepreneurial and are active in radio and television and cassette ministries as well as in campaigns and conventions. Another set of churches emerged from radical Christian student groups such as the Scripture Union, seeking a throughgoing discipleship amid well-established churches that they see as complacent, compromised, and powerless. A new African Christian asceticism is visible here, an emphasis on prayer and fasting and readiness to suffer. All the new movements share with the prophet-healing churches a quest for the demonstrable presence of the Holy Spirit and a direct address to the problems and frustrations of modern African urban life.

The Evangelical Succession

The fathers of the missionary movement undoubtedly expected that Christianity would assimilate Africans to a European style of life. Their apologetic was directed to those of their contemporaries who argued that this was impossible, that Africans did not possess the mental capacities to participate on equal terms in "civilization," that is, in the European discourse of life. Early missionary effort was thus devoted to proving that given the same opportunities, Africans could do just as well as Europeans. And by the middle of the nineteenth century they seemed to have made their point. At least one part of Africa, Sierra Leone, had produced a Christian community that had all the features of civilized life. People went to church dressed in European clothes. They sang their hymns and psalms in English. Their children went to school, where the brightest pupils learned Latin. Literacy was higher than in most European countries; there was even a girls' grammar school, which not many English boroughs had by mid-century. It looked as if an African Christian country would be like England in every particular—only better.[38] And when the Reverend Samuel Crowther, later to be bishop, came to London and people heard this grave and gracious black clergyman address public meetings in excellent English, when he visited the palace and answered Prince Albert's intelligent questions about African trade, missionary work appeared to have reached its final justification. Its aim henceforth must be to produce more of the same.

---

[38]Cf. the picture provided by Henry Venn, Secretary of the Church Missionary Society, in *West African Colonies: Notices of the British Colonies on the West Coast of Africa* (London: Darton and Lacy, 1865).

An African clergyman and an English clergyman should be identical in everything but color.[39]

But Sierra Leone was a special case. Its core population was descended from people taken from slaveships before they crossed the Atlantic—people of a hundred different languages, people uprooted from their lands with no expectations of seeing them again. They had lost their old identity and were too diverse to reestablish it easily. The alternative was a new identity: a Christian and basically British one. Of course, Krio identity was much more rooted in African soil than people realized; that discovery lay in the future. A quicker discovery was that Africans who had not shared the experience of uprooting did not often want to become black Europeans. They might take selected items from the European package; they might become Christians, but they did not reproduce Sierra Leone, the first model of missionary Christianity.[40]

As the various new models have been constituted, it has been with shared experiences that have not been part of Western Christian experience. African Christians face situations where integrity requires them to find a solution in Christian terms—that is, by the application of the word about Christ and of Scripture—where Western Christianity, the source from which Christian tradition has come, has no answers, because it has no parallel experience. And, by the same word about Christ and the same Scriptures, they face the task of penetrating an accumulated body of wisdom and ways of thought and action that in their way are as coherent as the Greek universe of ideas faced by early Hellenistic Christians.

There is no time for more than the briefest indication of some of the situations where the Christian experience of Africa has been different from that of the West.

God and the African Past

Christians are Gentiles (mostly) who worship the God of the Jews. Early Gentile Christians took over Jewish attitudes to the gods of the nations, and specifically to the popular divinities of Greco-Roman paganism. These were idols, not gods. Zeus or Jupiter was not God and Father of our Lord

---

[39]Cf. *An Appeal for a Great Extension of Missions to the Heathens . . .* (London: CBS, 1873), an anonymous book clearly written by an elderly and scholarly minded Anglican evangelical clergyman: "We have one black Bishop who is at home with his Greek New Testament, and administers his diocese of the Niger with zeal and judgment, like any bishop in England. I have a precious photographic picture of him and his son, his chaplain, in the midst of their evangelical work. Perhaps one or many of the African fathers were of the same colour" (32).

[40]Cf. J. F. A. Ajayi, *Christian Missions in Nigeria, 1841-1891: The Making of a New Elite* (London: Longmans, 1965).

Jesus Christ. But an important stream of native Greek thought had also rejected the gods of popular religion, and the Greek philosophical tradition developed the idea of God as highest Good, without name, best described in negatives. It was natural for Greek Christians to fuse this impersonal, nameless being with the God of the Bible, the God of the Jews.

This meant that the God of the Jews no longer had a personal name. He was just *ho Theos*, the God. As Christianity spread to the barbarian peoples of the north and west, they, too, abandoned the deities of their pantheons and substituted for all the gods the neutral term "God," the One for the many.

Generally speaking, however, the experience of African Christians has been different. Right across West Africa the first bearers of the Christian message, even when they assumed they were addressing a polytheistc, idolatrous society, found there the recognition of a creator God who was also the moral governor of the universe. The Mende called him Ngewo, the Akan Nyame, the Yoruba Olorun, the Igbo Chukwu or Chineke. The doctrine of the Fall was adumbrated too, for there were often stories that implied that God was once closer to earth than he is now, that some act of greed or folly on the part of people of old had made him keep his distance. For indeed, Ngewo or Olorun did not play much part in most people's daily devotion. Sacrifices to the Supreme Being might be rare or nonexistent, prayer made only in emergencies. Other deities appeared in dreams, possessed mediums—but not Ngewo, Nyame, or Olorun. For these people and others like them, there was thus an absolute class difference between the Supreme Being and the lower orders of divinities. There was no possibility of active rivalry between "God" and "the gods," no trace of the knockout competition among divinities that seems to have marked Semitic religious history. The lower orders could readily be accorded separate existence, perhaps limited autonomy; there was no doubt who was "God."[41]

It was natural, therefore, to use the name Ngewo, Nyame, Olorun, for the God of the Bible. (One may add in passing that Muslims have been very reluctant to do this. In Muslim Africa as a whole, only "Allah," no vernacular name, is used.)

In parts of East Africa there was a different situation. When the Arabs sought to bring a nineteenth-century Kabaka of Buganda to the knowledge of Allah, his reply was, "Where is there a God greater than I?" And he was talking in sober earnestness.[42] The Baganda worshiped no deity with more honor than the spirits of the Kabakas. But there was one spirit, Katonda, whose shrine had no fire, who did not appear in dreams, and who rarely

---

[41]Cf. P. J. Ryan, "'Arise O God': The Problem of 'Gods' in West Africa," *Journal of Religion in Africa* 11, No. 3 (1980): 161-71.

[42]J. V. Taylor, *The Growth of the Church in Buganda* (London: SCM, 1958), p. 9.

received offerings. He was really very much on the fringe of Ganda religion. However, it appeared that Katonda had been the worker of creation, and then he became identified with the God of the Bible. The effect was stunning. The half-forgotten Katonda, whom nobody much had been noticing, was- -according to the Christian proclamation—calling everyone to give up the worship of all other *muzimu*—indeed he had sent his son to cause them to do so. The effect was such, in fact, that many people hardly took in the bit about the son. This was hard for missionaries seeking to show Christ as the perfect sacrifice for sin and to lead on to holy living through the Spirit. But the construction of the Ganda auditorium did not immediately allow these words to be heard. It was the sudden appearance of the neglected Katonda that made the impact.[43]

We must not assume that the impact was therefore superficial. It is worth remembering the earliest proud chapter of Ganda Christian history. Christian profession was still young in Buganda when the Kabaka ("Where is there a God greater than I?") ordered his Christian pages to do acts they saw as forbidden by God. They refused, and numbers of Christian teenagers, Catholic and Protestant, were publicly mutilated and then burned alive.

We have not time to consider the later story, or the difficulty Ganda Christians have sometimes had in filling in the whole void—the pleroma, to use Paul's figure to the Colossians with an analogous problem[44]—between Katonda and themselves. Not everyone is quickly convinced that one brief visit to earth long ago is a sufficient basis on which to take over the whole business of representing the spirit world. The remarkable revival movement that East Africa has known for more than half a century past may represent another stage in the Ganda Christian itinerary. Let me point out only that in Buganda, as in most of Africa, God has a personal name, and that is a vernacular one. God is thus part of the African past; indeed, as Katonda or Nyame or Olorun, he is part of the Ganda, the Akan, the Yoruba past.

A good deal of current African theological debate is devoted to this question. African Christian scholars are searching the African religious heritage, not, as African Christians were once taught, to denigrate or despise it, but to see the ways of God with their own people. Some anthropologists, both European and African, complain of this as tending to Christianize African religion. A non-Christian African scholar such as Okot p'Bitek complains of being robbed.[45] Some Christian theologians have a different fear—that the process of seeking God in the African past will

---

[43]*Ibid.*, pp. 252-60.

[44]Colossians 1:19, where the *pleroma*—the entire sphere in which the intermediary powers between God and the universe operate—dwells in Christ.

[45]Okot p'Bitek, *African Religions and Western Scholarship* (Kampala: East Africa Literature Bureau, 1970).

render the Christian revelation unnecessary.[46]

Once again, we cannot go into the debate. It is worth noting, however, how parallel it is to the debate among second- and third-century Christians about the nature of their own past. Jewish Christians, who could proudly claim to be "circumcised the eighth day, of the tribe of Benjamin," and so forth,[47] knew their whole story from Abraham onward. But what of those Gentile Christians, but lately grafted into the olive tree?[48] Some of them began to point to those in their own tradition who had rejected the false gods and suffered for it, and some started to argue that philosophy was the schoolmaster to lead the Greeks to Christ even as the Lord led the Jews.[49] Second-century Hellenistic Christians who wished to present Christ to those who shared the same cultural heritage had to consider the relationship of Christ to that heritage, to their past as Greeks. No one can have a sense of identity without their past. Kwame Bediako has explored the parallel between the ancient Hellenistic and the modern African identity question.[50] Twentieth-century African Christians have to face the question, Where was God in Africa's past? It is the first question on the African theological agenda. And it is not answerable solely in terms of Western theological experience. Nyame, Ngemo, Olorun is the God of Scripture, the God and Father of our Lord Jesus Christ. Zeus and Odin never were.

The Healing Process

Consider this story from Uganda, as told thirty years ago by a scholarly missionary of great insight, later an English bishop.[51]

A married woman, a communicant member of the Anglican Church, who was childless, was suddenly seized by the *muzimu* of the prince Luyidde, son of Kabaka Mulando, whose shrine stands on a hill not far from her village. From her body, which was stiff and numb, two voices spoke, one repeating, "I am Luyidde," and her own saying, "I am a Christian; I cannot go." For days the psychosis continued, no one seemed able to help her, and eventually her brothers and her husband, also a communicant, agreed that nothing could save her but to let her go. She is living now at the shrine on the hill, separated from her husband because she belongs to Luyidde. Once in a while

---

[46]For example, the late Byang Kato, *Theological Pitfalls in Africa* (Kisumu, Kenya: Evangel Publishing House, 1975).

[47]Cf. Philippians 3:5.

[48]Cf. Romans 11:16-24.

[49]On Socrates and others who witnessed to the truth, cf. Justin, *Apology* 1.46; on philosophy as the tutor to Christ, Clement of Alexandria, *Stromateis* 1.5.

[50]Kwame Bediako, *Theology and Identity: The Impact of Culture on Christian Thought in the Second Century and Modern Africa* (Oxford: Regnum, 1991).

[51]Taylor, *Growth of the Church in Buganda*, p. 211.

she is possessed [*okusamira*] and speaks with his voice, but otherwise she is quite normal, regularly attends church, and is still a communicant.

Priests, priestesses, mediums, and diviners are often called to their life's work through an illness that yields to no treatment. They rapidly recover when they respond to the call and take up their shrine duties or begin the studies of their vocation.

In the case given, the person called was a Christian and did not want to go. Yet nothing in the church's armory availed her in her illness or gave her peace of mind. A recent thesis by Silas Ncozana, from Malawi, reveals how situations like this have now become a major pastoral problem in that country.[52]

In Africa, illness is regularly associated with spiritual powers, and with moral or social offenses and obligations, conscious and unconscious. The chief diagnostic question is not, therefore, What illness is it? but What—or who—caused it? Similarly, the way to recovery is to put right what is wrong (if the diagnosis shows it is one's own responsibility) or try to cope with the attack (if it is revealed to be the result of someone else's malice).

Traditional medicine has certainly used herbal remedies, but a traditional healer needs more than a knowledge of the pharmacopoeia. He must have a deep knowledge of human nature, the ability to ask probing questions, not to speak of his religious or magical expertise. Western medicine, in contrast, belongs firmly to the secular world. We have built our medical practice on the principle of treating the illness. African traditional medicine is based on the principle of treating the person.

But consider the effect of Christian preaching on healing in Africa. Magical practice is forbidden to Christians. Diviners, the heart of the diagnostic system, are equally forbidden. The whole apparatus of traditional healing is thus denied to the sufferer. The answer may be to take pills, and if these come from a pastor or a mission hospital, the pills may be seen as an instrument of God. But there is nothing particularly Christian about taking pills, considered as an act in itself. And in any case, what do you do if there is no medical supply in your area? Prophet Harris's converts, it is said, pressed the Prophet to give a course of action when they were sick—he had already described traditional healing as "nothing" if one believes God. His reply was, in effect, take native medicine if you have to, but while you gather the leaves, pray to God; while you prepare the medicine, pray to God; when you take it, pray to God.[53] The traditional specialist is in this way bypassed.

---

[52]S. N. Ncozana, "Spirit Possession and Tumbuka Christianity, 1875-1950." Ph.D. dissertation (University of Aberdeen, 1985).

[53]Haliburton, *Prophet Harris*, p. 54.

Harris was making a concession. If traditional medicine is ruled out completely by Christian conviction, the Christian has no defense against illness but prayer and trust in Christ. That stern ethic has carried many Christians through; the more radical Independent churches assert it with vigor, forswearing all medicines. What is the pill bottle but the formal equivalent of the traditional medicine, the white man's fetish substitute for faith? (One of the reasons why the Christ Apostolic Church split from the Apostolic Mission was disillusionment with missionaries who used quinine.)[54] But one can see how it was all too much for many people. So, when illness or trouble comes, a visit to the diviner takes place—but at night, and with a bad conscience, because the sufferers really think they ought not.

It is at this point that the prophet-healing churches speak with special force. They reflect an assurance that Christ is indeed Savior and still saves, that he heals in their congregation; the sympathetic moving of the congregation and the wrestling with evil of the charismatic leader take the illness of the sufferer and its likely causes seriously. The stress on response by the sufferer, in baptism perhaps, and continuing service of God in the church, underlines it further. It provides a framework in which those called as spirit dancers or mediums, like the one in the bishop's story, can be comprehendingly treated, in a battle royal with the spirits before, and with the aid of, the whole congregation.

It is said with truth that the prophet-healers use techniques and styles of interrogation characteristic of traditional diviners and healers. But among the prophet-healing churches are the most implacable foes of the traditional diviner and of those that quietly sneak to his house in the dark. They are insistent as to the source of their healing, locating it firmly with the work of Christ or the Holy Spirit. (They are not always clear about the distinction.) Placing a Bible against the sufferer's head or giving a bottle of water consecrated by prayer may be described as a fetish act, no different from applying a charm; yet when the source of power is so visibly identified with the God of the Bible and with the Spirit of Christ, there is a gap opened up with the old powers of Africa. The traditional African concept of healing the person rather than the sickness is retained, but it is transformed by locating the healing in Christ. It demands a more complete break with "the world" than going to church by day and to the diviner at night.

To tell the suffering woman that Luyidde is dead and cannot hurt her would be useless—she knew differently. Nor would it be Christian, for it would not be applying Christ to her need. Similarly, Western Christianity has effectively been disabled from helping in the desolating situation of witchcraft by the fact that its worldview had no real place for the objective reality of witchcraft. Its principal value has been in saving many people accused or suspected of witchcraft from undeserved suffering. But this does

---

[54]Turner, *History*, pp. 31-32.

nothing to reduce the fear of witchcraft; indeed, in some circumstances, it increases it. And it does nothing for the tortured soul who goes to the prophet-healer with the confession that she is a witch,[55] insists that she has killed people, names them, and begs to be delivered from this curse of destroying people. That the questioning of suspected witches can be brutal psychological bullying goes without saying, but the questions of the skilled healer can also bring to the surface things that are not only therapeutic but edifying. Witchcraft, after all, is hatred objectified. Skilled questioning may reveal the hatred and the jealousy that rejoices when a rival's child dies. By this means hatred can be brought to the surface, acknowledged for what it is. Forgiveness, even reconciliation, can then follow. Christ is thus applied to the needs of witch and victim alike and can be acknowledged as Victor, where rationalistic explanation would be futile and a generalized assurance of divine love fall flat.

The Evangelical Legacy

So various, and so luxuriant, has been the fruit of evangelical endeavor in Africa. Many more examples might have been given, some of them—notably the East African revival—closer to the evangelical tradition as it has developed in the West.[56] It has seemed, however, more important to indicate that the results of evangelical preaching have been much more widespread, and much more dynamic, than may be at first apparent. While some of the features of the evangelical religion that originated the missionary movement—certainly the high place given to Scripture and the recognition of immediacy in personal experience—have been regular features of African Christianity, it is important to note that the fruit of the work of evangelical missionaries has not simply been a replication of Western evangelicalism. The Christian message that they set loose in Africa has its own dynamic, as it comes into creative and critical encounter with African life with its needs and its hurts. Exactly the same thing happened when the Evangelical Revival bridged the culture gap for northern Protestantism with such spectacular effect. Africans have responded to the gospel from where *they* were, not from where the missionaries were; they have re-

---

[55]Cf. R. W. Wylie, "Introspective Witchcraft among the Effutu," *Man*, n.s. (1973): 74-79.

[56]The East African revival has been mentioned only in passing; in its origins this revival affected both European missionaries and Africans, and its antecedents can be found in both traditions. It has developed as an essentially African movement, though it has had a certain impact on evangelical life in the West, especially in Britain. See J. E. Church, *Quest for the Highest: An Autobiographical Account of the East African Revival* (Exeter: Paternoster, 1981); and P. St. John, *Breath of Life* (London: Norfolk Press, 1971); and for the influences, Western and African, R. Anker-Petersen, "A Study of the Spiritual Roots of the East African Revival Movement," M.Th. dissertation (Edinburgh: Centre for the Study of Christianity in the Non-Western World, 1988).

sponded to the Christian message as they heard it, not to the missionaries' experience of the message.

Nevertheless, the first hearing and the first response is not the whole, nor necessarily the climax, of the story. Perhaps we should give more attention to generational processes in Christian history, carefully observing communal religious itineraries that may take several generations. In many such cases it will be impossible to pass every milestone in one lifetime and dangerous to attempt shortcuts.[57]

As for the missionaries, they achieved—sometimes in spite of themselves—exactly what they believed they had been sent to do. After all, they had not gone to transmit evangelicalism to Africa, but the gospel.

---

[57]See Shank, "African Christian Religious Itinerary," esp. pp. 154-57.

8

Black Europeans — White Africans[1]
Some Missionary Motives in West Africa

Sierra Leone was the first success story of the modern missionary movement. The years from 1787 to 1830 saw it pass first from a green if not very fertile land supporting subsistence farmers and riverine slaving factories to Utopia in a disaster area; then transformed again as free blacks from Nova Scotia and Jamaica, full of evangelical religion and American republicanism, carried out a Clapham-inspired scheme in ways the men of Clapham did not always like; and again as this population was overwhelmed by new uprooted peoples from all over West Africa, brought in from the slaveships before they had ever seen the transatlantic plantations. The new population responded, sometimes with enthusiasm and rarely with prolonged resistance, to missionary preaching; and, with those same missionaries appointed to superintend their temporal as well as their spiritual welfare, adopted the norms and characteristics of their Nova Scotian and Maroon predecessors. Contemporary British sources do not suggest that at the time Sierra Leone was regarded as a huge success; people in England tended to think of the appalling loss of missionary life in the white man's grave, and the enormous expense of the Sierra Leone mission; besides, they heard stories which suggested that the serpent still dwelt in their West African garden. Nonetheless, here was the first part of Africa, one of the very few areas anywhere in the world to see a mass movement towards the Christian faith, where a whole non-Christian people became Christian.[2]

Looked at from another point of view, Sierra Leone saw the birth of a new nation and a new culture. In the Krio people and Krio culture, Euro-

---

[1]First published in D. Baker, ed., *Religious Motivation: Biographical and Sociological Problems for the Church Historian*, Studies in Church History, 14 (Oxford: Blackwood, 1978), pp. 339-48.

[2]See C. H. Fyfe, *A History of Sierra Leone* (London, 1962); J. Peterson, *Province of Freedom: A History of Sierra Leone 1787- 1870* (London, 1969); A. F. Walls, "A Christian Experiment: The Early Sierra Leone Colony," *The Mission of the Church and the Propagation of the Faith, SCH* 6 (1970), pp. 107-29.

pean and African elements were inextricably blended, and European institutions were adopted into an African context and transformed by it.[3] Again, this was only partially realized at the time, since what European eyes saw was the wholesale adoption of European institutions. The self-consciously Christian community flocked to buildings looking like English parish churches in villages called Leicester, Gloucester, Kent, or Sussex, or Wilberforce, Bathurst, Waterloo, or Wellington. (The patronal dedication of the church in the village of Wellington is the unlikely St. Arthur Wellington.) They wore European dress, as good as they could afford, for the purpose, and lived in houses influenced by European models. They were a literate community too, and as the years went by, developed their grammar schools, for boys and for girls; and their higher educational institution at Fourah Bay College in which by the 1870s it was possible to take degrees in arts and theology.

Such things perhaps concealed the extent to which the Krio community was also an African community: maintaining indigenous rites like circumcision,[4] clinging (though not usually with ecclesiastical approval) to forms of ancestor veneration, adapting funeral customs and friendly societies to African ideas of family solidarity and the living dead.[5] A distinctively Krio expression of Christianity emerged. If most churches, irrespective of denomination, used the Anglican liturgy, they also used the Methodist class meeting. Where observers saw Krio culture and church differ from that of Britain, it was assumed that the differences were imperfections due to ignorance, which would be remedied with time and patience. The question of language affords a paradigm here. Inevitably English became the language of administration, education, and worship in Sierra Leone. But a new lingua franca was growing up incorporating words from many sources, especially English, but developing a syntax which shows that it is an African language. When Englishmen heard it, they called it broken English, or bad English, or even (with a dig at the German missionaries who formed the staple of the CMS) "German English." It never occurred to them that it was a new language, with an English vocabulary and an African syntax. One result is that though every Krio speaks Krio at home, the Krio church to this day uses English—"good English"—for liturgy and preaching.

The Krio Church was built on recaptive Africans, uprooted from coherent societies and without the means of rediscovering their former cohesion. The only identity now open to them was a new identity. They took the only viable

---

[3]Compare A. T. Porter, *Creoledom* (London, 1963); L. Spitzer, *The Creoles of Sierra Leone: Responses to Colonialism 1870-1945* (Madison, 1974).

[4]*Ibid.*, p. 85.

[5]Compare Peterson, esp. pp. 259-63; H. Sawyerr, "Traditional Sacrificial Rituals and Christian Worship," *SLBR* 2, 1 (1960), pp. 18-27; H. Sawyerr, "Graveside Libations in and Near Freetown," *SLBR* 7, 2 (1965), pp. 48-55; compare S. Rowe, "Judas die don tidday," *SLBR* 7, 1 (1965), pp. 1-12.

al+ernative open to them, and adopted—and adapted—the package of Christianity and European civilization.[6]

It is not surprising if both they and their European contemporaries assumed that the Sierra Leone reaction could and should be typical of African reactions to Christianity. We can see now that the recaptives were very untypical of Africa; observers in the 1840s can be forgiven for not realizing this. Critics of Sierra Leone might see it as an inferior aping of European modes; its friends could see a "Black European" civilization, Christian, literate, using the English language with ease, differing from Europe only in being—potentially—more religious, more moral, more literate. Here was the triumphant demonstration of the repeated missionary assertion that given the same opportunities, Africans were as capable of "improvement" as anyone else. When the large, grave figure of Samuel Crowther, clad in immaculate clerical black, spoke convincingly on English public platforms, had audience with Queen Victoria, and answered all Prince Albert's intelligent questions about commerce in Africa, the whole missionary enterprise seemed justified. The future operations of missions in Africa must be directed to producing more of the same. There was nothing yet to force the question whether European civilization was the only standard by which attainment could be measured; nothing to suggest that the African ministry would, apart from its colour, look any different from the English. The African ministry would have the same sort of academic training as the English: a better academic training, therefore, than most of their English missionary mentors had received.[7] Not only was Sierra Leone beginning to produce a ministry that looked like that of England (possibly a little more like it than some of the rough-hewn artisan-catechists ordained via the mission field and Islington college), it was also producing a merchant class seeking culture as well as comfort, displaying godliness as well as gain. It was producing, in fact, the solid constituency reflected in the membership and leadership of the Church Missionary Society itself. So when the CMS grammar school began in Freetown, under a missionary principal, the hopes arising from it were for more than an educated ministry. It would teach biblical history and English history, mathematics and music, geography and Greek—and Latin. Greek was part of the plan for an educated ministry but Latin was there by public insistence.[8] Sierra Leone wanted everything that would be expected in England, and they made sure they got it.

---

[6]Compare A. F. Walls, "A Colonial Concordat: Two Views of Christianity and Civilization," D. Baker, *Church, Society and Politics, SCH* 12 (1975), pp. 293-302.

[7]Compare A. F. Walls, "Missionary Vocation and the Ministry: The First Generation," *New Testament Christianity for Africa and the World: Essays in Honour of Harry Sawyerr*, ed. M. E. Glasswell and E. W. Fasholé-Luke (London, 1974). Reprinted in this volume as chapt. 12.

[8]Fyfe, *Sierra Leone*, p. 237.

The last point is significant. Not only was it the missionary assumption that assimilation to the best norms of Protestant Europe was the highest good; not only was it the missionary intention to prove that Africans could be as good Europeans as anyone else; the intention of the exponents of Krio culture was the same. Later in the century would come the conscious search for more "African" forms of expressions; in the middle years of the century, this hardly showed. As early as 1830 the government announced its intention of gradually filling "all stations . . . by persons of colour"; in the early 1840s "persons of colour," notably Afro-West Indians, provided the governor, chief justice, and other major officials of the most important British possession in West Africa.[9]

The Krio church was to be of incalculable importance in Christian expansion in West Africa. In the first place, to a greater extent than has been commonly realized, it provided the labour force: a hundred or more ministers and missionaries in forty years for the CMS alone, and a very much larger number of schoolmasters, catechists, and artisans in mission service who might also do some teaching and preaching.[10] And the climax is reached when Sierra Leone can provide, in the CMS Niger mission, an all-African mission, and in Samuel Crowther, its own bishop. Such missionaries reflected the values of Sierra Leone, and when they set up a training institution hundreds of miles up the Niger, they called it *Institutio Causa Preparandi*.[11]

But the Sierra Leone missionaries, important as they are, are only a fragment of the Sierra Leone influence in the diffusion of Christianity in West Africa. As clerk, railwayman, mechanic, and above all as trader, the Sierra Leonean penetrated everywhere the British did, and often further. And wherever he went, he took his Bible, his hymn singing, and his family prayers. In area after area, well into the twentieth century, the first contact of African peoples with the Christian faith was through an itinerant or immigrant Sierra Leonean. And the mission to Yorubaland, which marked a turning point in bringing about a well-grounded church in inland Africa, came about because Sierra Leoneans had made their way back as traders over hundred of miles to the places from whence they had once been taken as slaves, and were missing their Sunday services.[12]

The background of the best missionary theory of the time was the

---

[9]*Ibid.*, pp. 178, 211, 220, *seq.* 229.

[10]Compare P. E. H. Hair, "Niger Languages and Sierra Leonean Missionary Linguists, 1840-1930," *Bulletin of the Society for African Church History* 2, 2 (London, 1966), pp. 127-38.

[11]See, for example, J. F. Ade Ajayi, *Christian Missions in Nigeria 1841-1891: The Making of a New Elite* (London, 1965).

[12]*Ibid.*, pp. 25 *seq.* There is still no full treatment of the Sierra Leone diaspora. On the nature and importance of the *Saro* in Yorubaland, see J. H. Kopytoff, *A Preface to Modern Nigeria: the "Sierra Leonians" in Yoruba 1830-1890* (Madison, Wisc., 1965).

conviction of the essential concomitance of Christianity, commerce, and civilization; the conviction—which seemed to have empirical evidence on its side—that it was essential for Christian expansion to abolish slave trading, and that this as an economic institution could only be overcome by economic means. Missionary theory and economic theory were thus consciously intertwined. The development of commerce will help to suffocate the slave trade and commend the gospel. And the work of preachers of that gospel is not simply to call out individual converts; it is, as the impeccably evangelical Henry Venn, secretary of the CMS, could say to missionaries as late as 1868, "to make disciples, or Christians, of all nations . . . that all nations should gradually adopt the Christian religion as their national profession of faith, and thus fill the universal Church by the accession of national churches."[13] To those with such a vision, Sierra Leone was a light upon the mountains.

It has often been noticed that the last quarter of the nineteenth century produced an unprecedented acceleration of the missionary movement. But not only were there throngs of eager young men to throw back the frontiers of mission: they also included a new breed of missionary. The standard product English missionary in the early part of the century had been a fairly homespun character with few formal attainments; by the end of the century, the victories of the gospel were being won on the playing fields of Eton. The devotional pattern and theological influences were also different; these men felt an evangelistic imperative which required the presentation of the gospel for decision by every individual, and to "lay all on the altar," a self-emptying in complete consecration to God. They had an ethic of self-denial, held with the doctrine (associated with the Keswick convention) of the availability of an experience of rest and victory over sin, received by faith; and an eschatology which saw the Lord's return as following the worldwide proclamation of the gospel.[14]

Such influences bringing such men with such motives at such a time meant a revolution in African missions. The story has often been told of how the young men with their new brooms swept away the all-African Niger mission and broke Crowther's heart in the process. And it is now being seen that it is not sufficient to write the story in terms of the abandonment of the theory of the self-governing church, or of the racist assumptions of the imperialist age

---

[13]Instructions of the Committee of the Church Missionary Society, June 30, 1868. The address is reprinted in W. Knight, *The Missionary Secretariat of Henry Venn* (London, 1880), pp. 282 *seq.*

[14]A full account of the background is still awaited. Some of the flavour is conveyed in the works (unfortunately undocumented) of J. C. Pollock: compare *A Cambridge Movement* (London, 1953); *The Cambridge Seven* (London, 1955); *The Keswick Story* (London, 1964). See also A. Porter, "Cambridge, Keswick and Late Nineteenth-century Attitudes to Africa," *JICH* 5, 1 (London, 1976), pp. 5-34.

replacing the more tolerant theory of an earlier period.[15] The influences which made these men missionaries implicitly challenged the priorities of west African missions and the assumptions which had underlain their methods for a generation past, not only highlighting the obvious failures of such missions but calling into question their very successes.

> We feel the absence of spiritual life out here in the Church. Conversion is practically unknown, and has certainly not been required as essential for admission to baptism. A mere knowledge of the Creed, Lord's Prayer and the Ten Commandments has always been reckoned as sufficient ground for baptizing anyone who offers himself. Can anyone be surprised if under such circumstances the Church is impure and rotten through and through.[16]

So wrote one of the young men, not long after his arrival. By this time, as the pyramids of gin bottles built up in villages and townships (especially, as mordant critics pointed out, in missionised areas, and very much less in Islamicised areas) it was no longer obvious that the interests of Christianity and commerce marched together. There was no Atlantic slave trade now to be counteracted by economic operations of missionary inspiration; and no place in missionary theology for such carnal activities. In symbol of the old alliance, the missionary travelled up river on a ship which put trade goods ashore:

> We have a large quantity of spirits on board, whisky and gin, and almost every place receives some. It is a frightful disgrace to our country to be daily pouring in oceans of foul liquor into a country where none is wanted . . . the [Royal Niger] Company place a very heavy duty on all goods except English goods, and so keep down very materially the supply of spirits in their Niger stations. They do, however, get rid of a good deal of their own, but are the only Company in West Africa who take any trouble at all in the matter. It certainly does make one ashamed of one's country to see this devilish trade going on. . . .[17]

---

[15]For a variety of interpretations, compare P. Beyerhaus, *Die Selbständigkeit der jungen Kirchen als missionarisches Problem* (Wuppertal, 1959), pp. 123-62; Ajayi, chapt. 8; J. B. Webster, *The African Churches among the Yoruba 1888-1922* (Oxford, 1964); P. E. H. Hair, *The Early Study of Nigerian Languages* (Cambridge, 1967), p. 60; G. O. M. Tasie, *Christianity in the Niger Delta 1864-1918*. Unpublished Ph.D. thesis (Aberdeen, 1969); G. O. M. Tasie, "The story of S. A. Crowther and the CMS Niger Mission Crisis of the 1880s: A Reassessment," *Ghana Bulletin of Theology* 4, 7 (London, 1974): 47-60.

[16]*Letters of Henry Hughes Dobinson* (London, 1899), pp. 49 *seq.* Dobinson, Repton and Brasenose College, Oxford, had just joined the mission from an English curacy a month or two previously.

[17]*Ibid.*, p. 40.

But it was not only, or even principally, the Royal Niger Company and the regular bugbear of the missionary, the white trader, which distressed the newcomers. It was the loose-living, gin-selling, hymn-singing Sierra Leonean entrepreneur or company clerk:

The question will face us at Onitsha, where some of the leading Church members deal largely in gin. It has been said publicly on the River and all here acknowledge, that any attacks on the gin traffic will ruin utterly all the Church work. Let the Church perish then, if she is here built on gin cases; but if she is founded on the Rock, she will not fall because we fight against and pull down a rotten prop or buttress.[18]

And so the young men set off to cleanse the Augean stables and the church rolls.

This group of men has been severely criticised, not least by themselves.[19] From some charges, however, they can be absolved. They were not inconsistent with their own principles, and those who accuse them of assumed superiority and of riding roughshod over African institutions should at least note that imperial aloofness, or the automatic assumption of the superiority of all things European over all things African,[20] did not determine their attitudes. They represented a radical criticism (though expressed principally in individualistic terms) of the nominally—but how far from really!—Christian society from which they came. And they desired identification with the life of the people with whom they now lived; to be, in fact, "all things to all men that by all means they might save some."

One of their instructive criticisms of the "Black European" missionaries from Sierra Leone—not less sincere because based on a misapprehension—was their aloofness from native life:

---

[18]*Ibid.*

[19]Dobinson, who lived longer than some of his companions (he died "of African fever" at Asaba in April 1897) came to argue for "more trust on God and more trust in the Africans," to deduce that "a European missionary is of little use unless he has a native agent alongside of him to help him for a year or two at least," and to reflect that "I certainly feel my ground more than I used to in the days of Brooke and Robinson; when I was hurried along in unknown depths of a fierce-flowing river" (*ibid.*, pp. 166 *seq.*).

[20]Graham Wilmont Brooke, often singled out as the representative of these men, indicates their assumptions about the peoples of the upper Niger: "our equals in intelligence, our superiors in courtesy, our inferiors in education" (CMS Archives G 3A 3/04, December 23, 1890). Brooke, Haileybury and "reading for Woolwich," had worked first as a freelance missionary before being accepted in 1889 as joint leader of the new Sudan mission. He was unordained, and like a number of the wealthy young men who entered missionary service, took no salary from the society. See A. Porter, "Evangelical Enthusiasm, Missionary Motivation and West Africa in the Late 19th Century: The Career of G. W. Brooke," *JICH* 6 (1977).

So far Mission compounds have been regarded by natives as absolutely sacred ground, in to which they are on no pretext to enter. We
hope to break down this absurd idea.[21]

This was essential to their missionary method: the tradition of Christian
life to which they belonged stressed the daily witness of the consecrated
life: whether in Cambridge or Onitsha, people would be influenced not
simply by preaching but by what they saw in a manner of life. If the "Black
European" clergy hid away in European-type houses, it was a further proof
of their 'unspiritual' life style:

The clergy have, we hear, no idea of people coming to them for help
and dread having their people close at hand *to see them live.*[22]

In fact, when the earlier missionaries, in the heyday of Christianity,
commerce, and civilization introduced western-style houses and developed Christian compounds in inland Africa, it was equally with the intention of demonstrating the advantages of the gospel: window frames and
family worship both had a part to play in this.[23]

If the Sierra Leoneans wore European dress, the principles which the
new missionaries had imbibed made them wish to appear as Africans.
Under the influence of Hudson Taylor and the China Inland Mission, the
"all things to all men" maxim was applied to dress.[24]

The young men on entering Hausa country adopted the tobe and
accepted the designation of *mallam*, or muslim teacher. They noted that the
Hausa dress, food, and houses could be adopted without serious danger to
European health.

The conditions of life thus enable the servant of Christ to live among
them on equal terms, by dress and manner making himself one of
them spending the day with them, learning their inner lives, their
interests, their needs; showing them hourly in his own person the
influence of an indwelling Christ to live among them and in such
homes as their own.[25]

There was some irony in all this when one considers that the tobe was
the symbol of burgeoning Islam in what was after all still a recently

---

[21]Dobinson, p. 39.

[22]*Ibid.*, p. 40 (italics mine).

[23]Compare Ajayi, chapt. 5.

[24]Thus the "Cambridge Seven," a few years earlier: "I have been laughing all
day at our grotesque appearance. Stanley, Monty and A.P.-T. have been converted
into Chinamen; we put on the clothes this morning, were duly shaved and pigtailed.
. . . Monty, Stanley and I make huge Chinamen; it makes us very conspicuous" (C.
T. Studd, quoted in N. P. Grubb, *C. T. Studd* (London, 1933), p. 55.

[25]*CMS Sudan Mission Leaflet* No. 1 (January, 1890).

Islamicised area; and there were serious inconveniences in the position of Christian *mallam*. They were expected to give *saraka*, make presents, as befitted people of such status. The African missionaries, however European in appearance, had understood the custom; the newcomers, with their insistence on "spiritual weapons" and their ethic of self-denial, were written off as tight fisted.[26]

While the African clergy explicitly recommended and personified the way of the west,

> We carefully avoid praising civilization or civilized powers to the heathen, and if they themselves are extolling civilization we tell them that they should not set their affection on things below.[27]

While the African clergy proudly accepted their designation as British subjects, the newcomers forswore British protection. They must be in the same peril as those they wished to induce to apostatize from Islam, and

> neither for them nor the converts should force or threat involving the possible use of force be employed.[28]

The alliance of Christianity and commerce was over: the Royal Niger Company, under the leadership of the acknowledged atheist Sir George Goldie, feared the Sudan party's potential to stir up militant Islam.[29] Crowther's longstanding policy of careful diplomacy with local rulers similarly took a new turn:

> It is our experience in this field that influence is not worth having; for it parts like a rope of sand the moment a faithful attitude is resumed.[30]

So sharp a change in motive and in method could mark a single field of a missionary society which had never wavered from its anglican or its evangelical allegiance.

---

[26]Compare A. C. Owoh, *CMS Missions, Muslim Societies and European Trade in Northern Nigeria, 1857-1900*. Unpublished M.Th. Thesis (Aberdeen, 1971), pp. 297 *seq*. Owoh also describes the difficulties when the white mallams like their muslim counterparts, responded to requests for written passages of scripture. (Quranic texts were much used as charms). The problem arose from the fact that the missionaries made no charge for their passages of scripture, and thus distorted the market.

[27]*CMS Sudan Mission Leaflet* No. 18 (February, 1891).

[28]*CMS Sudan Mission Leaflet* No. 1 (January, 1890).

[29]On Goldie, see J. E. Flint, *Sir George Goldie and the Making of Nigeria* (London, 1960). His alarm is indicated in letters of July 22, 1889, and August 9, 1889, appended to CMS general committee minutes of October 29, 1889. Brooke, meanwhile, was equally alarmed lest the CMS committee make an agreement with the Royal Niger Company and compromise him (*ibid.*, letter of September 16, 1889). The general committee resolved to forswear force or the threat of it (minutes, February 9, 1889).

[30]*CMS Sudan Mission Leaflet* No. 18 (February, 1891). Compare Owoh, p. 284 *seq*.

9

The Challenge of the African Independent Churches[1]

The Anabaptists of Africa?

We are just beginning to understand the complexity of African Christianity. Twenty years ago, while one could find missionaries and churchmen complaining of the activities of "sects," the African independent churches were not a subject of general interest. There was Bengt Sundkler's seminal study *Bantu Prophets in South Africa* (1948, revised 1961), and there were one or two area studies (notably Efraim Andersson's *Messianic Movements on the Lower Congo*). Terminology was very loose, words like "messianic," "separatist," "millennial," "syncretistic," and "prophetic" being used with great abandon as though they were interchangeable; indeed it was a great merit of Sundkler's book that he distinguished what he called "Ethiopian" from "Zionist" movements. Ten years later the situation had changed. On the one hand, H. W. Turner's two volumes on the Church of the Lord (Aladura) (*History of an African Independent Church* and *African Independent Church*, 1967) had given us not only a full and sympathetic account of one of these movements, but in the process the fullest account yet published of the life and worship of *any* group of African Christians. Partly by his influence, and aided by an International Missionary Council study (V. E. W. Hayward, ed., *African Independent Church Movements*, 1963), vocabulary was being tightened up. The phrase "independent churches" was now being widely used for those new movements that were recognizably Christian, by contrast with "older churches" (i.e., those that had maintained their mission connection); and Sundkler's earlier distinction (which had been designed for South Africa only) between "Ethiopian" and "Zionist" movements was being sharpened and made more widely applicable by the use of "prophet-healing" as a category. No longer could it be said that the

---

[1]First published in *The Occasional Bulletin of Missionary Research* 3 (April 1979): 48-51.

subject was a minority interest: such floods of articles appeared that there was a real danger that the solid block of African Christianity that could not be comprehended within the "independent" category would be neglected. The significance of the movements as vehicles of national identity excited some students; their significance as a bridge with the old religion attracted others. Among observers with a "missiological" interest, there was a notable change of attitude. One need only compare Marie-Louise Martin's hardline *Biblical Concept of Messianism and Messianism in Southern Africa* (1964) with her *Prophetic Christianity in the Congo* (1968), and later her *Kimbangu* (1975). D. B. Barrett attempted a continent-wide survey (*Schism and Renewal in Africa*, 1968), producing on the one hand tables of the variables that one might think could be used to predict the appearance of new movements scientifically, and on the other a religio-theological explanation of many of them in terms of (generally missionary) "failure of love."[2]

We are now, I think, in a new situation, where we must consider, first, What is the place of these movements within the history of religion as a whole? and second, What is their place within African Christianity? In both considerations, Turner has been a pioneer. In a series of studies less noticed than his African contributions, he has shown that the new religious movements in Africa, of which the independent churches are a part, have their analogues elsewhere—in North and South America, in Oceania, some in Asia, even a few in Europe. He has produced a carefully circumscribed definition: "a historically new development arising in the inter-action between a tribal society and its religion and one of the higher cultures and its major religion, and involving some substantial departure from the classical religious traditions of both the cultures concerned, in order to find renewal by reworking the rejected traditions into a different religious system" (*Encyclopaedia Britannica*, 1975, "Tribal Religious Movements, New"). His Project for the Study of New Religious Movements in Primal Societies, within the Department of Religious Studies at the University of Aberdeen, has identified and documented thousands of such movements. This work became the nucleus of The Centre for the Study of New Religious Movements in the Selly Oaks Colleges, Birmingham.

The worldwide nature of the phenomenon of new religious movements in primal societies should not, however, blind us to the fact that the distinction between the independent churches—which represent some of the many forms of new religious movements—and other forms of African

---

[2]"The root cause common to the entire movement of independency may therefore be seen in this single failure in sensitivity, the failure at one small point of the version of Christianity brought in by the missions to demonstrate the fulness of the biblical concept of love as sensitive understanding towards others as equals, together with the dawning African perception from the vernacular Scriptures of the catastrophic nature of this failure" (D. B. Barrett, *Schism and Renewal in Africa* [London: Oxford University Press, 1968], pp. 269f.).

Christianity can be exaggerated. It is worth considering Turner's definition again. "A historically new development arising in the inter-action between a tribal society and its religion" on the one hand, and an invader culture and its religion on the other, involving a substantial departure from both and a reworking of rejected traditions into something new—something like this is bound to happen whenever the Christian faith is effectively planted across a cultural frontier. Where it is thoroughly at home, where it has repaired the rent fabric of a shattered pattern of community life, where it is not simply an undigested "foreign body," African Christianity itself is likely to be a "new religious movement," reworking the old and the new. If this is true, the distinction between "independent" and "older" churches may be of decreasing value. We may also suspect that, when viewed as an aspect of Church history, the "historically new" movements are not "qualitatively new" but are new manifestations of "old religious movements" identifiable elsewhere in the Christian story.

Churches and Movements

It is perhaps necessary once again to indicate that "new religious movements" is a term much wider than "independent churches." Some of the movements are essentially renewal or adjustment movements within the old religion; one or two (even some called "churches") are abstractions from a romanticized tradition, patronized by intellectuals, attempts at a reformulated "intellectual" traditional religion; a good number are what Turner calls "Hebraist," making a clear and conscious break with vital aspects of the old religion, but without Christ holding any such place in their scheme as to enable them to be regarded as clearly Christian manifestations; a few (like Bayudaya of Uganda, who moved from mission Christianity via a "Hebraist" movement to a recognizable form of Judaism) represent developments into other major religions. Indeed it is vital to remember that motion is of the essence of movements; countless histories illustrate how new movements develop, sometimes toward a classical type of Christian affirmation, sometimes away from it.

We are concerned here only with those movements that are churches—organized expressions of Christian faith or practice—whether or not they originated as such. Along with these it is sensible to group the "para-churches," movements that do not claim to be churches but have the features of churches. Many important independent churches began in this fashion: not with a conscious desire to set up a new church, but with a society or movement within the old one. The Aladura churches of Western Nigeria spring from the Precious Stone Society—within the Anglican church until the church authorities took action on account of the members' views of infant baptism. On the other hand, the Martha Davies Confidential and Benevolent Association of Sierra Leone has remained throughout its substantial history, and despite its possession of a separate building, a supplement to the life of Freetown churches rather than a substitute for them. The *Kereke ea Mosheshoe* of Lesotho perhaps represents a transitional phase, a (well-established) movement in process of becoming a separate church; while the complex history of Kimbanguism of Zaire reflects one large church, the Eglise de Jésus-Christ sur la terre par le Prophète Simon Kimbangu (EJCSK), emerging, with some smaller ones, from the much more diverse Ngunzist movement, and effectively claiming legitimacy as the sole lawful legatee. It would not be hard, of course, to find parallels for each of these situations in Western Christian history. The history of Methodism and of the Salvation Army—each of which in its time was abused by churchmen as roundly as any African independent church has been—spring readily to mind.

Some Problems of Terminology

Even accepted terminology, which has been so helpful in sorting out past muddles and making clear distinctions, is now facing new strains.

First, what is an "independent" church? Nowadays most African churches are independent in the sense that their leadership is African, their ministry overwhelmingly African, and missionary direction minimal. Except, perhaps, in countries with white settlement, there seems therefore no longer any obvious reasons for "Ethiopian" secessions: virtually all African churches are now "Ethiopian." It has long been the case that life in the so-called "African" churches of Yorubaland (United Native African Church, Native Baptist Church, etc.) is virtually indistinguishable from that of the "mainline" churches from which they sprang: they are "new religious movements" only in a historical and no longer in a qualitative sense at all. (The end of the Ethiopian motive does not, of course, imply the end of schism, or even of ethnically or communally based schism—but that is another question.)

Second, the term "independent" must not obscure the fact that many (not all) "independent" churches consciously maintained a missionary legacy; they are often "mission-derived" churches as fully as the "older" churches. Some even claim fidelity to a particular form of missionary tradition as their raison d'être.

Again, with the passage of time, we now have independent churches with a substantial history. Many "independent" churches, with roots in the prodigious religious development of 1916-1930, are now in fact older than many "older" churches, some of which have achieved real independence of missionary control only in the last few years.

Changing Conditions

Present conditions help further to reduce the qualitative gap between "older" and "independent" churches.

The period when anyone desired complete assimilation to western cultural norms is now well past. One effect of this is to enhance the appeal of the independents, or of what they stand for, to *évolués* and intellectuals who in former times would have been embarrassed by any association with "primitivism." Partly for this reason, partly through a "routinization of charisma" in many older independent churches, the constituency of the independents is changing; some are institutionalizing and developing along the well-known lines of the older churches.

Further, the search for African identity, and the question of continuity of the African Christian present with the traditional African past raised by that search, are exercising younger leaders of the "older" churches. Some are evincing sympathy and respect for the independents as better reflecting or maintaining that continuity than some churches of the main line.

Word and Sacrament

But the most cogent factor working towards the reduction of the differences between "independent" and "older" churches is the presence in both of Word and sacrament within the same general cultural contexts.

The sacraments, indeed, have not been a prominent feature of many African independent churches; but it is also true that they have not been prominent in African Christianity as a whole. This results from the fact that the mission churches, Catholic and Protestant, have insisted on the practice of their countries of origin, that only a priest or minister is permitted to officiate at the sacrament, and there have never been enough of these to make sacramental worship more than a periodic experience for most African Christians. In some areas a further feature has been that Church discipline in conflict with local marriage custom restricts the Communion in practice to a minority,[3] often an older minority, of the congregation. It is not surprising if the independents have often taken the sacrament—and the creeds—as something that is part of being a church, part of tradition, but not as something near the heart of religious life. The EJCSK in Zaire in effect kept the Communion service in cold storage for years and then installed it, with great solemnity and an indigenization of the elements. But the communal meal, long prominent in African societies, has blossomed independently of the Eucharist. For instance, South African Zionists will break the Lenten fast with joy and gusto on Easter morning, but without the bread and wine or the words of institution. The Eurcharist came to Africa without emphasis on its aspect as a communal meal, and the Christian communal meal has gone on, in older and independent churches alike, developing without the Eucharist.

---

[3]Cf. J. V. Taylor's words about one Anglican area: "The rubric in the Prayer Book concerning the exclusion of the 'open and notorious evil liver' is applied to 87 per cent of married men in the church, and about 80 per cent of married women, and this quite irrespectively of the fact that in almost all peoples the congregation is not in the least 'offended' by what they have done" (*The Growth of the Church in Buganda* [London: SCM, 1958], p. 244).

The Word, however, has been central to African Christian experience. The independents have been marked above all by a radical biblicism—daring Christians in effect to live by what the Bible says. The Word is even visibly present when the charismatic person speaks, led by the free Spirit. Its visible presence is exalted even among groups who can barely read it; and more than one notable spiritual man has been anxious to demonstrate that, although illiterate, he can quote the Bible accurately and appositely. In some ways, the radical biblicists among the independents may be compared to the Anabaptists in Western Church history: the same wild variety, the same strong cohesion as "people of God," the same insistence on following the Word as they hear it.

This concern for the Word has perhaps been the main "catholicizing" factor for the independents, giving them a point of reference (and thus a potential source of change) and a recognizable common ground with the other churches. African Christianity has been from the beginning book-religion. The most effective bridge-building between independents and others has probably been in the area of shared Bible teaching—and is it coincidental that Mennonites, successors of the Anabaptists, have been so prominent in this? At this point, at any rate, the independents have simply heightened a feature which is common to most forms of African Christianity.

Differentia

Where, then, are the differentia between independents and older churches? Many external features of the independents come to mind when someone is asked to characterize them. We take here an arbitrary selection of them, and ask how far these are characteristic of African Christianity in general.

Other Sources of Revelation

A prominent feature of the independents has been the use of vehicles of revelation other than Scripture. Indeed, part of their appeal has been the accessibility of a direct personal "Word of God" to the enquirer. The background of this can be sought in two factors: the use of mediumistic trance in indigenous culture, and the presence of prophecy and revelation among the gifts of the New Testament.

A study of the "revelations" given in some churches, however, suggests that they are less integral to the life of the church than might be supposed. Most have a formal, a stereotyped character, even though uttered in ecstasy or received after rolling in the sand or some other technique for heightening the consciousness (and after all, did not the Old Testament prophets sometimes also employ techniques for the purpose? Cf. 2 Kings 3:15).

Dispute over the sources of revelation has been a regular feature of Christian history, and often enough the gap in practice between the "literals" and the "spirituals" was narrower than one would guess from the vituperation on the topic. In the early fourth century A.D., Phrygia (another culture where spirit mediumship was entrenched) developed, in Montanism, an indigenous form of Christianity. The orthodox fulminated against Montanus and his prophetesses. But they had reluctantly to admit that they used the same Scriptures as themselves. And when we try to find out what was done as a result of the New Prophecy nothing more dramatic is alleged against the Montanists than the institution of some supernumerary fasts.

As for dreams, certainly they are prominent in any profile of independency, and their interpretation is much sought after in African societies from any proficient person. But as Bishop Sundkler has illustrated,[4] dreams are important in the mainline churches too; countless of their priests or ministers first recognized their vocation in a dream in which they saw themselves robed, at altar or pulpit according to their tradition. And the independents point those who demur at these direct forms of revelation to the stories of Joseph or Daniel or other biblical examples.

Marriage

It is commonly said that the members of independent churches are fugitives from older churches with stricter discipline on marital matters, but it is hard to prove this. In fact, some independents, notably the EJCSK, preach monogamy as rigorously as anyone, and there must be few who consciously encourage polygamy. It is simply that the subject is not high on the agenda; they accept the facts of African married life as they are. Childlessness and its causes will rank higher in the minds of most couples. Now the older churches themselves are reappraising their own discipline amid changing economic circumstances. It is unlikely that the marriage question will long be an unbridgeable gulf between churches.

Healing

In traditional Africa, healing was usually performed in a religious context; the time and manner in which medical missions developed prevented (in most areas) a smooth transition from the old religion of healing to the new. It was the independents who made the logical connection: If the Christian was to trust Christ and not entreat the old Powers, should he not trust Christ for all the things for which he once entreated the Powers? But there is again nothing here that is incompatible with the life of the older churches. What the independents have done time and again is to challenge the half-Christian who goes to church respectably, but then in secret, and with guilty feelings, goes off to the diviner to seek the cause of sickness and the way of healing. The earthiness of African life demands that African salvation shall be as solidly material as biblical salvation.

---

[4]B. G. M. Sundkler, *The Christian Ministry in Africa* (London: SCM, 1960), pp. 25-31.

Examination of a whole range of other features of independents might be revealing, if followed by search of the same features in other forms of African church life. The sacredness held to attach to certain places and objects is strange—until one remembers that the same strictness of obser- vance may attach to many an Anglican sanctuary in Africa, where no lay person, above all no woman, may sit beyond the rails. The prescriptions laid down by independents often seem a strange mixture of African tradi- tion and Levitical law (and indeed very often it *is* African tradition reas- serted on the basis of the Levitical law). But in how many African Anglican or Methodist or Presbyterian churches are women simply quietly absent from Communion during the menstrual period, or do men in effect observe the rules of ritual purity laid down in the Old Testament?

One of the remarkable features of the independent churches for a westerner is their combination of the ritual and hierarchical with the charismatic and spontaneous. The West knows both types of religion, but—at least until recently—identifies them with different traditions. The independents combine them in the same tradition. But both features are part of African life. African life is ordered, has a sense of the appropriate time, place, and person; but it is also spontaneous, improvisatory, respon- sive. What is both more ordered and more spontaneous than the dances of Africa?

In the end, the history of African Christianity will be a single story, in which the missionary period is only an episode. The judgment of the churches of Africa will not be whether one can denominate them "older" or "independent"—that distinction, I believe, will in time, and perhaps soon, become meaningless. Their judgment, like that of all the churches, will be by the Lord of the Church on the basis of his Word.

10

Primal Religious Traditions in Today's World[1]

Immense difficulties lie in the way of any attempt at a comprehensive statement on the primal religions.[2] The sheer scale of the exercise: the vast number[3] of diverse peoples, cultures and environments, from the tundra to the rain forests, subject to the most widely different external influences; the absence of central authority or universally recognized texts or traditions; the bewildering variety of religious structure, the virtual impossibility of establishing even rudimentary statistics, inhibit the sort of account which can be attempted for most of the world's religious systems. The problems of definition are acute. For one thing, primal religions underlie all the other faiths, and often exist in symbiosis with them, continuing (sometimes more, sometimes less transformed) to have an active life within and around cultures and communities influenced by those faiths. What we call for convenience "religions" are not in any case self-contained, mutually exclusive entities which can be adopted or exchanged at will. From the standpoint of the believer or the community of believers, there is bound to be a continuum of perception and experience, even through periods of religious change; new ideas and activities, even the need for new ideas and activities, inevitably emerge in terms of the old. The influence of primal world views

---

[1]First published in Frank B. Whaling, ed., *Religion in Today's World* (Edinburgh: T&T Clark, 1987).

[2]For a general account and bibliographies see Joseph Epes Brown, B. Colless, P. Donovan, Aylward Shorter, and H. W. Turner, in J. R. Hinnells, ed., *A Handbook of Living Religions* (Harmondsworth: Penguin, 1984), pp. 392, 454. See also H. W. Turner, "The Way Forward in the Religious Study of African Primal Religions," *Journal of Religion in Africa* 12(No. 1, 1981): 1-15.

[3]G. P. Murdock, *Africa: Its Peoples and Their Culture History* (New York: McGraw Hill, 1959), lists 742 separate peoples in sub-Saharan Africa alone. For a geographical survey with bibliographies see W. Dupré, *Religion in Primitive Cultures: A Study in Ethnophilosophy* (The Hague: Mouton, 1975), pp. 57, 176.

thus continues long after adhesion takes place to Christianity or Islam, to Hinduism or Buddhism; but this is not the same as saying that the "conversion" is superficial or negligible. The major symbolic change may be highly significant, and marking a turning point in the religious development of a primal society. And thus, in one sense, in "primal" religion itself.

It has been the fate of the practitioners of primal religions to be classified and theorized over by others and rarely to be heard with their own story. At an earlier period they were pressed into the service of theories of the origin of religion and the early history of mankind, made the keystone of evolutionary interpretative schemes or the arsenal from which evolutionary schemes were bombarded. The modern controversies are, if anything, still more intense, for they now lie at the heart of questions of cultural identity and authenticity. The debates about them are no longer academic and historical: they affect how whole peoples perceive their present and its relation to their past. In Africa, in North America, and now in Australia new interpretations of the primal religions are arising from local scholars working in international languages, making an appeal to local popular consciousness, insisting that these religions have been misinterpreted through being forced into alien categories.[4] A particularly keen debate goes on between African scholars.[5] We will not be able to escape some reference to this process of re-evaluation, for in a sense it is part of the recent history of the religions themselves; but both this question, and that of the continuing effect of the primal religions within communities whose consciousness is formed by another faith (usually Christianity or Islam, but also Hinduism and Buddhism), lie outside the scope of this essay.

The Meaning of "Primal"

The very term "primal religions" is rejected by many. It is used here in the absence of any term which would be more widely acceptable when treating of a worldwide phenomenon not confined to any one region of the world. How else are we to bring together the religions of circumpolar peoples, of various peoples of Africa, the Indian sub-continent, South East Asia, Inner Asia, North and South America, Australia, and the Pacific? Suffice it to say that the word "primal" is not a euphemism for "primitive,"

---

[4]An African example is Okot p'Bitek, *African Religions in Western Scholarship* (Kampala: East African Literature Bureau, n.d., ca. 1971); a Native American example is Vine Deloria, *God is Red* (New York: Grosset and Dunlop, 1973).

[5]Cf. E. B. Idowu, *African Traditional Religion: A Definition* (Maryknoll, N.Y.: Orbis Books, 1975; London: SCM, 1973); J. S. Mbiti, *African Religions and Philosophy* (London: Heinemann, 1969); G. M. Setiloane, *The Image of God Among the Sotho-Tswana* (Rotterdam: Balkema, 1976). See also D. Westerlund, *African Religion in African Scholarship: A Preliminary Study of the Religious and Political Background* (Stockholm: Almqvist och Wiksell, 1985).

nor are any evolutionistic undertones intended. The word helpfully underlines two features of the religions of the peoples indicated: their historical
anteriority and their basic, elemental status in human experience. All other
faiths are subsequent and represent, as it were, second thoughts; all other
believers, and for that matter non-believers, are primalists underneath.

Content and Structure in Primal Religions

The above does not mean, of course, that the primal religions reflect a
single view of the universe or a common religious practice, nor that they
are without history or development. That idea has been kept in existence
by attempts to reconstruct the religion of particular peoples prior to contact
with the West as though that past was a static, timeless entity, and has been
reinforced by the common use of the "ethnographic present" in description.
It is the sheer quantity and complexity of the history, not its deficiency,
which makes it so hard to trace. Like all other faiths, the primal religions
have always known adjustments and alterations, fossilizations and revivals, prophets and reformers, new directions and new institutions.[6]

Until recent years, the tendency has been to designate types of religion
as characteristic of particular societies. Some have concentrated attention
on the phenomena of religion itself, identifying, for instance, a common
structure of religion across the African continent and sometimes beyond,
usually based on a fourfold pattern of Supreme Being, divinities, ancestors,
and objects of power.[7] Others have concentrated on the symbol systems of

----

[6]The work of Professor Åke Hultkrantz of Stockholm and his students has been
particularly fertile in its consideration of the historical aspect of primal religions.
See, for example Åke Hultkrantz, *The Religions of the American Indians* (Berkeley:
University of California Press, 1979); L. Bäckman and Åke Hultkrantz, eds., *Saami
Pre-Christian Religion: Studies on the Oldest Traces of Religion Among the Saamis*
(Stockholm: Almqvist och Wiksell, 1985); Åke Hultkrantz, "History of Religions in
Anthropological Waters: Some Reflections Against the Background of American
Data," *Temenos* 13 (1977): 81-97.

For a recent study of the history of the religion of an African people and its
continuity into the period of Christian interaction, see Janet Hodgson, *The God of the
Xhosa: A Study of the Origins and Development of the Traditional Concepts of the Supreme
Being* (Cape Town: Oxford University Press, 1982). One African institution that has
received particular attention from historians is the "cult-shrine"; see J. M. Schof-
feleers, ed., *Guardians of the Land: Essays on Central African Territorial Cults* (Gweru:
Mambo Press, 1979); and W. M. M. van Binsbergen, *Religious Change in Zambia:
Exploratory Studies* (London: Kegan Paul, 1981).

[7] This is expounded by Geoffrey Parrinder in *African Traditional Religion* (London: Hutchinson, 1954) on lines laid down in his *West African Religion* (London:
Epworth 1949). See H. W. Turner, "Geoffrey Parrinder's Contribution to Studies of
Religion in Africa," *Religion* 10 (No. 2, 1980): 156-164; and Andrew F. Walls, "A Bag
of Needments for the Road: Geoffrey Parrinder and the Study of Religion in Britain,"
ibid., pp. 141-150.

particular peoples.[8] Others again have concentrated on the functioning of
the societies themselves, and the place of ritual and religious specialists in
maintaining and cementing relationships;[9] while many, following old
precedent, have identified religious types according to environments—religions of hunter-gatherers, of pastoral nomads, of settled agriculturalists,
and so on.[10]

This is no place to pursue these methods of categorization. Bringing
them together, however, reminds us of four important facts that need to be
kept in mind.

1. *The elements of religious life are not the same as the structure of religious
life.* Most obviously, the tradition of a people may include a Being who,
when that people came into contact with a God-centered religious tradition,
will be invested with all the characteristics of the Supreme Being; or the
tradition may in some other way recognize the ultimate unity of the
transcendent world, a single principle underlying life. And yet such a
recognition may impinge very little on the life of most members of the
community, though ritual acts and words may be of regular occurrence. It
may be there in the margins of daily life; it may be locked in the specialist
knowledge of the experts in tradition. It is one thing, therefore, to identify
across many, perhaps most, primal religions, the fourfold series of elements
indicated above; the different patterns in which those elements are ar-
ranged result not only in different religions, but in different kinds of
religion. From the classical studies of particular peoples there appear to be
God-dominated systems, divinity-dominated systems, ancestor-domi-
nated systems, and systems in which the hypostatization of the transcendent is so slight that objects of power, or impersonalized power itself,
dominate them. At this latter point the line between religion and magic has
become of the thinnest.

In a study of the place of prayer among African peoples, Aylward
Shorter distinguishes six distinct types of religion, related to the way in
which prayer is directed.[11] He calls the first of these "strict theism," in
which, as with the Meru and the Pygmies of the central rain forest, the
Supreme Being is experienced directly in life and worshipped directly in
prayer. There is, however, a "relative theism," in which, as with the Nuer

[8]See G. Dieterlen, *Essai sur la religion Bambara* (Paris, 1951); M. Griaule and G. Dieterlen, "The Dogon," in D. Forde, ed., *African Worlds: Studies in the Cosmological Ideas and Social Value of African Peoples* (London: Oxford University Press, 1954). Cf. E. M. Zuesse, *Ritual Cosmos: The Sanctification of Life in African Religions* (Athens, Ohio: Ohio University Press, 1979), pp. 135-79.

[9]See comments of B. C. Ray, *African Religions: Symbol, Ritual and Community* (Englewood Cliffs, N.J.: Prentice-Hall, 1976), chapt. 1.

[10]See Zuesse, *Ritual Cosmos*, pp. 17-32.

[11]Aylward Shorter, *Prayer in the Religious Traditions of Africa* (Nairobi: Oxford University Press, 1975), pp. 8-13.

and Dinka, worship is rendered through a variety of beings conceived as modes of existence of the Supreme Being, and not as independent entities. Another type is "symmetrical mediation" in which intermediary spirits (usually ancestral) act as the vehicles of communication to and from the Supreme Being (Kongo, Tumbuka). With "asymmetrical mediation" the mediators receive prayer and there is little or no formal worship of the Supreme Being but its power and presence are acknowledged in life (Dogon, Shona, Zande). But it is also possible to have "strict deism" where there is no clear indication of a Supreme Being underlying such cult as exists (Acholi);[12] and very commonly there is "relative deism" in which neither the concepts of the Supreme Being nor of mediation play any prominent part in a religious life directed towards guardian divinities, cult heroes, or ancestors, but where the experience and worship of the Supreme Being are not ruled out (Yoruba, Ngoni, and many others). The same elements of religion appear in at least five of the six models; and yet the models reflect entirely different structures of religion.

2. As with all religious traditions, it is to be recalled that *there are different levels of religious knowledge and experience within the primal community*. In thinking of the religious life of a community as a whole, it may be necessary to take account of daily pieties, common observances, recognized means of recourse in emergencies, the special knowledge of experts, and the differing types of explanation offered in popular discourse and in the reflection of masters of tradition. The complexity of the African symbol systems elucidated by French anthropologists and the width of their field of reference can only be explained in terms of a succession of reflective commentators on the seen and unseen world, developing what in another context would be called philosophical method. Quite frequently, different types of divination are found side by side. Wider knowledge now available to outsiders of Ifa divination[13] lays emphasis not on the sleight of hand assumed by earlier Western observers, nor on the psychological insight always necessary in the diviner's task, but on the skilled application of a whole encyclopedia of myth covering every possible eventuality. This is essentially the "word of God" in a surer sense than can be derived from the apparently direct utterance of the spirit medium in trance sought by many ordinary people in need. It comes, as it were, from a deeper source in the divine world.[14]

---

[12]See Okot p'Bitok, *Religion of the Central Luo* (Kampala: East African Literature Bureau, 1971).

[13]See W. R. Bascom, *Ifa Divination: Communication Between Gods and Men in West Africa* (Bloomington, Ind.: Indiana University Press, 1969).

[14]Zuesse, *Ritual Cosmos*, chapt. 11; on divination as a "cybernetic" system, see V. W. Turner, *The Drums of Affliction: A Study of Religious Processes Among the Ndembu of Zambia* (Oxford: Clarendon Press, 1968), pp. 25-51.

3. It should be recalled that *since symbol system, religious ritual, and social system are interrelated, unassimilated stress in any of these areas will place strains upon the others.* Cataclysmic social changes leave an outdated symbol system and useless rituals which have lost their rationale—unless they can be adapted to take account of the new conditions. Additions to or drastic revision of the symbol system or ritual pattern call in question the established social order, or certain functions within it. Institutions must adapt to the new pattern or ignore it and produce a divorce between symbol and order.

4. *Living religion is likely to relate intimately to the basis of livelihood within a community.* This is not to say that it is determined by the community's environment; Åke Hultkrantz has indicated how ecological factors give shape to, indeed, "veil" religion, rather than provide content, which comes from that religion's own history and tradition.[15] Nevertheless, a change in the basis of livelihood either requires a new set of "veils" or leaves the religion without contact with the basis of the community's living.

Factors in Change in Primal Religions

These generalizations all point to important religious implications of any fundamental change in the society, whether environmental change, caused by migration or drastic alteration in the habitat; new modes of exchange, or anything else which alters the mode of personal relationships and the basis on which status is acknowledged; changes in kinship patterns or the community's order brought about by political or economic change or exposure to new pressures from an alien presence. None of these factors is new, nor a product solely of the conditions of the modern world. Primal societies have been open to such changes from time immemorial, and occasionally one can trace the pattern of change in the society and its religion over centuries. The Navajo, for instance, are descended from hunting peoples reaching northern New Mexico in the fourteenth or fifteenth century, necessarily turning to agriculture, and thereafter acquiring a matrilineal clan system, the use of sheep, and a complex mythic system under the influence of their settled agricultural Pueblo neighbors. In their case the new mythic system was superimposed on the rites and values appropriate to a hunting culture.[16] We must, therefore, proceed to six

---

[15]See Åke Hultkrantz, "An Ecological Approach to Religion," *Ethnos*, 31 (1-4): 131-50; "The Religio-Ecological Method in the Research on Prehistoric Religion," in *Valcamonica Symposium: Les Religions de la Préhistoire* (Capo di Ponte: Centro Camuno di Studi Preistorici, 1972). The idea of "veils" is developed in Hultkrantz's Gifford Lectures.

[16]See G. H. Cooper, *Development and Stress in Navajo Religion* (Stockholm: Almqvist och Wiksell, 1984), esp. chapt. 6.

further generalizations arising from the phenomenon of recurrent change in primal societies.

1. While models of distinct types of primal religion, such as Shorter's already referred to, are useful, they require certain caveats. In particular we must not assume that any given people's representation of a given model is static. The pattern of the elements, and thus, the structure, may be in flux, for instance, between his "relative theism" and "relative deism," or vice versa. We must in any case be cautious with the use of categories derived from other types of tradition. Geoffrey Parrinder has shown how misleading it can be to use the words "monotheistic," "polytheistic," and "pantheistic" of an African religion, for the very same society may produce examples of all three attitudes (or what in Western culture would be so designated) without any sense of the perceptions being incompatible.[17]

2. Where sufficient change occurs as to disturb the interrelated social, symbol, and ritual systems, the "expert" tradition is most in danger of marginalization. Its prestige, and that of its possessors, may remain high, but its application, or even the recognition of its application to daily life, becomes less obvious. Genuinely new questions and situations are beyond its scope; no longer, therefore, does it cover every eventuality. Unless it can be adapted or supplemented, it may become associated with a small elite or perhaps locked into durable but occasional practices, such as those associated with ruler cult, or become the esoteric possession of a learned class. (There have been instances, of which the Maori are perhaps the best known example, of the learned class deliberately choosing not to hand on their tradition.)[18] But popular religious knowledge and attitudes remain, to be reconciled with, or added to, elements derived from the new influences working in the society.

3. Such change does not necessarily affect all members of the society equally or in the same way. The society in change thus displays a series of symbolic worlds, which are not mutually exclusive but overlapping.[19]

4. There is, therefore, no inevitability about the nature of symbolic and ritual change under the pressure of social change. All societies tend to be conservative in matters of ritual and liturgy, and the mere presence of phenomena alien to a well-established world view does not immediately

---

[17]E. G. Parrinder, "Monotheism and Pantheism in Africa," *Journal of Religion in Africa* 3 (No. 2, 1970): 81-88.

[18]See James Irwin, *An Introduction to Maori Religion* (Bedford Park, South Australia: Australian Association for the Study of Religion, 1984), pp. 33ff. for a discussion of the historical basis of the precontact cult of Io.

[19]This is vividly conveyed in some of the outstanding African postwar novels, such as Chinua Achebe's *Things Fall Apart* and Ngugi wa Thiono's *The River Between*. Cf. the revealing biography of his father by S. D. Okafor, *A Nigerian Villager in Two Worlds* (London: Faber, 1966).

change the world view. There are various possible responses other than conservative affirmation. There may be a process of adjustment whereby elements derived from the forces influencing the society are incorporated into the traditional world view and modify its structure. There may be a radical break with that world view at some crucial point, an abandonment of major elements of the tradition. Such a break may occur in relation to "conversion" to one of the universal faiths, but it may also occur without such a movement; and it does not of itself alter all traditional perceptions.

5. Where the gap between the traditional patterns and the new experience of reality becomes inescapable, or where the traditional religious patterns prove powerless to cope with breakdown in the society, the society may enter a period of disillusionment and re-evaluation which might be described in religious terms as agnosticism. This "agnostic" condition, in which the traditional ritual pattern may be continued unchanged, may be the prelude to, perhaps is the essential precondition for, major religious change.

6. Where the gap between tradition and the new experience of reality is less severe, certain symbols or institutions may fall into desuetude, others may be retained largely for customary ceremonial purposes. Unless the traditional system is expanded or adjusted to take account of the new basis of life for most people in the community, this situation leads to effective secularization. The matters most affecting the life of the community have now fallen outside the sphere of religion. The remaining elements are no longer knitted into a living tradition, an all-embracing customary pattern for all occasions of life.

The Second World War and After

The period since the Second World War has been peculiarly productive of the factors which characteristically accompany change in primal religions. In many areas it has seen the acceleration of processes of change which were already in operation, and it has brought them to areas where they had been previously unknown.

In the Pacific, the Second World War itself had a dramatic religious effect. The Melanesian peoples in particular found themselves swept into a massive conflict between alien peoples, and suddenly exposed to displays far outside their previous experience. Daily events were on an apocalyptic scale; and Melanesian world views frequently had an eschatological element (return of the culture hero or the ancestors) which could illustrate or explain.[20]

The period since the War has seen the end of the European empires

---

[20]See especially F. C. Kamma, *Koreri: Messianic Movements in the Biak-Numfar Area* (The Hague: Nijhoff, 1972).

which had previously ruled most of sub-Saharan Africa, the Indian subcontinent, the Pacific, and most of South East Asia. In a few cases, revitalized or adapted primal religions took part in the process of decolonization. In Irian Jaya, new religious movements in which Christian elements sharpened traditional eschatological expectation helped to break down Dutch wartime rule and prepare the way for postwar independence.[21] In the Solomon Islands, the "Marching Rule" movement, strongly asserting traditional values (though perhaps not rejecting Christian teachings as such) long maintained virtually an alternative administration to the British, and seems to have faded only when its aims had been attained.[22] The religious aspects of the Mau Mau movement in Kenya are complex, but it certainly involved the assertion of Kikuyu traditional ritual as a means of mustering opposition to White rule (and specifically to White land ownership). Generally speaking, however, the leading role in mobilizing the movement for independence in Africa and the Pacific and in setting up the new states was taken by people educated on the Western model, usually in mission schools, confessedly influenced by Christian ideas and often identified with the Christian churches.

The colonial empires have been succeeded by nation states in Africa and the Pacific. These states are, however, colonial constructs, retaining the boundaries of the old colonies, frequently maintaining the inherited administrative system, and adding the idea of a national identity transcending the local and ethnic identities. The new states have thus been even more effective than the old colonies in encouraging mobility and setting up political, economic, and social structures which bring into contact with each other people of different interests and localities. The few exceptions have been states where central government has virtually broken down and where small-scale societies are able to live in certain areas virtually undisturbed by other than local factors. For most peoples, the universe has been permanently enlarged. Religious thinking can no longer be conditioned by purely local and ethnic factors. It must take account of other peoples and of national, not to say international, factors. It thus cuts across primal religions at the most critical point—the obligation of common custom for a common kin.

On the other hand, the rise of the new nation states has required African and Pacific peoples to establish identities; and identities can only be found by reference to the past. It has thus been a feature of the past generation to affirm the value and worth of the African and Pacific past, by contrast with

---

[21]See F. Steinbauer, *Melanesian Cargo Cults: New Salvation Movements in the South Pacific* (St. Lucia, Queensland: University of Queensland Press, 1979), pp. 10-17.

[22]See Darrell Whiteman, *Melanesians and Missionaries: An Ethnohistorical Study of Social and Religious Change in the Southwest Pacific* (Pasadena, Calif.: William Carey Library, 1983), pp. 250-273.

the denigration or rejection of it which often marked the colonial period. In consequence a new pride in traditional culture, including its religious aspects, has appeared even among people who were not fully nurtured in it. None of this implies rejection of the new, larger, entities such as the nation state (indeed, it reinforces still larger identities, such as "African"); nor of modern education, technology, and communication; nor of the use of international languages (English, French, Kiswahili). Nor does it necessarily imply rejection of the universal faiths (Christianity, Islam). The intellectual and religious demands come rather from the need to reconcile past and present.

The rise of the new nation states in Africa and the Pacific has been one factor in raising the consciousness of other peoples who through the centuries of European expansion became ethnic and cultural minorities in the lands which they had long inhabited. Native American and Australian Aboriginal cultural identity has been asserted in recent decades in a way unparalleled since the occupation of their lands. In each case this new confidence has arisen against the background of steady population increase after a period of decline; in each case it has been marked by the reclaiming of traditional religious institutions long in decline or even disuse. Once again the appeal to the past, through a quest for roots, appeals less to stricter local and narrowly ethnic considerations than to the larger identity as Native Americans or Aboriginals, over against White majority culture; and again it implies no rejection of the modern world as such; indeed, part of the motive for the revival is the improvement of the temporal lot of their peoples.

Another factor accelerating religious change has been the adoption by virtually all states of economic development models, centrally conceived and administered in relation to national considerations. The nature of the models differ: some have been explicitly capitalist, others explicitly socialist, some pragmatic and eclectic; but even those (such as Tanzania's "African socialism") which have claimed inspiration from indigenous tradition have led to the weakening of the traditional links of religion and society. Cash economy, production of surpluses for sale, mechanized exploitation of minerals, a degree of industrialization, large movements of population, and the break with the ancestral link with the land are features of virtually all modern nations and the path deliberately chosen—however imperfectly realized in practice—by most of them. Traditional value systems must adapt, wither, or be supplanted. Nor are the new nations the only ones affected. The rain forests of Latin America have seen massive penetration leading to development and clearing for cash crops and exploitation of minerals since the Second World War, and altering the basis of life for many forest peoples in Brazil, Colombia, Venezuela, and Central America.

Associated with pressures for economic development, but not solely caused by them, are major environmental changes. The world's tropical forests have sharply declined since 1945. This is due partly to the clearance for cash crops (or in the case of Central America, grazing), partly through modern technologically based warfare with its use of defoliants (notably in South East Asia), partly to the steady increase of population taking more and more land for food and fuel. All this involves a change in the basis of life to which religion must relate. A series of droughts across Central Africa, complicated in some parts by regional warfare, has altered the basis of life for many Sahel peoples, uprooting some from their land and eroding the basis of life of many nomadic and seminomadic pastoralists. Above all there is the factor of urbanization. Millions of people whose religious world, or whose parents' religious world, was formed in small agricultural communities recognizing common origin have been brought into vast modern cities of diverse population and subject to stresses, problems, and alienation lying far outside the scope of the traditional religious conception and its apparatus. This can apply even to cities which are in world terms quite small concentrations, such as Port Moresby in Papua New Guinea; but many African cities have reached populations of half a million or more since 1945.[23]

Finally, political pressures on primal peoples that were strongly applied during the colonial period have intensified since the European empires came to an end. In this connection the legislative sphere has probably been the least important. On the whole the successor states have maintained legislative provisions made by the colonial authorities making certain religious institutions, such as human sacrifice, illegal; but the religions concerned have long since adapted to the use of surrogates (indeed, it has been argued, were in process of doing so irrespective of legislation).[24] Certain forms of witchcraft detection and prosecution also remain outlawed. The prevalence of witch beliefs is unaffected, the scope for the suspicion of witch activity is probably increased by the stresses of urban life, but the new societies seek new means to cope with such activity.[25] Far more significant for primal peoples has been pressure, sometimes coercive, sometimes informal, to incorporate them into larger entities or recruit them into patriotic movements, or to employ them in conflicts directed by others. Before the independence of Malaysia the forest peoples of the peninsula

---

[23]D. B. Barrett, *World Christian Encyclopedia* (Nairobi, London, and New York: Oxford University Press, 1982) calculates that Africa has ten cities with a population of over a million and no less than 145 with over 100,000 (p. 780). That number has certainly grown since 1982.

[24]S. O. M. Adebola, *The Institution of Human Sacrifice in Africa and Its Analogies in Biblical Literature*. Ph.D. thesis (University of Aberdeen, 1985).

[25]Witch beliefs are not integral to primal religions (they appear, for instance, not to exist in Australia), and they can be accommodated within any religious frame. It is in the therapy used that the religious aspects appear. See R. W. Wyllie, "Ghanaian Spiritual and Traditional Healers' Explanations of Illness: A Preliminary Survey," *Journal of Religion in Africa* 14 (No. 1, 1983): 46-57.

became caught up in fighting between the British authorities and the communists. Since independence there have been government-sponsored attempts to bring these pig-rearing peoples within the fold of Islam.[26] The more recent endeavor to bring Irian Jaya and East Timor into closer harmony with the rest of Indonesia, including recent resettlement of Javanese populations in Irian Jaya, is fraught with immense consequences for primal peoples. Over centuries various Indian tribal peoples[27] have assimilated in greater or less degree to Hindu influence; but there remains still a sharp distinction between a tribe and a caste.[28] The status of tribal peoples is protected by law, but there are obvious advantages to the state in reducing the sharpness of the separate identity of tribal peoples; an advantage underlined by the potentially disturbing part played by border tribes in periods of tension between India and China. Small tribal groups such as those of Bangladesh are an uncomfortable surd in an essentially Islamic state, and they seem to have been subject to particularly intense pressure.[29] Marxist ideology has been officially adopted by many movements and some states in Africa, though there is little evidence of any sustained attempt to abolish religion (and, as far as the primal religions are concerned, a good deal to the contrary). Mobilization by means of party, military, or paramilitary organization provides yet another solvent for primal peoples with an agricultural basis of life. In Central America, Indian peoples have been the worst sufferers in the struggles for power in the various republics which have in various ways maintained the centuries-old tradition of seeking to assimilate the indigenous peoples to the ways of the majority culture. Both there and in some parts of South America such communities (partly primal, though largely Christian) continue to experience violence and disruption.

All these sources of change pose certain threats to primal religions. They

---

[26]Mustapa b.Hj. Daud, "The Religion of Two Negrito Peoples: A Comparative Study of the Semang of Peninsula Malaysia and the Andamanese of Andaman Islands." M. Litt. dissertation (1979), pp. 29ff.

[27]The oldest cultures in the subcontinent are "often in a stage of acute atrophy" (Dupré, *Religion in Primitive Cultures*, p. 76). Among the substantial studies of Indian tribal societies with their religion are P. Juliusson, *The Gonds and Their Religion: A Study of the Integrative Function of Religion in a Peasant, Preliterary, and Preindustrial Culture in Madhya Pradesh, India* (Stockholm: Acta Universitatis Stockholmensis, 1974); A. van Exem, *The Religious System of the Munda Tribe* (St. Augustin: Haus Völker und Kulturen, 1982); Barbara M. Boal, *The Konds: Human Sacrifice and Religious Change* (London: Aris and Phillips, 1982). Dr. Boal's earlier, more popular work, *Fire Is Easy: The Tribal Christian and His Traditional Culture* (Manila: Christian Institute for Ethnic Studies in Asia, 1973), contains a succinct outline of Kond religious life. The journal *Sevartham* provides a valuable series of studies of tribal religion in India.

[28]Juliusson, *The Gonds and Their Religion*, pp. 102-107.

[29]See *Inside Asia* 9 (July 1986): 28ff.

create disturbance of values, interfacing with the traditional ways of assessing worth, traditional lines of obligation, and traditional patterns of permission and prohibition. They create disturbance of hierarchy; they weaken the link with the land, and thus with the ancestors; they dissolve the link between traditional status and real power; they open new ways of acquiring status; they frequently obliterate vital distinctions (such as that between men and women's work). And they create disturbance of focus, rendering necessary a vision beyond the local; the community is manifestly part of a total world of events; perceptions of the transcendent world must now take account of this total world expanded vision of the total world.

None of these forms of disturbance is new in itself: the basis of life, and thus of perception, of primal peoples has constantly changed through war, conquest, migration, intermarriage, adaptation from neighbors, epidemic, environmental change. What is new is the extent, intensity, and universality of the forces of change.

Forms of Response

There is no sign yet of a common pattern of response to these forces of change. Since the Second World War there have been clear signs of processes which we may call Recession, Absorption, Restatement, Reduction, Invention, Adjustment, Revitalization and Appropriation.

Recession

This trend, begun long before 1945, has been the most marked. The disturbance of values, hierarchy, and focus induced by the processes of modernization has taken place alongside the presence of universal faiths which manifestly relate to the wider universe demanded by modernization. Large numbers of primal peoples have moved towards Christianity or Islam since 1945. In Africa, this continued a long-standing trend for both religions; and though there are signs of interconversion between Christians and Muslims,[30] instances of large-scale return to primal religions seem rare. In Melanesia and among primal peoples in Indonesia, the movement towards Christianity has accelerated since the war. India has seen movements of tribal people towards Christianity and towards Hinduism. In some cases the presence of one of the universal faiths has provided a means of maintaining the identity of a tribal people in the midst of pressures from a majority culture. Christianity, with its ready acceptance of vernaculars and preparedness for the Scriptures and the central acts of worship in the vernaculars, has been particularly attractive to groups which have felt themselves under threat of absorption or domination (some Indian tribals,

---

[30]J. K. Parratt, "Religious Change in Yoruba Society: A Test Case," *Journal of Religion in Africa* 2 (No. 2, 1969): 113-128.

for instance,[31] and minority peoples on the Nigerian plateau). African peoples who have long resisted Islam and shown little interest in Christian missions in their homelands have divided between church and mosque when migration has got underway to the cities. In Greenland and the Canadian Arctic, where the period of contact has been long, active practice of the primal religions seems to have died out altogether, and its most characteristic institution, shamanism, fallen into disuse.[32]

In some previous periods the move towards Christianity in particular was associated with the desire to participate in the power held by whites; the modernizing process was white-led and coincided with the activities of white missionaries. (Subsequent disappointment when access to such power was not achieved has affected both Christian and primal religious practice.[33]) Conditions since 1945, and particularly in the last twenty or so years, have progressively weakened such direct association. But Christianity and Islam, with their capacity to link into a wider universe, their provision of alternative codes of behavior, and their demand for symbolic change requiring some sort of act of decision, continue to provide keys to meaning and a means of adjustment to new conditions when a people's traditional lore is no longer able to do so. They are still the commonest refuge when agnosticism has set into a primal society.[34]

Absorption

One product of the process of recession has been the absorption of much of the configuration of primal religions into Christian and Islamic commu-

---

[31]Cf. Augustine Kanjamala, "Christianization As a Legitimate Alternative to Sanskritization," *Indian Missiological Review* 6 (No. 4, 1984): 307-331.

[32]I. Klevan and B. Sonne, *Eskimos: Greenland and Canada* (Leiden: Brill, 1985), p. 2. Cf. D. Merkut, *Becoming Half-Hidden: Shamanism and Initiation Among the Inuit* (Stockholm: Almqvist och Wiksell, 1985): "To the knowledge of Western observers, Inuit shamanism is today either extinct or obsolescent. Some few former shamans still live, but no longer practice. It remains to be seen whether a revival of shamanism will occur in the years and decades to come," (p. v). In view of recent Native American religious revivals the qualification seems wise.

[33]See H. W. Turner, "The Hidden Power of the Whites: The Secret Religion Withheld From the Primal Peoples," *Archives de Sciences Sociales des Religions* 46 (No.1, 1978); reprinted in *Religious Innovation in Africa: Collected Essays On New Religious Movements* (Boston: G. K. Hall, 1979): 271-288.

[34]A debate about the nature of African conversion has been initiated by Robin Horton, who stresses the aspect of the expanded universe. Among contributions to the discussion are R. Horton, "African Conversion," *Africa* 6 (2, 1971): 91-112; H. J. Fisher, "Conversion Reconsidered: Some Historical Aspects of Religious Conversion in Black Africa," *Africa* 43 (1, 1973): 27-40; C. Ifeka-Moller, "White Power: Social Structural Factors in Conversion to Christianity, Eastern Nigeria, 1921-1966," *Canadian Journal of African Studies* 8 (1, 1974): 55-72. See also the comments of Lamin Sanneh, "The Domestication of Islam and Christianity in African Societies," *Journal of Religion in Africa* 11 (No. 1, 1980): 1-12. For a closely argued case study, see C. C. Okorocha, "Salvation in Igbo Religious Experience: Its Influence on Igbo Christianity." Ph.D. thesis (University of Aberdeen, 1982).

nities. The results of this process properly belong to the study of these faiths, both of which have long historic experience of interpenetration with the primal religions. (Christianity, in particular, has from an early period made by far its greatest impact on primal religions, ancient and modern.) The modifications and rearrangement of priorities may be considerable, and many, perhaps most, live in overlapping worlds of spiritual perception. From one point of view, therefore, it may be proper to think of the primal religions having a continued life within the universal faiths.[35] But in another, more fundamental sense, the primal chapter of religious history has closed in such cases. The charismatic prophet may be the successor of the diviner, dealing with similar situations, perhaps using some of the same techniques; but if he does so in the name of the God of Israel, explaining his activities not from old tradition but from the Scriptures, and demanding rejection of both diviners and traditional objects of power, then historic change has come about.

Restatement

This is the hardest of the responses to identify precisely, and yet it occurs by the very presence of the world faiths. Contact with Christian and Muslim apologists forces on believers reflection and explanation, and this inevitably takes on some of the language of the outside faith and relates to the themes emerging most strongly in Christian and Muslim preaching and conversation. In the nature of things the topic most likely to occur is the nature of God. C. R. Gaba quotes the response of an Anlo elder commenting on the Christian identification of the God of the Bible with Mawu, the Anlo Supreme God:

> My son! Mawu is too big to be put into a small room and worshipped only at that place. In all Anloland, it is only the Christians who do this. How can we put into a room a Being we can never see and who is like the wind blowing everywhere? Our lesser gods we are able to house because they reveal themselves to us to see them and are locally connected with us just as other people also have theirs. Indeed I have my doubts if what you Christians worship in your churches is not the lesser god of the white man![36]

The elder affirms that Mawu has all the characteristics ascribed by Christians to God, and for that very reason decries the familiarity with him indicated in Christian worship. Christianity must be a cult, the worship of

---

[35] A complex case of interpenetration and symbiosis is traced by P. B. Steinmetz, *Pipe, Bible and Peyote Among the Oglala Lakota* (Stockholm: Almqvist och Wiksell, 1980).

[36] C. R. Gaba, "The Idea of a Supreme Being Among the Anlo People of Ghana," *Journal of Religion in Africa* 2 (No. 2, 1969): 64-79.

a cult divinity, and a foreign one at that. But his theology of Mawu, while probably containing nothing alien to pre-Christian Anlo tradition, is itself shaped in tension with the Christian presence. The presence of Christianity and Islam with their very positive and explicit affirmations about God must be one of the factors in the ongoing process of reflection and adaptation of myth and new explanation of terms and concepts. Actual conversion carries the process still further, especially among peoples becoming Christians. African Muslims characteristically avoid using vernacular names for Allah. Christians commonly make such identifications, thus strengthening the continuum between the old faith and the new, and in measure "converting" the past. Contentions common in current academic discussion about the characteristics of the Supreme Being and his place in worship in the pre-contact period of a particular people seem rather secondary; the religious process itself constantly reinterprets the tradition, and necessarily interprets the past.[37]

Reduction

Frequently a primal religion has become reduced or confined in its scope, either by the removal of major institutions or, conversely, by the institutions being cut off from the complex of tradition affecting the whole of life. The form of sacrifice may be kept, but carried out in token form, expensive beasts being only notionally immolated; in practice being presented, cropped in the ears, and returned. Initiation of youths may be too rooted in people's self-consciousness to be abandoned; but it must not interfere with education, and so is shortened to fit the school holidays. It must take account of knowledge of hygiene; so the circumcision itself may be carried out clinically.[38] The effect is to secularize an institution formerly at the heart of a body of living religion. Royal and chiefly cult has remained in many societies strongly influenced by the universal faiths (it has not been so readily assumed into Christian convention as it was in Europe), widely respected for historical and ceremonial reasons but no longer related to the main springs of religion. Those closely involved in it have often withstood conversion longer than most of their people simply because the cult (and sometimes the requirement of plural wives) was the last "irreconcilable"

---

[37]Cf. O. Bimwenyi Kweshi, *Discours théologique nègre Africain: Problèmes des Fondements* (Paris: Présence Africaine, 1981), pp. 61-5ff; and Kwame Bediako, "The African Evidence for a Christian Theology of Religious Pluralism," in J. A. Thrower, ed., *Essays in Religious Studies* (Aberdeen: University of Aberdeen Department of Religious Studies, 1986), pp. 44-56.

[38]F. B. Welbourn, "Keyo Initiation," *Journal of Religion in Africa* 1(No. 3, 1968): 212-232; see especially the remarks of D. K. Kiprono, himself an initiate, on latter-day events, pp. 230-232.

institution in the society.[39] Once again, it will be observed, reduction of scope is a mark of secularization.

H. W. Turner has indicated the way in which Christianity itself has been a secularizing influence in Africa, breaking into the "ontocratic" nature of a political entity functioning within a sacred universe.[40] But however far the secularization process proceeds, it is unlikely to remove the need for the diviner, the specialist in identifying causation and remedy.

Invention

From within the primal religions sometimes come bursts of new creative activity which transpose them into new settings, freely absorbing and adopting elements from other cultures. The most striking examples of this process developed long before 1945 in Haiti and Brazil.[41] The continuities with living religions in Africa are clear enough, but in the translation setting they have taken another dimension. In Brazil in particular, Umbanda and other spirit-religions strongly influenced by Africa have become increasingly important. They developed new features in recent decades, but with their large and systematic infusion of popular Catholicism it seems better to take these inventions as new religions rather than primal religions.[42]

Other forms of invention include the systematizing of cult and ritual elements in an attempt to produce a "universal" religious alternative to Christianity or Islam, often with written liturgy and apologia designed for educated people. Such movements had a certain popularity among the politically conscious in the period leading to independence, as providing an acceptable nationalistic religion.[43] New forms, such as Afrikania, founded by a former Roman Catholic priest,[44] are directed to appeal to a wider African consciousness.

---

[39]The case of I. B. Akinyele, Olubadan of Ibadan, a prominent figure in a Nigerian Independent church who was installed in 1955 without the traditional sacrifices, marks a turning point in that vast city's history. Cf. H. W. Turner, "The Late Sir Isaac Akinyele, Olubadan of Ibadan," *West African Religion* 4 (1965): 1-14; reprinted in *Religious Innovation*, pp. 129-32.

[40]Cf. H. W. Turner, "The Place of Independent Religious Movements in the Modernization of Africa," *Journal of Religion in Africa* 2 (No. 1, 1969): 43-63.

[41]R. Bastide, *The African Religions of Brazil* (Baltimore: Johns Hopkins University Press, 1978); R. F. Thompson, *Flash of the Spirit: African and Afro-American Art and Philosophy* (New York: Random House, 1984).

[42]A vast bibliography is included in I. Zaretsky and C. Shumbaugh, *Spirit Possession and Spirit Mediumship in Africa and Afro-America: An Annotated Bibliography* (New York: Garland, 1978).

[43]Take, for instance, Aruosa, associated with the then Oba of Benin and containing elements of the Benin cult and the National Church of Nigeria and the Cameroons (paralleling the political party with the same initials), vigorously directed by K. O. K. Onyioha.

[44]H. J. Becken collects and comments on Ghanaian newspaper reports, *Zeitschrift für Mission* 9 (1983): 233-239; cf. *Exchange* (Leiden) 13 (37-38, 1984): 98-106.

Adjustment

Attempts to adjust and expand world views to take account of new phenomena continue to be a feature of primal religions. Since 1945 this has been particularly noticeable in Melanesia, where the contact with the new influences has been relatively late and unusually drastic. It has now become common to describe as adjustment movements the plethora of movements once grouped together as cargo cults.[45] Over-emphasis on the cargo element, the most exotic and newsworthy from the Western point of view, can be misleading. But an existing religious framework including belief in the eventual return of the ancestors ushering in a time of health and happiness may be adjusted and harmonized to incorporate unparalleled new phenomena. The unloading of goods for a Papua New Guinea missionary in 1977 led to deputations to send more white people with cargo; the beginning of oil exploration reawakened the memory that the ancestors would return through a hole in the ground. The regular use of aircraft by another technologically minded missionary developed myth in a new way: "Mi Kristus has returned from the skyworld and has landed at Taiyeve. Airplanes are continually landing there, bringing cargo for the people of Taiyeve."[46] The aspect most often requiring adjustment is scale. It is remarkable how frequently the new movements in the Pacific transcend the old ethnic divisions, even between people long alienated from each other.

Revitalization

Primal religions today are not only adjusting; some have been revitalized. In part this results from the assertion of cultural identity and the regaining of cultural assurance on the part of non-Western peoples, with the rejection of European norms as the sole standard. African and Afro-American scholars, artists, and intellectuals are rediscovering and reaffirming the African culture heritage. In a few instances, usually for short periods, governments and political movements have used certain traditional rites (characteristically those strenuously rejected by local Christian groups) as tests of loyalty.[47]

---

[45]On these movements, see P. Worsley, *The Trumpet Shall Sound: A Study of Cargo Cults in Melanesia*, 2d ed., (New York: Shocken, 1968); K. O. L. Burridge, *Mambu: A Melanesian Millennium* (London: Methuen, 1960); K. O. L. Burridge, *New Heaven, New Earth: A Study of Millenarian Activities* (Oxford: Blackwell, 1969); J. G. Strelan, *Search for Salvation: Studies in the History and Theology of Cargo Cults* (Adelaide: Lutheran Publishing House, 1977).

[46]A. DeVries, "Cargo Expectations Among the Kwerba People," in Wendy Flannery, ed., *Religious Movements in Melanesia Today 1* (Goroka: Melanesian Institute, 1983): 25-30. "Mi Kristus" is Indonesian for Christ. The three volumes in this series document many other movements of the last decade.

[47]For example, Mau Mau "oathing" and at one period initiation ceremonies in Chad.

The most striking expressions of revitalized religion, however, are among Native Americans and Australian Aboriginals, minority peoples permanently deprived by white competition. When Joseph Epes Brown found the Oglala Sioux holy man Black Elk in 1948, he found him "lamenting the broken hoop of this nation," and it was generally believed, even by specialists, to be only a matter of time (very little time in fact) before the Indians with their seemingly archaic and anachronistic cultures would be completely assimilated into a larger American society convinced of its own superiority and the validity of its goals.[48] Black Elk's mission, which caused him so much suffering, "to bring to life the flowering tree of his people," may not have been fulfilled in the way that he labored for; but institutions characteristic of traditional religion, such as the sweat lodge and the vision quest, are reviving where they seemed about to die out.[49] And they are gaining the allegiance of younger people who drive cars and watch television.[50] With this comes a revived consciousness of the richness of the religious tradition and especially of its value and respect for the land. Environmental blight and other less-desirable features of Euroamerican culture values make assimilation not even desirable. Two features may be identified as especially interesting. First, the movement of revitalization, although a search for roots, is not centered on the consciousness of the narrow ethnic group; if anything, it is pan-Indian.[51] Second, the use of the hallucinatory drug peyote, formerly localized but becoming widespread for cultic purposes through the Native American Church, seems to be in decline. The new movement is not passive, but affirmatory.[52]

The Australian scene has some parallels. A major strand is the question of Aboriginal land rights, and a new political consciousness among Aborigines. The land rights issue is closely interwoven with the sacredness of ancestral sites. The very oppression that Aboriginals suffered in being driven away and forced to move has served in many cases to break the

---

[48]See Joseph Epes Brown's preface in *The Sacred Pipe: Black Elk's Account of the Seven Rites of the Oglala Sioux* (Harmondsworth: Penguin, 1971), p. xv. Black Elk died in 1950.

[49] Joseph Epes Brown, *The Spiritual Legacy of the American Indian* (New York: Crossroad, 1982), pp. 65ff.

[50]Cf. V. Dusenberry, *The Montana Cree: A Study of Religious Persistence* (Stockholm: Almqvist och Wiksell, 1962); for a bibliography of Native American Movements see H. W. Turner, *Bibliography of New Religious Movements*, vol. 2, *North America* (Boston: G. K. Hall, 1978).

[51]Brown, in *Spiritual Legacy*, notes the "double-edged'" nature of pan-Indianism: "The stimulus behind many of the movements is a reaction to EuroAmerican attitudes towards ethnic minorities. . . . The result is a complex of heterogeneous forms and practices that have popular appeal and commercial advantage, but risk sacrificing true spiritual content" (p. 67). Brown stresses, however, the way in which the rites provide outlets for central personal virtues, and the high personal quality of many of the leaders, including some of the new shamans.

[52]*Ibid.*, p. 18.

effective link between family and site; but a revival of traditional culture (not necessarily involving explicit rejection of acquired Christianity) has promoted a general Aboriginal awareness of the value of all the old sites. Once again new movements in primal religion move them from a locally ethnic to a wider consciousness.

Appropriation

Finally, we should note the phenomenon whereby primal religions are being adopted or recommended by those who historically belong to quite another tradition. The development in the West of the idea of responsibility for the environment has given a new appreciation of the world view of primal peoples without the sharp divisions of humanity vs. animals, animate vs. inanimate, and sacred vs. profane. This (combined, perhaps, with a new quest for meaning among people growing up effectively without religion in post-Christian Western societies) has led to a high valuation for Native American religion in particular, some of it expressed in somewhat bizarre and unrealistic terms. There has also been a lively international interest (expressed through such movements as Survival International) in the protection of small societies from exploitation or from more baleful results of contact with the Western world.[53] This movement sometimes focused attention on Christian missions as responsible for the erosion of the primal world view and for conditioning such societies towards a Western influenced culture and economy. The movement's journal documents these regularly, with special reference to Latin America.[54]

Not only is there a new confidence with the cultures historically associated with primal religions, there is a new self-criticism within cultures which formerly took for granted their own superiority. There is no sign, however, that this will significantly reduce the forces of change at work or the interaction of primal world views, the universal faiths, and the modern world. One observes, for instance, the pressure of the international women's movement, with women from African and Asian cultures well to the fore, for the abolition of clitoridectomy, a deeply rooted part of initiation to womanhood in many African societies.

All eight types of response have been found in primal religions since 1945, and all can be identified today. H. W. Turner has suggested a schema for Melanesian movements which includes the categories *Neo-primal* (those which seek only to remodel the traditional religions), *Synthetist* (those

---

[53]See C. Ahern, "Spiritualities on the Land." M. Litt. dissertation (University of Aberdeen).

[54]S. Hvalkof and P. Aaby, eds., *Is God An American? An Anthropological Perspective on the Missionary Work of the Summer Institute of Linguistics* (Copenhagen: International Work Group for Indigenous Affairs; London: Survival International, 1981); cf. G. Cano, *Los Nuevos Conquistadors* (Quito: CEDIS, 1981).

which are explicitly seeking to combine the old tradition with the newly perceived Christianity in a religion which differs from both), *Hebraist* (in which there has been a racial transference from the primal world to allegiance to the God of Israel, but in which Jesus Christ is not the means of salvation), and *Independent churches* (which seek to produce new Christian models).[55]

The last named is rare in Melanesia, though the characteristic form of new movement in modern Africa. The model would need expansion to take in relations with Islam and some of the reducing and secularizing movements we have mentioned. But it is worth noticing that the model allows for both a new situation, brought about by the permanent interconnection of cultures in this century, and for some fluidity between the categories. It points also to the principal change in primal religions since the Second World War: the search for a universal, not a purely local or ethnic, field of reference, a new focus suited to a village all now know to be global.

---

[55]H. W. Turner in Flannery, *Religious Movements 1*, pp. 1-6. For another version and an exposition see Turner's "New Religious Movements in Primal Societies" in V. C. Haves, ed., *Australian Essays in World Religions* (Bedford Park, S.A.: AASR, 1977), pp. 38-48; also in *Religious Innovation*, pp. 3-13; see also "A Typology for African Religious Movements," *Journal of Religion in Africa* 1 (No. 1, 1967): 1-34; also in *Religious Innovation*, pp. 79-108.

Part Three

THE MISSIONARY MOVEMENT

11

Structural Problems in Mission Studies[1]

The Critical Significance of Mission Studies

The proper definition of mission studies could occupy us a long time, but probably everyone could agree that certain topics belong to it. I am not concerned here with the relative importance of these topics within mission studies, nor with their degree of centrality to it, but with the fact that they illustrate the critical significance of mission studies as a discipline.

Let us begin with old-fashioned "missions." Studies of the activities of Western missionaries—and of the movement that produced them—nowadays often need an explanation or apology. Yet on any reading of history the missionary movement must have at least something to do with the most striking change in the religious map of the world for several centuries. One part of the globe has seen the most substantial accession to the Christian faith since the conversion of the northern barbarians; another, the most considerable recession from it since the rise of Islam. The most obvious centre of accession is tropical Africa, which even a century ago was statistically marginal to Christianity; the most obvious center of recession is Western Europe, which a century and a half ago would certainly have been identified as the most dynamic and significant Christian centre.

There must be some connection between these events and the missionary movement; and the modern missionary movement, though affected in important ways by earlier influences, took shape as recently as the nineteenth century. Yet how is the contemporary student of Christianity to understand this important motor of modern Christianity? It may be instructive to consider a standard work on British nineteenth-century church

---

[1]First published in *International Bulletin of Missionary Research* 15 (October, 1991): 146-55.

history, remembering that nineteenth-century Britain was the principal source of Protestant missionaries and the main base of the missionary movement.

Owen Chadwick's *The Victorian Church*[2] is a work of immense learning and profound scholarship. Furthermore, the author is perhaps the outstanding living example of a church historian not tied to a single specialization; he has even written a valuable work on missions to Africa.[3] The more noteworthy, then, that this splendid, many-sided study, of two volumes and 1,116 pages, contains no chapter or section on the Victorian missionary movement. The word "missions" (except for "missions, parochial, see also revival") does not even occur in the indexes. There is one reference to the Church Missionary Society (in relation to the early career of John Henry Newman) and one to the London Missionary Society (in relation to the Congregationalist interest in centralized funding). I have noticed the names of only three individual missionaries: Livingstone (in relation to burials in Westminster Abbey), and the South Africa bishops J. W. Colenso and Robert Gray—bishops with a reputation for heresy or schism, or who excommunicate other bishops, tend to make headlines.[4]

A valuable feature of *The Victorian Church* is its barometric sense of balance and movement; the events of the time, as seen by the central, normative ecclesiastical world of England, are displayed in the proportions accorded them by that world. In other words, Chadwick's work reveals that the British missionary movement at its height was only peripheral to the Victorian church. One of the features of the nineteenth-century Western Christianity that most determined the future of the faith made quite a small impression on its contemporaries, and has made a correspondingly small one on their historians.

This suggests that mission studies, and even the rather unfashionable "missions" studies, may now have a major interpretative role to play in the understanding of the history of the church in the West. (No doubt a history of Christianity composed in Jerusalem about A.D. 66 would have shown the Gentile mission as rather peripheral to Christian development. It is our possession of the "mission studies" documents by Paul and Luke that makes possible another interpretation).

---

[2]Owen Chadwick, *The Victorian Church* (London: Black, vol. 1, 1966, vol. 2, 1970).

[3]*Mackenzie's Grave* (London: Hodder and Stoughton, 1959) is a study of the early phase of the Universities' Mission to Central Africa. Professor Chadwick has more recently produced a revision of Stephen Neill's volume on *Christian Missions* in the Pelican History of the Church Series.

[4]G. A. Selwyn, Bishop of New Zealand, also occurs several times, but mainly by virtue of his later career as Bishop of Lichfield.

Subverting the Curriculum

But the change in Christianity's centre of gravity has still greater implications for Christian scholarship. Let us stay for the moment in the sphere
of historical study. The church history of Africa, of Asia, of Latin America,
of the Pacific, cannot be comprehended under "mission studies." The
missionary period in these histories is only an episode. In many cases it was
a very short episode, and in many others it is one that closed long ago. But
in relation to the various Christian communities of the Southern continents,
"mission history" and "church history" do not just represent different
periods, but different *kinds* of history.

Anyone who has used both mission archives and local church sources,
oral or written, will be aware of the totally different dynamics, perspectives,
and priorities these different sources reveal. The church histories of the
Southern continents are clearly of special concern to the churches, the
peoples, and the scholars of those areas. But they are not an exclusive
possession or interest; the whole history of the church belongs to the whole
church. This does not mean that Christian history in Africa or Asia is, for
people who are not Africans or Asians, simply a source of interesting
additional options in the curriculum. Still less does it mean that these
histories can simply be appended to existing syllabuses as though they were
an updating supplement.

The global transformation of Christianity requires nothing less than the
complete rethinking of the church history syllabus. Most conventional
church history syllabuses are framed, not always consciously, on a particular set of geographical, cultural, and confessional priorities. Alas, such
syllabuses have often been taken over in the Southern continents, as though
they had some sort of universal status. Now they are out-of-date even for
Western Christians. As a result, a large number of conventionally trained
ministers have neither the intellectual materials nor even the outline knowledge for understanding the church as she is. The only hope of such things
being acquired in perhaps the majority of theological institutions is from
what is currently thought of as "mission studies."

Indeed, the most recent phase of Christian expansion raises fundamental
questions about the very nature of Christian faith. This is not because the
issues raised by the global transformation of Christianity are new in Christian
history, but because they have recently been obscured by some aspects of
Western history—notably the Christendom model of the church and the
legacy of the Roman Empire. It is easier to recognize now than it was even a
century ago that cross-cultural diffusion has always been the lifeblood of
historic Christianity; that Christian expansion has characteristically come
from the margins more than from the centre; that church history has been
serial rather than progressive, a process of advance and recession, of decline
in areas of strength and of emergence, often in new forms, in areas of previous
weaknesses. Some of the implications of this, the relation to the themes of

translation and Incarnation (the great act of translation on which Christian faith depends) have been explored by Lamin Sanneh[5] and others. But the most obvious method of examining such basic questions about the Christian faith is by studying Christianity as expressed in the experience of the Southern churches. Such studies reveal how these shared and acquired attributes of a community which we call culture (and of which language is a working model) are the proving ground of Christian faith, the workplace of Christian theology. One much-needed contribution that mission studies can make to theological practice in the West is to raise the theological issues concerning Western culture with seriousness. (I take it for granted that such seriousness excludes simplistic instrumental views of culture which treat it as though it were some sort of evangelistic technique.)

The Workplace of Christian Theology

If culture is the workplace of Christian theology, it follows that the present Christian interaction with the cultures of the South—as intricate and far-reaching in their different ways as the Hellenistic Roman—marks a new creative stage in Christian theology. Once again there will be a tendency, as in the historical sphere, to try to add "African theology" or "Latin American theology" or even (*miserere nobis*) "Third World theology" to a preexisting syllabus. It is the very concept of a fixed universal compendium of theology, a sort of bench manual which covers every situation, that mission studies challenge. In mission studies we see theology "en route"[6] and realize its "*occasional*" nature, its character as response to the need to make Christian decisions. The conditions of Africa, for instance, are taking Christian theology into new areas of life, where Western theology has no answers, because it has no questions. But Christians outside Africa will need to make some response to the questions raised in the African arena. As Christian interaction proceeds with Indian culture—perhaps the most testing environment that the Christian faith has yet encountered—the theological process may reach not only new areas of discourse, but resume some of those which earlier pioneers—Origen, for instance—began to enter.

Lamin Sanneh's explorations of the nature of Christian faith have been

---

[5]Especially in Lamin Sanneh, *Translating the Message: The Missionary Impact on Culture* (Maryknoll, N.Y.: Orbis Books,1989). See also Lamin Sanneh, "Gospel and Culture: Ramifying Effects of Scriptural Translation," in *Bible Translation and the Spread of the Church: The Last 200 years*, ed. P. C. Stine (Leiden: Brill, 1990), pp. 1-23, and A. F. Walls, "The Translation Principle in Christian History," *ibid.*, pp. 24-39 (reprinted in this volume as chapt. 3).

[6]I borrow the expression from the title of K. Appiah-Kubi and S. Torres, *African Theology en Route: Papers from the Pan-African Conference of Third World Theologians* (Maryknoll, N.Y.: Orbis Books, 1979). On the occasional nature of theology, see also A. F. Walls, "The Gospel as the Prisoner and Liberator of Culture," *Missionalia* 10, no. 3 (1982): 219-33 (reprinted in this volume as chapt. 1).

striking because they have been presented in counterpoint with the character of Islamic faith.[7] It is in interaction that the nature of commitment
appears. Perhaps one of the most urgent areas of study at the moment is
the Christian interaction with the primal religions, the religious infrastructure of millions of Christians, historically the background from which most
large movements into Christian faith have always come. It is, however,
another issue, that of pluralism, which has brought the question of the
relations of Christianity with the other faiths into prominence in the West.

It can only be a good thing if Christian theologians are taking seriously
the other faiths of the world. And yet I confess to a good deal of unease
about the terms in which much of the Western debate is proceeding. There
are several related reasons for this. One is the lack of serious engagement
with the primal religions, the background of a large portion of the human
race and of multitudes of Christians. Another is an evident assumption that
we are suddenly at Day One of the interreligious encounter, an assumption
that bypasses the accumulated experience of many generations and, still
worse, implicitly locks Christianity into a Western framework. Worst of all,
and a direct result of that Western conceptual frame (shot through with
colonial guilt) is a shame-facedness about the missionary movement that
undercuts the position of the majority of Christian believers. For the majority of Christians live in the Southern continents, and their coming to
Christian faith is ultimately related to the missionary movement. No Western response to other faiths can hold water that does not take responsibility
for the missionary movement; no Western response to other faiths can show
Christian integrity if it by implication cuts itself off from the Christian
believers of the non-Western world. And a Western response must be
seriously impoverished that takes no note of the accumulated experience
of interreligious encounter forged in the missionary movement and in the
discourse of Christians who every day of their lives participate in cultures
shaped by the great non-Christian faiths of the world. Pluralism may be a
new issue for the West; it has been the normal experience for most of the
world's Christians.

A Renaissance of Mission Studies

We could go further. We have not, for instance, yet mentioned biblical
studies, where the Southern continents provide plenty of evidence of fresh
readings and understandings of the Scriptures. But perhaps enough has
been said to show the challenge that now lies before mission studies.
Contemporary theology needs renewal by mission studies. It needs the
knowledge, the disciplines, the skills, the sources within mission studies. It
needs to grapple with the history, thought, and life of the churches of the
non-Western world, the history and understanding of the missionary

---

[7]See Lamin Sanneh, *Translating the Message*, chapt. 7.

movement that was their catalyst, the understanding of Christian history and of the nature of Christian faith which studies of these topics bring, the constant concern with culture and regular critique of cultural assumptions that they encourage. The theological scholarship of the churches of the Southern continents needs these things; but at least it *knows* it needs them. The primacy of mission studies is well recognized there; it is the resources for it that are often lacking. Western theology, however, resembles Singapore in 1942: though well equipped with heavy weaponry, most of it points in the wrong direction. Western theological equipment requires to be turned—requires conversion, a fresh vision that could come from mission studies. The theological task throughout the *oecumene*, East and West, North and South, needs a renaissance of mission studies.

The nineteenth-century theological agenda was transformed by new discoveries. New dimensions in biblical scholarship were opened up by archeology, by the papyri, by new activity in text criticism, by deepened understanding of the worlds that surrounded old Israel and the early church. The theological task expanded to take account of new developments in the historical sciences and in the natural sciences, and of changes in society. While all this was happening, a still greater fund of new discoveries was coming to light in Asia and Africa, with the capacity for still greater impact on the Christian mind; but its importance for theology was not immediately recognized. It was secular learning that first felt the impact of the missionary encounter with Africa and Asia. Missionary scholarship established new boundaries, it established whole new disciplines (African linguistics is a direct fruit of mission activity) and revolutionized others. Scientific anthropology was made possible by the missionary movement; it was not something the early missionaries simply omitted to take with them. The same is true of the comparative study of religion and the phenomenology of religion that is its product. For a long time there was little understanding of other cultures. When Robert Morrison was appointed a missionary to China in 1807, the entire Chinese resources of British academic libraries consisted of one manuscript in the British Museum and one in the Royal Society, and not a person in Britain read or spoke Chinese. When Morrison returned on his first and only furlough (now the translator of the Bible and author of a massive Chinese dictionary), he took steps to establish an Oriental philological institute. Missionaries such as James Legge, the greatest English-speaking sinologist of the nineteenth century, and J. N. Farquhar, who did so much to interpret Indian literature in the twentieth, helped to open up the West to classical religious, philosophical, and historical texts of Asia. But no one, not even missionaries for the most part, realized the theological implications of all this learning. Theology was still a *datum*. Today, with a new phase of Christian history well launched in the lands that gave rise to this new knowledge, we have a theological El Dorado wholly comparable with the rich discoveries and new science of a century ago. It has fallen to those of us in mission studies to have our humble daily labour in the very territory that includes the path to El Dorado.

Mission Studies and the World of Learning

All this may seem an excessive prelude to an account of structural problems in mission studies. But it is not really a prelude. The root of many of our structural problems in mission studies lies in the relationships of mission studies to the rest of the world of learning.

The theological sector has not yet come to terms with that fundamental shift in the centre of gravity of the Christian world whereby the Southern continents have become the heartlands of the Christian faith. Even where the shift is recognized as a fact, the implication that this requires something analogous to a Copernican revolution in theological discourse is not recognized, and would certainly not be welcome. So theological institutions go on believing they are assisting the Third World by bundling African and Asian students into programs that take no cognizance of that world and have no intellectual space for it; and they minimize the benefit they themselves could gain from the contact by their assumptions about what their programs are able to do for such students. Or they compass sea and land to get a Third World professor as a figurehead and then think they have become ecumenical and comprehensive by including "the Third World" viewpoint. A distinguished historian of the impact on Europe of the discovery of the New World has pointed out how long it took for the discovery to register. The discovery of America did not mean that people threw their maps away and got new ones; still less did it mean that learned people abandoned ideas about humanity and society that were the product of European ignorance of the world beyond their own.[8] In fact, the new discoveries were intellectually threatening, requiring the abandonment of too many certainties, the acquisition of too many new ideas and skills, the modification of too many maxims, the sudden irrelevance of too many accepted authorities. It was easier to ignore them and carry on with the old intellectual maps (and often the old geographical maps too), even while accepting the fact of the discovery and profiting from the economic effects.

The modern "secular" world of learning poses problems of another sort. The nineteenth century, as already indicated, saw scholarship immensely enriched by the missionary movement in (one is tempted to say) every department of learning except theology. The legacy passed to the learned world in various ways; it helped to create new sciences (linguistics), helped to shape or was absorbed into new ways of organizing knowledge (anthropology), contributed to new clusters of subjects that brought the non-West-

---

[8]J. H. Elliot, *The Old World and the New, 1492-1650* (Cambridge: Cambridge University Press, 1970).

ern world within the parameters of Western learning (Oriental and African studies). But the other great modern religious development—the recession from the Christian faith in Western lands and the consequent marginalization of theology—has intervened. The secularization of thought has submerged the connection of learning with the missionary movement. The association of missions with colonialism has sometimes added a layer of embarrassment or even hostility; and several generations of secularism have blunted the capacity of Western scholars to cope with the sheer quantity, the resilience, and the ebullience of religion in the non-Western world. This is particularly the case when that religion is Christian. It is remarkable that the immense Christian presence in Africa is so little a feature of modern African studies, and how much of the scholarly attention devoted to it is concentrated on manifestations that in Western terms seem most exotic. (We know more about Bwiti than about Baptist religious life, and Jamaa is probably the best-illuminated aspect of African Catholic devotion.[9])

I propose that we recognize the renaissance of mission studies not only as a call from the church throughout the *oecumene*, but as a crying need of the whole world of scholarship, sacred and profane. That places certain responsibilities upon those who work in mission studies.

First, mission studies will need theological integration; we must insert the shape of the church as it is today onto intellectual and theological maps that were drawn according to the canons of what it used to be.

Something of the nature of the task may be deduced from pursuing the analogy of the revitalization of nineteenth-century scholarship through new discoveries. Revitalization did not take place simply by parading "discoveries," nor sloganizing them, nor by mixing conjecture and hypothesis with them in generous proportions. To abandon the labour of integrating old and new learning would have been simply destructive. The nineteenth century saw plenty of wild theorizing, plenty of unbalanced sloganizing. But the agents of revitalization, the abiding influences for good, were those with depth of scholarship, who sought its integrity with the ongoing faith and life of the church.

It is no accident that we can still turn with refreshment to the New Testament commentaries of J. B. Lightfoot and B. F. Westcott, or derive

---

[9]Bwiti, the Fong cult in Gabon, has been particularly thoroughly described, analyzed, and documented in numerous publications by J. W. Fernandez, e.g., *Bwiti: An Ethnography of the Religious Imaginations in Africa* (Princeton University Press, 1982) and by Stanislaw Swiderski. On Jamaa, an important devotional movement in Katanga originating in connection with the work of Fr. Placide Tempels, but often frowned on by the church authorities, see J. Fabian, *Jamaa: A Charismatic Movement in Katanga* (Evanston: Northwestern University Press, 1971) and W. De Craemer, *The Jamaa and the Church: A Bantu Catholic Movement in Zaire* (Oxford: Clarendon, 1977).

benefit from the insight of F. J. A. Hort and the lexical erudition of W. F. Moulton. It is no accident that the solidity of Lightfoot's patristic learning could crowd out the space for speculative theories of Christian origins. Such solidity combined with such sensitivity and wakefulness made the giants of those days open to visions beyond their natural sight. When Westcott predicted that the great commentary on the Fourth Gospel would come from an Indian Christian scholar, this was prophecy that comes from integrity of faith and scholarship.[10]

But the task cannot be performed solely with the acknowledged resources of theological scholarship. We have already recalled that part of the inheritance of the missionary movement has been absorbed into "secular" learning, and that the intellectual developments of the century have divorced this learning from the theological task. Our theological institutions taken alone do not have the resources within themselves to effect the needed renaissance. Mission studies must interact with ongoing work in the history, languages, political, economic and social organization, cultures, and literature of the Southern continents (not to mention many aspects of the Northern). Therein are some of the twentieth-century equivalents of Assyrian inscriptions and demotic Greek papyri with the potential to reorder much sacred and much profane learning.

A renaissance of mission studies will not be effected simply by increasing the number of faculty posts and the output of books and doctorates. It will require not just rigorous scholarship, but *depth* of scholarship, the depth of which the Lightfoots and Westcotts are exemplars. It will require integrated scholarship, which engages with all the existing theological disciplines and in doing so enriches them. It will need to bring to the task a range of disciplines and sources of which most even of the best theologians are innocent. It will need to demonstrate learning and professional competence in the phenomenology and history of religion and in the historical, linguistic, and social sciences too, for those disciplines also need the renaissance of mission studies.

We must also face a structural problem that is especially our own. Mission of its nature is about practice, and its ethos is frequently activist. Traditionally many teaching posts in mission are envisaged as providing

---

[10]David Newsome, *Godliness and Good Learning: Four Studies on a Victorian Ideal* (London: Cassell, 1961), pp. 105ff., shows how Westcott, Lightfoot, and E. W. Benson (also a fine patristic scholar and a future archbishop of Canterbury), fellow pupils at school and fellow students at Cambridge, dedicated themselves with missionary seriousness to the spiritual resuscitation of the English universities and the cathedrals, because (as Benson wrote later), "The conclusion was pressed on us with overwhelming force that there was no effective spiritual power in England able to bring the Faith into living contact with all the forms of human activity and thought" (A. C. Benson, *Life of Edward White Benson*, 2 vols. [London, 1899-1900], pp. 2:690ff.).

practical training for intending missionaries. The decline (happily now showing signs of reversal) in the number of teaching posts in mission partly reflected the decline in the number of missionaries sent by the older church agencies. But the agencies and traditions that seek to maintain missionary numbers naturally put a high value on the practical relevance of study. This is obviously not the place to discuss the proper place of the expatriate missionary in mission (nor even to discuss if and when the Koreans will take over that role). Whatever our view of that question, I do not see that good practice is remotely likely to suffer from the quest for such transforming, mission-related scholarship as is here proposed. But I am quite sure that good people, and financially influential good people, will fear that it may. It is necessary therefore to realize that the world of learning is a mission field too. Quality, depth, and range of scholarship are the marks of a vocation—and a collegial and demanding vocation, needing all the traditional missionary attributes of devotion, perseverance, and sacrifice.

The considerations advanced so far have arisen from the vocation of mission studies and the structural relationship with theology and other parts of the world of learning. What follows relates to structural problems of a lower order (many, indeed, might properly be called problems of infrastructure) that arise from the conditions under which as practitioners, we currently work. They are only a selection and reflect one person's, perhaps jaundiced, experience. They are raised with no order of importance or priority.

Instruments of Study

In view of the parallels offered in this paper with the movements that renewed theological study during the last century, let us turn to the large-scale compendium reference works that support the active student from day to day. The nineteenth century produced (or established the conditions which made possible) outstanding lexical works, grammars, and dictionaries, the great critical texts and large-scale assemblages of central scholarship drawn together in the great Bible encyclopedias. It produced—or led to the production of—the still larger fundamental works used mainly by specialists but used by them constantly: the repertories of inscriptions, the major collected editions, the great dictionaries of scholarship. Even the older established branches of learning produced excellent works of reference; think of the weight of patristic learning still made accessible behind the splitting spines of the four volumes of William Smith's *Dictionary of Christian Biography*[11] or the two of his *Dictionary of Christian Antiquities*.[12]

---

[11] William Smith, *Dictionary of Christian Biography* (London: Murray, 1877).

[12] *Dictionary of Christian Antiquities*, ed. William Smith and S. Cheetham (London: Murray, 1875). Westcott, Lightfoot, and Benson contributed both to this set and to the *Dictionary of Christian Biography*.

The devotion of such scholars as Otto Bardenhewer summarized sources of information and piloted the reader through the multitudes of patristic editions available in a dozen countries.[13] My own countryman James Hastings spent his working life as a theological toolmaker.[14]

I am sure there is no department of theological study in which the scholarly instruments are so few and so primitive as in mission studies. We all value the *Concise Dictionary of the Christian World Mission* of Neill, Anderson, and Goodwin[15]; but it is modest in size and now twenty years old. For a larger scale dictionary of mission (and even that is only of single-volume scope) it is necessary to go back to Dwight, Tupper, and Bliss[16] at the beginning of the century, though it was far from satisfactory even then. And these are only works of general handy reference, not scholars' tools.

There is a further price to pay for this: in the major general theological works of reference, such as *Religion in Geschichte und Gegenwart* (not to mention the smaller but more widely used ones, such as the *Oxford Dictionary of the Christian Church*), the mission studies sphere is inevitably under-represented. This in turn means that Africa and Asia and Latin America and the Pacific and the Caribbean—now major centres of Christianity—are under-represented in works that are meant to cover the entire field of Christian knowledge.

It is a propitious time for toolmaking. A vast amount of primary research has been devoted both to the missionary movement and to Southern Christianity that was not available to such scholars as Latourette (whose bibliographies are still turned to). Much of it is locked away in unpublished theses or little-known journals. Modern methods of data storage and transfer make large-scale cooperative work easier to handle than ever before. Surely a renaissance of mission studies will be marked by some first-rate instrument making.

Resources

This section will be brief, since libraries are the subject of another article. Let me refer only to some of the fundamental structural problems that arise partly from history and partly from geography.

---

[13]Otto Bardenhewer, *Patrologie* (Freiburg-im-Breisgau, 1901 and later editions).

[14]Besides the five-volume *Dictionary of the Bible*, an entirely distinct one-volume dictionary, and the vast *Encyclopaedia of Religion and Ethics* (until quite recently the only attempt in English at a full-scale survey of the phenomenon of religion), Hastings edited other specialist works, including *Dictionary of Christ and the Gospels* and *Dictionary of the Apostolic Church.*

[15]*Concise Dictionary of the Christian World Mission*, ed. Stephen Neill, G. H. Anderson, and J. Goodwin (London: Lutterworth Press 1971).

[16]See *The Encyclopedia of Missions: Descriptive, Historical, Biographical, Statistical*, ed. Edwin Munsell Bliss (New York: Funk & Wagnalls, 1891; 1904).

The first particularly affects those who study the missionary movement, especially in its Protestant aspects. The missionary movement was a transatlantic phenomenon. The influences shaping and sustaining it were the fruit of constant and complex interaction between Europe and America. The consequent fallout of resources (and this applies to library collection as much as to archives) and the development in different countries of distinct traditions of scholarship mean that study of the quality and depth we are considering will need application to resources held partly in North America, partly in Britain, and partly in Continental Europe. I know no single library—not even the Day Missions Library at Yale Divinity School, for which my admiration and gratitude are unbounded—that can be regarded as fully representative, let alone comprehensive in the field. I find myself, in order to do my job as a mission historian, a peripatetic, an academic equivalent of the Flying Dutchman. It will need both transatlantic thinking and a variety of cooperation, both formal and informal, in scholarship and fellowship, to overcome this structural divide. The real hazard comes from the fact that, unless you move on both sides of the dividing line, the built-up traditions mean that it is easy not to notice that the line is there at all.

A second major structural difficulty lies in the location of unpublished documentary sources. Generally speaking, the mission archives are in Europe and North America, in varying degrees of security and accessibility. Again generally speaking, the church archives are in the Southern continents under still more variable conditions. I leave out of consideration here the vital subject of the location and preservation of those records; the fact is that even now more are currently available for scholars than are ever used.

The result of this is that the scholarly task of interpretation can only be carried out by the activity in *both* areas with *both* types of material. Scholars from the Southern continents need access to mission archives; those resident in the North need access to those in the South. Two sets of considerations, one prudential and one ethical, arise. The prudential may be illustrated from an experience of the early 1960s, when I was involved in a project intended to recover materials for Nigerian Christian history. In one area of southeastern Nigeria, we found hundreds upon hundreds of documents registers, baptismal registers, discipline books, documents of every sort, kept by people in varying ways according to the standard of their education, documents in which a missionary hardly ever appeared: documents in which an African church could be observed worshipping and evangelizing and sinning and repenting over a period of fifty, sixty, seventy years. We collected that material in a safe place in reasonably environmentally sound conditions. We were always going to copy it photographically "next year"; photocopying was still a cumbersome matter in those days, and relatively expensive, and next year would do. Then came the Nigerian Civil War. The building took a direct hit and the entire collection was destroyed. What was meant as a gift to posterity became a sign of criminal folly. We had never made the photographic copies.

About the same time, the last expatriate bishop of another African country, transferring his authority to a national successor and not trusting the future, brought the diocesan records with him to Britain. They suffered in an unexpected flood. Hazards to documents are not confined to the Third World.

Ethical considerations arise from the acknowledgment that, in whatever degree of danger we believe materials to be, they belong to their owners. Scholars have no inherent right to any material and must be grateful for what they get. The documents of the Southern churches belong to those churches, whether they are presently being used or not. But, on reflection, do not the mission archives belong to them too? And is not the whole heritage of the church the heritage of the whole church? This is not the place for specific proposals, but in order to deal with these structural difficulties confronting mission studies, certain topics will need examination. One is mobility; much of the work in our field at doctoral level really requires work in more than one continent. This has implications for the way programs are planned, and perhaps for interinstitutional cooperation. Another is the possibility of team study. Yet another is investment in shared resources, using appropriate technology, whether photocopy or microform or electronic storage, so that the same records are accessible both North and South. Not only would this assist security; more importantly, it would undermine the principal contemporary disability of the Third World—colonialism of information.

Dr. Peterson deals with the substantive issues in this field, and therefore I will again be content with structural questions. The study of the missionary movements and of the Southern churches has suffered from the fact that the literature produced by both movements did not at the time seem sufficiently "academic" to interest major libraries. The literature from the Southern continents presents libraries with further problems—cataloging nightmares, storage anomalies, uncertain availability, "gray" material in abundance. We need, therefore, to give serious curatorial attention to what appears to be literary detritus. Researchers raised on the codex and the archival letter book will need to learn a new set of habits.

In many countries there is now a flourishing Christian literature that is not systematically collected even within those countries. Again the fine lines between trusteeship and colonialism will need consideration, but there are major collecting tasks ahead.

I will deliberatively eschew comment on mission studies bibliography to avoid saying too much. It is an area where international cooperation is being actively developed, not least under the aegis of the International Association for Mission Studies. Let me suggest only that the really urgent needs of the moment lie less in bibliography than in accessibility. We could face the possibility of drowning in information about items that cannot be obtained. Meanwhile a letter from a professor in Zaire includes a heartcry for a handful of items that would be in any Western library with the most modest pretensions to mission studies. The most important cooperative schemes for sharing information will probably relate also to sharing supplies.

Faculty and Students

For purposes of this chapter we are concerned with mission studies scholarship rather than with missionary training. When we think of the scholars and teachers who will be needed in the renaissance, we face a change from the situation that produced the great pioneers of missiology. Most of them (even then there were exceptions, including Gustav Warneck himself) had substantial missionary service, had learned a language at some depth, had acquired some inner knowledge of another culture. To a greater or lesser extent, similar considerations applied down to quite recent times; those involved in mission studies had a fair degree of active cross-cultural experience and had been in some way part, and a working part, of a church elsewhere than in their homeland. But now such experience is less readily available, and a new generation of mission scholars is arising with all the necessary skills and equipment but without the opportunity of overseas service. Perhaps one of the structural questions to be addressed in the renaissance of mission studies will be the development of means whereby those involved in teaching can gain the "immersion experience" denied them by their birth date.

Another set of structural problems affects students. Experience suggests that many who come to the West for advanced theological study are poorly served. They are taken into institutions where no one in the faculty has the knowledge or experience or the acquaintance with the relevant literature to link their course of study with the situation that concerns them. Respectable and respected biblical scholars or dogmaticians assume that the task can be done with a chapter at the end of the dissertation "relating the topic to Africa." Strong-minded students sometimes meet frustration in the face of conventional selection or formulation of topics. Other students are victims of what might be called the "Pity poor Africa" syndrome, which allows weak and unformed work to pass in order to "serve the Third World"—when better knowledge and guidance could have produced infinitely better performance and could have served the "Third World" infinitely better. Meanwhile, most of the institutions geared to the reception of such candidates and best able to help them, are aware of promising applicants held up by lack of funds.

These problems are interwoven into the deeper structure of theology that we have considered. There can be no final solution until those are overcome; but in the interim it may be worth considering ways to ameliorate the situation.

In the last three decades literally hundreds of Africans and Asians have qualified at doctoral or equivalent level in Western theological institutions.

Many of them did work of high quality in the process, and not a few contributed substantially to knowledge by their research. The expectation was that these would be the standard-bearers of the theological scholarship of the Southern continents. Clearly there are among them those who are standard-bearers in any company, who exercise an impact throughout the world. But equally clearly, the impact on scholarship of this corps of highly qualified people, taken as a whole, does not seem commensurate with their talents or training. Leave out of account those who have stayed in the West and those who are no longer teaching; there are still many serving in the universities, colleges, and seminaries of the Southern continents. But the rule of the palefaces over the academic world is untroubled. The expected publications do not materialize; or they have little international effect. And this seems to hold even in studies specifically directed to regional questions.

There are a variety of structural reasons for this. Teaching loads are often crushingly heavy. Persons of ability soon become burdened with a range of responsibilities for the institution, the church, the state. They will undoubtedly be subject to endless demands on time and energy from family and community. Ecumenical representative responsibilities may simply add to the consumption of time.

Economic and resource questions are still more desolating. The heady days when the Theological Education Fund aimed to spread first-class libraries throughout the Southern continents seem far distant. The reality for many African institutions now is a famine of important books, scrambles of students for copies of texts, books with missing sections, libraries that cannot begin to touch the cost of modern printed books, journal runs that terminated years ago when the national currency regulations changed. In all these difficulties, the wonder is, not that so little, but that so much research and publication is done in Africa. But even so African scholars do not have the weight that their number and ability indicate. The local journals may proliferate; in the international journals (even in the specifically African field) Africa is still underrepresented.

If Africa—and to varying extents the same applies to other parts of the Southern continents also—is to fill its proper place in mission studies, African scholars will need the time and the resources to renew their scholarship. Many a Western institution could be enriched by an African sabbatical visitor—not headhunted as a faculty acquisition and not burdened with heavy teaching, but welcomed as a colleague with a contribution to make and a scholarly task to pursue. The biggest single obstacle is financial. In many cases, national currency regulations prevent money being taken out of the country. Some investment in sabbatical schemes (sometimes, perhaps, on an institution-to-institution basis) could have multiple effects: in cross-fertilization, in cooperation, in collegiality (perhaps sometimes expressed in writing and publishing together), in raising sights and broadening vision, in deepening scholarship, and in enabling scholars from the Southern world to contribute internationally. It could be argued that the nurture and refreshment of scholars and teachers who are already at work is even more urgent than the quest for others.

Toward the Renaissance of Mission Studies

I am convinced that we stand at the threshold of an explosion of demand for mission studies (by whatever name) as the implications of the situation of the Christian faith in the world begin to dawn. It is the quality of the response that matters. It will need a depth and range of scholarship, and of library and resources provision, that do not at present exist. And it will need activity that is international, integrative, and cooperative.

It must be *international*, because the gifts of the church belong to the whole church. And as students of mission worldwide our histories are interdependent, our materials and our methods cross-cultural. We are all—Northern continents and Southern, American and European—dependent on one another. Each has resources, knowledge, skills, insights that the other needs.

In the Northern continents we have great mission archives; but it was the South that brought them into being. In the Southern continents we have vast quantities of material falling daily prey to time and termite, affording a view of the Christian story that often strikingly differs from that reflected in the mission archives. We have mountains of literature, daily increasing, that reflect the contemporary life of the Southern churches and that the great libraries pass over; and in the South there reside crucial representatives of a living (but also departing) oral tradition.

That is to say, neither in the North nor in the South can researchers be self-sufficient. Northern researchers need the resources located in the South; Southern researchers need the resources located in the North.

In the North we have many scholars who would benefit from the experience of living in a non-Western community. In the South there are scholars who never make the scholarly impact they should because the conditions of their ordinary work prevent it.

In the North we have a confident, if rather tired, tradition of theology, bearing the fossil marks of Western history and culture plainly upon it. We then sell this to students from the Southern continents as though the fossil marks were not there. In the South, processes are going on that require the redrawing of the whole theological map. These two traditions are both alike necessary for a universal church; but the people who might mediate between them—those from the South who have been theologically trained in the North—are sometimes incapacitated by their very training from doing so.

A possible test for the efficacy of the international aspect of the renaissance is the presence or absence of the principle of reciprocity.

But the renaissance must also be *integrative*. Mission studies do not exist in themselves; they cannot be separated from the other academic disciplines. They are potentially subversive because they are concerned with what happens elsewhere in the curriculum. Old texts may often be illuminated from the experience of Christian encounter today. The responses to Christianity amid the old religions of Europe that we meet in Patrick or Bede or Gregory of Tours are worth taking side by side with the Christian interaction with the primal religions of Africa. Biblical studies could receive an infusion of new research tasks; and only through mission studies are Western biblical scholars and theologians likely to learn of the work done in their own fields by their African, Asian, and Latin American colleagues.

This further underlines the point made earlier, that the resources of which workers in mission studies are trustees are the equivalent of the archeological and literary discoveries of the last century, of the Greek texts of the Renaissance. They have the same potential to redirect theological methods and perspectives. But it will be necessary also to build and sustain skills outside the sphere both of mission studies and theology as strictly interpreted. The study of the phenomenology and history of religion has been strangely neglected among us; this applies to the study of the primal religions in particular, despite their being historically the basis on which most large movements to the Christian faith have taken place. All the sciences dealing with language, history, and culture will occupy mission studies in the renaissance. Our duty to theology cannot be carried out with the resources of theology alone.

Finally, the response must be *cooperative*. It will demand teamwork, for none of us is self-sufficient. Such studies as we have envisaged here could produce a series of bilateral and plurilateral links, person to person, institution to institution, both within North America and intercontinentally. All this requires trust; the best arrangements are usually those between people who already trust one another and want to work together. But the aim will be to raise the quality, the range, and the depth of our scholarly work; the rigour and comprehensiveness of its method, its fidelity to sources, its attention to detail, its vision and insight, its sense of holy vocation. In the providence of God a renaissance of mission studies could be the prelude to the reordering of theology and the refreshment of the human and social sciences.

12

Missionary Vocation and the Ministry[1]
The First Generation

The modern missionary movement was a child of the Evangelical Revival, but it was a late child. In Britain half a century separated the period when John Wesley's heart was strangely warmed and the Countess of Huntingdon began to let Whitefield loose in fashionable drawing rooms, from the period when people met in conclave to consider, as a practical proposition, the evangelization of the world. They then estimated the world's population at 731 millions; and Protestant Christians were, for practical purposes, confined to western Europe and the North American eastern seaboard. They had no assembled missionary tradition, no gathered experience, little knowledge of the practical problems to be faced. The only reason they had to expect success was in the biblical prophecies: their conviction that in due time the earth would be full of the knowledge of God as the waters cover the sea.[2] It is hardly surprising that there was no rush to be in the first generation of missionaries, and a matter of interest to see where the founders of societies expected, and where they found, the personnel for the tasks which possessed them.[3]

In his *Enquiry*, an extraordinarily influential work for one published in the provinces by a man of only parochial reputation, William Carey assumes that the man who has accepted the call to the Christian ministry must be ready to receive it to the mission field also:

---

[1]First published in M. E. Glasswell and E. W. Fasholé-Luke, eds., *New Testament Christianity for Africa and the World: Essays in Honour of Harry Sawyerr* (London: SPCK, 1974), pp. 141-46.

[2]For the importance of prophecies, cf. J. A. de Jong, *As the Waters Cover the Sea: Millennial Expectations in the Rise of Anglo-American Missions 1640-1810* (Kampen, 1970).

[3]On the background of nineteenth-century missionaries, and helpful reflection thereon, see M. A. C. Warren, *Social History and Christian Mission* (London 1967), esp. chapt. 2.

And this would only be passing through what we have virtually engaged in by entering the ministerial office. A Christian minister is a person who in a peculiar sense is *not his own*; he is the *servant* of God. . . . He engages to go where God pleases, and to do, or endure what he sees fit to command, or call him to in the exercise of his function. He virtually bids farewell to friends, pleasures, and comforts. . . . It is inconsistent for ministers to please themselves with thoughts of a numerous auditory, cordial friends, a civilized country, level protection, affluence, splendour, or even a competency. . . . I question whether all are justified in staying here, while so many are perishing without means of grace in other lands.[4]

And he is ready to prove his point: for when, as a result of his influence, a missionary society is founded, he is ready to go as one of its first agents.

Carey was, of course, by any reckoning a remarkable man; yet he represents a type bred among the English Dissenters and the Scots seceders: independent, hard-working, developing their own tradition of learning. Many such ministers had practised trades or crafts before their call, and some might, as Carey had for some time done with his cobbling,[5] continue with them thereafter. There was certainly nothing incongruous in itself in a shoemaker becoming a missionary: this was the way men came into the home ministry.

People with this tradition did not have such a complicated view of missionary service as those ministers of the English and Scottish establishments who wanted to encourage missions. These took for granted, as Carey had done, that a missionary was essentially a preacher, and that a preacher should normally be a minister. But for them the minister was the representative of the established Church in society, and as such entitled to a measure of respect. This in turn implied a degree of education and social accomplishment which would not disgrace it.

Among early writers on missions with this background, it is remarkable to find that few seem to *expect* much response from ordained and beneficed clergymen as missionary recruits. Melvill Horne says in so many words that he does not expect it—though he immediately apologizes lest he has been too harsh on his own Church.[6] No, it is clearly too much to expect that a man who has a benefice, and the security which it provides—and which may have taken quite a bit of getting—will give it up for the hardships of Sierra Leone or Tahiti. Horne does not say so, but perhaps it was also expecting much of hopeful unbeneficed clergy that they should give up

---

[4]William Carey, *Enquiry into the Obligations of Christians to use Means for the Conversion of the Heathens* . . . (Leicester, 1792), pp. 71ff.

[5]"Not even shoemaker, sir: just a cobbler," said Carey to a sneering army officer. S. Pearce Carey, *William Carey D.D.* (London, 1923), pp. 34f.

[6]Melvill Horne, *Letters on Missions Addressed to the Protestant Ministers of the British Churches* (Bristol, 1794), chapt. 1.

their place in the queue, and lose, probably forever, that benefice which to the forty pounds a year curate must have seemed the best blessing of earthly existence. Jane Austen, always a most accurate observer of these things, puts the point well in the dénouement of *Mansfield Park*. Mary Crawford, surprised and abashed at Edmund Bertram's profound seriousness, says to him: "A pretty good lecture upon my word. Was it part of your last sermon? At this rate you will soon reform everybody at Mansfield and Thornton Lacey; and when I hear of you next, it may be as a celebrated preacher in some great society of Methodists, or as a missionary into foreign parts."[7] Edmund was a beneficed clergyman; and at the time (1811-13) that *Mansfield Park* was written, no former holder of an English benefice was, in the proper sense of the term, "a missionary into foreign parts."

A similar conviction is implied in a sermon by Thomas Haweis, one of the few prominent Anglicans to support the London Missionary Society, preached at the Society's inauguration in 1795.

> *Whom shall we send, and who will go for us?* I answer, such as the Lord hath prepared and qualified for the arduous task. Men, whose lives are not dear unto themselves, but ready to spend and be spent in the honourable service. Men, really moved by the Holy Ghost to devote themselves to the work. . . . Men, who have an internal evidence of the Spirit, *witnessing, with their spirits, that they are the children of God;*—a divine ardour, prompting them to prefer the salvation of men's souls to every earthly consideration. . . . Such are the men the great Shepherd and Bishop of Souls sends, such are the instruments we must seek.[8]

But where are such people to be found? Haweis has a quite explicit answer:

> Nor need we despair of finding them, if not in the schools of learning, or the seminaries of theology, yet among the faithful, in our several congregations.[9]

Haweis, that is, not only expects no recruits for the mission field from the home ministry: he does not expect that the ordinary sources of supply of the home ministry will produce recruits either.

> Not that the knowledge of the dead languages, however desirable, is essential to the communication of Gospel truth in the living ones. A plain man—with a good natural understanding—well read in the

---

[7] Jane Austen, *Mansfield Park*, vol. 3, chapt. 16 of the original edition; *Oxford Illustrated Jane Austen*, p. 458.

[8] A large section of the sermon, with many other addresses and documents associated with the birth of the LMS is printed in R. Lovett, *The History of the London Missionary Society 1795-1895* (London, 1899), 1, pp. 26ff.

[9] *Ibid.*, p. 27.

Bible,—full of faith, and of the Holy Ghost,—though he comes from the forge or the shop, would, I own, in my view, as a missionary to the heathen, be infinitely preferable to all the learning of the schools; and would possess, in the skill and labour of his hands, advantages which barren science would never compensate.[10]

The missionary needs spiritual qualifications, a knowledge of the Bible, and common sense. Competence with a mallet or a saw is all to the good, but formal education is not necessary—which is as well, for educated people are most unlikely to offer.

For many people who heard that sermon, this presented no difficulty: some outstanding Dissenting ministers did come from the forge or the shop, and had acquired much skill in dead languages as well. But Haweis was an Anglican, and knew quite well that no bishop was likely to ordain a man from the shop or the forge just because he knew his Bible. Haweis can answer this argument only with the big stick; unless the bishop (or presbytery) is born again, he cannot tell who is and who is not fit to be a missionary:

I am, my brethren, an Episcopalian, and by choice, as by education, attached to the Established Church, and wish to see a glory in the earth. . . . Yet I am no bigot. I neither suppose salvation restricted to her pale, nor the approbation of her rulers, however desirable, essential to an evangelical mission. Indeed it is an axiom, to which every real Christian will accede, that no dignity of office, whether Bishop or Archbishop, nor a whole Presbytery, however wise or learned, if they have not themselves experienced the divine call, and been inwardly moved by the Holy Ghost, to take the sacred ministry upon them. . . . such men, I say, can be no more capable of judging the qualifications of a missionary, than the stupid Omiah to solve the most difficult proposition in Euclid, or a deaf man to decide on the beauty of harmonical composition.[11]

This being so, missionaries will be chosen by

such as have themselves been taught of God; and whose age and experience, in the good ways of our Saviour, enable them to discern between the ebullitions of mistaken zeal and the deliberate devotedness of one truly sent and moved by the Holy Ghost.[12]

—in other words, by such people as shall form the London Missionary Society's committee. Haweis was a survivor of an older type of Anglican Evangelical who cared little for ecclesiastical regularity, and had many brushes with authority. For him, therefore, if the bishops were so obtuse as

---

[10] *Ibid.*, p. 28.
[11] *Ibid.*, pp. 28f.
[12] *Ibid.*, p. 28.

not to see where the interests of the gospel lay this was a pity, but neither
the missionary society nor its missionaries were any the worse for lacking
episcopal countenance.[13] But the newer generation of Evangelicals, that
typified by Simeon, could not so readily divorce the interests of the gospel
from the discipline of the Church.

It was such men who formed the society which became known as the
Church Missionary Society. For their purpose the preexisting Society for
the Propagation of the Gospel, the quasi-official organ of the Church of
England overseas, even if it were to undertake more obviously missionary
work (as indeed it had done at various times in its history) was inappropriate, for it was not committed to the gospel as the Evangelicals understood
it; and the ostensibly non-denominational London Missionary Society was
inappropriate since it was not committed to the Church as Anglicans
understood it.[14]

But the Church as Anglicans understood it had an episcopally ordained
ministry: it follows that an Anglican missionary society might be expected
to have episcopally ordained missionaries. If, however, such are not forth-
coming—and, as we have seen, there seems to have been little expectation
that they would be—and if those who do offer for service are not of the
social class and type of education normally expected of the clergy, would
it be right, even if it were possible, to seek regular ordination for them? To
those who argued that social refinements were unnecessary on the mission
field, others were quick to reply that once a man was ordained he was an
English clergyman for life; and if a vulgar man were ordained for missionary service, what would prevent his coming back and taking a benefice for
which he might be socially unfitted? Might not adventurers and social
climbers offer for missionary service simply as a short cut to higher status?

These questions are solemnly discussed in a memorandum drafted by
John Venn shortly before the foundation of the CMS:

> It is obvious that the Church of England can allow no persons to
> officiate in any respect as Ministers who have not been *episcopally
> ordained*. Episcopal ordination, bearing respect to the present im-
> proved state of society in this island, is justly conferred upon those
> only, whose education and learning qualify them for the rank the
> English clergy hold in society. It is evident, however, that a mission-

---

[13]Haweis had planned a Tahiti mission as early as 1789, employing two students
from the Countess of Huntingdon's Connexion; and he tried (at their insistence) but
in vain to secure for them episcopal ordination. See A. Skevington Wood, *Thomas
Haweis 1734-1820* (London, 1957), pp. 170ff., 177ff.

[14]On the origins of the CMS see Charles Hole, *The Early History of the Church
Missionary Society for Africa and the East to the End of A.D. 1814* (London, 1896) and
Eugene Stock, *History of the Church Missionary Society 1* (London, 1899), pp. 58ff.
Hole's book is often virtually a calendar of the documentary sources.

ary, dwelling among savages rude and illiterate, does not require the same kind of talents, manners or learning as are necessary in an officiating minister in England. But ordination admits not of distinctions correspondent to the degree of refinement in society. He who is once episcopally ordained, though with the sole view of acting as a missionary to the heathen, would possess the power of officiating, and holding any benefice to which he might be presented, in the English Church. This circumstance necessarily requires extreme caution in ordaining persons for the purposes of missions only. For what security can be afforded, that a person of inferior station, offering himself upon this ground for orders, is not influenced by a desire of a more elevated rank in society or of a life of greater ease, rather than by a pure zeal for the salvation of the heathen?[15]

Venn's answer is to suggest that a lower order of unordained missionary be created, with the title of catechist. Conscious of the breach with normal Anglican order, he enters on an excursus on early Church history to prove that there were catechists in the primitive Church who acted as evangelists, apologists, and instructors of converts—the very duties expected of missionaries. In the early Church too, the office of catechist was regarded as probationary for higher orders. Therefore, if a catechist should serve worthily on the mission field, there was excellent precedent for his eventual ordination.

The office of catechist was patently designed to permit the employment of unordained men in a missionary capacity by an Anglican society; and it was deemed necessary because at its commencement there was no real expectation of ordained or ordainable men coming forward in sufficient numbers. Even so, there was such strenuous opposition among the firmest supporters of the Society to so irregular an expedient that it was quietly abandoned.[16]

In the discussions which led to the formation of the Society it had been Simeon himself, that pillar of church order, who had said, apropos of missionary enterprise, "*When shall we do it?* Directly, not a moment to be lost. . . . *How shall we do it?* It is hopeless to wait for Missionaries. Send out catechists."[17] The abandonment of the catechist scheme seemed to bear out the truth of his words. It did appear hopeless to wait for missionaries. The Committee wrote to Evangelical incumbents all round the country, but none could produce any candidates. In Cambridge, Simeon put the question before his pious undergraduates, and was saddened to find not one responded.[18]

---

[15]Venn's memorandum is printed as an appendix to M. Hennell, *John Venn and the Clapham Sect* (London, 1958), pp. 280-84.

[16]Hennell, *John Venn*, pp. 243f.

[17]W. Carus, *Memoirs of the Life of the Rev. Charles Simeon M.A.* (London and Cambridge, 1847), p. 169.

[18]Hole, *Early History*, pp. 56ff., 61f.

The CMS was thus reduced for several years to the invidious position of issuing reports with nothing to report, and holding meetings about what they hoped to do in the future. No doubt, they could have made a start had they been able to send out men of the same sort of background as most of the early missionaries of the Baptist, London, and Scottish societies; but the insistence that none such should be sent except as, or at least in the company of, ordained men, effectively foreclosed any such possibility.

Meanwhile, the London Missionary Society had made its start with candidates recruited on the principles laid down by Haweis. A small operation was mounted in Sierra Leone, but the main thrust was to the Pacific islands and in 1796 a party of thirty missionaries, plus wives and children, set out.[19] Four of them were Dissenting ministers. The others included six carpenters, two weavers, two tailors, two bricklayers, two shoemakers, a harness-maker, a gardener, a cooper, a hatter, a shopkeeper, a gentleman's servant, a blacksmith, a surgeon (at that time, of course, an occupation mainly concerned with sawing off damaged limbs, and still associated with the barbers), a cotton worker, a linen draper, and a cabinet maker.[20] There were also six wives and three children. All had been examined by the LMS Committee. They were to live as a church and family, preach, maintain the mission, and teach European trades (which it was assumed the islanders were anxious to learn).

The first casualty was at Portsmouth; one of the wives was so seasick as to be unable to face another 27,000 miles of it, and her husband left too. The rest of the party made a quick passage, and distributed themselves between Tahiti, Tonga, and the Marquesas Islands. One refused to go ashore; two others left next time the boat came. At the first sign of violence erupting, eleven others left, and the thirty were reduced to fifteen, the wives to one. Three of the men were murdered in eruptions of violence, and four went back after a few years of service. Three married local women and settled down, two of them giving up all profession of Christianity.

Here were thirty people who apparently met the qualifications laid down by Haweis, yet only a handful were left after five years. The rest had collapsed under the strains, physical, mental, moral, spiritual, which a mission imposed. One of the many questions which this created for the promoters of missions must have been whether Haweis was right to say that education was irrelevant to missionary service. In the first place, there was a language to be learned, and only two of the Tahiti party ever mastered the island tongue as missionaries. Again, less obviously, there was what today we call culture shock; the experience of living in a society whose manners, customs, and values are quite different from one's own. Some of

---

[19]The story is told with frankness by Lovett, *London Missionary Society*, chapt. 3.
[20]The party are listed in J. Sibree, *London Missionary Society: A Register of Missionaries, Deputations etc. from 1796 to 1923*, Nos. 1-30; cf. Lovett, *London Missionary Society*, p. 127 for their trades.

the missionaries seem to have been incapable of the major intellectual effort required to grapple with this and work out its implications for their own life in that society, and conceivably their defective education and narrow experience—for some were very young—may have been partly to blame.

But having said all this, when one looks at the core of the party who remained, the generalizations collapse. The outstanding figure among them is Henry Nott. He became leader among them by sheer decision of character; he acquired the greatest mastery of the language, was the first to preach in the vernacular, and worked solidly for twenty-seven years at the translation of the Bible without leaving the island (save for a few months in Australia to get married), learning Hebrew and Greek to make himself a better translator. After twenty-seven years, and not before, he returned to Britain to see the Bible through the press; having done this, he returned to Tahiti, and worked there, with one sole break, till his death in 1844, a period of nearly fifty years in all. Yet Nott was a bricklayer by trade, had little formal education, and when the party sailed he was only twenty-two years of age.[21]

This is important because it shows that in a sense Haweis was right: some plain men with no obvious acquisitions but the Bible and common sense, were among the best missionaries. Apart from their personal qualities, their other skills were valuable: they were much more use at building churches and houses and schools than many a vicar from Eton and Cambridge would have been. And their background was an advantage in other ways. People like Nott, who were labourers or craftsmen, were not used to comfort at home; they never missed things which it might have been a privation to the beneficed clergymen to surrender.

Men of this type provided the staple missionary product in both England and Scotland for more than half a century. The Scottish establishment was not more accommodating than the English. From the famous 1796 Assembly debate, which by a masterpiece of minuting managed both to approve missions in principle and to prevent anything being done about them in practice,[22] until 1824, when the Assembly instituted its own mission, Scottish candidates could reach the field only through the Scottish Missionary Society,[23] or through English-based agencies such as the LMS. A goodly number did so; but a wholly disproportionate number of these came from the Secession churches, especially that of the Burgher Synod, and from the Scottish Congregational churches. Rather typical (in their

---

[21]See Sibree, No. 23; Lovett, *London Missionary Society*, pp. 117-305.

[22]*The Principal Acts of the General Assembly of the Church of Scotland* convened at Edinburgh, the 19th day of May 1796, Edinburgh 1796, sub 27 May.

[23]Originally separate societies were set up in various parts of Scotland; the Edinburgh and Glasgow societies both contributed men with the LMS to a Sierra Leone party in 1797. Later the Edinburgh society took the name Scottish Missionary Society.

background, not their careers) were the first four candidates of the Edinburgh and Glasgow societies, who all went to Sierra Leone:[24] a student from
the Burgher Divinity Hall, Henry Brinton of Selkirk; a Glasgow tailor,
Robert Henderson, who gave up being a missionary to become an atheist
lecturer;[25] a Clyesdale weaver, Duncan Campbell, who found a berth in the
Slave Trade in the Sierra Leone hinterland; and a gardener from Inverkeith-
ing, Peter Greig, who was murdered for his possessions.[26] In the course of
1802, the CMS did receive an application which could have transformed
the conception of the missionary: Henry Martyn, Fellow of St. John's
College, Cambridge, and Senior Wrangler the previous year, had become
convinced of his vocation, and the Committee rejoiced. But it was not to be.
The family fortunes collapsed and Martyn was left as the only support of
his family. He could no longer go as a missionary: he could not afford it.
Some years later, indeed, he was to reach India, and his brief life has become
one of the best known and most moving stories in modern missionary
hagiography. Yet technically he was never a missionary; he was a chaplain
of the Honourable East India Company, receiving a substantial official
stipend.[27] Some remarkable men, both before and after Martyn, with the
same missionary heart and outlook, served as chaplains to the British
monopoly company, and one of them, Claudius Buchanan, probably did
more than anyone else to arouse active and widespread public interest in
missions in India;[28] but they were not regarded as missionaries by their
employers, and they did not come through the missionary societies.

While Martyn was making his first application to CMS, the Society was
gaining its first regular recruits. Help had come from an unexpected
source.[29]

Through the German church in London, the Society made contact with
the Missionary Seminary in Berlin. The forces which had produced the

---

[24]Cf. William Brown, *History of the Propagation of Christianity among the Heathen*
(Edinburgh and London, 1854), II, pp. 415-56. Brown (a minister of the Burgher
Synod who was unable on health grounds to go to the mission field) was Secretary
of the Scottish Missionary Society.

[25]But he considerately repaid to the Society the money spent on his training—W.
L. Mathieson, *Church and Reform in Scotland* (Glasgow, 1916), p. 81.

[26]Greig's brief service has produced a brief biography. See George Smith, *Twelve
Pioneer Missionaries* (London, 1900), pp. 122-36.

[27]On Martyn's application see Hole, *Early History*, pp. 86f., 91, 93, which points
out that a formal candidature, as distinct from notice given, was hardly in question
in 1802; Martyn was still under age for priest's orders, and was not ordained deacon
until October 1803. Before this date the committee had already decided he would
be wasted in West Africa.

[28]Especially with his *Memoirs of the Expediency of an Ecclesiastical Establishment for
British India . . .* (London, 1805). (See the new edition with introduction by A. K.
Davidson, which indicates the effect of the *Memoir and Christian Researches in Asia
with Notices of the Translation of the Scriptures into the Oriental Languages* (Cambridge
and London, 1811).

[29]On what follows see Hole, *Early History*, pp. 84f., 114f.; Stock 1, pp. 82ff.

missionary societies in the English-speaking world were at work on the Continent also, where seminaries and systems of training for missionaries developed. What the Continental promoters of missions lacked was any means of stationing missionaries when trained. So an arrangement was concluded between the institution with the men but no means and the society with the means but no men, and the long period of co-operation between the Society and European agencies began. Should anyone cavil, the CMS could point to a long history of mutual recognition of the Church of England and Continental Protestant churches, especially Lutheran churches, and to the long-standing use by the impeccably Anglican Society for Promoting Christian Knowledge of Lutheran ministers, Danish and German, as its agents in India. There was even the understanding that (since there was no bishop nearer than London) the ordination of native ministers might be performed by Lutheran missionaries according to the Lutheran rite. And the practical problems which had bedevilled CMS recruitment from the beginning were settled at a stroke. There was no need now to labour along a tortuous and uncertain path to seek ordination for "plain men" with Evangelical principles unacceptable to most bishops; the missionaries could receive Lutheran ordination in Germany. There was no longer a need to rack the consciences of the sticklers for Church discipline on the Committee by expedients about catechists. And there was no longer a fear of an unsuitable person coming back from the mission field and aspiring to an English benefice. The advantages of accepting ordained Lutheran missionaries as though they were Anglicans were manifold.

The first two students from Berlin were accepted in 1802. They stayed in England for further study of theology, English (the first meeting with the Committee had been hampered by the fact that the candidates knew no English and the Committee no German), and Susu. They went back to Germany for Lutheran ordination and arrived in Sierra Leone in 1804, thus enabling the Society to get its first missionaries on to the field some five years after its institution.

The relationship—first with Berlin, then with Basel and St. Christhona and to a lesser extent with other continental bodies—was not always easy, and there were many abrasions.[30] But the German contribution to missionary operations was crucial. Of the twenty-four missionaries sent out by CMS in the period up to the end of 1815, no less than seventeen were Germans, and only three were ordained Englishmen.[31] If we take the earliest and most dangerous field, West Africa, in the same period, the total

---

[30]Cf. J. Pinnington, "Church Principles in the Early Years of the Church Missionary Society: The Problem of the 'German' Missionaries," *Journal of Theological Studies* NS 20 (2) (1969), pp. 523-32. Not all the students were Lutherans: some were Reformed. The Basel seminary was non-denominational.

[31]*Register of Missionaries (Clerical, Lay, and Female) and Native Clergy* (CMS, 1896 and 1905), Nos. 1-24.

is even more striking: all appointments except for one schoolmaster were Germans.[32] After 1815 the balance changes. That year saw the departure of the first two CMS missionaries to receive Anglican orders, both having been ordained on the title of English curacies,[33] and also of the first English university graduate, like Martyn an ordained Fellow of St. John's College, Cambridge.[34] The following year saw two more English clergymen setting out for India via English curacies;[35] and the only Germans who went out that year were recruited in London and not through the seminaries.[36] Next year, 1817, saw fourteen recruits getting out, much the largest number in any year so far; and seven were English clergymen and only four Germans.[37] From this point onwards the Germans, though they provide some of the most illustrious names, are only a supplementary source of recruitment, and it gradually became normal for missionaries from the Continental seminaries to receive Anglican ordination. But Lutheran ordination, which came to be a stumbling-block on the path of good relations between CMS and its Continental associates,[38] was in the early years a mighty convenience. As had been foreseen, it enabled the ordination of suitable

---

[32]*Register*, loc. cit. The first CMS missionaries, Renner and Hartwig, went first to Sierra Leone (the name then strictly applied only to Freetown and its immediate environs), but with explicit instructions to work in the hinterland. Until 1816 the centre of operations was in the Rio Pongas area, addressed to Susu-speaking peoples, with an entirely German staff, but there were occasional appointments to other places, such as the Isles de Los and even, during its British occupation, Gorée. Later attention was diverted to the new recaptive population in Freetown and the villages of the peninsula, and the Rio Pongas mission was gradually wound down, its staff transferred to Sierra Leone. Several English schoolmasters went to Sierra Leone, but no ordained English missionary before 1824.

[33]William Greenwood had been ordained deacon in 1813, and served eighteen months as curate at Knutsford; Thomas Norton was ordained deacon in 1813 and priest in 1814, and served a curacy in York. Both had previously offered for missionary service, and studied for some years under Thomas Scott, the commentator, who was in charge of CMS training. Both went to India (*Register*, Nos. 21 and 22).

[34]William Jowett (*Register*, No. 24) was Twelfth Wrangler in 1810. He was a missionary of the Society in Malta and later became Clerical Secretary of CMS.

[35]Benjamin Bailey and Thomas Dawson had served Yorkshire curacies, but for much shorter periods than their predecessors (*Register*, Nos. 29 and 30).

[36]Henry Düring and the celebrated W. A. B. Johnson were both Hanoverians who, like many of their compatriots, had sought work in the other dominions of the Hanoverian crown. Johnson underwent an evangelical conversion in London and was in attendance at Surrey Chapel when he offered as a schoolmaster (W. Jowett, *Memoir of the Rev. W.A.B. Johnson* [London, 1862]). Christopher Jost, who went out at the same time as Johnson and Düring, and like them as a schoolmaster, was a member of the Savoy church in London, whose minister, Dr. Steinkopf, had been the original link between the CMS and the Berlin Seminary.

[37]*Register*, Nos. 31-44. One of the English clergymen was sent to Malta, the rest to Ceylon or India. One German in Lutheran orders and two English lay schoolmasters went to Sierra Leone, the other Germans and one schoolmaster to India.

[38]Cf. Pinnington, "Church Principles." Many of the Lutherans, not unnaturally, objected to a second ordination.

local candidates as early as 1820.[39] It was also possible for lay missionaries, such as W. A. B. Johnson and Henry Düring, who had been discharging the pastoral office with great effectiveness, to be ordained on the field without the long journey to Britain and the uncertainties of appeal to bishops.[40]

We have already noticed a change in the CMS recruitment pattern after 1815. This is not the place to consider the reasons, save to say that these have nothing to do with any sudden attractiveness of the mission field to the younger sons of country gentlemen, but may have something to do with the Society's new method of organization which must have made many people in the parishes feel for the first time that the missionary cause was something to do with them,[41] and certainly something to do with a newly acquired accessibility to the episcopate.[42] But it is worth noticing that the period of improved recruitment from Britain takes place just at the point when missionary service is becoming notably dangerous: at the point when CMS has concentrated its African operations in the Sierra Leone Colony, and there is a fair presumption that anyone who goes to Sierra Leone will die there or be broken for life.[43] As at later times in the history of the missionary movement, it appears that, whatever factors adversely affect recruitment, the presence of physical danger does not necessarily do so.

But the typical missionary long remained, as he had been in the first generation, a man of humble background and modest attainments. Besides a sprinkling of men who might have, and in some cases actually did, minister in their own countries, it was the journeymen, artisans, and clerks who came to the mission field from England. From Scotland the missionaries came (much more frequently than in England) from the farm or the croft, like James Henderson, or from the factory, like Livingstone, or from

---

[39]The celebrated Muslim convert Abdul Massih had worked as a CMS catechist, and William Bowley (see *Register*, No. 68), a Eurasian, had done excellent work in Indian congregations. Bishop Middleton declined to ordain them on the ground that he had no authority to ordain natives of India. After receiving Lutheran ordination in 1820 they were given Anglican deacons' ordination in 1825.

[40]Johnson and Düring, who had not had seminary training, were given Lutheran orders by their Sierra Leone colleagues in 1817.

[41]Cf. Stock, *History of the Church Missionary Society* 1, pp. 129-43.

[42]The first Evangelical to be consecrated, Henry Ryder, became Bishop of Gloucester in 1815 (translated to Lichfield 1824). He was concerned in the ordination of six out of the seven English clergy who sailed in 1817, and for the first time English curacies were not required as a title to ordination. See G. C. B. Davies, *Henry Ryder, the First Evangelical Bishop* (London, 1958). Apart from Ryder, who was on the CMS Committee, several other bishops were by this time willing to lend the CMS more countenance.

[43]Of the twenty-seven missionaries sent to Sierra Leone before 1820, fifteen had died before the end of that year. In 1822 a total of twelve CMS missionaries (including wives) died in Sierra Leone. P. D. Curtin, "The White Man's Grave: Image and Reality 1780-1850," *Journal of British Studies* 1 (1) (1959), pp. 94ff., and *The Image of Africa* (Madison, Wisc., 1964), chapts. 3 and 5 offers evidence to suggest that many must have been the victims of treatment as much as disease.

the south-bound work-hunting emigrants, like Moffat, who was a gardener on an English estate. The mention of these names is itself a reminder, however, that many men who would not have been considered for ordination at home, in order to reach the mission field, or in order to be more effective there, set themselves to intellectual effort and acquired learning and skills far beyond anything which would have been required of them in their ordinary run of life. The fact that some of them became legends, and the not less important fact that many displayed the ministerial charismata in a high degree, were to have their own effect in the transformation of the ministry.

13

The Western Discovery of
Non-Western Christian Art[1]

Christianity is in principle perhaps the most syncretistic of the great religions. Unlike Hinduism, it does not have a unifocal religious culture belonging to a particular soil; nor, like Islam, does it have common sacred language and a recognizable cultural framework across the globe. Historically, Christian expansion has been serial, moving from one heartland to another, fading in one culture as it is implanted in another. Christian expansion involves the serial, generational, and vernacular penetration of different cultures.

The inbuilt fragility of Christianity and its vernacular nature have particular implications for Christian art, precluding the establishment of a normative Christian art in the sense that there is a normative Islamic art, a Christian civilization in the sense that there is an Islamic civilization. There was nothing distinctive about the earliest Christian art except its subject-matter: it brought no style, form, or technique that was not already employed in pagan Roman art. Christian art needs vernacular expression, a sense of locality. The Word became flesh and spoke Aramaic; presumably with a Galilean accent.

The massive shift in the demographic center of Christianity, most noticeable during the present century, has thus immense implications for the future of Christian art. It is likely that in 1900 over eighty per cent of professed Christians lived in Europe or North America, and that something approaching sixty per cent now live in Africa, Asia, Latin America, or the Pacific.[2] On the evidence of previous Christian history we can now expect

---

[1]First published in Diana Wood, ed., *The Church and the Arts*, Studies in Church History 28 (Oxford: Blackwell, 1992), pp. 571-85.

[2]Extrapolated from figures in D. Barrett, ed., *World Christian Encyclopedia* (Nairobi, 1982), esp. Global Table 2, updated by Barrett, in "Annual Statistical Table on Global Mission, 1988," *International Bulletin of Missionary Research*, 12 (1988), pp. 16-17.

a complete, though probably a gradual and certainly a multilayered, change in the manifestations of Christian art. This paper is therefore mainly concerned with prehistory, and with the early signs of recognition of one of the major implications of the modern missionary movement.

Around 1500, when the Christian West first came into prolonged contact with the cultures of the southern continents, Christianity was geographically more concentrated on Europe than at any time before or since. It could celebrate its triumph throughout the Continent, east and west; in the Christianization of Finland and the Baltic and the ejection of Islam from Iberia. The European triumph coincided with a twilight period elsewhere. Outside Europe, Christianity, once widespread across Asia and northeast Africa, was reduced to small enclaves. By 1500 European Christianity possessed a coherent, largely homogeneous artistic tradition. Art was, generally speaking, Christian art. "Secular" art certainly existed, but in an essentially subordinate role. There was a recognized range of appropriate themes of Christian art, and its iconographic register was settled. The Christianity which entered into engagement with the faiths of Asia and Africa was in confident possession of an artistic expression which had absorbed several vernacular European variations and had nowhere else to go. In Asia it met artistic traditions shaped by other faiths; in Africa artistic traditions that seemed uncouth and barbarous, perhaps childish.

By the middle of the twentieth century, the European adventure was over. The achievement of independence by India in 1947 heralded the addition of dozens of new nations to the roll of nation states as Europe opted for a continental future. Vasco da Gama sailed home. By this time both the religious and the artistic map of Europe had altered beyond recognition. The engagement of Christianity with Africa and Asia had an unforeseen outcome; Africans and Asians proved to have been adhering to Christianity at the very time Europeans were departing from it. And the European art tradition—so coherent, so secure, so Christian in 1500—was now fragmented, hesitant, and overwhelmingly secular in theme and outlook. Even when employing a theme from the Christian repertory, such as crucifixion, it was likely to do so as an illustration of the human condition rather than as a statement about the transcendent. The unity of theme, the common register of symbols, was lost beyond recall. So was European assurance in the face of other art traditions; for a generation past, Europeans had been moved by the power and mystery of African and Pacific art, without being able to adopt its indigenous significance or identify its ritual or cosmological context.

In terms of Christian art, the year 1950 witnessed an event of prophetic significance; the Vatican exhibition of Art in the Missions—which probably is still the most considerable celebration yet held of Christian art of non-Western origin. Its creator was Cardinal Celso Costantini, then Secretary of the Sacred Congregation for the Propagation of the Faith (the *Propaganda Fide*), and already the author of the most substantial comprehensive work yet devoted to the artistic expression of Christianity in the non-Western world.[3] Before he turned to theology, Costantini had begun work as an apprentice mason, bidden to read books on architecture and history of art. As a young priest he had brought artists and priests and others together in a Society of Friends of Christian Art, and he had combined parish and ecclesiastical duties with the directorship of a museum and the care of antiquities. From 1922 to 1933 he was Apostolic Delegate in China; years which, according to his own account, saw two revolutions, that of China itself and that of the missions. Among his contributions to the latter was an insistence that new churches and other Christian buildings reflect Chinese traditions in style and materials; he developed and published a substantial document of guidance on this. Equally significantly, he gathered a group of Chinese artists (none of them at that time Christians) to explore the painting of Gospel themes in Chinese style. Some of the group, notably Luke Ch'en, its most distinguished member, later became Christians.[4]

Costantini desired a renaissance of the arts which he saw emerging from reformation in the missions. The new generation of Asian Christian artists, he believed, presented a fresh vision of creation and of Christian faith, and Westerners, whose own aesthetic tradition was breaking down with fatigue, could turn to them (as to the Renaissance "primitives") with relief.[5] However, it would not be right to think of him as primarily an aesthetic reformer. His own account of his years in China concentrates on his concern for a Chinese episcopate. At his arrival, despite three hundred years of Catholic presence, there was no Chinese among the fifty Catholic bishops in China. His concerns about art and architecture (and also about music and liturgy) were part of a wider concern about the overwhelming foreign aspect of Christianity in China.[6] The neo-Gothic cathedral jarred with Beijing palaces and pagodas; the neo-classical cathedral in Hankow spoke of Europe as much as the synagogue in Rome spoke of the Jews.[7] Modern Christians should follow the practice of the early Church; Confucius and the other Chinese sages provided the same sort of preparation for the Gospel that Greek philosophy did in the Mediterranean world and offered a similar clothing for Christian thought. Instead of viewing local art as a threat to Christian integrity, and affirming Catholicism over against paganism by the consecration of alien styles, it would be well to return to the

---

[3]C. Costantini, *L'Arte Cristiana nelle Missioni* (Rome, 1940); *L'art chréiten dans les missions* (Paris, 1949).

[4]Constantini compiled five volumes of memoirs: *Foglie Secche* (Rome, nd);*Con i Missionari i Cina*, 2 vols (Rome,nd): *Ultime Foglie* (Rome, 1957). A French abridgement of the whole appeared as *Réforme des Missions au XXe siècle* (Paris, 1960). The account of his life before his appointment to China is given in *Réforme*, pp. 13-24.

[5]Costantini, *Réforme*, p. 242.

[6]*Ibid.*, pp. 27ff.

[7]*Ibid.*, p. 239.

principles which Gregory the Great commended to Augustine of Canterbury,[8] and indeed to Propaganda's original principles that missionaries should not transport France, Spain, and Italy with them.[9] The three vital principles are: evangelize, not colonize; respect the art and culture of the country; and remove foreign forms from sacred art.[10]

Costantini's appointment to Propaganda brought these ideas to bear well beyond China. They assisted the development of the theology of adaptation which became the conventional wisdom in Catholic missiology in the period that produced the Second Vatican Council and that made its own contribution to that event. The search for indigenous art forms was extended to other areas. In Nigeria, for instance, an experiment began which has been credited with the rescue, just in time, of traditional Yoruba woodcarving by bringing traditional carvers to work on Christian themes.[11] In India the hierarchy was generally supportive, and the Jesuit Fr. H. Heras took initiatives which led to the development of interest in Christian painting, architecture, and scholarship, using Indian cultural resources.[12]

Behind Costantini's thinking is the idea of art as essentially a *language*. It is in a sense value free, neither "pagan" nor Christian; it can be equally the vehicle for the expression of sentiment, prayer, or blasphemy.[13] In the same vein, the founders of the Nigerian experiment insisted—in contradiction of some loud voices of the time[14]—that traditional Yoruba art was "humanistic" rather than "religious," and thus could express Christian themes without danger of confusion with pre-Christian ideas.[15] Such simplicity of approach was hardly possible in dealing with Indian art; but such questions rarely surface in Costantini's exposition of the meaning of culture.

The Protestant world, without apostolic delegates or sacred congregations, reveals, on the one hand, a good deal of quite adventurous practice and, on the other, remarkably little public discussion and exploration of principles.

As far back as 1883, the Church Missionary Society opened a church in Peshawar, in the Punjab, not far from the border with Afghanistan. All Saints Memorial Church was built on a grand scale, with a huge square façade, a central arch scalloped (as frequently in Islamic architecture), and

---

[8]See, among many passages, *Réforme*, pp. 223-36.

[9]*Ibid.*, p. 238.

[10]*Ibid.*, pp. 237-42.

[11]K. Carroll. *Yoruba Religious Carving: Pagan and Christian Sculpture in Nigeria and Dahomey* (London, 1967). See the foreword by the ethnographer W. B. Fagg.

[12]Cf. J.F. Butler, *Christian Art in India* (Madras, 1986), p. 124. Heras (1888-1955) was primarily a historian, but his work touched many aspects of Indian culture. See the tributes in *Indica 25* (1988), pp. 83-91; and M. Lederle, *Christian Painting in India through the Centuries* (Bombay: Heras Institute, 1987).

[13]Costantini, *Réforme*, p. 243.

[14]Especially Ulli Beier, *Art in Nigeria 1960* (London, 1960).

[15]Carroll, *Religious Carving*, pp. 70-2.

smaller arches either side of it, each surmounted by a large star. Across the façade, in fine Arabic calligraphy, was set the words, "Amen, Blessings and glory and wisdom and thanksgiving and honor and power and might, be unto our God for ever, Amen." Each corner of the building had a slender minaret, and a great dome sat over the whole. Only the gilt cross over the dome proclaims that the building is not a mosque but a church. The interior was equally designed to provide landmarks for Muslims. A delicately-carved screen of local wood, in local style, by local craftsmen, was set behind the communion table, with an ambulatory across the apse behind it; and another screen across a transept allowed the purdah rule to be observed by women.[16] Another area of the church allowed space for observers who did not wish to uncover either head or feet. The walls carried biblical texts—in Arabic, Urdu, Persian, and English—in the way that Islamic buildings bear Qur'anic inscriptions; representational decoration was avoided. Altogether, All Saints, Peshawar, may seem an extraordinary production on the part of a rather conservative missionary society in the 1880s. Yet it seems to have attracted no great heart-searching or controversy; and the Society's magazine for the general home constituency felt confident in providing a full description[17] of the opening of this "remarkable building in Saracenic style, designed to adapt a Christian place of worship to Oriental ideas."[18]

That home constituency was even more aware of another building half a century later; the great cathedral built at Dornakal and designed by Bishop V. S. Azariah, the Indian churchman best known outside India.[19] Azariah was well known as a spokesman for Indian Christian identity; a cathedral for a largely new Christian community must reflect that identity. But in India it is less easy than in China to adopt Costantini's principle of art as a language which is religiously neutral. An Indian cultural identity must surely mean Hindu cultural identity—unless it takes Islamic identity. Which of the traditions most readily accords with specifically Christian needs and symbols? Azariah's answer was to essay a deliberate combination of the two: an Indian Christian building should reflect the whole of the nation's past without being tied to any one of its separate traditions. Azariah's building thus has both Muslim domed minarets and Hindu open court;[20] the most obvious analogies are in the palaces of south Indian princes. This recalls another feature of Dornakal Cathedral, its grandeur of

---

[16]Photographs of exterior and interior in D. J. Fleming, *The Heritage of Beauty* (New York, 1937), pp. 67-8.

[17]*Church Missionary Gleaner*, Nov. 1884.

[18]E. Stock, *History of the Church Missionary Society*, 3 (London, 1899), p. 471.

[19]See C. Graham, *Azariah of Dornakal* (London, 1946). For the cathedral, see pp. 11f., 99f., 114f. Miss Graham rather stresses the Hindu aspect; but the minarets are unmistakable.

[20]Illustration in J. F. Butler, *Christianity in Asia and America = Iconography of Religions*, 24:13 (Leiden, 1979), plate XIX.

scale and concept. Yet the Christian community to be served consisted mostly of desperately poor subsistence farmers. Azariah wanted to bring a touch of splendor into these contracted lives. On the one hand, the great building was a declaration that Christianity was there to stay, whatever happened to the government of India. On the other, it was a sign that even the poorest Christians owned a share in magnificence. Azariah was facing and resolving in his own way an issue that has been raised more recently by the doyen of Indian Christian artists, Jyoti Sahi: the proper artistic expression of a Christian counter-culture in a setting where the dominant culture is associated with oppression.[21]

Church building, the provision of appropriate space for worship, obviously forces Christians into making artistic choices. But in India, in particular, pictorial art was raising theological issues of immense importance—and it was not only Christian artists who were raising them.

In the earliest phase of the Indian renaissance, the figure of Christ as presented in the Christian Scriptures was an unmistakable influence. In the twentieth century, art came explicitly into the sphere of the renaissance, with Rabindranath Tagore's university of Indian culture at Santiniketan and its school of art headed by Tagore's nephew Abanidranath.

Some of the outstanding artists who came from Santiniketan use Christian themes. Janini Roy, the greatest of them all, regularly painted Jesus—a Jesus who is greater than us, and who is not tied to a particular period. He walks on the water (like other deities, he is at home in the elements, in air, in fire, in water). It is a Hindu reading of the Gospels. K. C. S. Panikkar (not a Christian but a former student at Madras Christian College) is another Indian renaissance artist who regularly paints the Christ figure; a Christ who belongs to India, for he stands with the other peace-makers, the Buddha and Gandhiji, giving his blessing to the poor, the sick, and the naked.[22]

But Christian artists went to Santiniketan also; indeed one, V. S. Masoji (d. 1977), became a professor there.[23] Among the important early figures are the Roman Catholic Angelo da Fonseca[24] (who was associated with Father Heras, already mentioned) and the Anglican A. D. Thomas. The latter may be specifically mentioned at this point, since his paintings

---

[21]Jyoti Sahi, "Reflections on Biblical Images/Symbols in Relation to Indian Christian Spirituality," *Image*, 37 (1988), pp. 10-11.

[22]On Roy and Panikkar, see R. W. Taylor, *Jesus in Indian Paintings* (Madras, 1975), and Butler, *Christian Art*, pp. 125-9.

[23]Examples of Masoji's painting in A. Lehmann, *Afroasiatische christliche Kunst* (Berlin, 1966), plates 161-6.

[24]See *The Art of Angelo da Fonseca* (Bombay, 1980). This booklet, written for an exhibition of da Fonseca's paintings at the Heras Institute, includes a statement by the artist and an account of his life and work by M. Lederle. Da Fonseca, born in Goa and brought up in Pune, lived from 1910 to 1967.

attracted some attention in the West through the publication in 1948 by the Society for the Propagation of the Gospel of *The Life of Christ by an Indian Artist*,[25] containing twenty-four pictures. Thomas attributed his inspiration to a verbal picture of Jesus by a Western missionary, that by E. Stanley Jones in *The Christ of the Indian Road*.[26] Thomas's portraits of Christ certainly present him as an Indian figure on the Indian road, but it is a serene, soft-colored Christ. He has the smile of the Buddha, untouched by earth and all that earth can do.

The Indian Christian artist works in perhaps the most testing environment that Christianity has yet met. That environment includes a religious culture in which the divinity of Christ, the superlative status of his teaching, and his right to worship, devotion, and love, can be readily conceded, so long as that recognition is not held to imply a unique or exclusive status or to demand a transition from one community to another. Christianity in India walks a tightrope. On one side, is the condition of a foreign, alien, and entirely detachable institution. On the other, lies the threat of absorption as one more of the multifarious forms of Hinduism.[27] The Indian Christian artist has to expound the person of Christ in the land that both gave birth to one of the most powerful innovators in religious history, Gautama Buddha, and that reinterpreted him as one of the incarnations of Vishnu. The image of Christ has long had a place in Indian art far outside the Church. Sacred pictures with salvation themes were a principal evangelistic instrument of the Jesuits at the court of Akbar, who loved paintings. In later Mughal painting the Christian themes take on a life of their own, independent of the traditional iconographic register.[28] The Indian renaissance takes Christ along Indian roads not mentioned in that register. Panikkar's portrayal of Christ alongside the Buddha and Gandhiji (and as Indian as they are) can be paralleled in dozens of popular bazaar prints.[29]

All this illustrates the quite considerable degree to which non-Western art over the last century (in church architecture and furnishing especially, but in other ways too) has been a means of exploration of the relations of Gospel and culture and of the relation of Christianity to other faiths. Indeed, artists and architects and church designers were facing these questions at a deeper level than that reached by many of the theological commentators,

---

[25]The pictures are also reproduced in A. Lehmann, *Die Kunst der Jungen Kirchen*, 2nd ed. (Berlin, 1957). The SPG had earlier published *The Life of Christ by Chinese Artists* (London, 1943).

[26]E. Stanley Jones, *The Christ of the Indian Road* (London, 1925).

[27]The issues discussed at length by Taylor, *Jesus in Indian Paintings* and by Butler, *Christian Art* throughout their studies.

[28]See the examples in F. zu Löwenstein, *Christliche Bilder in altindischer Malerei* (Münster, 1958).

[29]Examples in the Butler Collection, Centre for the Study of Christianity in the Non-Western World, University of Edinburgh.

and sometimes raised issues before the high theologians reached them. But Christian art figures only marginally in the general discussions on the impact of Christianity on Africa and Asia during the period when the great demographic shift within Christianity was beginning.

Christian art does not seem to have reached the agenda of the great Protestant missionary conferences until the Tambaram meeting of the International Missionary Council (IMC) in 1938. It would indeed be surprising to find it in the conferences of the late nineteenth century. In 1910, the Edinburgh World Missionary Conference was too concerned with the impact of Western education and "civilization" upon the non-Western world to take much account of the independent cultural heritages of the newer churches. And although the Jerusalem meeting of the IMC in 1928 paid attention to the religious consciousness of Asia, the question of how that consciousness might surface within Christianity was not at the forefront. Even at Tambaram the treatment is tentative and perfunctory. The clearest reference comes in the section on "The Inner Life of the Church." In the subsection on worship, recommendation 7 begins:

> Having noted that there is in some of the younger churches extreme eagerness and in others extreme reluctance to use in worship indigenous forms of art, such as music and architecture, we urge the publication of literature at a price within the reach of all, giving examples of the music or other arts of different nations as used in the life of the Church, and passing on the inspiration and joy of bringing out native arts as an offering to our Lord.[30]

Here one scents the unmistakable odor of the hot potato, especially as no suggestions are made as to who is to write and produce this economically priced literature. The impression of tentativeness is reinforced when the recommendation continues.

> We hope that some guiding principles on the connection of architecture with worship and witness may be made available for any church or mission desiring to study them.[31]

The only hint about what these principles might be is a bibliographical footnote referring to two books by Daniel Johnson Fleming (to be mentioned later) and one article in the *International Review of Missions*. The footnote is clearly editorial; the article had not even appeared when the conference met.[32] With manifest relief at being able to be specific at last, the recommendation concludes with a reprimand to missionaries who are still

---

[30] *The Life of the Church International Missionary Council Meeting at Tambaram, Madras* (Tambaram, Series 4), p. 6.

[31] *Ibid.*

[32] But the author, J. Prip-Moller, was a delegate at Tambaram and may well have had his say on the subject.

eager to transplant the music, architecture, or art of their home churches, and an affirmation of "the duty of helping the younger churches to express their Christian life in forms that are part of their nation's heritage."[33]

Among the notes preserved from the preliminary papers for this section are commendatory references to T. C. Chao's Chinese hymnbook, with its use of Chinese tunes and other liturgical experiments in China, with the non-committal statement, "There is also Dr. K. L. Reichelt's *Ritual Book of the Christian Church among the Friends of the Tao* and Dr. Chu Pao-yüan's *Book of Indigenous Worship Forms*."[34] Another paper refers to Indian melodies used in Lutheran liturgies in Andhra,[35] and another carries a suggestion from the Congo Protestant Council that Christian worship might more closely reflect African rhetorical practice by employing antiphonal singing and interweaving song and speech as in traditional story-telling.[36] On the other hand, a multidenominational conference in South Africa concluded:

> It is difficult for us at the present stage to conceive of worship in the younger church in South Africa taking a form other than the present one. We cannot think what a form of worship more closely related to the life of the African people would be, though through time it may evolve.[37]

The thinness of treatment of art and architecture at Tambaram is quite in line with the modest appearance the subject makes in the missionary literature of the time. It is very little in evidence through the 1930s in the *International Review of Missions*, the IMC's own organ, and the principal Protestant missiological journal. The article referred to in the editorial note on the Tambaram report was by an architect, J. Prip-Moller.[38] Prip-Moller had worked with Karl Ludvig Reichelt in his endeavors to establish a setting in which Chinese Buddhist monks could approach and study the Christian faith, and had helped to construct the striking Hong Kong building for Reichelt's Tao Fong Shan institute.

The article reflects Chinese experience, pleading for entry into the "spirit" rather than the "details" of Chinese architecture. That involves

---

[33]*The Life of the Church*, p. 6.

[34]*Ibid.*, p. 8. Reichelt's controversial views (set out in, for example, *Truth and Tradition in Chinese Buddhism*, 1st English edition [Shanghai, 1927], and posthumously in *Religion in Chinese Garment* [London, 1951]), were expressed in equally controversial practice. See E. J. Sharpe, *Karl Ludvig Reichelt, Missionary, Scholar, Pilgrim* (Tao Fong Shan, Hong Kong, 1984); H. Eilert, *Boundlessness: Studies in Karl Ludvig Reichelt's Missionary Thinking* (Ringkobing, 1974).

[35]*The Life of the Church*, p. 12.

[36]*Ibid.*, p. 15.

[37]*Ibid.*, pp. 15f.

[38]J. Prip-Moller, "Architecture: A Servant of Foreign Mission," *International Review of Missions*, 28 (1939), pp. 105-15.

more attention to how buildings are groups, and how they fit into the landscape, and to the effect of shadow created by long, overhanging eaves, than to painfully copying curved roofs or multiple brackets. It may be true that some Christians are inoculated by missionary practice against their local styles; but it is surely more important to consider the effect on the far greater number of non-believers. The less the effect of foreignness is paraded before them, the author apparently believes, the more likely are they to reflect on the central concerns which are the reason for the Christian buildings' existence.

Among British contributions relating directly to the arts are an article in the Anglican review *The East and the West* from 1927 on "African Art and Its Possibilities" and a three-part series on "The Arts in the Mission Field" in *The Church Overseas*, a magazine of the Society for the Propagation of the Gospel, in 1931.[39] Edward Shillito, a Congregational minister of poetic attainments who did literary work for the London Missionary Society, produced a small book called *Craftsmen All*. A better-known book[40] by another LMS writer, Mabel Shaw, attracted attention by its accounts of African initiatives in worship within a girls' mission school in what is now Zambia. In 1933 the SPG published *Worship in Other Lands: A Study of Racial Characteristics in Worship*, put together by a member of the Society's home staff, H. B. Thompson, from examples supplied by SPG missionaries. The author expressed a hope that other missionary societies would take the story further from their own resources; none seem to have done so. Much of *Worship in Other Lands* is concerned with liturgical acts in the narrower sense, and the influence of Bishop W. V. Lucas of Masasi, with his somewhat archaizing ideas about African rituals,[41] is evident. But there are specific examples of architecture, music, drama, and the visual arts. Of its nature it is a thing of shreds and patches. It is slightly disturbing to find the Black Madonna of the frontispiece, carved in a mission workshop in South Africa, described as "perhaps the most notable work of art that can so far be shown" from Africa. It is certainly African in facial features, but in other respects pure Percy Dearmer.

The strand of Anglican tradition represented in the SPG believed, as the preface of a manifesto volume of the time puts it, that Christianity could "absorb and transmute all that is good and of permanent value in other religions, cultures, and institutions."[42] In fact, it is fashionable to exaggerate the cultural insensitivity of the missionary movement of this period as a

---

[39]There were contributions on Africa (by W.V. Lucas, Bishop of Masasi), China, and Japan.

[40]Mabel Shaw, *God's Candlelights* (London, 1932).

[41]See his contribution, "The Christian Approach to Non-Christian Customs," in E. R. Morgan, ed., *Essays Catholic and Missionary* (London, 1928); reprinted as late as 1950 in *Christianity and Native Races* (London).

[42]Morgan, ed. *Essays*, p. v.

whole. And, as we have seen, there was by the time of the Second World War and the close of the Vasco da Gama era, already a substantial corpus of non-Western Christian artistic expression. Much of the experimental work had been in church building; yet Prip-Moller in 1939 makes a plea for "beautiful architecture" to take its place alongside the Chinese poetry, calligraphy, and music already being used to the glory of God.[43] Another contributor to the *International Review of Missions* says in 1942 of Indian music that, "No missionary of my acquaintance is averse to its use. Most advocate it, even belligerently."[44] His plea is for a far deeper understanding of it, rather than for its recognition and use.

Yet questions of art, whether in themselves or in their wider implications, figure little more in the literature of the post-war period, so concerned first with the autonomy of the Asian and African churches and then with Gospel and culture, than they do in the pre-Tambaram period.[45] There are some splendid studies of the earlier aspects of the Christian presence in the non-Western world—Mughal painting, Japanese Namban art, Congo ivories—and recent years have produced valuable accounts of development in particular areas, notably India.[46] But—if we leave aside Costantini's work and what it produced—only three writers in the whole of the twentieth century appear as consistently drawing attention to what was happening in Christian art in the non-Western world as a whole and to its theological and artistic implications. They are the American Daniel Johnson Fleming, the German Arno Lehmann, and the Englishman J. F. Butler.

Fleming had recently graduated from college when, travelling in India, he saw All Saints Church, Peshawar, and thought it was a mosque. It fixed his interest in "the naturalization of Christianity in national homes of the spirit and the manifold expression of Christian experience as found in houses of God."[47] In *The Heritage of Beauty* (1937) he gave photographs and commentaries of three dozen or so such houses of God, all but two or three of them Protestant, all over the world. Asia predominates, but Alaska and the Pacific are not forgotten, and there are some telling items from Africa.

---

[43]Prip-Moller, "Architecture," p. 115.

[44]M. Pitt, "Take, for Instance, Indian Music," *International Review of Missions*, 31 (1942), pp. 205-10.

[45]There is a rather embarrassed reference in the report of the World Council of Churches Assembly in 1961 to the close historical association of the Church with the arts and the open questions about art and society. The conclusion appears to be that the subject is important, but the council currently without machinery for pursuing it. There is no reference to the possible contribution in this field of the newer churches: *The New Delhi Report: The Third Assembly of the World Council of Churches 1961* (London, 1962), pp. 181ff.

[46]The works of M. Lederle, R. W. Taylor, and J. F. Butler have already been mentioned: see nn. 11, 19 above.

[47]Fleming, *Heritage*, p. 17.

(The latter included one by then already vanished, the first cathedral at Namirembe, Uganda; entirely an African hut in design, but of gigantic proportions.) Fleming, who was a professor at Union Seminary, New York, was aware that what was involved was not "a relatively simple matter of the use of brick and mortar."[48] The theme of much of his writing is the essential connection between the diversity of world Christianity and its catholicity. "World Christianity" is a favorite phrase of his (his other books include *Marks of a World Christian* and *Ethical Issues Confronting World Christians*), and his view of the nature of Christian mission is essentially permeative. He also has a strong view of world citizenship (he wrote on *Ways of Sharing with Other Faiths and Contacts with Non-Christian Cultures*). But if a liberal (and there are frequent reminders of Hocking) he was not a naïve liberal. It is a feature of *The Heritage of Beauty* that sensitive issues raised by particular buildings are identified and succinctly set out. He is also concerned about aesthetic issues, and not simply in architecture. The *Heritage* includes one painting (by Luke Ch'en), and Fleming went on to produce *Each with His Own Brush*[49] and to consider wider issues of religious symbolism.[50] He also had the prescience to see a new future within Christianity for indigenous African arts threatened with destruction by Western influences.[51]

Arno Lehmann had seen missionary service in India, and wrote an important history.[52] In his later work as Professor of Missiology at the University of Halle-Wittenberg he developed the systematic study of the Christian art of Africa and Asia (which for these purposes included the Pacific). A stream of studies proceeded through the 1950s and 1960s, especially dealing with pictures from Africa and Asia illustrating biblical incidents or themes. Whereas Fleming had emphasized architecture, Lehmann's chief concern was with painting and the plastic arts. Two encyclopedic surveys (as well as an article in *Religion in Geschichte und Gegenwart*[53]) came from his later years: *Die Kunst der Jungen Kirchen* (1957) and *Afroasiatische christliche Kunst* (1966). Both are profusely illustrated. Lehmann, more than any other single person (with the possible exception of Costantini), documented the sheer extent and richness of modern non-

---

[48]*Ibid.*

[49]Daniel Johnson Fleming, *Each with His Own Brush* (New York, 1938).

[50]Daniel Johnson Fleming, *Christian Symbolism in a World Community* (New York, 1940).

[51]Fleming, *Heritage*, p. 85. On Fleming's theology and place in American mission history, see W. R. Hutchison, *Errand to the World. American Protestant Thought and Foreign Missions* (Chicago, 1987), pp. 150-8.

[52]Arno Lehmann, *Es begann in Tranquebar* (Berlin, 1955); E.T. *It Began at Tranquebar* (Madras, 1956).

[53]"Malerei und Plastik VII: Christliche Kunst in den jungen Kirchen," *RGG*, 4, cols 702-4. For Lehmann's other articles see the bibliography in *Afroasiatsche christliche Kunst*; E.T., *Christian Art in Africa and Asia* (St. Louis, 1969).

Western Christian art, and the innovative nature of much of it. His achievement is the more remarkable in that the collection of data on which it was based was compiled in the German Democratic Republic.

John Francis Butler was appointed Professor of Philosophy at Madras Christian College in 1937, the year in which *The Heritage of Beauty* appeared. He later served with the Christian Literature Society for India, which dealt not only with books, but with the posters, pictures, and ancillary material used by hundreds of congregations and thousands of ordinary believers. In 1951 he returned to Britain and never held another academic appointment. For most of the rest of his life he was a Methodist circuit minister, filling the studies of a succession of manses with books, journals, slides, and exemplars of what he called "missionary art." He used the term advisedly. Missionary art, he argued, is the use of art in mission; the nationality of the artist is a secondary consideration. Over a thirty-year period came a stream of articles, both learned and popular, and a handful of books, some published, others remaining in manuscript.[54] Architectural historians sometimes noticed him when theologians did not.

Of the three prehistorians of the non-Western phase of Christian art (if the considerations with which this chapter opened are valid), Butler is probably the most important. He has far more depth than Fleming, and more breadth of treatment than Lehmann. His approach was grounded in a philosophical interest in aesthetics and backed by a detailed knowledge of Western art and architecture. More than either of his seniors, he set the art of the churches of Africa and Asia in their context in the history of art and the history of Christianity. For the same reason, he was more aware than they of the special importance of Latin America in the history of Christian art and of the aesthetic and theological issues involved in mixed traditions. He was interested in Mughal art, in Castiglione and the Jesuits in China, in "Jesuit pottery," and in Namban art. In his later work, he came to argue that the theological problems of cultural transmission and syncretism in art should be posed historically. The questions facing Christian artists and decision-makers in Africa and Asia were endemic to Christianity, and to him Christian history revealed a succession of more or less successful solutions to analogous problems. His chosen title for an article with this thesis was "Nineteen Centuries of Missionary Art."[55] The issues he raises range from the economic one, "How is an Asian Christian artist

---

[54]The most important books are *Christianity in Asia and America* in the Brill *Iconography of Religions* series and the posthumous *Christian Art in India* already referred to. See also his contributions to G. Cope, *Christianity and the Visual Arts* (London, 1964), and G. Frere-Cook, *The Decorative Arts of the Christian Church* (London, 1972). A collection of his articles is in the Butler collection at the Centre for the Study of Christianity in the Non-Western World, University of Edinburgh.

[55]The actual published title became "Nineteen Centuries of Christian Missionary Architecture," *Journal of the Society of Architectural Historians*, 21 (1962), pp. 3-17.

to live?" to that of the influence of "international" styles in architecture, to whether Africa and Asia can make better use of ferro-concrete than the West has done.

He also took up a question which Costantini had hinted at: Whether non-Western Christianity might be the matrix for a new artistic renaissance. Butler once wrote an article entitled "Can Missions Rescue Modern Art?"[56] In it he contrasts the old cultures of Africa and Asia—tired, perhaps, but the basis of national pride and self-confidence—with a dying culture in Europe. That culture has lost its ultimate values, its social solidarity, and any viable economic basis for the arts; Western art, accordingly, is in a perilous state. The churches of Africa and Asia seethe with problems, but by their possession both of the Christian faith and the resources of cultures of the non-Western world, they can provide the clash of ideas and techniques from which renaissance springs. It could well happen that missions would prove to be the source from which salvation came to modern art.

Butler lived to see the foundation of the Asian Christian Art Association in 1978.[57] The number of Asian countries which now have their own associations of Christian artists or societies for promoting Christian art attests the vigor of the movement. Whether or not salvation will come from the East to Western art, as he and Costantini envisaged, it is still impossible to know. But that a new phase of Christian art has opened, with its focus in the southern continents, is beyond doubt. Costantini, Butler, and Lehmann are among its few prehistorians.

---

[56]J. F. Butler, "Can Missions Rescue Modern Art?" *Hibbert Journal*, 56 (1958), pp. 371-87.

[57]The association arose with the support of the East Asia Christian Conference, later the Christian Conference of Asia, and the active promotion of the Sri Lankan churchman D. T. Niles. Niles commissioned Masao Takenaka of Doshisha University to collect work by Asian painters on Christian themes. Takenaka's *Christian Art in Asia* (Tokyo, 1975), was a manifesto volume. See R. O'Grady, "The Tenth Anniversary of the Asian Christian Art Association," *Image*, 37 (1988), p. 2.

14

The Nineteenth-Century Missionary as Scholar[1]

The first generation of missionaries did not possess a high degree of formal education, and the average of the second generation was not outstandingly higher. Even powerful advocates of missions made it clear that they did not expect to recruit largely from the ranks of the educated, and in England (this study will use English and Scottish models for the most part) for many years churchmen expected the average run of missionary candidates to be neither ordained nor (in terms of the parish ministry in England) ordainable. The Continental recruits who formed so important a section of the early recruitment of the Church Missionary Society relieved its Committee in this respect of a great embarrassment.[2] Theological education (and often wider education) for missionaries was, however, taken seriously from the beginning: very seriously if one considers the training of much of the home ministry. The London Missionary Society—oddly enough, in spite of its overwhelmingly Dissenting character, the most clerical of all missionary societies in its conception of the missionary office—provided a very substantial academic discipline for such of its candidates as had not received one in Scotland or elsewhere; and the Anglican Church Missionary Society also made its own arrangements for surveillance and tuition long before this was formalized into the Church Missionary College.[3] It was the Wesleyans, with their tradition of "on the job"

[1]First published in Nils E. Bloch-Hoell, ed., *Misjonskall og Forskerglede: Festskrift till Professor Olav Guttorm Myklebust* (Oslo: Universitetsforlaget, 1975), pp. 209-21.

[2]Cf. A. F. Walls, "Missionary Vocation and the Ministry: The First Generation," in M. E. Glasswell and F. W. Fasholé-Luke, eds., *New Testament Christianity for Africa and the World: Essays in Honour of Harry Sawyerr* (London: SPCK, 1974), pp. 141-56 (reprinted as chapter 12 of the present volume).

[3]On one phase of Islington College, see A. Hodge, "The Training of Missionaries for Africa: The Church Missionary Society's Training College at Islington, 1900-1915," *Journal of Religion in Africa* 4 (2) 1971: 81-96.

training for preachers, who were probably slowest in this respect; but even here the principle, once it was established, produced what was effectively a separate missionary college.[4] Nonetheless the standard missionary product for the first half of the century remained a person of humble origin and, with the exception of those of the Church of Scotland (and after 1843 the Free Church of Scotland) and to some extent the other Scottish churches, of more modest education than his counterpart in the home ministry. The better his education and mental attainments, the more likely he was to be sent to India (or later to China), the less likely to Africa or the West Indies (only once in 60 years did the CMS for instance, send an English graduate to Africa, and even then the circumstances were special).[5] It was only in the great burst of missionary recruitment of the last two decades or so of the nineteenth century that the victories of the Gospel were demonstrably won on the playing fields of Eton, and crowds of eager young men came from the universities, the public schools, and the Keswick Convention to throw back the frontiers of mission in every continent. A corresponding increase (out of the 1859 revival and its aftermath, among other factors) of candidates without education came in the same period; the new "faith" missions to which most of them went were slow to institute formal training, but came eventually to do so.

The patterns of recruitment changed during the nineteenth century, but certain literary factors remained constant. In the first place the missionary movement developed and sustained a quite remarkably informed constituency. It was a grass roots movement, centred on penny a week collectors and local enthusiasts and auxiliaries; its principal agency was the missionary magazine. But the magazine was not the only literary deposit of the movement. The missionary best-seller—"missiography," if one may use such a term to denote the type of popular literature which portrayed the missionary work as the *Acta Sanctorum*—became established early and continued throughout the century. Some highly esteemed items were composed by literati in the home country—Miss Tucker's popular *Abbeokuta or Sunrise within the Tropics* (1853) is a good example, and she did more such; but some of the most effective were accounts of their work by missionaries themselves: John Williams, *Narratives and Missionary Enterprises in the South Seas* (1837) and Robert Moffat's *Missionary Labours and Scenes in Southern Africa* (1837) were constantly reprinted and imitated. Such accounts were written for the home missionary constituency, for the same people as read the magazines; but in the nature of things they sometimes introduced material, recorded with varying degrees of insight and observation, new to human knowledge in the west. Some works of this character passed beyond

---

[4]Richmond College, Surrey.

[5]E. G. Irving, M.D., a retired naval surgeon, with experience of the British Government service in West Africa, was appointed to the Yoruba Mission in 1853 "to act as adviser of the missionaries in temporal matters."

simple missiography into "researches" of interest to a very much broader category of reader: Livingstone's *Missionary Travels and Researches in South Africa* (1857) is perhaps the best known example, but it was by no means the first. Works such as William Ellis' *Polynesian Researches* (1829) and even his earlier *Narrative of a Tour through Hawaii . . . With Observations on the Natural History of the Sandwich Islands and Remarks on the Manners, Customs, Traditions, History and Language of Their Inhabitants* (1826) were beginning to introduce the Missionary as Scholar, and in the process to produce a new type and dimension of scholarship.

LMS Authors

The last four names mentioned—Williams, Moffat, Livingstone, and Ellis—were all, as it happens, missionaries of the London Missionary Society. None held a university degree, and Livingstone's modest and hard-won acquisitions in Glasgow represented the most considerable paper qualifications of the four. They were fairly typical. From the Society's first valedictory in 1796 until 1900, it sent out 1,120 missionaries (including women missionaries who later married LMS missionaries but excluding other missionary wives).[6] Of these, on a conservative estimate, at least 146, or 13 percent, produced books in English (with a few in Welsh) or in the languages of the countries in which they served. If we discount Bible and other translations, and restrict the list to those known to have written original works, there are still 115, more than 10 percent of the total missionary force, who were authors of this sort. In the same period 151 LMS missionaries went to the field holding university degrees or obtained them during their service, 66 medical and 85 non-medical (including at least one with both qualifications), well over half of them in the last thirty years of the period. There is no obvious correlation between the university training and the literary production: though it is probable that China tended to receive the best equipped candidates intellectually and certain that it stimulated some of the best missionary scholarship. Naturally, in the first half of the century and longer, with the older English universities closed to Dissenters, most of the LMS missionaries with university training were Scots.

If we look at the literature produced by these missionaries, 22 of the 115 produced linguistic or lexical studies, grammars, dictionaries, etc., some of an elementary, some of an academic, character. The languages presented include Chinese (in many forms), Sanskrit, Hindi, Samoan, Motu, Herero, Bemba, Malagasy, and Modern Greek. The studies include the pioneer Chinese dictionary of Robert Morrison (originally published in six volumes between 1815 and 1822 with the assistance of William Milne), and the works

---

[6]J. Sibree, *London Missionary Society: A Register of Missionaries, Deputations, etc., from 1796-1923* (London, 1923) gave a full list with skeletal biographical information from the LMS candidates' records.

of other Sinologists like Medhurst, Legge, Edkins, and Eitel. Nine missionaries (four of them also in the 22 already mentioned) produced English
editions, with varying degrees of scholarly apparatus, of texts from the
countries in which they worked. In this way not only Confucius, Mencius,
and Lao-Tze appeared in English, but collections of proverbs from China,
from Madagascar, from Polynesia, which provided a means of insight into
primal societies not readily obtainable elsewhere, and even collections of
Chinese scientific texts. The most considerable single achievement was
undoubtedly James Legge's scholarly editions of the Chinese classics.[7] (The
LMS missionaries of this period seem to have been less notable as translators of Indian than of Chinese literature; though they produced historians
of and commentators on Indian literature like E. P. Rice, who wrote *A
History of Kanarese Literature*,[8] Edwin Greaves,[9] who shared in a descriptive
catalogue of Hindu Christian literature, and, above all, John Nicol Farquhar, who was both a historian and an interpreter of Indian religious
traditions.

Nearly half the missionary authors (55) produced works which might
be called "Descriptive, Historical, Anthropological, or Literary." This ad-
mittedly broad category covers works of very varied degrees of pretension,
quality, and level; it shades toward "missiography," but is distinguished
from it by some claim to analysis or close description of another culture, or
the church within it, or both. It includes some famous names and some
famous books: the Milnes, father and son, Ellis, Moffat, John Williams, John
Philip, George Turner, Livingstone, Chalmers, MacKenzie, MacGowan,
Slater, Gilmour, Sibree, Matthews, W. C. Willoughby, and Farquhar, some
reflecting considerable scientific detail, some presenting serious anthropological recording, and some displaying careful historical research involving
knowledge of oral and literary traditions.

It is thus somewhat of a surprise to find only eleven missionaries in the
list who compose works on what one might call "comparative religion,"
reflecting scholarly study of the *religions* of the peoples among whom they
worked or the religious implications of their encounter with Christianity—
and few of these works are early. (It would not be right to deduce from this
that missionaries as a whole did not produce studies of non-Christian
religions—indeed, they deeply influenced the standard mid-century descriptions.) LMS writers in this field include some eminent names: Legge,
Wylie, Edkins, and Eitel on Chinese religions; Mullens, Slater, and Farquhar

---

[7]*The Chinese Classics with Critical and Exegetical Notes, Prolegomena and Copious
Indexes*, 5 vols. (Hong Kong, 1861-1872); *The Chinese Classics Translated . . . with
Preliminary Essays . . .* 3 vols. (London, 1869-1876); *The Sacred Books of China*, Sacred
Books of the East series, 6 vols. (Oxford, 1879-1885), etc.

[8]In Azariah and Farquhar's Heritage of India series (1915; enlarged ed. Calcutta,
1921).

[9]Cf. *Sketch of Hindi Literature* (Madras, 1918).

on Indian; and we should remember also the descriptive works of Ellis, Turner, and others who depicted primal societies as they saw them, with their religious aspects, which we have included in the earlier category.

Another category which is smaller than might have been expected is that of the tracts on political and cognate contemporary issues relating to missions. I find only four, (though I suspect I have undercounted) dealing with opium or the effect of the presence in the mission areas of other powers (France or Cecil Rhodes). Some other issues, notably slavery, form, of course, a substantial theme in the descriptive works.

After the descriptive, the largest category of writers (42) is that of authors of "missiography" among whom are included all the writers of juvenilia. In view of the vast market for such material and the large number of deputation addresses which most missionaries on furlough gave (and must have been tempted to permanize), it is perhaps surprising that this category is not larger. In the circumstances one may be surprised that so high a proportion of more serious and demanding works of description and analysis were composed by missionaries.

The memoir, and the hagiographical memoir in particular, was a well-established literary form before the missionary movement, but was readily taken over by it. If we include autobiographies (other than those "narratives" which belong properly to the category of descriptive works), eighteen LMS missionaries in the period produced works of this kind. Most of these represent a specialized form of missiography for edification, emulation, or family *pietas*, but one or two works are more ambitious in scope (and at least one consisted of biographies of significant African Christian chiefs).

The missionary movement produced its own apparatus, and perhaps became statistically conscious rather earlier than the Western churches as a whole. At any rate, five men in the LMS list produce works on missionary administration and statistics; they include Joseph Mullens, one of the pioneer missionary statisticians, and Thomas Cochrane, who was to become one of the twentieth-century exponents of the missionary survey.

A small group of five medical and scientific writers (there are probably far more of the former whom I have not located) occurs, providing monographs on tropical diseases, leprosy in China, the geology and flora of Madagascar, and similar topics. Numerous others wrote schoolbooks, especially for use in mission schools; one or two wrote verse or English hymnody (vernacular hymnody, which many missionaries wrote, and in which LMS missionaries in South India were especially creative, has not been considered here) or produced editions of early divinity. The versatile James Sibree, who was an architect by training, produced two illustrated volumes on English cathedrals.

Perhaps the oddest feature is the small number of missionaries who seem to have written works of a theological character, though if that is taken to include more popular works in the vernaculars of their areas or college textbooks, there must have been more than the twelve authors I have been able to trace. The list of their theological works is even less impressive: of the five authors who produce works of theology or philosophy, only one, T. E. Slater, wrote a solid work of obvious significance.[10] Only three names are attached to works of biblical study: the authors of a Bible dictionary (based on Hastings) and a concordance in Malagasy, and Joseph Pearce, also of Madagascar, to whom are attributed commentaries on the epistles which I have not been able to trace.[11] There is one work of general (as distinct from local or mission) church history, and there are two "devotional" writers (both women missionaries).

Church of Scotland Authors

It is interesting to compare this LMS literary productivity with that of the Church of Scotland missionaries in the same period: interesting both because the Church of Scotland represented a generally higher standard of ministerial education, both at home and abroad, than was common in the churches and societies based in England, and because so high a proportion of Church of Scotland work in the period was invested in the colleges in India to which ministers from Scotland were specifically appointed. An unusually high proportion of missionaries were accordingly engaged in higher education as professors in the Indian colleges.

Sixty-two ministers of the Church of Scotland (including those sent prior to the Disruption who later joined the Free Church, but excluding HEIC and Government chaplains and missionaries to the Jews) served under the Foreign Mission Committee up to 1900.[12] Half of these held a university degree. (Six of the remainder were later awarded the degree of D.D. *honoris causa*, and one of them an honorary M.A. also). No less than 24 out of the 62 were, as missionaries or later (in one notable case before) also authors. By contrast with the LMS men, however, only three contributed significant lexical or linguistic studies, Bailey in Punjabi and Hetherwick in Chinyanja together with John Wilson's early work in Marathi (many others made translations); and only one seems to have translated Indian literature. Five authors produce comparative studies in religion. These include some very substantial studies, but all but one are from the earlier part of the period—

---

[10]Cf. *God Revealed* (Madras, 1876); and especially his *The Higher Hinduism in Relation to Christianity: Certain Aspects of Hindu Thought from the Christian Standpoint* (London, 1902).

[11]Sibree (p. 598) speaks of commentaries on 1 and 2 Corinthians, Philippians, and 1 and 2 Thessalonians. I have not found these; perhaps they were in Malagasy.

[12]The names will be found in Hew Scott, ed., *Fasti Ecclesiae Scoticanae*, vol. 7 (Edinburgh, 1928).

Duff, Wilson, John McDonald, and Murray Mitchell. Descriptive, historical, anthropological, and literary studies come from eight missionaries, including Duff and Wilson, and Duff MacDonald, whose *Africana, or the Heart of Heathen Africa* is a pioneer work of anthropological study and recording of African religion.[13] Three, Wilson, Duff, and John Morrison, all well-known figures, write tracts on political and social questions cognate to Indian missions, one missionary writes on missionary administration, six write memoirs, and ten, including some very well-known names, "missiography."

The traditional theological disciplines were notably better served than by the LMS, at least fourteen, approaching a quarter of the total list of missionaries, contributing productions of this sort. But much of the philosophical and theological material is popular, and the most substantial works of William Hastie were written after he had left India for good. There are three church historians (not counting one ex-missionary who became a distinguished Scottish antiquary and genealogist), and three devotional and pastoral writers (including John MacDonald, whose reputation in this field was established before he became a missionary). Hastie translated acres of German theology and Thomas Smith produced editions of Rutherford and the English Puritans. There was also a mathematician and (probably) a poet.

The differences in literary output between the LMS and the Church of Scotland reflect primarily their different preoccupations within their mission service. The Church of Scotland missionaries with less involvement in evangelism in the vernaculars in the period do not make so distinguished a linguistic contribution as those of the LMS; with their involvement in higher education they found themselves in a literary confrontation with Hinduism and other major religious traditions in India, producing works of comparative religion based on examination of the literary sources; with their constant contact with the intelligentsia, and fortified by the particular traditions of Scottish churchmanship, they produced a relatively high proportion of literary theology for the general reader, be he convert, enquirer, or opponent. The two missions overlap in their production of solid, detailed works of observation, analysis, and interpretation of the cultures and societies in which they work.

The CMS and Scholarship

Both Scotland and English Dissent had their own traditions of education and scholarship; but missionary scholarship of the nineteenth century was not simply the fruit of these. The Church Missionary Society, for instance, Anglican and Evangelical, reflects something very similar. It did have on

---

[13]London, 1882.

its staff from time to time some highly equipped Continental, especially German, missionaries, including, for instance S. W. Koelle, the father of comparative African linguistics,[14] and K. G. Pfander, the learned controversialist with Islamic doctors; from the old universities of Oxford and Cambridge and from Trinity College, Dublin, there came in the early part of the century a trickle, by the end of the century a flood, of candidates; but the CMS missionary staple for most of the century consisted of men of humble education, who would not have met the normal expectations of the home ministry.[15] Yet men of this character, as well as those much better equipped, contributed to the new missionary scholarship.

For instance, among the contributors to Trubner's prestigious Oriental Series are three CMS missionaries. A. B. Hutchinson gives a translation of Faber's *Mind of Mencius*. The same man was responsible for a considerable quantity of literature both in Chinese and Japanese. Yet Hutchinson was already 30 years of age when accepted by CMS and his highest education was in the CMS College in Islington. The same was true of Edward Sell, who contributes the volume *The Faith of Islam* to the Trubner series, and who also wrote a Persian grammar and directed revision work in Indian vernaculars. All his considerable Oriental learning was acquired in the field (The Archbishop of Canterbury conferred a Lambeth B.D. upon him in 1881). James Hinton Knowles, who produces the Trubner volume *Folk Tales of Kashmir*, had even less by way of initial qualification: he had to spend a time in the CMS preparatory institution before he could even be admitted to Islington College; yet he, too, was widely recognized as a scholar in his own field.

Another unlikely scholar is John Batchelor, who was one of the members of an unusual party of missionaries experimentally trained in Hong Kong. He was then appointed as a "Lay Helper" to the CMS Japan Mission in 1879; not till 1887 was he ordained deacon, by which time he had had a few months of study at Islington and at Ridley Hall, Cambridge, before returning suddenly to Japan "in the exigency of the Mission." Yet Batchelor was the first missionary living permanently in Ainu country, and he became the first Western exponent of the Japanese Ainu language and culture. The 25-column article "Ainus" in Hastings' *Encyclopaedia of Religion and Ethics* bears witness not only to the extent of his knowledge but to his insight and discipline.

The list could be lengthened indefinitely. Gilbert Walshe of the Christian Literature Society for China, also a contributor to the *Encyclopaedia of Religion and Ethics*, was a 39-year-old clerk on the Irish railways when

---

[14]See especially his *Polyglotta Africana* (London, 1854), and cf. P. E. H. Hair, *The Early Study of Nigerian Languages: Essays and Bibliographies* (Cambridge, 1967).

[15]CMS missionaries are listed in *Church Missionary Society: Register of Missionaries, Clerical Lay and Female, and Native Clergy from 1804-1904* (London, n.d.).

accepted by CMS and sent to Islington College. John Roscoe, described in the CMS register as "an engineer," went to the preparatory institution and after a year at Islington was sent as a lay missionary, not receiving ordination until nine years afterwards in 1893. Yet Roscoe became a considerable anthropologist, his work on *The Baganda* (1911) resting on long and careful observation, the later studies of neighbouring peoples applying the principles he had learned from James Frazer against the background of his intimate knowledge of Ganda society.[16]

Language and Culture

Roscoe illustrates the conditions which forced the pioneer missionary to some of the preconditions for scholarship, and to acquaintance with two— at that time undeveloped—fields of scholarship.

> Having spent twenty-five years as a missionary in the heart of Africa in intimate relations with the natives, I have had greater opportunities for obtaining some knowledge of their mode of life and habits of thought, as well as becoming intimately acquainted with their old religious ideas, than falls to the lot of most men. None of the Baganda who gave me information about their early institutions knew English, nor had they come into contact with Englishmen; their minds were uninfluenced by foreign ideas.

In a pioneer situation the missionary was faced either with complete ineffectiveness or with a course which, if it did not make him a scholar, would give him, in spite of himself, scholarly instincts and disciplines. And throughout the nineteenth century, missionaries were in pioneer situations. Roscoe in the 1880s and 1890s was experiencing in Uganda what Henry Nott and the select few to survive the disastrous beginnings of the early Polynesian missions knew in the century's earliest decades. Their response to this situation was a central factor to their survival: the inability of some of their colleagues to cope with the implications of culture contact was the cause of their collapse.

Linguistics, as we have seen, was not the only branch of scholarship to benefit indirectly from the missionary movement, or the only one into which missionaries were forced as a function of effective work. The great nineteeth-century anthropologists were armchair men, and whatever their views on the origin or on the future of religion, they laid the work of field missionaries under regular tribute. Roscoe speaks of the gratitude he owes

---

[16]Cf., e.g., *The Bakitara or Banyaro* (Cambridge, 1923); *The Banyankole* (Cambridge, 1923); *The Bagesu and Other Tribes of the Uganda Protectorate* (Cambridge, 1924); all parts of the report of the Mackie Ethnological Expedition. Roscoe received an honorary M.A. from Cambridge.

to his friend and "illustrious teacher" Professor J. G. Frazer;[17] but Frazer owed as much to the careful collection and classification of reliable information by people like Roscoe. It is worth remembering that the word *mana* first passed into anthropological argot through the interpretation of its significance by a missionary in Melanesia, R. H. Codrington.

The Recognition of Scholarship

It was probably the linguistic work of missionaries which first gave rise to the recognition that they were opening up new branches of scholarship. Glasgow University gave a D.D. to Robert Morrison in 1817, followed by the same honour for his colleague in the Chinese Dictionary, Milne, in 1820. In fact some twenty LMS missionaries whose service began before 1900 received honorary doctorates (Livingstone received two and James Legge three): a few came from North American universities, one (Livingstone) from Oxford, most from Scotland. Of the 62 Church of Scotland missionaries, no less than 19 received doctorates (Duff and Thomas Smith each received two). Many of the awards had, of course, little to do with any scholarly contribution of the missionaries, and in the case of some of these in the Church of Scotland, little to do with their missionary service (many of those appointed to professorships in the Indian colleges served a relatively short period before returning to parish work in Scotland); but a list which includes such names as Morrison, Medhust, R. C. Mather, Legge, Mullens, Edkins, John Chalmers, W. H. Rees, T. G. Bailey, Duff, Hetherwick, Duff MacDonald, Thomas Smith, and John Wilson as well as pioneer translators like Nesbit, McFarlane, and Turner cannot be regarded as deficient in scholarly achievements.

It is of more interest to note the areas in which missionaries went to academic posts in the west. From LMS missionaries whose service began in the nineteenth century, there came no fewer than four professors of Chinese in British Universities: Samuel Kidd at University College, London (1837), James Legge at Oxford (1876), George Owen at King's College, London (1908), and William Hopkyn Rees, also at London (1921). Of these, only Legge ("I looked forward to your arrival here with the greatest interest," wrote Max Müller to him, "Oxford wants scholars more than anything else, if it is not to diminish down to a mere High School")[18] had had a university education. J. N. Farquhar, like Legge a product of Aberdeen University, became the first Professor of Comparative Religion at Manchester in 1923, and W. C. Willoughby, a missionary anthropologist, became Professor of African Missions at Hartford Seminary Foundation,

---

[17]*The Baganda*, preface.
[18]Quoted in H. E. Legge, *James Legge: Missionary and Scholar* (London, 1905), p. 243.

Connecticut, in 1919. The only other example I have noted was that of Andrew Davidson, who pioneered medical services in Madagascar under LMS (where he wrote a Therapeutika in Malagasy), took a colonial service appointment in Mauritius, and then was "Lecturer on Oriental Diseases" at Edinburgh, where he composed books such as *Geographical Pathology: An Enquiry into the Geographical Distribution of Infective and Climatic Diseases* (1892) and *Diseases of Warm Climates* (1893).

The Church of Scotland Missions produced one academic linguist, T. G. Bailey, who became Reader in Hindi and Urdu at the School of Oriental Studies, London, in 1920, after 25 years' service in the Punjab. Otherwise there is Duff's special chair, for the establishment of which he had pleaded, in Evangelistic Theology at New College, in Edinburgh, in which he was succeeded by Thomas Smith. Professor Myklebust has illuminated this history.[19] The only other appointment and the only one in either list to an academic appointment in the traditional theological disciplines, is that of William Hastie to the Divinity Chair at Glasgow in 1895, which probably owed little to his troublesome and unhappy five years in Calcutta.[20]

Missionaries and Theology

Which brings us to a last curious reflection. The groups of missionaries we have examined produced some major scholars, a few of the first rank, and a large number of competence and industry. They also had a major impact on the development of new disciplines and fields of study. But relatively few of them wrote significantly in biblical studies, in dogmatics, or even in the field of philosophy of religion; and few of those who did show any radical influence from their missionary service and knowledge. Theology was a *datum* to be explained and demonstrated in the new cultural setting, not something which would develop in it. As a generalization, this seems to be true of the British missionary movement as a whole. Continental scholarship received a much more direct impact from the missionary movement; and continental missionaries reflecting on their work produced a tradition of theological scholarship, invented "missiology" in fact.[21] The sad fate of the Chair of Evangelistic Theology pioneered by Alexander Duff, the nearest thing to a British missiologist the nineteenth century saw, is a

---

[19]O. G. Myklebust, *The Study of Missions in Theological Education* 1 (Oslo, 1955), chapt. 4.

[20]I have left out of account Robert Jardine, who had been a professor at the University of New Brunswick before his missionary service but who seems not to have returned to teaching afterwards; and the learned John Morrison who did temporary teaching at St. Andrews and Edinburgh.

[21]Cf. Myklebust, *Study of Missions.*

symbol. The British movement produced scholarship but it was never integrated into theological scholarship. Farquhar's view of Christianity as "The Crown of Hinduism" had profound theological implications,[22] but Farquhar and most of his disciples pursued them from the Hindu rather than the Christian side. The late and lonely figure of A. G. Hogg remains to suggest what might have been.

---

[22]E. J. Sharpe, *Not to Destroy but to Fulfil: The Contribution of J.G.N. Farquhar to Protestant Thought in India Before 1914* (Lund, 1965).

15

Humane Learning and the Missionary Movement[1]

"The Best Thinking of the Best Heathen"

It is now a common-place that the typical early nineteenth-century missionary—visualized by David Livingstone as "a dumpy sort of man with a Bible under his arm"[2]—was a fairly homespun character, from the forge or the shop (if he were English), or from the croft, the farm, or the factory (if he were Scots). His formal education was not high and, if an Anglican, his social and educational attainments were not such as would have brought him ordination to the home ministry. It is almost equally accepted that by the end of the nineteenth century the situation had changed; not only were the numbers of missionaries immensely swollen; but the universities and the public schools could now supply a quota, for Africa as well as for the lands of the ancient Eastern civilizations.[3] The evangelization of the world in one generation was to be accomplished essentially by the international student community.[4] The typical missionary was now a conventionally educated

---

[1]First published in K. Robbins, ed., *Religion and Humanities*, Studies in Church History 17 (Oxford: Blackwell, 1981), pp. 341-53.

[2]Cf. A. F. Walls, "Missionary Vocation and the Ministry: The First Generation," in M. E. Glasswell and E. W. Fasholé-Luke, eds., *New Testament Christianity for Africa and the World: Essays in Honour of Harry Sawyerr* (London, 1974), reprinted as chapter 12 of this volume; Sarah Potter, "The Social Origins and Recruitment of English Protestant Missionaries in the Nineteenth Century." Ph.D. thesis (University of London, 1974).

[3]Cf. A. F. Walls, "Black Europeans, White Africans: Some Missionary Motives in West Africa," in D. Baker, ed), *Religious Motivation: Biographical and Sociological Problems for the Church Historian* (SCH, 1978), pp. 339-348 (reprinted as chapter 8 of this volume).

[4]The American veteran A. T. Pierson, expounding "the plan of God in the ages," told a student conference of the multiplication of facilities and instrumentalities whereby world evangelization could now be effected. "Not one of you who is twenty-one years of age, but has substantially lived longer than Aristotle or Plato.

man, and if that did not imply conspicuous intellectual attainment, nor did entrance to the home ministry.[5]

The missionary movement produced some major scholars, a few of the first rank and a large number of competence and industry. Some developed new fields of study and pioneered new disciplines, but few of them made any significant contribution to theological or biblical studies, and of those who did even fewer showed much obvious influence from their cross-cultural experience.[6] It may be worth considering the relationship of all these trends with current secular learning.

An obvious place to begin is India, for towards the end of the eighteenth century India was for a time adopted into the Western tradition of humane learning, and in a quite different way from that in which the Chinese and the noble savage became topics of academic discussion.[7] Dr. Johnson might describe the contemporary idealized pictures of life in Tahiti as canting in defence of savages,[8] and thought nothing of importance could be learned from Pacific exploration;[9] but when Warren Hastings promoted Oriental learning, Johnson corresponded gravely, almost enviously, with him as with a patron of high learning.[10] When Sir William Jones produced his pioneer translations of the Sanskrit classics, he was following the usual avocations of a gentleman scholar, applying to the Vedas the faculties which similar literary gentlemen in England were applying to Pindar or Macrobius.[11]

There is not one of you who is blessed with University training, but knows more in the general province of knowledge than the great philosophers of a thousand years ago" *(Make Jesus King: The Report of the International Students Missionary Conference, Liverpool, January 1-5, 1890* [London, 1896]), pp. 25f.

[5]Cf. World Missionary Conference, 1910, Report of Commission V. "The Training of Teachers" (Edinburgh and New York, 1910), p. 67 ". . . it is evident that the Church does not secure an adequate proportion of the best intellectual results. The proportion of Pass-men to Honour-men ordained is about half as high again as amongst university men generally."

[6]Cf. A. F. Walls, "The Nineteenth Century Missionary as Scholar," in N. E. Bloch-Hoell, ed., *Misjonskall og forskerglede. Festskrift till Professor Olav Guttorm Myklebust* (Oslo, 1975), pp. 209-221 (reprinted as chapter 14 of this volume).

[7]Cf. D. E. Mungello, *Leibniz and Confucianism: The Search for Accord* (Honolulu, 1977).

[8]Boswell, *Life of Johnson*, sub 1784 (Hill iv, p. 309).

[9]*Ibid.*, sub 1776 (Hill iii, pp. 49f.); cf. sub 1769 (Hill ii, p. 73) and *Rasselas*, chapt. 2.

[10]*Ibid.*, sub 1781 (Hill iv, pp. 68-70): "I shall hope, that he who once intended to increase the learning of his country by the introduction of the Persian language, will examine nicely the traditions and histories of the East; that he will survey the wonders of its ancient edifices, and trace the vestiges of its ruined cities; and that, at his return, we shall know the arts and opinions of a race of men, from whom very little has been hitherto derived. . . . It is a new thing for a clerk of the India House [his friend John Hoole] to translate poets [Tasso and Aristo]; it is new for a Governor of Bengal to patronize learning."

[11]In John Courtenay's poem "Moral and Literary Character of Dr. Johnson" occur the lines:

Chairs of Sanskrit could be created in Western universities since Sanskrit could be seen as a somewhat recondite branch of Greco-Roman learning.[12] But in India there was another, utilitarian motive, too. Sanskrit and Persian were the languages of government and administration. Oriental languages were not therefore just a hobby for learned lawyers like Jones and Colebrooke; prosaic but dutiful characters like Sir John Shore, the future Claphamite Lord Teignmouth, acquired their little stock.[13] And even the most erudite were utilitarian. Jones, for instance, a judge of the High Court of Calcutta, devoted long years to an *Institutes of Hindu Law, or Ordinances of Manu*, in the hope—baseless as it proved—that the administration of justice could be improved by a codification, by recovering a sort of Indian Justinian.[14] (In parenthesis we may note that there is no evidence that the humanist tradition of scholarship had much practical effect in developing understanding, or even the desire for it, for *contemporary* Indians.)[15]

It has been argued that Indology met a sudden death by the 1830s.[16] If Indology is seen narrowly as the study of Sanskrit texts, there is some basis for this (though one can exaggerate both the suddenness of the demise and the duration of the period before its resurrection). The change from the classical Oriental languages to English as the language of Indian administration removed the utilitarian motive. But the change did not mean the death of all Indological learning. Already long before the 1830s, a new type of expert on India was appearing, and his interest and acquisitions were quite different from those of Sir William Jones.

Harmonious JONES! who in his splendid strains -
Sings Camden's sports, on Agra's flowery plains:
In Hindu fictions while we fondly trace
Love and the Muses, deck'd with Attick grace.

[12]Boswell and Johnson decided to have Oriental learning (taught by Jones) in the imaginary ideal college which they based on the members of The Club (*Journal of a Tour to the Hebrides* 25.8.1773; Hill v., p. 108).

[13]*The Life of Lord Teignmouth by His Son* is full of examples. Cf. P. Woodruff, *The Men Who Ruled India* I, 2d ed. (London, 1963), p. 153: "Perversely virtuous, obstinately middleclass. Shore spent his leisure mugging up Persian—and did not even pretend to be idler than he was." Shore compiled the first memoir of Jones (London, 1804).

[14]See A. J. Arberry, *Asiatic Jones: The Life and Influence of Sir William Jones* (London, 1946); P. J. Marshall, *The British Discovery of Hinduism in the Eighteenth Century* (Cambridge, 1970). After Jones' death, H. T. Colebrooke was set to produce a translated digest of Hindu law, and for this purpose was transferred from the revenue to the judicial branch of the East India Company's service. Cf. T. E. Colebrooke, *The Life of H.T. Colebrooke* (London, 1873), pp. 71-108.

[15]Cf. Woodruff, p. 383. T. S. P. Spear, *The Nabobs: A Study of the Social Life of the English in Eighteenth Century India*, 2d ed. (London, 1963) implies a different view.

[16]H. H. J. Swanson, "The Development of British Indology 1765-1820." Ph.D. thesis (University of Edinburgh, 1979), which discusses Jones and Colebrooke at length.

The new expert was a missionary. The first and greatest of them, William Carey, worked both on Sanskrit and a wide range of vernaculars; but for most missionaries it was the vernaculars which were most important: the languages of bazaar preaching and of the little congregations of predominantly low-caste converts. The authority of the missionary expert as a writer lay in his essentially descriptive method: he gave a direct account of what he could see in India, with those topics most prominent which were most likely to appal a British reader—especially the sort of reader whose moral indignation had already been aroused by the stories of the Slave Trade. They described widow burning, temple prostitution, ecstatic worshippers throwing themselves before the colossal car of Jagganath—and all with the connivance, nay, the active support, of a government ultimately responsible to a Christian nation. The convictions, the constituency, the agents, and the methods employed in this form of writing were essentially those of the movement for the abolition of slavery. People like the East India Company chaplain, Claudius Buchanan, came to play the part that Stephen and Macaulay played in the earlier controversy: marshalling descriptive material until the reader is unable to avoid its impact.[17] In fact Buchanan was the popularizer of the new type of missionary-originated oriental scholarship, and the measure of his success, is the way in which the missionary picture dominates the standard works of reference until well after the Mutiny.[18]

This missionary image of India, of which the most learned example, and the fount of many Western accounts, William Ward's *Account of the Writings, Religion and Manners of the Hindoos* (which is confessedly based almost entirely on Bengal) was a world away from the Augustan humanism of the earlier scholars with their base in East India Company administration. The Augustan dream faded in India as it did in Britain. To many earnest people, administrators as well as missionaries, the world of the Sanskrit classics must have seemed utterly remote from the daily realities of Indian life. As though to prove it, Jones' masterwork on ancient Indian law lay unused by judge or judged, European or Indian.

It is necessary to stress that the missionary picture of India was undergirded by knowledge of the living vernaculars, since so much attention has been paid to that aspect of missionary operations which most obviously coincided with the Anglicist revolution and which flowered most notably

---

[17]Jane Austen is a fair barometer: though not enthusiastic about Evangelical literature, she read and was moved by Buchanan (Letter to Cassandra Austen, January 24, 1813, in R. W. Chapman, ed., *Jane Austen's Letters*, 2d ed. [London, 1952], p. 292). It is perhaps significant that Buchanan's name is linked here with that of Thomas Clarkson, writer on the Slave Trade.

[18]A. K. Davidson, "The Development and Influence of the British Missionary Movement's Attitudes Towards India, 1786-1830," Ph.D. thesis (University of Aberdeen, 1973), assesses the effect of Buchanan's writing.

in the Scots Colleges.[19] It is worth remembering that, influential as they were, these colleges, aiming essentially at Brahmin youth, were always a minority exercise, and were frequently criticised in missionary circles as wasteful in resources. In origin they were almost a necessary product of Scottish ecclesiastical circumstances. Moderate and Evangelical could reach a consensus on an educational mission where agreement on other activities might have been more difficult. Few in either party would have seen much difference between the state of a Hindu and of a Catholic Highlander, and there was ample precedent for taming the latter and leading him to the courtyard of heaven by the medium of schools in which the Bible was the centre and the sun. Duff, an Evangelical commissioned as a missionary by an Assembly with a Moderate majority, followed this model precisely, bringing together the Western learning already desired by young Brahmins, the English language which they needed to acquire in order to enter government service, and a Christian metaphysic where the Bible was the reference book. The whole formed a mine which he trusted would one day blow up the citadel of Hinduism, whose outworks had already been dented by western scientific thought.[20]

It is interesting to see Duff's successor, Thomas Smith, obviously feeling embattled at the 1860 Liverpool Conference on Missions. He refuses to accept the easy way out, that of arguing that preaching and teaching are just different modes of evangelism; the real point, he insists, is whether it is right for a missionary to teach *other things than the Gospel*. He concludes that this is a proper use of a missionary's energies, provided that the teacher's ultimate aim is to introduce and establish Christianity. "I maintain that education, in its proper sense, if at once storing the mind with instruction, cultivating all its faculties and powers, is a legitimate method of fulfilling the great obligation of Christian missionaries." At the very least it must be legitimate where heathenism itself is embedded in the educational system, when, as in India, a whole people were brought up to believe that there is no distinction between moral good and evil, no difference between God and creation, and thus no responsibility. And in that country there is not only the desire for learning but other secular agencies which can supply the apparent want without ever touching the real need.[21]

---

[19]See M. A. Laird, *Missionaries and Education in Bengal 1793-1897* (Oxford, 1972) for a study of both vernacular and English education.

[20]Duff, speaking in Scotland after twenty years in India, says of his educational theory: "We thought not of individuals merely; we looked to the masses . . . we directed our view not merely to the present but to future generations. . . . While you engage indirectly separating as many precious atoms from the mass as the stubborn resistance to ordinary appliances can admit, we shall, with the blessing of God, devote our time and strength to the preparing of a mine, and the setting of a train which shall one day explode and tear up the whole from its lowest depths" (George Smith, *The Life of Alexander Duff* [London, 1881], p. 68).

[21]*Conference on Missions Held in 1860 at Liverpool* (London, 1860), pp. 118-120.

In other words, the logic and moral philosophy which formed the backbone of the Scottish Arts degree was a natural *praeparatio evangelica* for India. A missionary in such a setting needed that equipment himself—not as a means of understanding India's traditional thought but as a means of providing India with a substitute for that traditional thought. One can understand the sense of betrayal which Duff felt as he watched his mine being defused by neo-Hegelian biblical critics within the Church colleges of Scotland.[22]

Smith's Liverpool Conference audience were polite, but clearly not all convinced about higher education as a missionary method, and in particular about whether it was a good use of resources. But an Indian in the conference, the Rev. Behari Lal Singh, complained that when it came to the training of the Indian ministry the Scots colleges, far from being too learned, were falling short of the standard required if they were to produce ministers able to meet Hindu and Muslim religious leaders on equal terms. A Christian minister should be as learned in Hebrew and Greek as they in Sanskrit or Arabic; and Singh recounts on occasion when he would have been sadly worsted by a *maulvi* had he not acquired some additional Hebrew, not from the college of the Scots mission, but from a converted Jew.[23]

The Scots apart, comparatively few missionaries of that time could have had more Hebrew than the Scots colleges gave Indian ministers: for as we have seen, a missionary was for at least another decade more likely than not to be a person who had escaped a humanist education.[24] But throughout the century the missionary was thought of as primarily a minister. Special missionary operations, medical, educational, industrial, might involve laymen; and women were essential for certain missionary tasks; but the *typical* missionary was always a minister who happened to have an overseas station. Missionary colleges, whether informal (like the earlier arrangements of the London Missionary Society), or formal (like the Church Missionary College at Islington), were not places for special missionary study; they were places for providing a liberal and theological education as near as possible to what the home ministry would get. Henry Venn of the CMS, for instance, said that there would be no need of a training college, if

---

[22]Duff's daughter describes his distress after hearing Robertson Smith lecture in Aberdeen. "He had been obliged to read all manner of sceptical books, because there was not a book of the negative sort which did not find its way to Calcutta, or an argument advanced by the sceptical school on the continent which was not soon in the mouth of Hindoos. *But they were outside the Church* and he always regarded the two things as widely different, the coming out of midnight darkness—when individuals were groping their way. . . and the deliberate turning from the noontide blaze of gospel light into the mischievous questionings of carnal reason" (Smith, *Duff*, pp. 450f.).

[23]*Conference at Liverpool*, p. 216.

[24]*Ibid.*, p. 264. "The larger proportion of the missionaries have been drawn from the lower ranks of the middle classes, and the classes immediately below them."

one could get enough missionaries from the universities and the regular clergy.[25] In other words, any special missionary training which the Islington College supplied would be incidental, and in a sense accidental; its main function was to provide enough language, literature, theology, and good manners for a man from the lower middle class to pass muster as a clergyman.

Conversely, a man who had attended a university needed little extra learning to equip him as a missionary. The common stock of a liberal humane education would be the foundation on which men of quality (and increasingly missionary societies stressed the intellectual as well as the spiritual quality required for the mission field) would confront the questions raised by confrontation with other religious traditions or the complexities of new pastoral situations. As waves of missionary enthusiasm deluged the universities in the 1880s and 1890s, great stress was placed on the study of missions and missionary literature,[26] but it was assumed to be informal, private, study. The spirituality which underlay the movement laid great stress on bringing the best to Christ, and much was said about the best men being needed for the mission field;[27] but when such speakers talked of "the best men intellectually" they seem to have implied simply a good standard of general education. At the Conference of the Student

---

[25]Letter to F. Monod, February 5, 1855, quoted in W. Knight, *Memoir of the Rev. H. Venn: The Missionary Secretariat of Henry Venn* (London, 1880), p. 247. On the training of missionaries in this period see C. P. Williams "The Recruitment and Training of Overseas Missionaries in England between 1850 and 1900." M.Litt. thesis (University of Bristol, 1976).

[26]The American wing of the volunteer movement laid particular stress on this; Harlan P. Beach of Yale gave a special explanatory talk at the 1896 Conference (*Make Jesus King*, pp. 135-144). The conference organizers claimed to be presenting "the most complete set of missionary literature ever brought together," and provided bibliographies for missionary libraries to cost respectively £1, £3, £5, £10 or £20 (*ibid.*, pp. 276f). The London Conference of 1900 went further with addresses on the topic by J. H. Bernard and George Robson, editor of the United Presbyterian *Missionary Record: Students and the Missionary Problem. Addresses Delivered at the International Student Missionary Conference, London, January 2-6, 1900* (London, 1900), pp. 230-245, and offered libraries ranging in value from £5 to £63 (*SMP*, p. 547). The conference report included a fourteen-page catalogue of recently published missionary books (*SMP*, pp. 549-562).

[27]"Long ago it used to be thought that if a man was not good enough for the home ministry he might be sent out as a missionary. Thank God that . . . the question today is not 'Is he good enough to stay at home' but 'Is he good enough to go out?' No man is too good to go to the mission-field, and very few are good enough" (F. Gillison, *Make Jesus King*, p. 34). "Half the good in a university or college course is not the learning gained, but what it makes the student, and the work among the lowest in the missionfield needs often times the best equipped. . . . Do not think that a life spent among the outcasts of God's children will be a throwing away of your talents. Jesus Christ threw Himself away, but what was the result?" (Georgina Gollock, *ibid.*, pp. 95f).

Volunteer Missionary Union in 1896 there was a paper on the intellectual preparation of the volunteer. It was entrusted to a medical missionary. Dr. Thomas Gillison of the LMS believed God had laid a message on his heart through his thirteen years of service in China: it was of the imperative need for missionary candidates to get a full medical training even if it meant delaying reaching the mission field for a further three years.[28] His reasons, *mutatis mutandis*, might have been held to apply equally to preparation in other disciplines also, but subsequent speakers at the conference rather took occasion to say how well they had managed without a full medical training.[29] And Gillison, while firm on the requirement of the would-be missionary to train his intellect (and his physique)[30] was temperate, to say the least, about specifically intellectual pursuits. . . .

> Study history, study science, study divinity if you will. . . . But, friends, do not let the study of science overbalance the study of your Bible. To see a minister or missionary giving himself to collecting butterflies, or going on geographical excursions when he ought to be studying his Bible, is a sad sight.[31]

The Bible, and man—these are for Gillison the proper study of missionary mankind. All other topics, any other topics, are useful ancillaries but simply because they teach *method*, and method is for a busy missionary *sine qua non*.[32]

There was a special two-hour meeting for professors and tutors at the Conference. Reportedly this was "imbued almost more than the rest with that intense yet quiet glow of enthusiasm which characterized the whole Conference." This meeting of teachers does not seem to have been much concerned with the intellectual preparation of candidates; the report says that all the speeches at it converged on the question "How best may the spiritual life and work of the students be promoted without that interference which might defeat its own object?"—a development seen by the student committee as an answer to prayer.[33]

---

[28]*Make Jesus King*, pp. 33-37. Thomas Gillison, M.B., C.M. (Edin.) was in charge of the hospital in Hankow from 1883 to 1918 (See J. Sibree, *London Missionary Society: A Register of Missionaries, Deputations etc. from 1796 to 1923* [London, 4 cd, 1923], No. 801).

[29]See Egerton R. Young, *Make Jesus King*, p. 51; and, more guardedly, C. F. Harford-Battersby, *ibid.*, p. 236.

[30]"God has given us our bodies to take care of, and a man is sinning against God, who thinks it of no importance to look after his physical health. The man who neglects to train his intellect, is throwing away five out of the ten talents which God has entrusted to his care" (*ibid.*, p. 34).

[31]*Ibid.*, p. 35.

[32]"There is nothing more important for a man who is going to the mission field than to learn to be methodical. He will find duties pressing upon him, and if he does not know what to do first, he will find a great many left undone" (*idem*).

[33]*Make Jesus King*, p. 264.

Gillison had said "Study divinity *if you will.*" Some saw theological study as having special perils for the enthusiastic missionary volunteer. "I do not know that the study of Hebrew or of theology is any more divine in itself than the study of mathematics" said A. J. Gordon, a man much respected by the missionary constituency. "I go further, and affirm, what the history of the church is constantly proving, that the pursuit of these studies without a humble and prayerful dependence on God may be absolutely injurious to one's Christian life." It was not the brilliant and cultured sceptics and agnostics who were destroying the foundations of Protestant Christianity; it was the holders of theological chairs.[34]

A different note was sounded at the SVMU's London Conference in January 1900. The student committee who organized it included not only another address on the mental preparation of the missionary[35] but a whole session entitled "The need of thinkers for the mission field." Their speakers for this session were the celebrated Baptist John Clifford, who combined evangelical warmth with liberal theological sentiments and an outspoken Liberalism in politics; and R. H. Glover of Bristol, a Baptist of the evangelical heartlands. Clifford begins with a comparison of two great evangelists lately passed away. D. L. Moody was a robust intelligence but not in the ordinary use of the word a thinker: but Henry Drummond's evangelism took account of the intellectual conditions affecting thinking men. The mission field needed Drummonds as well as Moodys:

We need students—men who will work upon the facts of religion as Richard Owen among fossils and Sir Joseph Hooker on plants; scientific students, exact, severe, painstaking, hating inaccuracy as they hate a lie, as devoted to truth as to God; rigid in their scrutiny and flawless in their reasoning. . . eliminating the possibility of error by the repetition of experiments and the accumulation of observations, and so furnishing the churches and their workers with that knowledge of the realities of life without which energy is wasted, mistakes are made, and work is marred. (*SMP*, p. 212)

The mission field thinker is here primarily a scientific observer, collecting facts; but he must not be a bookworm, nor turn a blind eye to the difference

---

[34] A. J. Gordon, *The Holy Spirit in Missions* (London, 1893), pp. 201f. Gordon did not approve of Xavier's theology or methods but acclaimed this utterance of his: "It often comes into my mind to go round all the universities of Europe crying like a madman to all the learned men whose learning is greater than their charity, 'Ah what a multitude of souls is through your fault shut out of heaven!'" (*Ibid.*, p. 39). The SVMU organizers had hoped that Gordon would address the 1896 conference, but he died before it took place (*Make Jesus King*, p. 5).

[35] *SMP*, pp. 173-180. It was given by T. W. Drury, Principal of Ridley Hall, who had been an effective Principal of the Church Missionary College at Islington (E. Stock, *History of the Church Missionary Society* [London, 1899], 111, p. 262).

between the teachings of the sublime texts of the ancient east and the popular religion of the east today. Further, he must be a philosopher on the Pauline model, who can recover the hidden universals of our common humanity and thus open the closed doors that separate eastern from western minds; and he should be a master builder, able to cope with the complex problems of social life and development which arise on the mission field (*SMP*, p. 214).

The last aspect was developed by Glover: matters like polygamy and ancestor cult were not simple issues to be solved with a smile and a text or by what he calls "cockney" (i.e., culture-bound) methods. Furthermore, thorough mental preparation was necessary to produce the essential respect for non-Christian peoples and for the discovery of what he called the "temple-building materials" already to hand in the religion and culture of non-Christian peoples (*SMP*, p. 266).

How can one effect the necessary mental preparation? By studying, says Glover, the best thinking of the best heathen (*SMP*, p. 229). The greatest name in philosophy is still that of Plato, a heathen man; and the study of Plato, Sophocles, and Euripides (in translation, for Glover evidently did not overrate the competence of his audience in the ancient tongues) is the way to follow through the volunteer's consecration to God (*SMP*, pp. 222, 229). It is also the best preparation for reading Confucius. Englishmen do not make good metaphysicians, and therefore need plenty of practice before trying conclusions with Chinese. The Buddha is "in many directions the greatest of moral philosophers" who "has tracked, with such subtlety and strength, the influence of action on character . . . and of the automatic influence of character on destiny" (*SMP*, p. 222).

In the end, then, the best way of preparing for the mission field is to make the best use of a gentleman's education. As regards specifically theological education, the Rev. J. H. Bernard, Fellow of Trinity College, Dublin, who spoke next on "The need of advance in missionary education," admitted that the clergy had not given the duty of world evangelization its proper place. Only better ministerial education could cure this; but this did not imply the extension of the theological curriculum. "It is not practicable to introduce the history of missionary enterprise during the past hundred years into the official programme of our Divinity Schools and Theological Colleges."[36] Nor does he appear to envisage special academic provision for more than a handful of missionary candidates—and such special souls are evidently as likely as not to be Germans.[37] For the rest, all ordinands, whether intending the home or the overseas ministry, should be encouraged in the voluntary

---

[36]*SMP*, p. 231. "You cannot teach *everything* in two or three years to a young clergyman any more than to a young doctor or lawyer."

[37]In particular he thought of the study of Arabic, and the production of a critical edition of the Qur'an "which shall point out the sources from which its puerilities are derived. . . . Is it unreasonable to think that in this great assembly of students there may be *one*—perhaps of our own race, perhaps from Germany, that nursery of scholars—*one* who could take up this sorely needed task?" (*SMP*, p. 230).

study of missions, ancient and modern, with particular reference to the ancient. (Bernard was, after all, a sound patristic scholar himself.) And above all let them acquire a sound theological competence. The Councils of Ephesus and Chalcedon are highly relevant to the Muslim controversy, and, rather curiously

> The Eastern mind is just the same now as in the days of Athanasius, and we shall do unwisely, if we think we can escape, in India and Africa at least, from facing the difficulties which Christian men had to face then. (*SMP*, p. 237)

By the time of the Edinburgh World Missionary Conference of 1910, the missionary societies were clearly unhappy about the lack of specifically missionary material in the theological curriculum (*WMC* V, 39). The typical missionary, however, was still a minister.[38] (The commission of the conference which dealt with the preparation of missionaries was somewhat perplexed by the fact that ordained missionaries had necessarily to superintend educational institutions, when they did not necessarily have the professional competence of their lay colleagues.[39]) There remained a general desire that missionary and home ministry candidates should be trained together, and "the theological curricula would be enriched for all students by fuller treatment of missionary subjects, even if that involves some revision of the traditional curriculum."[40] The missionary must have the best education which his own country and Church can give him (*WMC* V, 107) and that should include, wherever possible, a university education, including the study of languages, history, moral science, and philosophy.[41] When the commission considered the proper subjects of study in detail, they gave pride of place to the Bible, then to natural science, then to philosophy, and then to elementary medicine and hygiene (*WMC* V, 109-114).

Philosophy received particular stress. "A leading missionary in India" described a philosophical training as being more valuable to a missionary than a theological one. It enabled theology to be studied with ease and breadth, reduced the dogmatism so counter-productive on the mission field, and enabled the missionary's ideas to be better understood, whether by opponent or by convert (*WMC* V, 111f.).

> Other experts have stated that the ideal training is furnished by the School of *Literae Humaniores* at Oxford, inasmuch as it develops best the general and thoughtful appreciativeness of students, and that an

---

[38]"In the vast majority of Societies, as in the denominations they represent, the ordained missionary is, and will always be, recognized as the representative figure and the most powerful factor in the whole movement" (*WMC* V, 115f.).

[39]Cf. *WWMC* V, 42f.

[40]*WMC* V, 80; cf. 122f., recommendations 3 and 4.

[41]*WMC* V, 122, recommendation 2. But of the minority report by Father Kelly of Kelham, 240-245.

Honours man in that school requires only the addition of a moderate amount of theology strictly so called in order to be qualified for work on the mission field. (*WMC* V, 118)

So ultimately, it is for the mission field as for the Civil Service: the best preparation for anything is Oxford Greats. Those who cannot get that must get what they can. And theology can be left as an occupation for theologians, the Household Cavalry of the Church Militant.

16

The Domestic Importance
of the Nineteenth-Century
Medical Missionary[1]
"The Heavy Artillery of the Missionary Army"

The history of medical missions is an epiphenomenon of the history of the medical profession. On the one hand they can be seen as a late growth in the missionary movement, and throughout the nineteenth century they required explanation and apology; on the other, they can be seen as present from the movement's earliest days. After all, when William Carey sailed for India in 1793 his only colleague was a medical man;[2] and a "surgeon" was specifically included among the first party sent by the London Missionary Society to the Pacific in 1796.[3] Indeed, generations of missionaries carried out a form of pillbox ministry, gravely administering draughts, lancing excrescences, and proceeding by trial and error ("We soon discovered the unfitness of calomel for African fevers," observed the Rev. Hope Waddell of Calabar, "by its prostrating effect upon ourselves").[4] Some, like David Livingstone, studied medicine as part of their missionary training, without thereby becoming any special sort of missionary, or one whit less the minister of the Gospel that the ordinary missionary was assumed to be.

---

[1]First published in W. J. Sheils, ed., *The Church and Healing*, Studies in Church History 19 (Oxford: Blackwell, 1982), pp. 287-97.

[2]John Thomas (1757-1801), enfant terrible of the Baptist mission, had studied at Westminster Hospital and had been a naval surgeon as well as a surgeon-apothecary in private practice. See C. B. Lewis, *The Life of John Thomas, Surgeon of the Earl of Oxford East Indiaman, and First Baptist Missionary to Bengal*, (London, 1873).

[3]John Gilham (1774-?), surgeon, appears as No. 13 in J. Sibree, *London Missionary Society: A Register of Missionaries, Deputations, etc. from 1796 to 1823*, 4th ed. (London, 1923).

[4]Hope Masterton Waddell, *Twenty-nine Years in the West Indies and Central Africa* (London, 1863), p. 452.

The difference between this and the developed medical missions which were all but universal by the First World War was created less by developments in missionary thought than by developments in the medical profession. By 1914 that profession had not only become immeasurably more effective in the treatment of disease and the promotion of health than could have been dreamed of even in 1830; it had also become a monopolistic institution in western society. One result of ennobling Mr. Sawyer and Mr. Allen into Dr. Finlay was the axiom that no one should apply himself to draughts and excrescences without a diploma authorizing him to do so. When the professional medical missionary first became noticeable in the middle of the nineteenth century he was a humble lay auxiliary worker alongside his clerical brother; by the end of the century missionary societies were taking responsibility for an entire university medical faculty and teaching hospitals to serve the entire Chinese Empire. As far as British missions are concerned, the development was made virtually inevitable by the powers given in 1850 to the General Medical Council.

Broadly speaking, the reasons for medical missions canvassed by their apologists[5] may be comprehended under four heads, and while the emphasis doubtless changes from time to time all four types of motive are found from the beginning of medical missions onward. There are imitative or obedientiary reasons urged for missions; the texts about the example of Christ "who went about doing good" and the dominical command to "heal the sick" are quoted endlessly. There are humanitarian or philanthropic reasons, the necessary response to unnecessary suffering; utilitarian reasons, relating medical provision to missionary mortality and efficiency; and strategic reasons, arising from the acceptability of medical missions when no other form of mission could gain a hearing.

It is interesting that the humanitarian motive is most obvious in the period of intense missionary recruitment during the last two decades of the century. It is urged by and upon the same constituency as was moved by calculations of the numbers of heathen passing annually into a Christless eternity. A little book by the American George D. Dowkontt circulated widely from the very offices that published *The Christian* and the Keswick

---

[5]Perhaps the most important single apologia is John Lowe, *Medical Missions: Their Place and Power* (Edinburgh, 1886, many later editions). Lowe (1835-1892) served LMS in Neyyur, South India, from 1861-1868 (he is No. 569 in Sibree's *Register*). Like his predecessor C. C. Leitch, he was both medically qualified and ordained. He did much to build up the Neyyur Hospital. From 1871 to his death he was Secretary of the Edinburgh Medical Missionary Society which provided background and practical training and financial assistance for the studies of medical missionary candidates and from whom medical missionaries for many societies were recruited. Lowe's book has a commendatory preface by the notable Indian civil servant (and by this time Principal of Edinburgh University) Sir William Muir, which contains just a hint that such sober authorities believed Lowe might have overstated the general *necessity* for medical missions.

movement's literature.[6] Entitled *Murdered Millions*, it argued that murder was worse when committed by neglect than by intent, and hence that if Christians failed to reduce the world's mortality by means of medical missions they would be guilty of murder on a massive scale. There is little point, Dowkontt remarks, in speculating on the eternal future of the heathen wh~ . their present is so pitiable; it would be more appropriate to reflect on that of those who, in possession of both the gospel and medicine, withheld them from the needy.[7]

At the "first missionary soirée" at the Liverpool Conference on Missions in 1860, William Lockhart, FRCS, the first genuine medical missionary to be appointed by the London Missionary Society, responding to hearty cheering (for he was a Liverpudlian himself), said of medical missions:

> They were commenced by the various Missionary Societies in England and America, in imitation of the example of Him "who went about doing good," and "healing all manner of sickness and disease among the people." The experiment thus made was to send out surgeons to various heathen lands, to endeavour to win the affections and confidence of the people, by healing their infirmities; while at the same time their minds were directed to Him who is the "Great Physician," and who can cure them of their deeper malady of sin."[8]

Lockhart gives prominence, like countless other apologists, to the strategic motives for medical missions—they are means of making an opening. Time and again it is insisted that this is not their primary motive, that they need no such justification; but the fact remains that historically it was probably the most decisive one, at least for determining when and where medical missions began. Lockhart himself had been the first Protestant missionary in North China; he had been able to convey any idea of his purpose only after opening his house for free medical treatment. At the time of the Liverpool Conference, the Church Missionary Society was finding Kashmir virtually inaccessible. The Lahore Missionary Conference of 1862 put it to Henry Venn, who was cautious, not to say sceptical, on this subject, that a medical man could provide the needed opening; and the CMS was eventually led to the unusual step of appointing a doctor from the Free

---

[6]G. D. Dowkontt, *Murdered Millions* (London, 1894). The American edition was earlier. Dowkontt, an M.D., was Secretary of the International Medical Missionary Society from 1881.

[7]*Ibid.*, p. 20.

[8]*Conference on Missions Held in 1860 at Liverpool. . .* edited by the Secretaries to the Conference (London, 1860), p. 100. Lockhart (1811-1896) is No. 384 in Sibree's *Register*. He wrote an account of his work entitled *The Medical Missionary in China* (1864).

Church of Scotland.[9] Young Dr. Elmslie[10] found he could conduct public prayers and his catechist could preach daily to the patients, their relatives, and all the carriers, if he was seen to be offering an effective medical facility—and this in an area where evangelistic missionaries had been effectively inhibited. Before long a local rajah was offering to pay for a doctor of his own, to work on the same terms as in British India, and with no strings attached as to what else he did; and the Punjab Medical Missionary Society was beseeching Edinburgh Medical Missionary Society to find such a one.[11] Medical missionaries, said an enthusiastic speaker at a Student Volunteer Missionary Union conference many years later, "are the heavy artillery of the missionary army."[12]

It was as heavy artillery that medical missions were used above all: in the less responsive fields, in Islamic societies, and above all in China. The London Missionary Society, for instance, sent out some 80 medical missionaries and 27 nurses between Lockhart's commissioning in 1838 and the outbreak of the First World War. That is 107 out of a total of 987 missionaries over the whole period, no mean proportion. Of the doctors, only 8 served in the Society's Central African field, and another 6 in Madagascar, where the LMS could point to a notable response to their preaching; and in the Pacific, the Society's oldest field, with the best-established church and most significant Christian population, only two. However 20 served in India, and no less than 48 in China.[13] A lady doctor of the Church Missionary Society in Persia cried out to the Student Volunteers "In the whole of this land there are but eight qualified medical missionaries."[14] Persia was far from responsive soil. There must have been many larger and more responsive populations with many fewer doctors.

This leads to the observation that all the motives for setting up medical missions were arguments for heavier and heavier commitment to them. To be committed to providing a doctor implied a commitment to more doctors, or a mission might collapse if the doctor were sick or on leave.[15] Even so,

---

[9]CMS Archives GAC 1/16 49-50 Venn to Balfour, November 27, 1863, April 7, 1864, June 1, 1864. Cf. CMS CI 1/26, 356, Venn to Sir D. F. McLeod KCSI: "Our past experience of medical missionaries has been uniformly unhappy. I will indulge the hope that in this case we may have better success."

[10]On William J. Elmslie (1832-1872) see Anon. [John Lowe], *Medical Missions as Illustrated By Some Letters and Notices of the Late Dr. Elmslie* (Edinburgh, 1874) and *Church Missionary Society Register of Missionaries and Native Clergy from 1804 to 1904* (London, 1905), No. 657.

[11]CMS Archives GAC 1/16, Letter of November 7, 1866.

[12]Herbert Lankester, M.D., *SMP*, p. 494.

[13]Calculations are based on Sibree's *Register*. The aggregate credited to the various fields is more than 80, since several served in more than one field.

[14]Emmeline M. Stuart, who had been the SVMU Women's Travelling Secretary, sent this appeal from Isfahan (*SMP*, pp. 512f.).

[15]Cf. R. Fletcher Moorshead, *"Heal the Sick." The Story of the Medical Mission Auxiliary of the Baptist Missionary Society* (London, 1929), p. 50, for an account of an Indian hospital faced with an epidemic in the absence of the only doctor.

the volume of work imposed on them, and the conditions under which it was carried out, could produce intolerable strains. Five doctors of the Baptist Missionary Society in China, young men for the most part, died at their posts through illness or overwork within a period of six years.[16] Consequently the call went out for more and more doctors to replace casualties or provide relief—let alone for those needed to follow up new and clamant opportunities.

Nor was it simply a matter of doctors. Not only did the idea of providing ministerial missionaries with some medical training fade, as did the idea of a doctor whose primary function was to maintain the health of the mission's staff;[17] increasingly it was argued that to send doctors without hospitals was an inefficient use of medical personnel. And whereas in the days of Lockhart and Elmslie a hospital might be set up in the doctor's house, a generation later a hospital implied buildings, equipment, qualified nursing staff, training facilities for local staff—certainly for auxiliaries, probably for nurses, sometimes for doctors.[18] And as standards went up and medical knowledge increased, so did the demands for the replacement of obsolete buildings[19] and the introduction of new, and comparatively expensive, equipment that could be taken for granted in the progressive hospitals at home where the young—they were usually young—missionary doctors had received their training or experience. Back in the 1860s Elmslie was employing anaesthesia in the remote Kashmir mission, thanking God that he had attended J. Y. Simpson's class in Edinburgh. The time was to come when his spiritual successors were calling on their supporting societies for X-ray apparatus.

---

[16]H. S. Jenkins and C. F. Robertson died in 1913, John Lewis in 1916, Thomas Scollay in 1918, and G. K. Edwards in 1919.

[17]The Baptist Missionary Society originally conceived the medical function in the Congo Mission as medical attendance on the missionaries, with gratuitous help to "any European or Native in the neighbourhood who may be ill or send for help" (Moorshead, p. 28). There was plenty of contemporary evidence in decimated missions to some parts of Africa, of the dangers of not having specialist medical advice. Cf., e.g., *The Catholic Church and Zimbabwe*, ed. A. J. Dachs and W. F. Rea (Gwelo, Zimbabwe, 1979), chapt. 1 and M. Gelfand, *Gubulawayo and Beyond: Letters and Journals of the Early Jesuit Missionaries to Zambesia 1879-1887* (London, 1968), *passim*. The first ten years of Baptist missions in Zaire were very costly in life and health.

[18]Elmslie read a paper at a CMS conference at Amritsar as early as 1866 proposing a Punjab equivalent of the Edinburgh Medical Missionary Society to assist the formation of indigenous Christian doctors (Lowe, *Elmslie*, 79). The significance of the small number of "national" Christians accredited as medical missionaries needs study of its own.

[19]"The old hospitals with their inefficient equipment and structural deficiencies, were in the position of the old wineskins in the familiar parable of our Lord" (Moorshead, p. 129, on the Baptist hospitals immediately after the First World War). The deputations from the home committee in fact brought back frightening accounts and urgent recommendations for renewal.

And the arguments for medical missionaries were also arguments for having the highest quality. Fletcher Moorshead, the long-serving Secretary of the Baptist Medical Missionary Auxiliary, pointed out the remarkably high average of formal qualifications attained by the medical missionaries of the immediate post-war period, as well as their contributions to the advancement of knowledge, and this tradition was of some standing.[20] Even in the most enthusiastic period of missionary volunteering, medical students were urged to complete the full course, and, if possible, to get appropriate postgraduate experience. After all, "he will usually have to be general practitioner, consulting surgeon, oculist, aurist, dentist and everything else."[21] But a long medical training was expensive. Dowkontt lamented that good volunteers were not getting the medical training due to the heathen world, while any number of theological seminaries were endowed to give theological teaching free.[22]

One of the speakers at the SVMU Conference was the celebrated Duncan Main of Hangchow. Main was fully aware of the humanitarian motive for his work; he recalled when as a student he had proffered a tract in an Edinburgh slum, and received the answer "It's a pity I can't eat it." But his instructions were evidently to highlight the strategic motive, and show how it brought people to Christ. "That is the aim and object of all hospital practice, to work through men's bodies to get to their souls" (*SMP*, p. 501).

And it soon becomes evident that the strategic, ultimately evangelistic, aspect of medical missions requires investment in medical technology. Itinerating medicine or outpatient work is not efficient either medically or evangelistically.

Take a man suffering from a broken leg; you go in and say "What is your hope of a future life?" He says, "What about this pain?" Take the man into a little room, get his leg set, put him into a comfortable bed, and leave him. Go back in half an hour, and he will say, "What was that you were saying about a future life?"[23]

---

[20]R. Fletcher Moorshead, *The Way of the Doctor: A Study in Medical Missions* (London, n.d., ca. 1926), pp. 181ff.

[21]Lankester, *SMP*, pp. 49ff. Similar advice was given at the 1896 Liverpool Conference by Dr. Thomas Gillison of the LMS in China *(Make Jesus King*, pp. 33-37). At the Cleveland Student Volunteer Conference of 1891, one of the themes was "Immediate Sailing: Its Advantages, and How Secured." Nevertheless Dowkontt, who spoke on medical work, said in answer to a question as to whether one should take a full or a short course, "I would say, never go out unless you have a full medical course. And unless you have a degree, do not allow people to call you a doctor, and do not dare to assume the title" *(Report of the First International Convention of the Student Volunteer Movement for Foreign Missions*, 1891, p. 91; reprinted Pasadena, Calif., 1979). There were cases of contrary advice about full training, notably in the policy of the China Inland Mission.

[22]Dowkontt, *Murdered Millions*, p. 20.

[23]*Ibid.* On David Duncan Main (1856-1934), like Elmslie a Scot who entered the service of the CMS, see K. de Gruchè, *Dr. D. Duncan Main of Hangchow, Who Is Known*

Another missionary in China, mystified by the growth of objections to anaesthesia on the part of patients' relatives, discovered that it was due to the high incidence of patients who received it who became associated with the church.[24] In other words there was a direct relationship between the seriousness of the operation or the length of stay in hospital and the religious response to treatment. Main was quite clear about the implications.

> Every medical missionary who is sent out, as soon as he passes his language examination, should have a grant to build a hospital. He should be not only thoroughly qualified, but thoroughly equipped. (*SMP*, pp. 501f.)

The Committee treasurers in his audience must have been stirring a little uneasily. The brutal fact was that medical missions were immensely expensive, especially if they were to be equipped as the medical staff insisted was essential. From hospitals it was a natural step to teaching hospitals and then (in China) to regular Christian Faculties of Medicine with professors of medicine and science, pharmacists and other requirements furnished through the missionary societies.[25] What better legacy for missions to leave to a country, what better gift to a new church, what surer way of providing for their work to be continued? Yet even much simpler hospitals placed great strain on resources under the relentless pressure of improved medical standards. It might be true that the money would go further and be more efficiently used than in many hospitals in the West, but it required a major effort to raise it, and separate appeals by the medical mission auxiliaries ran the danger of competing with general mission giving. The London Missionary Society's medical mission in Madagascar made a prosperous beginning, but its security depended on a single donor. When the donor changed his mind, the mission collapsed, and the missionary doctor went off to be Government Surgeon in Mauritius.[26] Many suggested that medical missions could be made self-supporting. Too many medical missionaries, argued Dowkontt, were wearing themselves out giving free service when, if they would spend a little time with the half dozen private patients a day who could afford realistic fees, they could relieve their missions of the

---

in China as *Dr. Apricot of Heaven Below* (London, n.d., ca. 1926) and A. Gammie, *Duncan Main of Hangchow* (London, n.d., ca. 1934).

[24]Moorshead, "*Heal the Sick*," p. 94.

[25]The post-war appointments of the LMS, e.g., included an Associate Professor of Physiological Chemistry and two pharmacists for the Union Medical College, Beijing (Sibree, Nos. 1388, 1428, 1429).

[26]Cf. R. Lovett, *The History of the London Missionary Society*, vol. 1 (London, 1879), pp. 771-773. The doctor concerned, Andrew Davidson (Sibree, No. 584), wrote a massive *Geographical Pathology: An Inquiry into the Geographical Distribution of Infective and Climatic Diseases*, 2 vols.(Edinburgh, 1892) and lectured at Edinburgh University.

burden of their support.[27] Later, and in the context of the need for hospitals to have materials and equipment, Fletcher Moorshead was indicating that a policy of "superior accommodation" and "remunerative fees" for private patients could produce a local income.[28] Thus financial dilemmas led to moral ones, until the post-war conditions, the quite unexpected impact of the high rupee and Chinese dollar, and then the Great Depression, brought about far-reaching changes in this as in most other aspects of Western missions.[29]

The high unit costs attached to medical missions and their special nature led naturally to separate funding. By another route medical missions had another substantial effect on mission administration: they radically assisted the declericalization of the missionary.

As early as the Liverpool Conference of 1860 it was being argued that the ministerial and the medical professions should be kept separate. "That [profession] to which I belong," said a medical man, "is sufficient to fill an angel's mind, and if you attempt to graft upon it the higher and nobler profession of divinity you will at the same time, spoil a divine, and make a quack."[30] In the light of this, it is interesting to note that several clerical missionaries returned home to qualify medically, and there are signs that others wanted to and had to be dissuaded.[31] It is also interesting that no less than 19 LMS medical missionaries before 1914, almost a quarter of the whole, were the children of clerical missionaries.[32]

However, the professional autonomy of the medical missionary did not mean that he was divorced from evangelistic or spiritual concerns. Indeed, as Duncan Main indicated to the Student Volunteers, the doctor remained as much an evangelist as any ministerial missionary; and, in view of the close relationship of the medical and evangelistic aspects of the work, the doctor must have charge of both. It was generally recognized that a medical missionary must be suitable in both aspects of his work. Herbert Lankester,

---

[27]*Murdered Millions*, chapt. 4.

[28]Moorshead, *The Way of the Doctor*, p. 191.

[29]Moorshead, *"Heal the Sick,"* pp. 122f. gives some account of the Baptist position, including a requirement on hospitals to raise 80 percent of their expenditure from local services.

[30]J. D. Macgowan, American Baptist Missionary Union, Ningpo, *Conference on Missions Held at Liverpool*, p. 275.

[31]E.g., Samuel Hickman Davies of the LMS (Sibree, No. 640), an ordained missionary, served in Samoa (where medical missions were not developed) for twenty years before going to study medicine in Edinburgh in 1805. He qualified (LRCS and LRCP) and served five more years in Samoa before, following health troubles, he took a post with the St. Pancras Medical Mission. He later stood *locum tenens* at the Neyyur Hospital, South India (1900). For Henry Venn cooling the ardour to study medicine of a hard-pressed missionary in the Turkish Empire, cf. CMS Archives GAC 1/16 49-50, Venn to O'Flaherty, December 26, 1864.

[32]A twentieth, T. T. Thomson, was the son of a medical missionary.

Physician to the CMS and Secretary of its Medical Committee, came to advocate the attachment of evangelistic missionaries to hospitals to relieve the overburdened medical staff—but it is clear that he still envisaged the medical superintendent as being in charge of the whole of his mission's ministrations, bodily and spiritual (*SMP*, pp. 497ff.). The World Missionary Conference of 1910 found it necessary to allude to the problems of educational institutions, where it was desirable to have a ministerial head who might not have the professional competence of his lay colleagues (*WMC* V, p. 42f.) It is a sign of the remarkable development of the medical profession that the Conference did not have to discuss the desirability of ministerial headship of medical institutions.[33]

Thus the doctor—and increasingly the doctor might be a woman—moved over into a sphere once unchallengeably the preserve of the minister; both in the field and in home administration (where many missionary societies developed medical committees as auxiliaries, with medical men as secretaries who were well aware of what committees consisting of godly non-professional men were capable)[34] medical missions effectively moved to a quite special position in missionary polity. In the meantime, the day of the pillbox missionary gradually died away. The ministerial missionary who used draughts and lancet stood in danger of being denounced as a quack.

What all this meant for the relation of Christianity and healing for those affected by the missions is a quite different, much wider matter. It is perhaps sufficient to note in closing that medical missions were earlier, stronger, and far more numerous in those parts of the world where, as in the West, healing and religion could be mentally separated with relative ease. Conversely, they were later and less noticeable in those parts where healing and religion are most intimately connected in the traditional world view.[35]

---

[33]The commission recognized that in a busy hospital the medical missionary might be absorbed in the professional side of his work, but even so acknowledged his "general spiritual oversight" of that "directly spiritual" work which he might need to delegate to others (*WMC*, p. 138).

[34]Cf. Lankester, *SMP*, p. 499: "As a rule the well-qualified medical realises full well how little he knows, whereas sometimes a non-professional Committee thinks that as long as a legal qualification has been obtained it is sufficient," and Moorshead ("*Heal the Sick*," chapt. 2, where the author clearly relishes the young medical man's triumph over the venerable Candidates Committee). Lankester (CMS) and Moorshead (BMS) were G.P.s who had not been serving missionaries but who serviced the medical departments of their respective societies. Lankester was called in to advise on the setting up of the Baptist auxiliary.

[35]It is interesting that the establishment of the Baptist medical mission in Congo in 1907 arose spontaneously from a public meeting in Birmingham where the elderly chairman spoke eloquently of the recent death in Congo of that city's distinguished Baptist George Grenfell. The committee had planned the meeting to support the work in China (Moorshead, "*Heal the Sick*," p. 56).

Perhaps it could not have been otherwise; and it is at least arguable in the light of experience of the "White Man's Grave," that (save for the dreaded surgery) Western medicine demonstrated little obvious superiority over African before the days of the General Medical Council. Be that as it may, the huge proportion of those professing and practising the Christian faith which Africa now provides, causes the special relationship of religion and healing there to be one of the utmost significance for the future of Christianity, and medical missions are only one of the elements in its story—and not the principal one.

17

The American Dimension
of the Missionary Movement[1]

Can Americans Teach Religion?

Americans themselves know all too well that their genius is not in religion. . . . Americans are great people; there is no doubt about that. They are great in building cities and railroads, as ancient Babylonians were great in building towers and canals. Americans have a wonderful genius for improving the breeds of horses, cattle, sheep and swine; they raise them in multitudes, butcher them, eat them, and send their meat-products to all parts of the world. Americans too are great inventors. They invented or perfected telegraphs, telephone, talking and hearing machines, automobiles. . . poison gases. Americans are great adepts in the art of enjoying life to the utmost. . . . Then, they are great in Democracy. The people is their king and emperor; yea, even their God; the American people *make* laws, as they make farms and farm implements. . . . Needless to say, they are great in money. . . . They first make money before they undertake any serious work. . . . To start and carry on any work without money is in the eyes of the Americans madness. . . . Americans are great in all these things and much else; but *not in Religion*, as they themselves very well know. . . . Americans must *count religion* in order to see or show its value. . . . To them big churches are successful churches. . . . To win the greatest number of converts with the least expense is their constant endeavour. Statistics is their way of showing success or failure in their religion as in their commerce and politics. Numbers,

[1]First published in Joel A. Carpenter and Wilbert R. Shenk, *Earthen Vessels: American Evangelicals and Foreign Missions, 1880-1980* (Grand Rapids: Eerdmans, 1990), pp. 1-25.

numbers, oh, how they value numbers! . . . Americans are essentially children of this world; that they serve as teachers of religion . . . is an anomaly. . . . Indeed, religion is the last thing average Americans can teach. . . . Americans are the least religious among all civilized peoples. . . . Mankind goes down to America to learn how to live the earthly life; but to live the heavenly life, they go to some other people. It is no special fault of Americans to be this-worldly; it is their national characteristic, and they in their self-knowledge ought to serve mankind in other fields than in religion.[2]

The year is 1926; the source, the first volume of the *Japan Christian Intelligencer*; the writer, Kanzo Uchimura, one of the outstanding Christian figures of his day in Japan. He was a first-generation Christian, converted through American missionaries, and full of honour and respect for certain Americans. Of "my own teacher in Christian religion," as he called him, Justus H. Seelye, Uchimura wrote, "I could not but bow myself before such a man, place the care of my soul in him, and be led by him into light and truth. The Lord Jesus Christ shone in his face, beat in his heart."[3]

There are reasons for beginning an assessment of twentieth-century American evangelical missions with this view from the outside. Uchimura speaks as a Christian, as a disciple of Christ whose knowledge of Christ has come from American sources. But for him, as for a good part of the world, to hear the words *American missions* is to hear first the word *American*. This chapter is concerned with the prehistory of our subject and will say little directly about the evangelical societies of the past hundred years that lie at the heart of it. The flowering of American missions that began a century ago is in full continuity with the American missions of an earlier period. "Evangelical" missions as such belong, as it were, to Volume Two. Volume One of our story is the American-ness of American missions.

And to one highly intelligent and not unsympathetic observer of sixty years ago, one who had drunk deeply of American missions, it seems that the word *American* conveys, first of all, immense energy, resourcefulness, and inventiveness—a habit of identifying problems and solving them— and, as a result, first-rate technology. In the second place it reflects an intense attachment to a particular theory of government, one that does not grow naturally in most of the world. Third, it stands for an uninhibited approach to money and a corresponding concern with size and scale. Fourth, it stands for what Uchimura calls "materiality," a somewhat stunted appreciation of certain dimensions of life, notably those relating to

---

[2]Kanzo Uchimura, "Can Americans Teach Japanese in Religion?" *Japan Christian Intelligencer* 1 (1926): 357-61. For other views of Americans see W. R. Hutchison, "Innocence Abroad: the 'American Religion' in Europe," *Church History* 51 (1982): 71-84.

[3]Uchimura, "Americans Teach Japanese," p. 357.

the transcendent world. Americans have a tendency to translate those very dimensions into technological terms, problems to be solved, something that can be all worked out—big boots in the Temple, as one might say. Uchimura, a Christian and a convert, not a Buddhist or a Shintoist, senses in the religious culture of his country (traditions that as to their content he has rejected) a recognition of transcendent reality compared to which most of these vigorous, confident American missionaries, in common with most of their countrymen, are on the beginner's slopes.

America as the Ultimate Development of the West

A British commentator can take no comfortable pride in his own position on hearing such an analysis. No doubt much of what Uchimura says would apply to the whole of the Western presence in the East; America looms largest in his consciousness because America has the leading Western presence in Japan and because so many of his own contacts were American. But insofar as America stands for the West, America is the West writ large, Western characteristics exemplified to the fullest extent. Americans themselves have always been aware that they represent the decisive and ultimate development of the West. None other than Rufus Anderson, an American missionary thinker almost a century before Uchimura, has said:

> The Protestant form of association—free, open, responsible, embracing all classes, both sexes, all ages, the masses of the people—is peculiar to modern times, and almost to our age. Like our own form of government, working with perfect freedom over a broad continent, it is among the great results of the progress of Christian civilization in this "fulness of time" for the world's conversion. Such great and extended associations could not possibly have been worked, they could not have been created, or kept in existence, without the present degree of civil and religious liberty and social security, or without the present extended habits of reading and the consequent wide-spread intelligence among the people; nor could they exist on a sufficiently broad scale, nor act with sufficient energy for the conversion of the world, under despotic governments, or without the present amazing facilities for communication on the land, and the world-wide commerce on the seas. Never, till now, did the social condition of mankind render it possible to organize the armies requisite for the world's spiritual conquest.[4]

---

[4]"The Time for the World's Conversion Come" first appeared in the *Religious Magazine*, Boston, in 1837-38. It has been reprinted several times, most recently and accessibly in *To Advance the Gospel: Selections from the Writings of Rufus Anderson*, ed. R. Pierce Beaver (Grand Rapids: Eerdmans, 1967), pp. 59-70. The passage quoted occurs at pp. 65-66 of that version.

This passage comes from a sermon of 1837 called "The Time for the World's Conversion Come." It is an attempt to discern the signs of the times. Many contemporary Western European Christians were engaged in a similar exercise; but their energies were usually directed to new schemes of interpretation of Daniel and Revelation, their applications to the conversion of the Jews, or the Eastern Question in European diplomacy.[5] Anderson's identification of the signs of the times is perhaps characteristically and pragmatically American—though to some extent it had been adumbrated half a century earlier by William Carey, himself wide open to the American influences of his own day.[6] The signs that Anderson identifies are those of opportunity and capability providentially furnished for direct evangelization of the whole world. It is a practical, activity-directed style of argument of American advocates of mission that runs through A. T. Pierson and John R. Mott to Ralph Winter.[7] What is especially interesting in the passage quoted is that Anderson does not base his judgment that the time for the world's conversion is come solely on what one might call technological criteria—improved communications, ready maritime access, and so on. Equally important are the political, economic, and ecclesiological developments of his day.

Anderson expects the Great Commission to be fulfilled by means of what he calls the Protestant form of association, that is, the voluntary society. And one sign that the time for the world's conversion is come is

---

[5]Cf. the influential preacher John Cumming, minister of the Scots Church in London, whose *Apocalyptic Sketches: Lectures on the Book of Revelation* first appeared in London in 1848. He argues that the drying up of the Euphrates under the sixth vial portends the decline of Turkey: "From 1820 down to the present time, Turkey has been wasting—the crescent waning. . . . Contemporaneous with the wasting of the Turkish power, there should be the rise of an interest in the Jewish race. . . . And such an interest is actually taken in their destiny at the present day" (12th ed., 1850, p. 494). Cumming was much indebted to E. B. Elliott, *Horae Apocalypticae; or, A Commentary on the Apocalypse, Critical and Historical*, 5 vols. (London, 1844); Elliott began the work in 1837, the same year Anderson's tract appeared. On the changed position of Turkey following the French Revolution, and its wasting from 1820 (see 4th ed., 3:310, 415-17), Elliott is particularly severe on Moses Stuart ("the American professor," as he calls him) for resolving "even what seems more specific into generalizations" (5:522).

[6]Cf. William Carey, *An Enquiry into the Obligations of Christians to Use Means for the Conversion of the Heathens* (Leicester, 1791), facsimile ed. with introduction by E. A. Payne (London: Carey Kingsgate, 1961), pp. 67-69.

[7]Cf. Pierson's contribution at the Liverpool student conference, *Jesus King!* (London: SVMU, 1896); John R. Mott, *The Evangelization of the World in This Generation* (New York: SVMU, 1900), chap. 6: "The Possibility of Evangelizing the World in this Generation in View of the Opportunities, Facilities and Resources of the Church," and *The Decisive Hour of Christian Missions* (New York: SVMU, 1910), chapt. 8: "Possibilities of the Present Situation"; Ralph D. Winter, *The Twenty-Five Unbelievable Years, 1945-1969* (Pasadena: William Carey Library, 1970).

that social organization has now reached a stage at which voluntary associations can flourish. As Anderson indicates, this cannot happen under despotic governments; one would not expect to find societies for the evangelization of the world arising in the Kingdom of the Two Sicilies. But for voluntary societies to flourish more is necessary than the absence of despotism. One needs a social system that allows for plurality and choice, in which people are not required or prepared to act in the same way as all their neighbours, in which there is a highly developed sense of the individual and of individual autonomy. The voluntary association is part of a wider community but does not act solely by means of that community's recognized channels of activity. Many communities that are by no means despotic do not provide these conditions. In nineteenth-century America they were provided as never before and as nowhere else.

For the voluntary society to operate overseas implies the existence of cash surpluses and freedom to move them about. It cannot operate if the surplus of production is marginal or if the movement of surpluses is controlled by the wider community. America provided *par excellence* the economic capability for voluntary societies to operate overseas, just as it had provided a favourable social and political climate for their development.

Explicitly *Christian* voluntary societies imply a conception of the church that does not inhibit their birth and a style of church organization that is not embarrassed by their activity. Anderson recognizes that it is only in his own time that Protestant Christianity had produced an organizational form that was capable of sustaining overseas mission. His description of this new Protestant form of association as "free, open, responsible, embracing all classes, both sexes, all ages, the masses of the people"[8] hardly applies to any of the classical forms of church government, whether Episcopal, Presbyterian, or Independent. In fact, the churches of Christendom were *not* organized for overseas missions in Anderson's time or long afterwards; they were outflanked or subverted for this purpose by the Protestant association, the voluntary society. Voluntary Christian societies flourish through the atomization of the church, the decentralization and dispersal of its organization. Nineteenth-century America produced just those conditions; and by the twentieth century the line between church and association had in America become so fine that the church itself often came to be seen almost in terms of a voluntary society.

Anderson's analysis refers to the whole Protestant world of his day; but note how easily he passes from the whole Protestant Christian world to a statement that could apply only to the United States: "The voluntary society is peculiar to modern times, and almost to our age. Like our own form of

---

[8]Anderson, "Time for the World's Conversion," p. 65.

government, working with perfect freedom over a broad continent, it is among the great results of the progress of Christian civilization."[9]

There must have been many devout English supporters of missions in 1837 who would have been shaken by the suggestion that American democracy was the finest fruit of Christian civilization. It was manifest to them that it owed not a little to demoniacal French atheism. Anderson, however, has no compunction in associating American governmental theory, American continental expansion, and the providential direction of the Holy Spirit. The United States of America represents, under God, a new and higher phase of civilization. And he grasped that the missionary movement in which he was so important a figure at such a formative stage was the product of a particular phase of Western political and economic development, the characteristics of which were to be demonstrated most dramatically in the United States. It was not in his power—or his responsibility—to offer guidance for the period when that phase ended.

When Anderson wrote, Americans were a minority among missionaries. Britain was much the largest source; Germany and other parts of Europe provided others. From the late nineteenth century the American proportion increased, until soon after the First World War North America had become the principal source of missionaries.[10] Since the Second World War that proportion has rapidly increased.[11]

In twentieth-century missions, then, North America plays an increasingly dominant role, and in the last section of that century an overwhelming one. That same period has seen an increasing proportion of missionaries from missions not only unmistakably American but insistently claiming the title "evangelical." Here we must return to Uchimura and remind ourselves that among the words *American evangelical missions* the word that most people will hear first and loudest is the word *American*. For the moment we can leave on one side the political associations that must inevitably cling to this word and thus to the words with which it is linked. Perhaps we can restate one of Uchimura's observations and put it in less provocative form by saying that Christianity as represented by Americans has been shaped by essentially American cultural influences. American missions are thus both products and purveyors of American culture.

A leading characteristic of historic Christianity is that, though it crosses cultural frontiers, it rapidly acculturates and takes new forms dictated by the culture in which it becomes rooted. It is, then, only to be expected that

[9]*Ibid.*

[10]W. Richey Hogg, "The Role of American Protestantism in World Missions," in *American Missions on Bicentennial Perspective*, ed. R. Pierce Beaver (South Pasadena: William Carey Library, 1977), pp. 354-402.

[11]See the successive editions of *Missions Handbook: North American Protestant Ministries Overseas*, published since 1967 by Missions Advanced Research and Communications (MARC) Centre, Monrovia, California.

a specifically North American form of Christianity should arise. It is the inevitable consequence of a genuine rooting of Christian faith in North America. And here we recall a striking fact. Latourette rightly calls the nineteenth century "The Great Century of Missions." But in no part of the world did that century see such a striking outcome as in North America.[12] The main missionary achievement of the nineteenth century was the Christianizing of the United States.

There was nothing inevitable about all of this. After all, modern Australia, New Zealand, and to some extent South Africa were also the products of European emigration, often from the same sources as North America; but their religious history has been quite different. They produced no indigenous "religious tradition." New Zealand, even though large sections of some of its founding communities were shaped by strong Christian influences, soon developed into what one of its own historians has called "a simple materialism."[13] The secular nature of Australian universities of the 1890s was defended with an antireligious verve that shocked John R. Mott, accustomed as he was to the principle of church-state separation and to "secular" state universities in the United States.[14] In the present century, although the elements of the church life of Australia, New Zealand, and the English-speaking community of South Africa have been reordered from the European forms, the total religious history has borne much more resemblance to Europe's than to that of North America.

Missions and the Frontier

American overseas missions were a continuation and extension of home missions. The Christianity displayed in twentieth-century American missions was determined by the nineteenth-century Christian movement along the frontier and the evangelization of new cities. The whole climate of American Christian thinking was conditioned by expansion. As early as 1837 Anderson spoke of "working with perfect freedom over a broad continent" and of both religious influences and "our own form of government." Contemporary Europe saw little systematic thought about expansion; newly acquired territories were likely to prove expensive liabilities.[15] Not until the last quarter of the century did imperial acquisition become a

---

[12]Kenneth Scott Latourette, *A History of the Expansion of Christianity*; see esp. vol. 4, *The Great Century in Europe and the United States of America*, A.D. 1800-A.D. 1914 (New York: Harper, 1941). Vols. 5 and 6 deal with the "Great Century" in other parts of the world.

[13]K. Sinclair, *A History of New Zealand* (Hammondsworth: Penguin, 1959), p. 278; but note Sinclair's remarks on the molding of moral attitudes in New Zealand by Puritanism.

[14]C. Howard Hopkins, *John R. Mott, 1865-1955: A Biography* (Grand Rapids: Eerdmans, 1979), p. 161.

[15]Anderson, "Time for the World's Conversion," p. 65; cf. the minute of James Stephen, Under Secretary for the Colonies, to Lord John Russell in relation to Africa

major concern. Chronologically, America was the first modern imperial power, or perhaps second after Russia, the former expanding eastward as the latter expanded westward, until the two met.[16]

The specifically Christian aspect of that expansion was vigorous evangelism—primary evangelism, the delivery of the elements of the Christian gospel. The delivery was couched in terms which sought individual commitment yet recognized the family unit and created and strengthened local *communitas*, which both channeled emotion and permitted the development of a popular culture, and which suggested a continuity with old traditions while being manifestly free of old institutions. This concern with primary evangelization differed from most European thinking of the same period. Contemporary Europeans were aware of a religious crisis, but they generally thought of it as a *pastoral* crisis. Their concerns were about building churches large enough and in the right places and getting the right sort of ministers to staff them, about the place of the church in a national system of education, and about preventing state countenance of antichurch or anti-Christian influences. The fundamental desire of European Christians was the preservation of a Christian society such as Western Europe had been since the Dark Ages. Its earnest evangelicals, who in Britain reached their peak of influence toward the middle of the century, were still thinking of the provision of the gospel for a Christian, if apostatizing, society.

Perhaps this could not be where a new society was manifestly arising, as on the American frontier. At any rate, the primary evangelism in such conditions had to be innovative and adaptive; established East Coast practice offered little guidance for work under frontier conditions. Europe, despite its unchurched urban working class, was not impressed by the American experience and did not expect to learn much from it; even English Methodists who bore Wesley's name reacted with horror to the device of the camp meeting.[17]

---

in 1841: "If we could acquire the dominion of that whole continent, it would be but a worthless possession" (quoted in Christopher Fyfe, *A History of Sierra Leone* [London: Oxford University Press, 1962], p. 217).

[16]Sir John Seeley, in *The Expansion of England* (London: Macmillan, 1883), saw America and Russia as the two coming world powers; Britain might take a third, but only if it developed proper relationships with its empire.

[17]The Methodist Conference of 1807 produced the following question and answer:

Q. What is the judgment of the Conference concerning what are called Camp Meetings?

A. It is our judgment that, even supposing such meetings be allowable in America, they are highly improper in England, and likely to be productive of considerable mischief; and we disclaim all connection with them.

The insistence of some leading working-class Methodists in Midland industrial areas on using this method was a cause of their exclusion and the formation of the Primitive Methodist Connexion. The catalyst seems to have been the American

As the century proceeded, the focus moved from the expanding frontier to the expanding cities. American Christianity produced the same concern with expansion, the same basis of primary evangelism, backed by the same innovation and adaptation. The evangelistic campaign arose from the special conditions of urban America, just as special modes of Christian thinking—adventism, apocalypticism, the holiness movement—were transmitted in its atmosphere. Christianity expanded in urban America; the great new centres of population in Europe saw little comparable response.

American Christianity and the Voluntary Association

One fundamentally different constituent in the experience of Europeans and Americans is space.[18] Nineteenth-century American Christianity developed in a setting of apparently limitless space. In these circumstances it could be expansive and effective only by being entrepreneurial. Ponderous strategies on a continued wide basis, tight control by hierarchical bodies, were likely to be as self-defeating as the European tendency to think in terms of the parish as "territory." North American Christianity became pluriform and diffuse. There was always room for an inspired individualist; there was even promising scope for the eccentric. Well might Rufus Anderson see America as the natural sphere of the voluntary society. The principle of the voluntary society is: identify the task to be done; find appropriate means of carrying it out; unite and organize a group of like-minded people for the purpose. When this principle was applied to the business of making and sustaining congregations of Christian disciples, the distinction between church and voluntary society, always fundamental in Europe, sometimes all but disappeared in America. A congregation, or a whole denomination, might in principle be no different from a voluntary society. In strife or disagreement, one could always leave and join—or even start—another.

In one respect the United States actually preceded Europe in centralizing missions and relating them to home-church structures. In Europe and America alike, effective overseas missions began not with the official machinery of the churches, but with voluntary societies. To a remarkable degree societies continued in Europe (and notably in Britain) to be the principal means of conducting missions, even when the idea of overseas mission had become universally accepted in the churches so that the denominations effectively "adopted" their denominational societies. By the Civil War period in America, however, most denominations had formed their own mission boards (in the process leaving the American Board to the

---

irregular evangelist Lorenzo Dow. See Holliday Bickerstaffe, *The History of the Primitive Methodist Church* (London: Joseph Johnson, 1919).

[18]Clyde Curry Smith has developed this point in "Some Demographic Considerations in American Religious History," *Bulletin of the Scottish Institute of Missionary Studies*, n.s., 3 (1986): 14-21.

Congregationalists by default).[19] But once more the voluntary principle took over: the apparent ecclesiasticization of American missions was the prelude to the emergence of a surge of new societies outside the major denominational boards. One effect of this vast outlay of energy was to transfer overseas many of the attitudes and values that had produced the evangelization of the frontier.

Missions and Money

Another aspect of American life that was to shape American Christianity and be expressed in American missions was the transformation of the nation's economic base in the course of the nineteenth century and its emergence in the twentieth as the world's greatest industrial nation. Certain differences emerge in any comparison with similar processes in Europe. In the economic and social sphere, the connection between entrepreneurial effort and efficiency on the one hand and financial and social reward on the other was much clearer in America. In Europe there have always been sources of status other than money and sources of wealth other than industrial output. Furthermore, the American industrial transformation took place in the same period as the christianizing of the cities to which we have referred. In Britain and in most of Europe, the industrial process accompanied Christian decline. For whatever reasons, the linking of entrepreneurial activity, efficient organization, and conspicuous financing, which was characteristic of American business, became characteristic of American Christianity. The loose structure of American religious organization, essentially societal rather than ecclesiastical, enabled powerful laymen (and what more powerful layman than a substantial businessman?) to play a major part in the shaping of activities. One of Mott's last works has a chapter on "the greatest evangelist of the nineteenth century."[20] One reason Dwight L. Moody was the greatest evangelist was that he produced and mobilized Christian businessmen, who munificently supported missions at home and abroad. Mott himself used a network of wealthy laymen, vigorously and unashamedly solicited funds from the well-to-do as a normal part of student organizational work, and relied for the funding of many special projects on a few exceptionally wealthy people.[21]

---

[19]Valentin H. Rabe, *The Home Base of American China Missions, 1880-1920* (Cambridge: Harvard University Press, 1978), pp. 15-17.

[20]John R. Mott, *The Larger Evangelism* (Nashville: Abingdon-Cokesbury, 1944), chapt. 3.

[21]For Mott's use of solicitation as part of normal travelling organization, see Hopkins, *John R. Mott*, pp. 172-173. On Mott as fundraiser, see Rabe, *Home-Base*, pp. 152-154. For the successive interventions of Mrs. Nettie McCormick to fund posts at Mott's behest, see Hopkins, pp. 205-7, 220, 273, 454. Mott's expensive world tour (*inter alia*, to bring Edinburgh to Asia) of 1912-13 was financed by fifty friends, including Mrs. McCormick and John D. Rockefeller.

In the period in which the new American missions were coming to life it is plain that a whole aspect of American culture—the association of business methods, efficient organization, and financial reward—was unquestioningly accepted not only as a fact of life but as something that could be consecrated to God and employed in Christian activity. One of the officers of the American Board even wrote a book called *The Business of Missions*. Enough, he wrote:

> . . . of armies, of strategies, of firing lines, of trenches, of conquests, of crusades! We are living in a business age, we believe as never before in business results. It is a working, rather than a fighting church to which we belong.[22]

This is a characteristically American perspective. European missions were always glad enough for wealthy supporters and sometimes relied heavily on them for new projects. And unusual donors such as the eccentric Robert Arthington could facilitate a whole new direction of effort.[23] But the British faith missions of the period that saw the American missionary expansion typically feared lest organization crowd out the Holy Spirit, lamented Mammon as the god of this world, stressed the sacrificial aspect of missionary vocation (often in financial terms), were often hesitant about any form of solicitation, and saw their help rather in the tithes of the (relatively) poor rather than in the abundance of the rich. Extended organization and a "worldly" concern about money were the sort of characteristics

---

[22]Cornelius H. Patton, *The Business of Missions* (New York: Macmillan, 1924), foreword. This dedication states, "If you are a Christian and also a practical man this book is dedicated to you." Chapter headings include "A Going Concern," "The Great Partnership," and "Do We Mean Business?" Patton scornfully rejects a printed appeal suggesting that "Christianity abroad is the best business proposition for America" (p. viii) but invites his readers to look forward "to the day when you can support your missionary as your personal representative, your substitute abroad, when you can erect or equip a hospital, build a Church, a school, or a residence, when, possibly, you can endow an institution which will bless mankind in countless ways after you are gone" (p. 264). On Patton, see Rabe, *Home Base*, pp. 136-37.

[23]Gustav Warneck, *Abriss einer Geschichte der protestantischen Missionen* (Berlin, 1901), p. 222, characterizes Arthington as "a generous but often eccentric [opferwilliger aber oft phantastischer] rich English friend of missions." Arthington's gifts were responsible for persuading the (British) Baptist Missionary Society to begin its operations in Zaire. He left an immense legacy to the BMS and to the London Missionary Society but specified that it be used for new work. The Society had to explain to supporters that it could not use Arthington money to maintain the work commenced by its agency. See *114th Annual Report of the Baptist Missionary Society. . . to 31st March* (London, 1906), pp. 10-11, 17.

they deplored in the older missions.[24] It would need an extended investigation to compare the actual relative importance of solicitation and wealthy donors in mission accounting; but the difference in style is unmistakable. American religious culture had no *inhibitions* about money.

Church and State

If there is one doctrine characteristic of American Christianity as a whole, distinguishing it from the European stream that in so many respects it continues, it must be that of the separation of church and state. The widespread acceptance of this doctrine was due to a civil rather than a theological proposition, arising from the historic situation of the infant United States. American churches have come to adopt it as an article of faith, and American missions have carried it into a variety of overseas spheres. The effects have been paradoxical. American missions have tended to think of themselves as nonpolitical: how can it be otherwise if church and state live in different spheres? Non-Americans have seen continual political implications in their activities: how can it be otherwise if church and state inhabit the same sphere, or at least overlapping spheres?

Colonial authorities often, with varying degrees of justification, looked askance at American missions as potentially undermining the subjection of subject peoples.[25] In the days of the National movement in India, the British administration was particularly sensitive about Americans working in the

---

[24]Thus J. Hudson Taylor, founder of the China Inland Mission, the prototype of the new societies:

> I had determined never to use personal solicitation, or to make collections, or to issue collecting books. . . . We are convinced that if there was *less* solicitation for money and *more* dependence upon the power of the HOLY GHOST and upon the deepening of spiritual life, the experience of Moses [having to call a halt to gifts for the Tabernacle because of the excess] would be more common. . . . Perhaps in many cases what GOD wanted was *not* a money contribution but personal consecration to His service abroad, or the giving up of son or daughter (*A Retrospect* [London: CIM, n.d.], pp. 110-13).

[25]After 1920, North American mission organizations seeking to work in India were required to recognize explicitly that "all due respect should be given to the lawfully constituted Government, and that, while carefully abstaining from political affairs, it is its desire and purpose that its influence, insofar as it may be properly exerted in such matters should be so exerted in loyal co-operation with the Government of the country concerned, and that it will only employ agents who will work in this spirit." Missionaries from continental European countries were required to make still stricter individual pledges. See George Thomas, *Christian Indians and Indian Nationalism 1885-1950: An Interpretation in Historical and Theological Perspective* (Frankfurt: Peter Lang, 1979), p. 132. On the American missionary Ralph Keitahn, expelled from India in 1930, and the pressure on his mission to disown him, see Thomas, 191-92, and Keitahn's own *Pilgrimage in India* (Madras: Christian Literature Society, 1973).

country. We have spoken of America as the first of the modern empires; it was also the first colonial independence movement, and one can see how powerfully the American movement appealed to the first generation of nationalist leaders in both India and Africa. The insistence on the separation of church and state can give encouragement to deny Caesar what is not thought to be his; and in such situations Caesar readily takes offense.

Another side to the separation doctrine as expressed in American missions was readily allied to premillennial thinking. This was a tendency to posit an entirely "spiritual" concept of the church, which annexed it to a condition distinct from the world in which political action takes place. The old European Anabaptists who first formulated the separation of church and state were at least aware that in itself it is a highly political doctrine; indeed, when insisting on it could get you thrown into the Rhine in a sack, the political implications must have been vividly recognized. By contrast, modern American missions have sometimes displayed a curious political naiveté, as though by constantly asserting that church and state were separate they have somehow stripped mission activity of political significance. Even the elementary political implication of their presence, let alone of patriotism, has not always been recognized.

Theology and Common Sense

We have little space in which to allude to a related and highly complex matter, the development of specifically North American theologies. In this area we must pay tribute to the work of Mark Noll, who has explored the influence of Scottish common sense philosophy in America and especially what he calls the "methodological common sense" that was rigorously applied to theology.[26] He points to an eloquent statement by Charles Hodge at the very beginning of his *Systematic Theology*: "The Bible is to the theologian what nature is to the man of science. It is his storehouse of facts, and his method of ascertaining what the Bible teaches is the same as that which the natural philosopher adopts to ascertain what he teaches."[27]

The dispensational schemes of C. I. Scofield (who had the needs of missionaries particularly in mind) and others proceed on the same principle; and their influence has been continued in the present century in a major stream of American religion. Why has this method of using the Bible as a quarry in which the gems are statements of unconditioned fact been so much more characteristic of America than of any other parts of the world? Does it owe something to the new-style Christianity of the frontier, the emergence of new Christian communities that, as it were, started Christi-

---

[26]Mark A. Noll, "Common Sense Traditions and American Evangelical Thought," *American Quarterly* 37 (1985): 216-38.

[27]Charles Hodge, *Systematic Theology*, 2 vols. (New York, 1872), 1:10. Hodge's very first paragraph is headed "Theology a Science."

anity all over again and saw no need to relate to nineteen centuries of church history?

At any rate, "methodological common sense" led to two features of American Christianity that are particularly relevant to the study of modern evangelical missions. First, it has made a great part of American Christianity immensely conscious of statements of belief, often set out as catalogs of unconditioned fact; and a progressive definition of the Christian faith in these terms has followed until the range of succinctly defined topics runs from the mode of creation to the relation of the Lord's return to the other "last things." Here we see again the characteristically American problem-solving approach at work: identify the problem, apply the right tools, and a solution will appear. Then move on to the next problem. By contrast, European movements born out of the evangelical revival have rarely been creedally creative; when they have wished to define their faith and witness to their distinguishing beliefs, they have generally looked to the ancient creeds and to the sixteenth-century Reformers.

The other, and related, result of the application of methodological common sense to theology has been the American tendency to use the new extended creeds as tests for fellowship and a basis of separation. Perhaps this principle of separation is the converse of the principle of free association that lay behind so much of nineteenth-century American Christianity and provided so much of its dynamic. In the peculiar historical circumstances of American church growth, with the church concept often nearly absorbed in the voluntary society, it was easy to identify fellowship with association. The inevitable result was the atomization of the church. This again has been in contrast to the European continuators of the evangelical revival tradition.

Only Uchimura himself could say whether these features have anything to do with the tendency that he thought the least developed of all American excellences, that which we have called wearing big boots in the Temple. Another type of investigation might raise the question whether North America produced a new major branch of the Christian family; whether the separation between evangelicalism-fundamentalism, shaped very much by North American cultural factors, and the older, essentially North European evangelical Protestantism was similar in kind to the latter's breach with Latin Christianity. Such an investigation might also reflect on the special nature of American liberalism (though its direct connection with the mission movement is more problematical), which evidently has been distinct from the European phenomenon.

An American Christianity

Without plunging into such deep waters, we may still recognize a specifically American Christianity, an expression of Christian faith formed within and by American culture. Among the features that mark it out from other such Christian expressions are vigorous expansionism; readiness of invention; a willingness to make the fullest use of contemporary technology; finance, organization, and business methods; a mental separation of the spiritual and the political realms combined with a conviction of the superlative excellence, if not the universal relevance, of the historic constitution and values of the nation; and an approach to theology, evangelism, and church life in terms of addressing problems and finding solutions.

None of these marks, and none of their effects, is nearly as important as the universal Christianity, the gospel of the risen Christ, to which historic American Christianity witnesses. But no one ever meets universal Christianity in itself; we only ever meet Christianity in a local form, and that means a historically, culturally conditioned form. We need not fear this; when God became human, he became historically, culturally conditioned man, in a particular time and place. What he became, we need not fear to be. There is nothing wrong with having local forms of Christianity—provided that we remember that they *are* local.

Sometimes local features can have an important effect, either direct or catalytic, outside the locality. If the evangelization of North America was the most signal success of the great century of missions, its full significance was not evident until North America became the chief source of missionaries in the early part of the twentieth. Within the nineteenth century the sudden emergence of the United States as a Pacific power produced an American missionary consciousness at a period when Britain was still the leading missionary-sending nation. But British perspectives on the Far East were formed by the China trade; Japan seemed just too far away for immediate concern. American innovation beyond the regular church structures was often extremely influential in the quite different church setting of Europe. For instance, the Student Volunteer Missionary Union is very much part of British domestic church history, as well as British mission history, and in many ways a thoroughly "indigenous" institution; but it owed something to the American student movement.[28] The American business sense of John R. Mott produced the international organization of missions, with all that this was to lead to; one has only to reflect that the sole contemporary alternative would have been the British "old boy" network to realize how important was this contribution. Mott's business sense even realized the need to invest in research, and as a result, J. N. Farquhar was seconded for scholarly study of Hinduism—and even in those steamship days he divided his time, for the sake of mission, between India and Oxford.[29] And the direct American approach to a particular problem by a

---

[28]Ruth Rouse, *The World's Student Christian Federation: A History of the First Thirty Years* (London: SCM, 1948), chapt. 1; and John C. Pollock, *A Cambridge Movement* (London: John Murray, 1953).

[29]Eric J. Sharpe, *John Nicol Farquhar: A Memoir* (Calcutta: YMCA Publishing House, 1963), pp. 61-63.

specified method has been endlessly demonstrated, for instance, in the emergence of such enterprises as the Wycliffe Bible Translators.

Even markedly local features can be transmitted to another culture and take on a life of their own there. A historian of religion might judge Adventism to be unmistakably a product of the conditions of nineteenth-century America; but it was Adventist teaching that led African communities in Malawi to seek to realize the kingdom of God.[30] Adventist teaching has also given a new form to religious movements in Melanesia;[31] and the special form of Adventism associated with the Jehovah's Witnesses has been potent in millennial movements such as Kitawala[32] in East and Central Africa and the God's Kingdom Society in Nigeria.[33]

In the early 1900s, pentecostalism appeared to be a minor aberrant form of American Protestantism; now it is the natural expression of faith and practice for millions of Latin Americans. John Alexander Dowie was a Scot, but had he stayed in Scotland, no one ever would have heard of him. Only in the United States could he have carried out his great experiment in Zion City.[34] I once spent Easter with the Christian Catholic Apostolic Church in Zion of South Africa (Bantu); as they danced in the Lord's resurrection with the words "We have a Zion which is our home," I knew I was watching a thoroughly Zulu Christian development. Yet when the very aged leader showed me his ordination certificate, it bore the signature of J. A. Dowie and the stamp of Zion City, Illinois. And in all of this we have not even mentioned the many side effects of the Christian enterprises of African-Americans in Africa. This demands a study in itself. The whole story of Ethiopianism[35] in Africa over several generations, the rise of South African

[30]George Shepperson and Thomas Price, *Independent Africa: John Chilembwe and the Origins, Setting and Significance of the Nyasaland Native Rising of 1915* (Edinburgh: Edinburgh University Press, 1958).

[31]Gottfried Oosterwal, *Modern Messianic Movements as a Theological and Missionary Challenge* (Elkhart, Ind: Institute of Mennonite Studies, 1973). On Adventists in the Pacific, see Charles W. Forman, *The Island Churches of the South Pacific* (Maryknoll, NY: Orbis Books, 1982), pp. 52-54.

[32]H. J. Greschat, *Kitawala: Ursprung, Ausbreitung und Religion der Watch-Tower-Bewegung in Zentralafrika* (Marburg: Elwert, 1967).

[33]D. I. Ilega, *Gideon Urhobo and the God's Kingdom Society in Nigeria*. Ph.D. dissertation (University of Aberdeen, 1983).

[34]On Zion City, see Grant Wacker, "Marching to Zion: Religion in a Modern Theocracy," *Church History* 54 (1985): 496-511. On Zionist churches in South Africa, and the connection with Dowie, see Bengt G. M. Sundkler, *Bantu Prophets in South Africa*, 2d ed. (London: Oxford University Press for International African Institute, 1961).

[35]See Sundkler, *Bantu Prophets*; for different types of black American influence, see Walter R. Johnson, *Worship and Freedom: A Black American Church in Zambia* (New York: African Publishing, 1977); Theodore Natsoulas, "Patriarch McGuire and the Spread of the African Orthodox Church to Africa," *Journal of Religion in Africa* 12 (1981): 81-104.

black theology[36] in the present generation, in each of which black American influence has been crucial, are permanent reminders of how relevant and dynamic some local phenomena may be in a quite different locality.

A Changed World

Hitherto our concern has been with origins and prehistory—with the factors that have given American Christianity, and the evangelical missions that are the special subject of our study, a distinctive shape. We can hardly conclude without a glance at the world in which they function today. It goes without saying that it is a world transformed in the course of a century. It is one in which the sea-based empires of western Europe have passed away. It is also one in which the whole center of gravity of the Christian world has been changed. Not only has there been an unprecedented Christian expansion in all of the southern continents and in Africa in particular; there has correspondingly been an almost unprecedented recession in some of the older Christian heartlands, most obviously in western Europe.

Let us consider some of the results.

1. Christendom, the centuries-old concept of certain nations belonging to the Christian society and others lying outside of it, has come to an end. Christians are now much more diffused throughout the world than they ever have been; yet they are also much more diffused *within* societies. Despite burgeoning numbers of new Christians, we are not seeing many new Christian *states*, certainly not in the manner of old Christendom. No longer does the word *Christianity* have a territorial connotation.

But it was the concentration of Christians into certain geographical areas that brought the missionary movement into being. As recently as 1910 the World Missionary Conference could distinguish between "fully missionized" and "not yet fully missionized" lands. The missionary movement was Christendom's last flourish. Today some of what in 1910 appeared to be "fully missionized lands" are most obviously the prime mission fields of the world.

2. In the high days of the missionary movement Christianity was associated with a particular form of civilization and an advanced technology. That technology was offered in all sincerity as undoubtedly beneficial in its effects and was widely accepted in the same conviction. The association is now much less obvious. In the first place, the countries most clearly connected with high technology are not necessarily also connected with Christianity. Second, most Christians now live in areas relatively low in technological capacity and with little hope of ever having access to what the

---

[36]See Basil Moore, ed., *Black Theology: The South African Voice* (London: Hurst, 1973), published in the U.S.A. as *The Challenge of Black Theology in South Africa* (Atlanta: John Knox, 1974). The catalytic figure was James H. Cone.

nations of high technology possess. And third, the confident assertions that Christians once made about the gospel-associated blessings of technology have given place to doubts of its efficiency, consciousness of its demonic power for destruction, and desire for its control.

3. But some countries have a special relationship between missions and technology. In some broken-backed nations, those marked out by poverty of resources, technological breakdown, political instability, or economic disaster, the missionary bodies, often working in concert (Missions Incorporated, as one may say), now have the most flexible, powerful, and efficient organization in the country. They can fly people around the country and in and out of it; they can bring in machinery and service ailing plants; they have radio telephones that work; they can arrange currency, get foreign exchange, and send an international message quickly. They can sometimes do things that the government itself cannot do. And the local church, however independent or indigenous, can do none of these things, except insofar as it can act as a link to an outside mission.[37] In the end, what will be the implications of all this power held by Missions Incorporated?

4. The missionary movement occurred when it did through the co-existence of a certain religious condition with political systems that permitted free association and economic structures allowing movement of capital and export of surpluses. In Europe that co-existence is no more; at present it continues in North America. As a result, the "overseas missionary" is now more North American than European. But America's position in the world is quite different from that of the missionary movement a century ago, in the high days of the European empires, when Robert E. Speer could rejoice in situations where American missionaries could operate as neutrals without the obloquy attached to Britons.[38] A missionary's effectiveness, or even sincerity, will sometimes be measured by the extent to which the message preached is reflected in the nation from which he or she came; the higher that nation's visibility in the world, the more likely is this measure to be used. We do well to ponder that inasfar as the missionary movement continues *as a separate* identifiable phenomenon, it is bound to be seen, for good or ill, as part of the United States presence overseas.

5. In the older missionary movement, missionary life was represented in terms of the ideals of Christian sacrifice. The missionary was the person

---

[37]See W. McAllister, "The Heart of Africa Mission and the Unevangelized Fields Mission and the Subsequent Churches." Ph.D. dissertation (University of Aberdeen, 1986).

[38]See also G. E. Post (of the Syrian Protestant College, Beirut) in *Report of the Centenary Conference on the Protestant Missions of the World*, ed. James Johnston, 2 vols. (New York: Revell, 1889), 1:322: "The English hold the hands—the physical forces; and God has given to the other branch of the Anglo-Saxon race, untrammelled by your political complications, a control of the brains and of the heart."

who renounced all for Christ, turned his back on nation and family, risked privation and disease. Nowadays Missions Incorporated generally makes it possible to maintain life at a tolerable level. The people who now risk privation are those so-called tent-makers who have taken a position (perhaps even with similar daily duties to those they might have as missionaries) at a local salary, sharing the housing and frustrations and insecurities of national colleagues and left to their own devices when their contract ends.

6. The Protestant missionary movement developed by means of the voluntary society, and America perfected its application to the purposes of overseas mission. The resultant mission agencies were admirably designed for their task: to direct the resources of Christians in one country to the preaching of the gospel and the establishing of churches in another country. That is, the task in hand was principally giving; the design was essentially for one-way traffic. But with the new shape of the Christian world, there are needs for which the perfect instrument was not designed. Instruments are now needed for *two*-way traffic: for sharing and for receiving.

7. We have argued that Christianity developed in America in a specifically local form. But the rooting of the Christian faith in Africa, Oceania, and in large areas of Asia and its reformulation in Latin America have produced other local forms of Christianity. This means that North American Christianity often will be one of several local forms in juxtaposition. Will we see a competition among local Christianities? The process of encounter will always present difficulties as well as excitements and discoveries. The principal dangers of the encounter come when one party insists that its own local features have universal validity.

Conclusion

The missionary movement is one of the turning points of church history; the whole shape of the Christian faith in the world has been transformed by it. America's contribution to it has been incalculable. But the history of the missionary movement has never been at the center of Christian historical scholarship; like the practice of missions, it has been in the sphere of the enthusiasts, not of the main tradition. Consequently we know curiously little about some of the most crucial events and processes in Christian history. Conferences such as this, entitled "A Century of World Evangelization: North American Evangelical Missions, 1886-1986" enable us both to explore what we can know and to prepare for what we cannot yet know. There can be few more rewarding tasks in contemporary scholarship.

The historians of African and Asian Christianity are already seeing the missionary period as an episode, sometimes a rather distant one, in a continuing story. The missionary movement itself will have its own continuity; Christian people of one nation will continue to hear the word from people of another; Christian people will continue to share their faith and life and work. But the movement will change beyond recognition and it will need all that adaptability to situations that was the genius of its American manifestation. Christian expansion hitherto has often involved a period of cross-cultural transmission, followed by the emergence of a new local form of Christianity. But all our local forms are provisional, part of the local Christian process whereby "we all attain to . . . a perfect man, to the measure of the stature of the fullness of Christ" (Eph. 4:13).[39]

---

[39]In this chapter I have not considered perhaps the most important of all aspects of the American dimension of missions: that related to the Native Americans. Properly speaking, it is here that the modern missionary movement starts; it was in North America that Protestant Christians first found themselves in daily contact with a culture uninfluenced by the Judeo-Christian tradition. In another respect, like Australia, it illustrates one of the sadder and more admonitory passages of missionary history. I am conscious also that I have left aside the special features of American Catholic missions and have made only passing reference to the long, and to some degree separate, tradition of African-American missions, on which see Walter L. Williams, *Black Americans and the Evangelization of Africa 1877-1900* (Madison: University of Wisconsin Press, 1982).

18

Missionary Societies and the Fortunate Subversion of the Church[1]

I

It is surprising how little attention the voluntary society has attracted in studies of the nineteenth-century Church, considering the immense impact on Western Christianity and the transformation of world Christianity which (through its special form in the missionary society) it helped to effect. The origins of the modern voluntary society lie in the last years of the seventeenth century. It was put to new uses in the eighteenth century and in the nineteenth developed new ways of influencing, supplementing, and by-passing the life of Church and State alike. Let the American missionary statesman Rufus Anderson describe its progress. Writing in 1837 on "The Time for the World's Conversion Come,"[2] he lists the signs of the times that seem to him to indicate that the time is at hand when the prophecies will be fulfilled and the earth will be filled with the knowledge of God as the waters cover the sea.[3] Some of these signs have to do with technological progress; never before had the logistics of access to the whole world been so easy. "It was not until the present century that the evangelical churches of Christendom were ever really organized with a view to the conversion of the world."[4] Anderson identifies the characteristically Protestant form of organization for this purpose as the voluntary association:

---

[1]First published in *The Evangelical Quarterly* 88 (No. 2, 1988): 141-55.

[2]This tract has been published several times since it appeared in the *Religious Magazine*, Boston, 1837-38. It is most recently reprinted in R. Pierce Beaver, ed., *To Advance the Gospel: Selections From the Writings of Rufus Anderson* (Grand Rapids: Eerdmans, 1967), pp. 59-76, and since this is also the most accessible version the references given are to it.

[3]*Ibid.*, p. 61.

[4]*Ibid.*, p. 64.

. . . what we see in Missionary, Bible, Tract and other kindred societies, not restricted to ecclesiastics, nor to any one profession, but combining all classes, embracing the masses of the people; and all free, open, and responsible. . . . It is the *contributors of the funds*, who are the real association . . . the individuals, churches, congregations, who freely act together, *through such agencies* for an object of common interest. . . . This Protestant form of association—free, open, responsible, embracing all classes, both sexes, all ages, the masses of the people—is peculiar to modern times, and almost to our age.[5]

Anderson here recognizes several important features of the voluntary association: its instrumental character, its relatively recent origin, and its special structure. It differed from all previous structures in that it was open in its membership, that lay people were as much involved as ministers, and that its organization was rooted in a mass membership, who felt responsibility for it and contributed generously to its support. Like the New England Congregationalist he was, he states that such associations could only arise in countries which had an open, responsible form of government, where Protestantism had prepared the way for civil liberty; and that missionary facilities were the beneficiaries of vastly improved land communications and of vastly increased international seaborne commerce. He is right, of course, that a voluntary society could hardly have flourished in contemporary Spain or Naples; and he gives us an early hint that the missionary society as we know it arose from seizing the opportunities offered by a particular phase of Western political, economic, and social development.

Let us return to the instrumental nature of the missionary society. As Anderson puts it, in a voluntary association, individuals, churches, and congregations freely act together for an object of common interest. It is essentially a pragmatic approach, the design of an instrument for a specific purpose. The first of the modern religious societies arose in sober High Church congregations in London at the end of the seventeenth century. They arose in response to the preaching of men like the German-born Anthony Horneck who called the congregations to a more devout and holy life. Companies of earnest people met to pray and read the scriptures and visit the poor; others to "reform the manners" of the nation by rebuking profanity and seeking to keep prostitutes off the streets.[6] They were seeking a practical response to serious preaching; answering, as it were, the question "What shall we do?" They encountered a good deal of suspicion and hostility—why were certain people meeting together? Why were the meet-

---

[5]*Ibid.*, p. 65.

[6]On the background see W. K. Lowther Clarke, *Eighteenth Century Piety* (London: SPCK, 1946); N. Sykes, *Edmund Gibson, Bishop of London 1669-1748: A Study of Politics and Religion in the Eighteenth Century* (London: Oxford University Press, 1926).

ings necessary? Were the Church services not good enough for them? Against the background of the times any sectional meetings took on the appearance of political disaffection or ecclesiastical discontent. Yet societies for mutual support in the Christian life, or for more effective expression of Christian teaching, grew more and more. They were important in John Wesley's spiritual formation, and essential to the development of his work.[7] Meanwhile those (relatively few) Churchmen who thought seriously about evangelization outside the normal sphere of the Church realized that nothing could be done without a new structure: hence the foundation of the Society of Providing Christian Knowledge and the Society for the Propagation of the Gospel. These were not voluntary societies in the true sense of the term; they held Parliamentary charters, and care was taken to link their management with the bishops of the Church of England.[8] As a result, the things they could do well were largely things that the Church had always done: that is, ordain and equip clergy. The Societies did enable these equipped clergy to be sent abroad, mostly to the Americas, where they were applied to the rescue of English colonists from Presbyterianism and vice. The visions of a wider missionary sphere caught by some of the founders were not realized until into the nineteenth century, and even a bishop of London anxious to see such enterprise started by the societies found himself utterly frustrated.[9]

The Church structures could only do what they had always done; a new concept needed a new instrument. The title of William Carey's seminar tract of 1792 is itself eloquent. He calls it *An Enquiry into the Obligations of Christians to Use Means for the Conversion of the Heathens. In Which the Religious State of the Different Nations of the World, the Success of Former Undertakings and the Practicability of Further Undertakings, Are Considered.*[10]

---

[7]See, e.g., J. S. Simon, *John Wesley and the Religious Societies* (London: Epworth, 1921), and *John Wesley and the Methodist Societies* (London, 1923).

[8]See W. K. Lowther Clarke, *A History of the S.P.C.K.* (London: SPCK, 1959); and H.P. Thompson, *Into All Lands: The History of the Society for the Propagation of the Gospel 1701-1750* (London: SPCK, 1951). It is significant that Thompson's first section after his account of SPG origins deals with "The American Colonies 1701-1783," and the first four sections of "The Years of Awakening, 1783-1851" deal with the home scene and with Canada. The primary tasks of the SPG were with English colonists. Thomas Bray, the moving spirit in its formation, had a much wider vision (cf. Thompson, p. 17); but in practice men like Thomas Thompson (cf. Thompson, pp. 67ff), a chaplain in Maryland who travelled to West Africa in the 1750s to visit the place of origin of the plantation slaves, were rare. The young John Wesley hoped to preach to the Native Americans when he became a missionary in Georgia; in fact he was able to see little of them.

[9]Cf. G. D. McKelvie, *The Development of Official Anglican Interest in World Mission 1788-1809, With Special Reference to Bishop Beilby Porteus*. Ph.D. thesis (University of Aberdeen, 1984).

[10]Published in Leicester, 1792, and several times reprinted. A facsimile edition with introduction by E. A. Payne was published by the Carey Kingsgate Press (London, 1961).

The crucial words are "the obligation to *use means.*" There is theology in Carey's pamphlet, and there is history, and there is demography; but at the heart of it lies the responsibility of Christians for means to seek the appropriate instrument, to accomplish a task which God has laid upon them.

In the final section of the *Enquiry*, having established the obligation of Christians, traced the history of former attempts to fulfil it, indicated its scope in the then contemporary world, and demolished the arguments for deciding fulfilment to be impossible, Carey seeks to identify the appropriate means. The first of these is united prayer. "The most glorious works of grace that ever took place, have been in answer to prayer, and it is in this way, we have the greatest reason to suppose, that the glorious outpouring of the Spirit which we expect at last, will be bestowed."[11] He is writing against the background of a movement for regular prayer which had been sparked off through the reading of Jonathan Edwards' call for a "concert of prayer" more than forty years earlier.[12] Edwards himself had been led to make his call on learning of the groups of young men meeting for prayer following the revival at Cambuslang in the West of Scotland in 1742.[13] Carey goes on to illustrate his argument of united prayer as an efficient means. Since the monthly prayer meetings had started in Carey's own Midland Baptist circle, "unimportunate, and feeble as they have been, it is to be believed that God has heard, and in a measure answered them." The first evidence is that the churches involved have in general grown. There is no thought of distinction between home and overseas mission here—those praying for "the increase of Christ's Kingdom" will be concerned for both.[14]

Other evidence concerns the clarification of issues that had long perplexed and divided the Church, and from opportunities to preach the Gospel in unaccustomed places. Even more opportunities could be expected from "the spread of civil and religious liberty, accompanied by a diminution in the spirit of popery." English Dissenters like Carey were not afraid to pray for the spread of civil and religious liberty, and some of them saw in the aspects of the French Revolution the shaking of the power of antichrist. Indeed, one of the objections raised against missions, in the General Assembly of the Church of Scotland and elsewhere, was their association with such people, who were thought to have revolutionary aims under their cloak of "civil and religious liberty." In like vein, Carey rejoices at the first Parliamentary attempt "to abolish the inhuman slave trade," and

---

[11]Carey, *An Enquiry*, pp. 78f.

[12]*An Humble Attempt to Promote Explicit Agreement and Visible Union of God's People in Extraordinary Prayer for the Revival of Religion and the Advancement of Christ's Kingdom on Earth, Pursuant to Scripture—Promises and Prophecies Concerning the Last Time* (Boston, 1747).

[13]A. Fawcett, *The Cambuslang Revival: The Scottish Evangelical Revival of the Eighteenth Century* (London: Banner of Truth, 1971).

[14]Carey, p. 79.

hopes it may be persevered in; and at the establishment of the free Christian settlement of Sierra Leone.[15]

What, then, can one see from even a modest attempt to bring groups together for a common purpose in prayer? Revival in the churches, clearer theological understanding, new evangelistic openings, the French Revolution, the assault on the Slave Trade, a Christian outpost in West Africa? These, says Carey, "are not to be reckoned small things." He sees no incongruity in grouping together events in his own circle of Baptist churches and events in the great movements of the time. God works in both, and

> if an holy solicitude had prevailed in all the assemblies of Christians in behalf of their Redeemer's kingdom, we might partially have seen before now, not only an *open door* for the gospel, but *many running to and fro*, and knowledge increased; or a diligent use of those means which providence has put in our power, accompanied with a greater blessing than ordinary from heaven.[16]

Prayer, he goes on, may be the only thing which Christians of all denominations can unreservedly do together; but we must not omit to look for the use of means to obtain what we pray for. Then he takes an analogy from the contemporary commercial world. When a trading company have obtained their charter, the promoters will go to the utmost limits to put the enterprise on a proper footing. They select their stock, ships, and crews with care; they seek every scrap of useful information. They undergo danger at sea, brave unfriendly climates and peoples, take risks and pay for it all in anxiety, because their minds are set on success. Their *interest* is involved; and does not the interest of Christians lie in the extension of Messiah's Kingdom?

And so he comes to his proposal:

> Suppose a company of serious Christians, ministers and private persons, were to form themselves into a society, and make a number of rules respecting the regulation of the plan, and the persons who are to be employed as missionaries, the means of defraying the expense, etc., etc. This society must consist of persons whose hearts are in the work, men of serious religion, and possessing a spirit of perseverance; there must be a determination not to admit any person who is not of this description, or to retain him longer than he answers to it.[17]

From the members of this society, a committee might be appointed to gather information—just like the trading company—collect funds, scruti-

---

[15]*Ibid.*, pp. 79-80.
[16]*Ibid.*, p. 80.
[17]*Ibid.*, pp. 82-83.

nize possible missionaries, and equip them for their work. All this sounds so trite today, because we are used to the paraphernalia of committees and councils of reference and subscriptions and donations. So it is hard to remember that the average eighteenth-century Christian was not used to such things at all. Most Christians thought in terms only of a parish church, with its appointed minister or, if English Dissenters or Scots Seceders, in terms of a congregation which called its minister. The "instrumental" society, the voluntary association of Christians banding together to achieve a defined object, was still in its infancy. It is significant that Carey—a man of the provinces and of humble station—takes his analogy from commerce; organizing a society is something like floating a company. He is looking for the appropriate means to accomplish a task which cannot be accomplished through the usual machinery of the Church. We could take the other early missionary societies one by one; whether the Church Missionary Society, formed by evangelical supporters of the established Church of England, or the London Missionary Society, enthusiastically maintained by English Dissenters, or the various enterprises in Scotland. They are all equally pragmatic in their origins. The simple fact was that the Church as then organized, whether episcopal, or presbyterian, or congregational, *could* not effectively operate mission overseas. Christians had accordingly to "use means" to do so.

There never was a *theology* of the voluntary society. The voluntary society is one of God's theological jokes, whereby he makes tender mockery of his people when they take themselves too seriously. The men of high theological and ecclesiastical principle were often the enemies of the missionary movement. When (or rather, if) the elder Ryland barked out at Carey, "Young man, sit down; when God wants to convert the heathens, He'll do it without your help or mine" (one of those stories which is probably not true but which *ought* to be true), he was simply expressing a standard form of Protestant doctrine formulated a century earlier as an apologetic against Roman Catholics. When Roman Catholics pointed to their propagation of the faith in the Americas and in Africa and Asia in the seventeenth century and said to Protestants, "Where are *your* missionaries?" there was an accepted theological answer. It began with the well-known Protestant argument that the apostolic office was once and for all. Since therefore, the command "Go ye into all the world . . . " was addressed by the Lord to the apostles, that commission was fulfilled in the days of the apostles. To take it upon oneself to fulfil it now was presumptuous and carnal; it was taking to oneself the office of the apostle, the very error of the Pope himself. Carey has no difficulty in reducing this argument to absurdity. Where, he asks his fellow Baptists, is there then any justification for baptizing—is not that equally an apostolic office?[18] The (Anglican) Church

---

[18]*Ibid.*, pp. 8ff.

Missionary Society was commenced at the insistence of devout pragmatists such as John Venn and Charles Simeon. They had trouble from some of their more doctrinaire evangelical brethren who feared that the Anglican Prayer Book might not always be adhered to on the mission field; while many Irish Churchmen regarded the Society as a distraction from the "real" work of combating Rome.

II

Untheological development as it may have been, the voluntary society had immense theological implications. It arose because none of the classical patterns of Church government, whether episcopal, presbyterian, congregational, or connexional, had any machinery (in their late-eighteenth-century form anyway) to do the tasks for which missionary societies came into being. By its very success, the voluntary society subverted all the classical forms of Church government, while fitting comfortably into none of them. To appreciate this we have to remember how fixed and immutable these forms appeared to eighteenth-century men. They had been argued out for centuries, each on the basis of Scripture and reason—and still all three forms remained, putting Christians into classes, categorizing them unambiguously. People had spent themselves for the sake of the purity of these forms, had shed their blood for them, had been on occasion ready to shed the blood of others for them. And then it suddenly became clear that there were things—and not small things, but big things, things like the evangelization of the world—which were beyond the capacities of these splendid systems of gospel truth. The realization removes some of the stiffness from the theological ribs. Here is Carey:

> If there is any reason for me to hope that I shall have any influence upon any of my brethren, and fellow Christians, probably it may be more especially amongst them of my own denomination. . . . I do not mean by this, in any wise to confine it to one denomination of Christians. I wish with all my heart, that every one who loves our Lord Jesus Christ in sincerity, would in some way or other engage in it. But in the present divided state of Christendom, it would be more likely for good to be done by each denomination engaging separately in the work, than if they were to embark in it conjointly. There is room enough for us all . . . and if no unfriendly interference took place, each denomination would bear good will to the other, and wish, and pray for its success . . . but if all were intermingled, it is likely that their private discords might . . . much retard their public usefulness.[19]

Carey's reasons for basing a mission denominationally are thus entirely

---

[19]*Ibid.*, p. 84.

pragmatic. He has no *theological* objection to a united mission; indeed he invites all Christians to the work. But to form a society you must begin where you are, with people who already form a nucleus, with people who already have some cohesion, mutual trust, and fellowship. Let suspicion and lack of trust enter, and the society is doomed. It was, of course, possible to start from the same ecumenical theological premise as Carey and reach a different conclusion about the basis for the missionary society. So it was with the founders of The Missionary Society, so-called because it was hoped that it would comprehend all men of good will, whether episcopal, presbyterian, or congregational. As other societies appeared, however, it soon became known as the London Missionary Society. At its inauguration one of the preachers cried "Behold us here assembled with one accord to attend the funeral of *bigotry*. . . . I could almost add, cursed be the man who shall attempt to raise her from the grave."[20] In witness to this the founders devised what they designated the "fundamental principle":

> Our design is not to send Presbyterianism, Independency, Episcopacy, or any other form of Church Order and Government (about which there may be difference of opinion among serious Persons), but the Glorious Gospel of the blessed God to the Heathen: and that it shall be left (as it ever ought to be left) to the minds of the Persons whom God may call into the fellowship of His Son from among them to assume for themselves such form of Church Government, as to them shall appear most agreeable to the Word of God.[21]

It would be possible to argue that this fundamental principle was in fact a Congregational principle—especially with that parentheses "as it ever ought to be left"; and one might go further to give this as the reason why the LMS became substantially, though never in name or completely, a society supported by Congregationalists. However it is far more important to note that the foundation of the LMS demonstrates at the end of the eighteenth century something that would have been inconceivable at its beginning: a common ground of action for Episcopalians and Presbyterians, Independents and Methodists. The common ground is a society, a common means for people who start from different bases but have a common aim.

The society becomes the vehicle for catholic spirit. It is not the source of that spirit, but a product of it and a means of expression for it. Carey proposes a denominational society for the most ecumenical reasons; the fathers of the London Missionary Society produce a non-denominational society for very similar reasons. But in these days Churchman and Dissenter might meet at

---

[20]David Bogue. The sermon is summarized and quoted in R. Lovett, *The History of the London Missionary Society 1795-1895* (London: Oxford University Press, 1899), 1:55f.

[21]Lovett, *History*, pp. 21f.

the dinner table or the coffee house and talk, but there was no means whereby they could ever *act* together till it was provided in the voluntary society. But the challenge of the society to the traditional structures went still deeper than this, and it was the missionary societies that presented the challenge most acutely. There were created for the spread of the Gospel; which was one of the reasons for which parishes and congregations in principle existed. But they were *not* parishes or congregations, and they worked in a quite different way. They could not be digested by any of the classical systems whereby parishes or congregations were linked—even when the societies were themselves explicitly denominational.

A new type of church government was growing up alongside the old, parasitically attached to forms that had seemed permanent, argued over till there was no more to say.

It is no surprise, then, that throughout the nineteenth century societies multiplied to deal with specific social abuses or meet special social needs. Nor is it surprising that in the wake of the 1859 Revival a new group of missionary societies arose, many reviving the old hope of a non-denominational structure for all of good will; nor that the same period saw many new societies for aspects of home mission and evangelism in sectors that were not being noticeably covered by the regular church machinery.

III

According to Anderson, part of the special significance of the voluntary society is that it is not restricted to ecclesiastics. This points to another way in which the voluntary society subverted the old Church structures: it altered their power base. It was the voluntary society which first made the laymen (except a few who held office or special position in the state) of real significance above parish or congregational level. As the societies developed, people, whether clerical or lay, who had previously been of no particular significance in their churches, came to be of immense significance in the societies. This is well illustrated in the history of the Church Missionary Society. The CMS was begun by a group of clerical nobodies. They were a handful of London ministers, not all of them even beneficed, a Fellow of a Cambridge College, a few people from the country—not a bishop, or a dean, or an archdeacon among them. From the point of view of influence, their only strong point was that they had the support of some notable laymen, prominent members of Parliament like William Wilberforce and Henry Thornton, who would make well-sounding Vice-Presidents or competent treasurers. And indeed, when it becomes necessary to speak to the Archbishop of Canterbury about the Society, the layman Wilberforce has to do it; there is no clergyman in the group with sufficient weight to talk to an archbishop.[22] But in the whole of the nineteenth century, did any

---

[22]See Michael Hennell, *John Venn and the Clapham Sect* (London: Lutterworth, 1958), chapt. 5.

archbishop hold a more extensive or more important *episcope* than Henry Venn? Venn, the Secretary of the CMS for thirty years in the middle of the century, never held more than a small prebend in the Church, but no bishop had so wide a diocese. Few can have had more clergy, none had nearly so much direct influence on his clergy.[23] Some of his predecessors and successors were laymen, of whom the best known is Dandeson Coates. As the century proceeded, still more dramatic developments took place. Medical and other specialists personnel in certain societies came to take the executive places once thought the sphere of the minister and the theologian. And then came women, to take place in the leadership and organization of societies, far earlier than they could decently appear in most other walks of life. A mother-in-Israel such as Mrs. Grattan Guinness was not just a patroness, a species of sanctified Baroness Burdett Coutts, but an animator, a motivator, an organizer. The vision of the need which led to the Mission of Lepers (now the Leprosy Mission) came to the missionary Wellesley Bailey, but the organizer and the focus was the redoubtable Miss Pym of Dublin. And so another quiet revolution took place in the Church; and just because the society never became properly digested within the systems of the Church, no one raised difficulties about the ordination of women, or even about their being silent in the church. If the voluntary society was one of the Lord's theological jokes, the stately structures of Church government, hallowed by centuries of doctrinal exposition and smothered in polemical divinity, had by the end of the nineteenth century become the scene of a hilarious comedy.

IV

Anderson speaks also of the voluntary society "embracing the masses of the people." This points to another vital feature of the voluntary society. It depended for its very existence on regular participation; it developed means of gaining that participation at local level. Carey's proposals were implemented on the basis of a small group of Baptists in the English Midlands who already knew each other well. The LMS was a much bigger affair, partly because its sponsors, men like David Bogue and George Burder, were more eminent in their denominational constituency than was Carey in his; even so, for its coherence and dynamic it depended on committed groups of people in certain areas, especially London and Warwickshire. The Church Missionary Society illustrates the point best of all. It began as a result of discussions in a ministers' fraternal, and for a long time it was a congeries of ministers who met in London and corresponded with their evangelical clerical friends round the country. For nearly fifteen years it could get hardly any candidates from within Britain. Almost all

---

[23]Cf. W. R. Shenk, *Henry Venn, Missionary Statesman* (Maryknoll, N.Y.: Orbis Books, 1983).

their employable candidates came from Germany, as a result of correspondence with the Continental missionary societies.[24] From about 1814, the situation slowly changed, and one reason must surely be that the CMS had put into practice a new form of organization already pioneered by the Bible Society: a network of locally organized auxiliary associations. Local Church Missionary Associations could vary from large cities like Bristol, where they might be supported by prominent noble and civil figures, to quite small rural parishes or other natural units (there was, for instance, a Cambridge Ladies Association from 1814, before there was any general association for the city or the university). The CMS was transformed. It ceased to be a committee of clergymen meeting in London; it became the group of people meeting in the parish to learn of the latest news from India or West Africa, and the eager readers of the missionary magazines. Its lynchpin was no longer a distant distinguished secretary, but the collector in the parish who went round collecting—perhaps only a penny a week from some—and promoting the sales of the *Missionary Register*. People of the most modest position and income became donors, supporters of the overseas work, felt themselves to be sharing in it. And the recruiting pattern of the society changed. It began to get offers for missionary service from within the nation. And this at the very point when missionary work was becoming visibly dangerous, when the missionary mortality in certain fields was at its height. The reason must surely be related to the development whereby the society was rooted locally among Christians all over the country. The society took a local embodiment, developed a broad spread of participants, gave scope to lay commitment and enthusiasm.

V

The part played by the missionary magazines in this process has not yet received sufficient attention from scholars. The voluntary societies, and the missionary societies in particular, created a new reading public and used it to sensitize public opinion. The roots of the process lie in the Slave Trade abolition movement, which was, of course, promoted by many people who also actively supported missionary societies. The abolition of the Slave Trade was perhaps the first victory won by modern propaganda methods, by the use of the media to educate and mobilize public opinion. The missionary societies gradually took over the same role. The year 1812 saw the birth of the first of the great missionary magazines, *Missionary Register*. The *Register* printed news from all over the world and, in the catholic spirit of missionary endeavour, from all agencies. It was eagerly read all over the country. The circulation of such magazines was much wider than that of other prestigious journals like the *Edinburgh Review* and the *Quarterly*

---

[24]On early missionary recruitment, see chapter 12 of this volume, "Missionary Vocation and the Ministry."

Review which went into the libraries of the country houses of the gentry. The missionary magazine went to many people who had never previously been periodical readers at all. The magazines helped to form opinion, they developed images and mental pictures, they built up attitudes. Their effect on popular reference books in the nineteenth century was considerable. The average reader of the *Missionary Register* or the other missionary magazines knew exactly what he thought the British government should do about the temple tax in Bengal, or about the *sati* of Hindu widows, or the opium trade, or slave running. And a mass readership was produced, a readership concerned and informed about the world outside their own country as perhaps no other group in the nation.

One example must suffice. In the middle of the century the CMS became involved in one of the first modern churches in inland Africa, in the Egba state of Abeokuta in Yorubaland. When the Egba looked in danger of being overwhelmed by the Kingdom of Dahomey and the interests of the Slave Trade, the CMS used its influence in government circles to gain moral and a degree of logistical support for the Egba.[25] The mighty Dahomian army withdrew, and Henry Venn noted universal satisfaction in Britain "from the ministers of Her Majesty's government to the humble collector of a penny a week." He was not exaggerating; Her Majesty's ministers had acted because of evidence marshalled by the missionary society, and doubtless countless penny-a-week collectors followed the events in Africa with bated breath, and gave thanks with the missionaries for the deliverance of Abeokuta and its church. But how many people in Britain in the 1850s would have heard of Abeokuta, or been able to distinguish the King of Dahomey from the Queen of Sheba? Most of those that could do so would have gained their knowledge from the window on the world provided by the missionary magazines.

VI

The later years of the nineteenth century saw the development of a multitude of new missionary societies, many of them belonging to the new category of "faith missions" of which the China Inland Mission was the pioneer and prototype. They represent a development of the voluntary society rather than a totally new departure. They embody and take to their logical conclusion principles which were already present in the older societies. To some extent they represented a reform movement, going back to first principles; rather as Cistercians and Carthusians reasserted the Benedictine ideal when they thought that Jeshurun had waxed fat and kicked. They continued the revolutionary effect of the voluntary society on

[25]S. O. Biobaku, *The Egba and Their Neighbours 1842-72* (Oxford: Clarendon Press, 1957); cf. J. F. Ade Ajayei, *Christian Missions in Nigeria 1841-1891: The Making of a New Elite* (London: Longmans, 1965), pp. 71-73.

the Church, assisting its declericalization, giving new scope for women's energies and gifts, adding an international dimension which hardly any of the churches, growing as they did within a national framework, had any means of expressing. After the age of the voluntary society, the Western Church could never be the same again.

The missionary society was, as Carey indicated, a use of means for a specific purpose. The original purpose was what Carey called "the conversion of the heathens." The purpose of both the older and the newer societies was essentially evangelistic; inasfar as it was formulated, the theory was that when the church was founded the mission would move on. In practice it did not, perhaps could not, happen that way. As new churches appeared, the society remained as a natural channel of communication, through which flowed aid, personnel, money, materials, technical expertise. The societies, as we have seen, developed other roles, as educators of Church and Public, as a conscience for peoples and governments. All these roles were already established in the missionary societies before 1830, and they are all there still.

But neither the fears of nineteenth-century Churchmen nor the hopes of nineteenth-century missionaries comprehended a situation so soon in which Africans, Asians, and Latin Americans would form the majority of Christians, and that on them would lie so soon the main responsibility for the evangelization of the world. The new chapter of Church history which has begun arises, not from the failure of the missionary movement, but from its success. It may now be appropriate to re-examine the "obligation to use means," and the purpose for which our "means" is directed. Societies established for an evangelistic purpose may produce strictly bilateral connections, so that churches formed as a result of "our" work have relations only with "us." Is this a measure of the fullness of the Body of Christ? And relationships so easily become finance-dominated; it is hard to keep relations on an equal footing when the regular topic of conversation is money, and how much. And the societies were designed for one-way traffic; all the assumptions were that one party would do all the giving and the other all the receiving. Now, our desperate need in the West is to be able to receive, and we have also an "obligation to use means" for the sharing of all the gifts that God has given to all his people.

The voluntary society, and its special form in the missionary society, arose in a particular period of Western social, political, and economic development and was shaped by that period. It was providentially used in God's purpose for the redemption of the world. But as Rufus Anderson noted long ago, it was but the modern, Western form of a movement that has periodically reappeared from an early period of Christian history. In one sense, monasteries were voluntary societies, and "it was by means of associations such as these that the Gospel was originally propagated among our ancestors, and over Europe."[26] From age to age it becomes necessary to

---

[26]Beaver, p. 64.

use new means for the proclamation of the Gospel beyond the structures which unduly localize it. Some have taken the word "sodality" beyond its special usage in Catholic practice to stand for all such "use of means" by which groups voluntarily constituted labour together for specific Gospel purposes. The voluntary societies have been as revolutionary in their effect as ever the monasteries were in their sphere. The sodalities we now need may prove equally disturbing.

19

The Old Age of the Missionary Movement[1]

Christian faith is missionary both in its essence and in its history. At the heart of the Christian faith lie assumptions about the Lord and Ground of the universe and the common nature of humanity and affirmations about Jesus Christ that forbid its appropriation to any person, group, or community as a private possession. The conviction that Jesus is Lord and the testimony that Christ is risen cannot mean that much unless they are to be shared. But both the faith of Christians and the nature of the church are missionary in a much deeper sense, more closely related to the "sending" idea from which the word "missionary" came. "As the Father has sent me," said Jesus to the first apostles, "so send I you." The Father sent his Son into the world not simply to speak, but to be and to do. The Son, for all that his own work was unique, sends his people as he was sent: to be light to the world, to give healing and hope to the ill and the weak and the unwanted, to suffer, perhaps unjustly, on behalf of others. The mission of the church is not simply to add to itself but to bear witness that by his cross and resurrection Christ bought back the whole creation and defeated the powers that spoil it. In this sense all Christian life is missionary, as is the work of Christians and their commerce and habits of life, their art and music and every activity that demands choice.

But historical circumstances have required a special, technical meaning of the word "missionary." The missionary movement from the west in recent centuries has introduced us to the idea of the representative of the total Christian community who has in principle exactly the same faith, testimony, and responsibility as all other Christians, but who exercises these in a cross-cultural situation.

---

[1]First published in *International Review of Mission* 77 (January, 1987): 26-32.

It is a feature of Christian faith that throughout its history it has spread through cross-cultural contact; indeed its very survival has been dependent on such contact. This is not true of all the great faiths; not of Judaism, for instance, found throughout the world, but almost entirely in ethnic communities; nor of Hinduism embracing countless millions in the oldest faith in the world, but overwhelmingly concentrated in one nation and people. Buddhism and Islam have indeed repeatedly crossed the cultural divide, but of Christianity we may almost say that it exists today only *because* it has crossed it. For Christian expansion has not been progressive, like Islamic expansion, spreading out from a central point and retaining, by and large, the allegiance of those it reaches. Christian expansion has been serial. Christian faith has fixed itself at different periods in different heartlands, waning in one as it has come to birth in another.

The first Christians in Jerusalem, Jews to a man and woman, did not change their religion when they accepted Jesus as Messiah. To be a Jesus person was to be a Jew in a fuller sense; to find new delight in the law and in that temple to which they daily resorted. Then somehow, some people— we do not even know their names—introduced the Jewish national saviour to some pagan Greek friends in Antioch. Though this was to lead to some heart searching in the Christian community, its real significance was not clear until thirty years later when the Romans destroyed the Jewish state and the temple and the original Christian community faded into the margins of Christian history. Had Christian faith remained as in the early chapters of Acts, Christianity would never have survived the Roman holocaust. What saved it was the action of those people in Antioch. By the time the Jewish state collapsed, most Christians were no longer Jews, but Greeks.

In time, the tables were turned. In A.D. 600 the Christian heartlands, already justly claiming antiquity, lay predominantly among Greek-speaking people in the eastern Mediterranean; but the whole of that empire that had crushed the Jewish revolt now acknowledged the lordship of Christ. By A.D. 800 those eastern Greek-speaking heartlands were not only under Muslim rule; large sections of their populations were becoming Muslims. Latin-speaking Christians were deluged in fierce, ugly little wars; and Latin-speaking African Christians were dying out altogether. How did Christianity survive the collapse? Because by the time those events took place Christian faith was taking hold among the northern and western barbarians whom civilized Christians had long feared and despised. New Christian lands emerged, replacing the old and shifting the Christian centre of gravity as drastically as it had shifted after A.D. 70.

For several centuries Christian presence was concentrated (not exclusively, but principally) in Europe. The western Christians, after seeking for a time to impose their faith where possible, began slowly to seek to offer and to share it. This process reached a sustained pitch of effort during the nineteenth century. A glance at a religious map of the world at the time of the World Missionary Conference of 1910 might suggest that what they had accomplished by then was noticeable, but hardly overwhelming; the conference still thought in terms of (western) lands "fully missionized" and of the challenge of the other "not yet fully missionized." We can see now what was still hidden from them and which gives the missionary movement most historical significance. Over a long period Christianity in Europe was receding; only after World War II did it become clear how far that recession had gone and how it was accelerating. At present it seems that Europe and North America are the only continents where Christian faith and commitment is statistically receding. Everywhere else it is expanding. Sub-Saharan Africa provides a massive Christian population. In the Pacific there are now Christian nations of the sort that Europe used to have. In Latin America lies the largest single Christian culture group. The new Christian heartlands are in the south, in Africa, Latin America, parts of Asia, in the Pacific; and the European empires that looked so permanent in 1914, nay in 1940, have all disappeared. This vast shift in the Christian constituency, parallel to those that followed the fall of Jerusalem, the western progress of the Arabs, and the fall of the western Roman Empire, could not have occurred without that previous cross-cultural diffusion of Christian faith centred in the missionary movement.

We cannot eliminate the theme of crossing cultural frontiers from Christian history. Cross-cultural transmission is integral to Christian faith. The first Christian frontier breakers, those "men of Cyprus and Cyrene" in Antioch, were simply talking to their friends. They themselves were immigrants, indeed refugees, earning their living in new surroundings. The barbarians of the north and west learned Christ through all sorts of means. Christians kidnapped and made slaves brought Christianity to the eastern Goths; Christian survivors from a shipwreck took it to Ethiopia. Official missions sponsored by the church authorities did exist, but were only one means among many. The preaching of wandering monks was the contact for some centres; others met Christians through the strange, severe life of some who appeared to do little but pray. The expansion out of Europe brought new methods and special organization. The Roman Catholic Church adapted the religious order to missionary purposes. Protestant Christians in the late eighteenth and nineteenth centuries developed the voluntary society, which was to prove so powerful and efficacious that even the Catholic missionary orders found something to copy. The societies organized the systematic channeling of western Christian energy, work, prayer, and giving, and built up, trained, and equipped a force for cross-cultural mission. This force established churches, often pastored them, and usually led them. When the operation began, such missionary service was costly in life and health and dubious in outcome or result. It was not long, in terms of total Christian history, before there were resultant churches all round the world and western church leaders were talking of "daughter" churches, and then of "younger" churches; and missions had become a means not only of planting churches but of servicing a huge international network with educational, medical, social, industrial, translational, and many other branches.

We can thus see that, while the element of cross-cultural diffusion runs throughout Christian history, it has never been dependent on any one instrument. The "missionary" in the technical sense is one present, and historically important, example of a recurrent Christian phenomenon.

The recurrence of the phenomenon is itself a sign of its temporary nature in any given situation. When Barnabas came to Antioch he evidently judged that the converted rabbi Saul was the person most needed by the new gentile church there; but it was not long before Paul was elsewhere and the Antiochene church without either of its famous names. The cross-cultural agent is vital, but catalytic and temporary and must be ready to move on. Anyone who works in the field of African Christian history becomes conscious of how in so many cases the missionary period is now an episode, often an increasingly distant one, in an ongoing story. Yet the same story often reveals how missionaries had sometimes to be shaken out—by international warfare, political change, economic depression at home, or simply by schism—before the story could proceed.

Any consideration of the future of the missionary movement must take account of the factors that originally produced it. And here we must remember that its origin lay in the territorial idea of Christianity, the association of the faith with one part of the world, the "fully missionized lands" of 1910, from which the word may go forth to the "not yet fully missionized lands" elsewhere. The missionary movement is in some respects the last flourish of the Christendom idea, and, in its early days at least, it was borne forward by the hope of adding to Christendom. But now the idea of territorial Christianity, of geographically contiguous Christian states, lies irretrievably broken. It was itself the product of the special historical circumstances of the conversion of the western barbarians. Now the lands of their successors show marked recession from Christian commitment and western Europe has become a prime area, perhaps *the* prime area, for identification as a mission field. It would be easy to adapt some of the nineteenth-century descriptions of the need of the heathen—the ignorance of religion, the immorality, the proneness to warfare, the inhumanities and injustice widely accepted in society—as a stirring call to Christians of the southern continents to undertake the salvation of the west.

But the southern Christian lands do not constitute a new Christendom. Few of them have become homogeneous Christian states. Christian faith is now more diffused than at any previous time in its history; not only in the sense that it is more geographically, ethnically, and culturally widespread than ever before, but in the sense that it is diffused *within* more communities. The territorial "from-to" idea that underlay the older missionary movement has to give way to a concept much more like that of Christians within the Roman Empire in the second and third centuries: parallel presences in different circles and at different levels, each seeking to penetrate within and beyond its circle. This does not prevent movement and interchange and enterprise—these things certainly marked Christians in the pre-Constantinian Roman Empire—but it forces revision of concepts, images, attitudes, and methods that arose from the presence of a Christendom that no longer exists.

The older missionary movement was the product of a particular phase of western political, economic, and religious development. The Christendom idea, which so radically affected its shape, was only one aspect of this. We have seen that the characteristic organization developed by the movement was the voluntary society, which developed into the mission agency with its board, its constituency of concerned supporters, and the body of agents and representatives that it sent and maintained abroad. This itself was a product of the concomitance of certain political, economic, and religious conditions at a certain period of western history and not always present even in all parts of the west. In political terms it required regimes permitting free association, a climate in which such association was not perceived by the state as a threat, a type of society in which individual consciousness was highly developed, in which it was not necessary or appropriate that all should be like their neighbours. In economic terms it required the existence of surpluses, their enjoyment by a fairly broad spread of the population, and the freedom to move them around. In religious terms it implied not only a substantial Christian base with enthusiasm needing outlets, but a sufficiently centralized or relaxed (or ineffective) style of church organization for such energetic religious activity to be tolerated outside its formal structures, especially as the societies created new power bases and new (often lay) leadership. And for the agencies to operate implied a certain relationship between the west and other parts of the world, whereby agents of the societies could normally freely travel and settle and, if not necessarily welcomed, at least be tolerated.

The nineteenth and early twentieth centuries saw a high degree of convergence of these conditions in certain western countries. For most of these countries that phase of development is now past. In one respect it is clearly past for all of them; no longer can their citizens take for granted the right of entry or settlement where they choose. Nor are the social, political, or religious conditions what they were in the high days of the missionary movement. But the most marked difference is in the economic sphere. Missionaries are now expensive commodities; in terms of the countries that they serve, sometimes astronomically so. There is already a notable number of missionaries from third world countries serving in countries other than their own, but there are good reasons for not expecting a general burgeoning of third world "overseas mission" societies. Such societies can only emerge, whether in the west or elsewhere, against the background of a certain type of economy. They cannot operate where the economy is based on marginal agriculture, or in countries with chronic economic disabilities, or in countries with tight monetary controls.

Despite the formidable economic obstacles to the continuance of the older missionary movement, there are nevertheless countries where the missionary is a symbol of economic power. There are "broken-back" states, crippled economies, areas unattractive to or vacated by all large investors, where the missions have the largest and most efficient technological and communications capability in the country. They are the sources of foreign money; they have means of transport and travel and outside communication. The immense power has little to do with the local church, except insofar as that church may call in people from outside: it remains foreign in its nature.

The changed world situation thus requires us to examine some of the unintended consequences of a continued projection of the missionary movement. But there are changes also in the church, which must be taken into account. The older missionary movement, as we have already seen, developed a characteristic form of organization, the mission agency based on the model of the voluntary society. Back in 1792, when voluntary societies were by no means so common as they were to become a generation later, William Carey described how such an association might be formed in his *Enquiry into the Obligation of Christians to Use Means for the Propagation of the Gospel Amongst the Heathen*. The formation of the mission society was a "use of means" for a specific purpose. As it developed it became a quite efficient means of achieving certain ends: sending and equipping people for the purpose of Christian proclamation and service overseas, and mustering "home" interest and support for their work. No one would claim that this exhausts the needs of the Christian world today, or even that it expresses its primary needs; nor that it appropriately reflects the true relationship between the Christians of the north and of the south. The original organs of the missionary movement were designed for one-way traffic; for sending, for giving. Perhaps there is now an obligation of Christians to "use means" better fitted for two-way traffic, fellowship, for sharing, for receiving, than have yet been perfected.

The older missionary movement produced its own spirituality. At the nineteenth-century apex of the movement this was expressed in the self-denying life of the ideal missionary, sacrificing country, comfort, prospects, and perhaps health for the sake of the gospel. But this does not necessarily reflect today's reality. The missionary no longer answers a lifetime call, and certainly does not get a visa for it. Missionaries are often protected from the worst inconveniences of life in the place where they are by the sheer efficiency of mission organization and its capacity to apply foreign funding to meet emergencies. Expatriate Christians who take on overseas contract posts on local terms know at least that they are wanted: had a local person been available they would not have been appointed, and when one is available they will not be reappointed. They share all the local frustrations—and perhaps some of the vulnerability that lay at the heart of the former missionary ideal.

The missionary movement is now in its old age. It is not a useless and decrepit old age. There are situations where it provides the most effective, perhaps the only foreseeable means of making any witness to Christ or any proclamation about him. There are many others where the surviving apparatus of the missionary movement is all that remains, till better means appear, to express and realize the universal fellowship of Christ's church and to make possible real sharing between its various parts. But the conditions that produced the movement have changed, and they have been changed by the Lord of history. And the church has been changed out of all recognition by the agency of the missionary movement itself.

It can be misleading to refer to this as the end of an era, for this implies some sort of historic finality. In fact the continuities are far more important. The task of world evangelization that formed the declared programme of missionary movement is not over; it never is. The essentially missionary nature of the church, the essentially missionary calling of the Christian, is where we began; and perhaps the twentieth-century fading of territorial Christianity enables us to see better that recession is as much a part of Christian history as expansion, part of the vulnerability, perhaps, of the means God has ordained to make the human witness to Christ. It is, after all, the One who holds the seven stars in his right hand who takes away the lampstand of a church. What is changing is not the task, but the means and the mode. Changing, too, are some of the accompaniments. In its heyday the missionary movement came hand-in-hand with forms of education and technology seen as themselves the fruit of Christian influences and as unquestionably beneficial in their results, and often received as such. It now seems increasingly likely that the bearers of the gospel will bring no gifts with them, except the gospel itself. And that again was the situation of the early church.

Nor does the old age of the missionary movement imply the end of cross-cultural mission—though it may raise questions about who does the crossing. We are now aware that there are more uncrossed cultural frontiers than the best-informed strategists of 1910 realized. And many of the most significant developments in Christian history, movements opening that serial penetration of cultures by the gospel of which it is made up, have begun with a period of cross-cultural contact. The period has sometimes been confused, sometimes traumatic, and almost invariably short. It will be quite in accord with the previous story of the Christian faith if the second evangelization of the west, the true penetration of a culture as alien to the gospel as any in the world, were to be effected by means of cross-cultural Christian contact.

Index